POLITICS AND SOCIAL CHANGE IN THIRD WORLD COUNTRIES

POLITICS AND SOCIAL CHANGE
IN THIRD WORLD COUNTRIES

310976

F. LaMond Tullis

Brigham Young University

JOHN WILEY AND SONS, INC.
New York • London • Sydney • Toronto

COVER: Designed and Illustrated by ROY JONES
TEXT: Designed by ROY JONES

Library of Congress Cataloging in Publication Data:

Tullis, F   LaMond, 1935-
  Politics and social changes in third world countries.

  Bibliography: p. 331
  1. Underdeveloped areas—Politics and government—Case studies. 2. Underdeveloped areas—Social conditions—Case studies. I. Title.

JF60.T85   309.1'172'4   72-10961
ISBN 0-471-89230-0
ISBN 0-471-89231-9 (pbk)

Printed in the United States of America

10 9 8 7 6 5 4 3 2 1

FOR SHARMAN,
        AND RICHARD, MICHAEL, AND ERIC.

PREFACE

Contemporary political, social, and economic changes in Asia, Africa, Latin America, and the Middle East provide the background for this textbook. The book describes and analyzes not only transformations in the physical environment of Third World countries and the way people relate to and think about them, but also alterations in the structure of whole societies and their underlying institutions. The main focus, however, is on the rise of new social forces and their relationship to the political institutions that they hope to create or with which they must deal. The approach is theoretical and empirical, and it includes extensive case studies on Brazil, Libya, and Peru.

Within this subject-matter focus I have set three objectives.

1. My first objective is to provide students of modernization and political and social change with material with which they can empathize. The case studies are directed partly toward this end. Departing from the traditional academic approach of conveying factual material, I have added a new dimension—a story—that is exciting and factually informative.

2. I have also examined the main ideas and concepts that social scientists have formulated as they attempt to understand the political and social aspects of modernization. Scholars have carried out an enormous amount of exciting original research. They have attempted to explain the phenomena of contemporary environmental and value change, and sometimes they have given policy insights into the subject. In most instances, however, their research and writing have been directed toward professional colleagues and graduate students. I have "translated" some of these insights to make them readily available to nonspecialized undergraduates.

3. My final objective is to introduce the beginning student to the way in which many social scientists frame their analytical tools, to the use of hypotheses and variables, and to the use of qualitative case-study data for illustrative purposes. My experience has shown that subsequent readings in the theoretical literature on modernization can be done with a higher degree of comprehension.

Effort is required to move from concept to theory—or even to simple analytical tools. Also, effort is required to gain an understanding of how these tools can alert us to more than we already know in the practical world and how they can help us to refine our thinking and to save time in making coherent sense out of the facts we do discover. For this reason, I have included an introductory chapter dealing with theory building, with the use of dependent and independent variables, and with the manner in which one relates indicators to them. An analogous purpose is to sensitize students to the social scientists' "way of looking" at the rapid changes in economy, society, culture, and politics that are now confronting much of the world.

However, I must give a word of caution. This book does not purport to deal with all aspects of modernization, and it does not give equal space or competence to all those that are included. The themes I have selected relate generally to fundamental concepts and, particularly, to the rise of new social forces and to the ability of political institutions to cope with or adapt to them.

The cases that illustrate the concepts and theories are presented with substantial ecological backgrounds. Thus, beginning students, having at hand fairly complete factual materials that assume little prior knowledge of the respective countries, will be better able to grasp the conceptual and analytical meanings that the facts are intended to illustrate or clarify. Subsequent reading of additional factual material will thereby be made more meaningful.

Samuel P. Huntington made helpful suggestions for a revision of an earlier draft of the manuscript. Richard Kennedy ably assisted in the preparation of the Brazilian case study. To both of these colleagues I offer what must, in the final word, be a selfish thanks. Others who made helpful critiques of parts of the manuscript include David E. Bohn, David Chaplin, Wesley W. Craig, Jr., Mark O. Dickerson, Richard F. High, Louis Midgley, Alma Don Sorenson, Berkley Spencer, and Edward J. Williams. While I am responsible for any errors in fact or judgment in this work, all of us can share in its virtues.

Without making institutions responsible for the result of their financial generosity, I thank the Social Science Research Council and American Council of Learned Societies (Foreign Area Fellowship Program), which funded a year's research in Peru, and the Research Division of Brigham Young University, which made the preparation of the Libyan case possible.

F. LaMOND TULLIS

List of Figures

CONTENTS

POLITICS AND SOCIAL CHANGE
IN THIRD WORLD COUNTRIES

INTRODUCTION

Much of the world has been afflicted with a massive appetite for new things. Indeed, no country now seems to be immune from the desire to secure a better life founded on material well-being if not spiritual awareness. To satisfy some of the resulting hungers, nations are making substantial efforts to industrialize, to increase the productivity of their labor and capital, and to create the necessary technology to help production meet demand. The consequences, and frequently some of the causes, entail fairly massive shifts in people's environment and often in many of the values that they or their fathers have held dear. It is a search for "modernity," we are told. Yet, if that is the modern life, when can we know that we have "arrived"? When everyone consumes to the value of $10,000 yearly? A hundred thousand? More? What would such an arrival, if that is what it is, imply for life-styles, behavior, cultural norms and values, and political and social organization? Or, should we characterize modernity by describing—as is frequently done—the conditions of life that *now* exist in the most advanced sectors of countries of the North Atlantic region? But if we do so, a strange paradox results. The processes of change and adaptation that have made these nations what they are seem to be singularly unimpressed with the need to "stop." Relentlessly, engines of change appear to be pushing all of us into the yet unknown. Definitions, obviously, will therefore be altered. Change is everywhere; indeed, we are led to expect it.

On whole nations as much as on individuals, changes in technology, society, culture, and politics increasingly impinge with adventures and excitement, frustrations and despair. By all appearances the whole process is accelerating, progressively affecting more people on the cosmic dust speck that its English-speaking inhabitants have chosen to call Earth. Even if, fortuitously, we do not succeed in upsetting the delicate balance of our planet's life-support systems (deferring, as well, what might be interpreted as a planetary inclination for atomic suicide), a horizon of environmental and value stability and nonchange will probably not appear. Perhaps such stability is a luxury—or a burden—that our world will never again—if it ever did—experience.

"Modernization" is the term generally used to describe these processes when one is referring to Asia, Africa, Latin America, or the Middle East. But how should one classify analogous changes affecting nations already technologically advanced? More modernization? Decay? Spiritual renaissance? Self-destruction?

Whatever the case may be, a great many people in economically advanced nations and people in nations struggling to progress actively seek "modernizing" change. Others, however, detest not only the technological changes but the alterations in culture, life-styles, politics, and society that tend in one form or another to accompany them. If the lament seems loud it is because no country—indeed, few people—are entirely immune to the impact of contem-

1

porary change and, for good or bad, to the consequences that accompany it.

Modernizing change, at least in the world of Asia, Africa, Latin America, and the Middle East—the regions on which this book focuses—is currently advancing relentlessly. It is a drama filled with excitement, frustration, success, and frequent failure, partly because it coincides with an attempt to marry an archaic yet sometimes cherished past with a future that is only partially disclosed. Some people aspire. They change. Sometimes they progress. Yet frequently their new hopes and aspirations are cruelly disappointed. Stunned, but frequently unwilling to give up, they—or perhaps their children—rise again and again to thrust themselves into the traces.

In the so-called "Third World" of Asia, Africa, Latin America, and the Middle East, many of the early changes were introduced by colonial powers, such as France, England, and Spain. Yet now, most of their colonial empires are extinct. In all probability the termination dramas for the remaining few will be played out within the lifetime of the present generation, and the last die-hards will be pushed back to their native homeland. To be sure, the great modern, technically nonimperial powers—Russia and the United States—will continue to exert great influence in other regions of the world for the foreseeable future, but probably not like the British exerted 30 years ago over a domain on which the sun never set, nor like the Spanish two centuries ago exerted over nearly one half the Western Hemisphere.

The modernization of former colonial and other Third World peoples has led, as one of the by-products of their experience, to a search, indeed a demand, for self-identity, development, and freedom. From the peasant of Peru to the modernizing Shah of Iran the story of change is similar in quantity if not in style. The "dormant" peoples of the world are on the move; the stable sanctity of past colonial days is gone forever. "Modernizaion" has seen to that.

The search for identity, development, and freedom has been a lengthy story; nearly always it has entailed a struggle. The American colonies were able to free themselves from England in 1783 and to become "the first new nation" only after a costly and bitter eight-year war. In the early part of the nineteenth century, the whole of Spanish and Portuguese America finally liberated itself from the bonds of the Iberian monarchs. While the liberation of Brazil cost little more than a shout, the bloodshed in the Spanish colonies was plentiful enough. Similar independence movements arose in Asia and Africa nearly 150 years later; and, following World War II, Britain, Belgium, France, and Holland were all forcibly turned back to their North Atlantic homes.

Similarly, the United States, a sometime supporter of twentieth-century British and French colonialism in Asia and Africa, has also been overextended. In 1969, President Richard Nixon made a "triumphant" tour of South and Southeast Asia, not to wield the historical big stick or assert continued military and economic dominance in much of the developing world but, instead, to announce that his country was "willing" to reduce the size of its economic, military, and cultural empire. In fact, the President could just as well have said that Americans no longer can either afford such extended activities or handle their consequences. The reason, of course, is that many of the less economically developed areas of the world, which for several centuries have been not only largely subordinated by Western powers but relatively quiet as well, are now restive. No longer content with backwardness, powerlessness, or the lack of an acceptable self-identity, they seek change and they want it now. Correspondingly, it has become more costly for big powers, colonial or otherwise, to maintain their traditional dominance. Dormant people are easily exploited and inexpensively controlled. Mobilized people create a different history, and only recently have we begun to assess the implications.

In the last 15 years, as in Latin America more than a century ago, backwater lands in Asia and Africa have emerged from colonial status to nationhood, if not in fact, at least in name. Contemporary traditional monarchies (such as Iran), although they have not suffered the "blessings" of a full-fledged colonial occupation, have also thrown themselves into one of the most important political, social, and economic activities that has captured the imagination and energies of millions of people in our age—the struggle for freedom, identity, and material progress. This aura of change with its accelerating aspirations has likewise enveloped anew the old republics of North and South America. Indeed, even the seemingly most modern of all modern nations has not escaped its influence. Many of America's blacks, Chicanos, and Indians are now pursuing a similar course. "Modernity" may not be understood—but it is wanted by nearly everyone who thinks that he does not have it.

Depending on historical time and place, a country's experience with modernizing change may be different, even unique. The kind experienced in today's Third World nations, for example, is extraordinarily unlike most of that recorded in histories of the United States. There are some noteworthy exceptions, of course, but for the most part newer nations of Asia and Africa, the old republics of Latin America, and the traditional monarchies of the Middle East and Southeast Asia have gotten off to a different start in their independent or modernizing life. Generally, they have different and more rigid social structures, more antagonistic cultural mores and norms, more complicated historical positions vis-à-vis modern technology, more dependent and vulnerable economies, more complex relations with the so-called "superpowers" and more basic problems with ethnic and language diversity and religious tradition. Indeed, when the processes of change occurring in the Third World today are compared in intensity and quality with those of North America's formative years, many of the apparent similarities with early experiences in the United States rapidly fade. Samuel P. Huntington speaks of America as being "historically a new society but an old state."[1] Conversely, Asia and Africa are *old societies* but *new states.*[2] Whether you begin as a new society with old political institutions, or as an old society with new political institutions does make a modernizing difference. And a differing historical evolution frequently lays the foundation for major differences in the social and political consequences of modernization.

Louis Hartz emphasizes an important historical factor. North America is the product, after Columbus at least, of a "fragment society," one that evolved from a particular system of values largely established by social rejects from Great Britain.[3] The country inherited a somewhat unique and relatively close-knit value system (aside from the religious denominational question) because most of the early "Yankee" colonizers not only started with the so-called Protestant "this-world ethic" but they also established the cultural and social norms to which all latecomers were expected to pay deference. This occurred *before* America became an industrialized state.

Industrialization with all of its associated social dislocations and political antagonisms, is a very difficult task even when the process is extended over two or three centuries and is built on substantially compatible values. Most of the citizenry, by gradual change and accommodation from generation to generation, have adequate time to be converted to the material benefits of technology and to become resigned to their social costs. But when one chooses to speed up that process, to attempt to do in 20 or 50 years what others have taken 300 years to accomplish, and to do so when social values are not compatible, then the story is entirely different. Hatred and dissent become incredibly intense as new groups, forcing their way up the development ladder, push aside, thrust down, or exterminate older established ones. Modernization is greatly facilitated when a country is first, when it can take a long time to do it, and when the process, though always generating conflict, nevertheless does not occasion frequent and absolute antagonisms among large groups in its society. North America was reasonably fortunate in this regard; today's Third World, for the most part, has not been. Historically, the United States has had only a handful of major political purges—and thus far only one civil war. In much of the Third World, purges are almost a daily experience; civil violence and guerrilla warfare are commonplace; and political instability and frequent chaos are a way of life. Indeed, these are the basis for the international news stories of the early 1970's.

Although America's history does not provide a universal model, its contemporary period is nevertheless ripe with analogies. When we reflect on its current protest movements—on the challenges to tradition and the time-honored virtues of the past, and the systematic rejection of the sacred and the profane—we begin to get a better "feel" for what the Third World is experiencing. The great difference, of course, is that the United States is already rich and industrialized. Moreover, it has reasonably powerful and flexible political institutions that can heal the wounds of dissension and can make necessary reforms. Most of the Third World has neither the wealth nor the institutions. This is a simple fact that makes the modernizing problem of our Asian, African, Latin American, and Middle Eastern friends perhaps a hundred times more excruciating than the modernizing problem of our American forefathers.

These are a few of the reasons why the United States' historical model for modernization is not really suitable for "transfer" to the Third World of today. As things stand, therefore, we must look for new models to explain the phenomena of social and political change in these regions. Such models today are mainly analytical constructs that extract the rich variety of human experience and attempt to explain it in a generalized form. The shift, therefore, is away from an over-reliance on the "lessons-of-history" of any single country and toward a testable theory that can be generally applied to all modernizing countries. In this book we investigate a number of theoretical propositions, some of the research approaches and important aspects of the mood of modernization.

PART I

Some Preliminary Concepts and Analytical Tools

Before we can comprehend much about *what* scholars say regarding modernization and political and social change we must learn about *how* they say it. This requires our knowing something about variables and hypotheses, and having, at least, a minimal grasp of how theories are formed and used (since those who study modernization habitually come up with scores of them). Equally important is the need to gain insight into how all these academic approaches can be linked up to the world of reality.

If we do not have an understanding of these tools and concepts, we will probably not understand the literature very well. Moreover, we will probably have scant capacity to analyze, except in the most intuitive and general way, the case studies that we read. Chapter 1, therefore, conveys, in an informal "simulated" way, an understanding of variables and hypotheses and suggests insights into how some social scientists, using these tools, frame their questions and seek their answers. Chapter 2 then examines some of the fundamental concepts that students of modernization use. With these tools and concepts in mind we shall be able to move on to a more specialized consideration of social forces and political institutions and, finally, to the case studies that complement them. Those already acquainted with these preliminaries can move directly to Part II (Chapter 3) without loss of continuity in the discussion.

CHAPTER 1

Analysis, Variables, and Theory

The early 1960's ushered the modernizing world of Asia, Africa, Latin America, and the Middle East into a period of considerable international attention. The Cold War had suddenly become hot again. "Liberation fronts" were making headlines. Hundreds of American universities began to develop "area-study programs." Research and study grants became increasingly available, most from legitimate academic sources, but a few ultimately from CIA funds channeled through front foundations.[1] Everyone, frequently for differing reasons, wanted information and knowledge. Very little was available. Yet this happy coincidence of "need" and "exciting things to study" set the stage for the birth of one of the fastest growing fields in the social sciences today—modernization and development.

The efforts invested in learning about "underdeveloped" foreign areas were supreme. So also was the struggle to remove them from that state. If the results of the studies and development projects fell appreciably short of quality goals —and they frequently did—in large part, the blame can be laid not only to the ignorance the studies were meant to dispel but to a nearly total lack of understanding of what modernization in "old societies" means. Only today is that ignorance being dissipated. And yet we still know very little in terms of actual facts, or what the facts mean once they are uncovered. The consolation, however, and it is an important one, is that the level of knowledge and understanding is considerably better now than it was 15 years ago.

The initial stages of academic and applied interest were accompanied by some impressional conclusions regarding the Third World, conclusions mainly based on models and concepts derived from studies of and experience in the North Atlantic nations. But soon many observers dramatically began to shift their theoretical gears on the entire subject of modernization, so much so, in fact, that one might even argue that as much "modernization" occurred in the academic disciplines and fields involved as in the modernizing countries that had captured their interest.

Thus agricultural and community development technicians are now as concerned with people's values and attitudes as they traditionally had been with the technical requirements of their working environment. The shift derived from some painful reflections. Scores of casebooks relate the unhappy story of "technically sound" demonstration projects that were rejected by the peoples they were supposed to influence, and of progressive community development programs sabotaged by one or another of the groups receiving the aid.

The economists have become equally alarmed. In the last few years they have moved to supplement their theoretically sound but failing-in-practice growth formulas with social and political factors that have been proved to play a major role in economic development—or nondevelopment. As with the technicians, the economists' shift was also preceded by certain frustrations. There are numerous examples of economic growth formulas which, when applied to concrete situations in the developing countries, were so undermined by cultural traits and political institutions as to render virtually useless the standard models for national development.

After a considerable amount of practical experience in this regard, the famed Brazilian economist, Roberto Campos, came to this conclusion:

"The anguished study of the principles, problems, and policies of economic development has brought economists to a humble acceptance of the inter-disciplinary approach to social sciences, an approach which they resisted for a long time. . . .I am more and more convinced that the foundation of the theory of growth has much more to do with psychology, social institutions, and ethical values than with the laws of rational economic behavior."[2]

My own field, political science, has also suffered from serious failures in explanation and concept formation. Indeed, in the past several years so much dissension has arisen among us over these and related problems that some observers, in all seriousness, have announced that we are a nondiscipline. Of course, this oversimplifies the matter considerably; but we are, indeed, a discipline in transition, moving from a preponderant concern with formal political institutions (such as courts, legislatures, and executives) toward an understanding of the relation of politics to culture, attitudes, and values. The need for a changed focus is particularly evident when politics and society are in a state of rapid change. Accordingly, when a political scientist looks hard at the Third World he feels a need to accelerate the discipline's transition, precisely because the old political science formulas do not work, any more than did the old growth or demonstration formulas.

Modernization studies are now highly interdisciplinary. Considerable adopting and adapting from one discipline or field to another is currently in vogue. In particular, political scientists have found it helpful to incorporate into the study of politics many of the insights of the sociologists, psychologists, and anthropologists. We have also greatly profited from the rigorous analytical methods of the economists.

It is only natural that "ecological" or "systems" studies should emerge from these interdisciplinary considerations. The question now is not one of just looking at economics, *or* politics, *or* social relations, *or* culture, *or* technical administration but, instead, of determining how these relate to one another within the society. Generally, a scholar will focus on some aspect of politics, social relations, economics, culture, or administration that he wishes to explain and then will enlist relevant social, political, economic, cultural, and perhaps other data to clarify the problem and tender an explanation for its existence or a prescription for its solution. This is a new road. At times it is also one that can have a rough surface. Nevertheless, even though there is considerable methodological and theoretical paving to do, the indications are strong that, in general, it is one of the more potentially productive routes.

DESCRIPTION VERSUS ANALYSIS

One of the noticeable trends in modernization literature is a consistent shift away from primarily descriptive studies toward those that emphasize rigorous analysis. In the strictest sense, a descriptive study describes events and facts but explains no "whys" regarding them. Few studies, of course, are this descriptively "pure." Most contain some kind of analysis. Nevertheless, one finds in earlier approaches a preponderance for description whereas today the growing emphasis is on tight analysis and hypothesis testing. It is worthwhile to illustrate some of the basic differences in these two approaches so that the contents of this book will be better understood. Perhaps an "applied parable" will serve this purpose.

Suppose you had an opportunity to study patterns of agricultural technology in one of the millions of peasant villages existing on this planet. We might as well place the capstone: You also are to write a book in which you will relate your findings. Your study will require that you reside in a village for several months, thereby enabling you to become acquainted and conversant with the villagers, observe what they do as they farm their plots of land, and perhaps even participate with them in some of their endeavors.

Having selected a village and taken up residence, you quickly become aware of the peasants' primitive agricultural technology. You observe that they plow the ground with a pointed stick drawn by yoked oxen, that the seeds they use are not of good quality, and that they do not use commercial fertilizers or insecticides even though mechanized equipment, hybrid seeds, and agricultural chemicals are readily available in the country. If you observed only to describe, your book would relate these and numerous other findings in depth and color so that your readers would know exactly what you had seen. You would have been there, and "this is what I saw." If you wrote well, no doubt you would become the author of an extremely interesting and chromatic book, one which might even function as an important source of knowledge about agricultural practices in the village.

On the other hand, by taking a purely descriptive approach your book will fail to tell us *why* the peasants do not use hybrid seeds, *why* they seem disinterested in mechanized equipment, *why* they have an aversion to the use of chemical fertilizers and insecticides, or *why*, in short, they go on employing traditional agricultural practices when more modern ones not only are readily at hand but the villagers obviously know about them.

"Why" suggests analysis; yet this is not simple. Does one accomplish it by saying that "peasants are stubborn, tied to the traditions of the past and, therefore, find it difficult to change"? Although it hardly does justice to the questions, such an explanation is exemplary of the superficial kinds of analysis that some observers employ. You, however, are not content with pure description or superficial analysis and, accordingly, have decided to investigate all the circumstances or factors you can that in any way might explain the peasants' failure to adopt new forms of agricultural technology. You will still do a lot of describing. And in this regard your book may still be "colorful." Yet you are going to try to answer some very difficult questions about the "whys" of what you have seen. Through investigation you find several interesting particulars. To these you now direct us. In so doing you are moving toward analysis.

Surprisingly, you find your particular peasants not to be ignorant at all about small-scale agricultural machinery, quality seeds, fertilizers, or insecticides. In fact, not only have several villagers already investigated the possibility of adopting these modern agricultural inputs but they would like to do so immediately if it were not for several impossible situations automatically accompanying their use. The peasants' awareness of or desire to adopt new technology is, therefore, no problem in your village (although it quite frequently is in many others).

As you dig into the "impossible situations," you discover some interesting facts. For one thing, the villagers have already sampled the hybrid potato being pushed by the government's agricultural development agency (potatoes being the main staple in the region. In other parts of the world it may be corn, beans, or rice). The peasants consider the hybrid potato to be greatly inferior in taste to that of their own native yellow potato. Although the yield from the yellow is low compared to that of the hybrid, for the villagers the taste of the yellow is sufficiently better to dampen any desire for change in plantings for home consumption. Moreover, the peasants' traditional fertilizer—corral dung —is adequate and sufficiently plentiful for the native variety. Besides, insects have not proved to be much of a problem. As long as the yellow is planted, therefore, there is no real reason to incur the expense of commercial fertilizers and insecticides.

On the other hand, you ascertain that the villagers certainly do wish to increase their marketable surplus and, therefore, their cash income (now at an annual amount equal to $120 per family). Because each family's farming plot is small (1 to 3 acres) and already intensively cultivated by traditional standards, the peasants realize that the only way to increase their marketable production is to adopt higher producing inputs. They have considered using the hybrid potato and its related technology for this purpose.

Contrary to your earlier suppositions about peasants in general, you now find that those of your village not only are aware of new inputs and desirous of using them for *cash* crops but also have a basic perception of the technological requirements for such a venture. You are satisfied on this point when they tell you that to make the new technology work they must apply specific amounts of commercial fertilizer to the hybrid. They also recognize the need to use proper insecticides (because as production concentration increases so do field pests), to apply fungicides (because the hybrid is not as resistant to a local blight disease as is the yellow), and to employ mechanical spreading devices (to assure that the chemicals and fertilizers are applied in the prescribed concentrations).

The peasants also inform you that they know how to count. They relate the following: last year a government agricultural technician visited the village, disseminating information regarding the new potato technology. The technician also took several interested villagers to a demonstration station near the provincial capital (several hours' travel away) where the new seed had been planted and the resulting crop was then ready for harvest. After seeing the results, the villagers had little doubt that the technology would work. The government technician returned with them to their home, looked over a sample plot, and advised them that for best results 300 pounds of hybrid seed should be planted.

The seed was readily available from the government field distribution stations but, of course, it had to be purchased. Unlike the traditional practice with the yellow, it could not be taken out of last year's storage bins "free of cash expenditures." The cost of the seed was equal to $30.00, that is, $0.10 per pound. The technician also stated that 100 pounds of chemical fertilizer were required. That would come to an additional $10. Then, in order to insure a good crop in the event of a bug invasion, $10 must be invested in insecticides. Moreover, an additional $15 would be needed to purchase fungicides to combat the local blight disease to which the hybrid was highly vulnerable. The mechanical spreading tools for the fertilizer and chemicals would cost another $20, bringing the required total investment to $85.

Eighty-five dollars may seem a small sum unless one remembers that the average annual cash income per family in the village is only $120, hardly a grand reservoir from which to extract investment funds for new technology. One might invest the meager savings on hand and borrow the balance. But what if something should go wrong and the entire crop should be destroyed—floods, drought, frost?

All this was a year ago. You have since found, however, that several of the more young and daring villagers who were not so fearful of a capricious environment had looked thoroughly into the question of obtaining credit for swinging into the new technology. Most of these families had about $20 in savings literally tucked away in their own "banks." (Some had it buried, others had it sewn into their straw mattresses, and still other heads of families carried it with them at all times.) They had planned to use their savings and borrow the balance.

The peasants related an interesting finale to this episode, however. When they approached the banks in the provincial capital to ask about borrowing the remaining funds needed for the investment ($65 on the average), they were summarily turned away. They could offer no security acceptable to those lending institutions. So the motivated villagers went to the government-sponsored agricultural development association. But officials there told them that their institution was accustomed only to dealing with large landowners and had no facilities to handle small-loan requirements. As the government had no other subsidized credit facilities in operation, that left, as a last resort, only the truckers. These were marketing "middlemen" who sometimes made financial advances to a peasant if he guaranteed to sell them his entire marketable surplus at preestablished prices—and also to pay 100 percent interest on the loan advance, a standard rate for peasants in the area.

The daring villagers made a not-too-unexpected analysis: in order to switch to the new technology they would need $85 for inputs and machinery, and an additional $65 to cover the 100 percent interest charges on the truckers' loans. Now that adds up to $150. Whether the investment under these conditions would pay off depended on the expected harvest income. And it is here that you found another interesting factor bearing on the peasants' decision not to adopt the new technology.

That additional factor dealt with price controls. Potatoes are a staple food in the country, not only for the peasant but for the workingman in the nation's cities. In an attempt to curb growing urban unrest, the government had found it advantageous to control the prices of basic foodstuffs; potatoes, of course, qualified. The result was the establishment of prices considerably lower than what free-market forces would suggest they should have been. Although costs of other less basic commodities had been rising dramatically in the past few years, the price of potatoes remained stable: $0.07 per pound.

If your peasant planted the recommended amount of seed and was blessed with a good harvest, he could expect a return of about 5000 pounds of the new potato. Of course, he would not receive the government-controlled price of $0.07. He must sell to the trucker. That would be the agreement as a condition for the trucker's credit, and he, you remember, is the only one willing to offer it. The trucker will receive the top price, not the producer. Moreover, because of the credit arrangements, the peasant cannot even bargain for competitive freight rates. Indeed, under the circumstances he could not even hire another trucker. The shippers have made a compact not to undercut one another when credit is involved, and so the peasant must sell at prices the trucker is willing and able to pay.

The trucker is in business to make money, naturally, and he considers that any return on his own investment appreciably less than 100 percent will not permit him to stay solvent. He has to consider his operating expenses, vehicle upkeep, and replacement costs (which are considerable, owing to the primitive nature of the roads). Also he has his own time investment and, of course, he does incur a certain risk in finding a good potato market. Under the circumstances he feels that the most he can offer the peasant is $0.04 per pound, weighed in at the village.

The resulting arithmetic may not be exactly simple, but it is not over the heads of your villagers. A 5000-pound harvest selling at 4 cents comes to $200. However, the original investment, including interest on the loan, would have been $150. For a $50 net profit the peasant should adopt modern agricultural technology and do all the work and run all the risks involved in the adventure? For no more work and, perhaps, considerably less risk he makes more than twice as much doing business as usual with his yellows. Thus the traditional practices in your particular village go on as before and the people continue to live at a level slightly above subsistence, growing enough yellows for their own personal needs and a little surplus for the town market. (They market yellows themselves at $0.07 per pound because, by using the old technology, they are not forced into financial ties with the middlemen.)

On the potato technology question, you have found your villagers not to be "stubborn people tied to the traditions of the past." On the contrary, within the environment in which they live you have found them to be quite rational and rather pragmatic.[3]

From one place to another in the Third World there are complex and diverse explanations for the "backwardness" of peasants, but quite frequently it becomes apparent that the peasants' love for traditional life is only part of the problem. Indeed, in your village you found that traditional attitudes were no problem—at least, as far as modern agricultural technology was concerned. The failure of your peasants to adopt the new forms derived from the following factors, each working in combination with the other: (1) low family income that made savings for an initial investment difficult if not impossible, (2) the high cost of credit, a functional substitute for insufficient savings, (3) government price controls which discriminated against the peasant producer, (4) the need to market through a "high take" middleman, and (5) the relatively high costs of the required inputs.

Most other villages that you might have studied would not have permitted explanations as simple as those above. Quite frequently many other complex factors are at work. In general, however, it is only fair to acknowledge that the peasant behaves in his environment in a very rational way *from his points of view*. The traditional practices of the past have, at least, kept him alive; a sudden change in those practices may not do as well for him. However, if by one means or another his rational horizons have expanded, as they obviously had done in your village, this still may not be sufficient to occasion a change in his behavior. Your "ecological analysis" has made the point rather well.

So you write your book. By not only describing what you saw but explaining it as well you will have created an analytical study. You will have focused very tightly on specific factors that seem to explain, more so than any of the others that you discovered, the "whys" of the reluctance of your peasants to adopt modern agricultural technology. Your book will not read exactly like a descriptive travelogue but, for those whose interests lie in analysis, your study may very well be exciting.

There are added benefits. These relate to the very real practical and moral considerations that governments, organizations, and individuals face as they search for solutions to developmental problems. To solve a problem one must first understand why it exists. Unfortunately, decisions are frequently made without that understanding, and the resulting wastes in money and manpower, with their attendant hardships for many people, are sobering indeed. Your study, however, will have filled the analytical gap on the subject of adoption of agricultural technology in your village. Aided by it, decision makers can be rational in terms of practical necessities and moral consequences.

Suppose that you were consulting with the nation's food-production board and were asked how one could go about increasing the marketable surplus from your village without his having to impose on it a coercive social organization (as some communist states and dictatorships have done when confronted with similar problems). You would have something quite concrete to say. It would be considerably more than "well, you have to change their old attitudes before anything." And "what we need to do is establish (or expand, or reorient, or refocus—the list is long) a school in the village," the standard catchall proposal.

You could say: "Fine. While I see a lot of good coming from an improved educational opportunity in my village, I must say that it will probably not have much effect in the short run on agricultural productivity. If you really want to see some dramatic changes on this point you must create production incentives. This will automatically initiate a substantial increase in marketable output. You must consider one or more of the following: (1) how to facilitate reasonably-priced credit, (2) how to facilitate marketing practices that allow a higher return to the producer, (3) the elimination of price controls on potatoes, and (4) how to facilitate lower costs for hybrid seeds, fertilizers, insecticides, fungicides, and equipment."

Since you are the researcher and the analyst you would know that if these decisions could be operationalized (and there are numerous ways in which they could be if the effects in terms of political and economic costs vis-à-vis other groups in the society could be contained), the peasants of your village would be highly motivated to adopt the new potato technology and to begin producing considerable surplus for the urban markets.

DEPENDENT AND INDEPENDENT VARIABLES

In all the disciplines, modernization studies have progressively become more rigorous. Scholars are working with "variables" and are creating "models" in order to better explain and predict behavioral, environmental, and value changes. You will be introduced to several perspectives in this book. For the moment, however, let's look at some simple variables to understand more fully the contemporary analytical trends.

A variable isolates and abstracts something that varies. For example, temperature varies. Accordingly, it is a variable against which objects, gasses, or solutions may be measured and compared. The results may be reported in a relative sense, such as "high," "low," "medium," and so forth. Or the exact temperature may even be specified in degrees. Most variables with which the social sciences deal are not nearly as exact as the "ratio" variable of temperature. Even with these limitations, however, their use facilitates a better handling of relevant facts that are discovered through research.

Reflecting on the parable of your peasant village study, you now can see that "the adoption of modern agricultural technology" may be considered a variable. The level of adoption may be high in one village but low in another. In yours it happened to be low. By ascertaining the adoption level of a number of villages (one way would be to measure the per capita use of fertilizers, insecticides, hybrid seeds, mechanical farming devices, and other appropriate "indicators" of modern agricultural technology) the villages may be placed on an "adoption dimension" somewhere between a "low" and a "high" position relative to each other. Thus, on this very tightly focused topic, many villages may be compared. Similarly, hundreds of other variables relevant to the study of modernization may also be specified. Villages or other units of analysis may then be compared on these dimensions.

As an example, suppose that you have measured the relative position of a number of villages on the adoption-of-modern-agricultural-technology variable. Suppose, further, that on this variable you are in a position to make some rather rigorous village comparisons. This is a necessary *descriptive* step in the formulation of rigorous analytical studies, since it prepares the way for you to proceed to an explanation of a logical ensuing question: Why, on this variable, does one village place higher or lower than another? It is at this point that you begin an analysis of the comparisons you have made. There are obvious practical benefits. By discovering *why* some villages rank high and others rank low, you might be able to prescribe solutions to some of their problems.

Your own single-village research discovered several factors explaining the village's low adoption-of-technology position. These were (1) family income—the peasants placed so low on this factor that they were unable to save sufficiently for investment, (2) availability of low-cost credit—very low also, (3) price incentives—very low because of government controls, (4) availability of direct urban markets—very low because of agreements among the truckers, and (5) availability of moderately priced agricultural inputs—very low as well.

These five factors may *also* be called variables because, although your village placed low on all of them, other villages, when compared to one another, may place low, medium, or high, depending on their particular circumstances. In your case the "outside world" indirectly or directly caused the village's low positioning on each of the five variables. These variables, taken together, then explained the village's low position on the main variable that had first captured your interest: adoption-of-modern-agricultural-technology.

To simplify the exposition at this point as well as to clarify what is meant by "dependent" and "independent" variables, you must think of all your village-related variables as being dichotomous, that is, as reflecting only high or low positions. We shall indicate this with plus and minus signs. In this way we can note your village's position on each variable, and also can show what we would expect to happen, in terms of your analysis, if certain changes were made. Line A in Figure 1 shows the variable relationships that you found. Thus it shows that the village placed low on variables one through five. Line A also restates, with explicit variables, the nature of your argument to the government agency. The result, as you have shown, was a self-reinforcing chain of causation that prevented villagers from adopting modern agricultural technology (and why, therefore, the village placed low on variable D).

The *changes* you proposed to the government agency are summarized in line B of the figure. The result is a graphic representation of a predictive

	1. Income	2. Low–cost credit	3. Price incentives	4. Direct markets	5. Moderately priced agricultural inputs	(Leads to a high probability of)	D. Adoption of modern agricultural technology
A. Village's observed position on the variables (showing the causal relationship	–	–	–	–	–	⟶	–
B. Village's hypothesized position immediately following the introduction of incentives	–	+	+	+	+	⟶	+

Figure 1. Your village on six variables.

"hypothesis," that is, a postulation of likely changes on variable D if the indicated changes are made on variables one to five. You urged the agency to take measures to increase the availability of low-cost credit; to remove price controls and thereby increase price incentives; to facilitate direct marketing; and to make available moderately priced agricultural inputs. You predicted (hypothesized) that, as a consequence of these changes, the village would move to a "plus" on adoption variable D.

You also implied that one result of these changes, aside from increased agricultural productivity, would be a rise in family income which would reinforce the adoption cycle after the first harvest. Thus a new D variable (income) emerges from your analysis and is explained in terms of hypothesized relationships shown in Figure 2.

What you have experienced is a very simple exercise dealing with *independent* and *dependent* variables cast into empirical and hypothetical relationships. Your first dependent variable (D in Figure 1) was the abstraction of that piece of village reality you wanted to explain, that is, the village's low adoption of modern agricultural technology. Your explanation *depended* on the relationship of this variable to the five independent variables (1 to 5 in Figure 1) that you found to be relevant. Such variables are said to be independent not because they are "free floating" and do not relate to other factors in the environment but rather because they state a relationship with a variable you wish to explain.

Independent variables attempt to explain the dependent variable. Yet these, in turn, depend on other factors in the environment. In your case, credit depended on the truckers, not on the peasants' adoption of agricultural tech-

	Independent Variables			Dependent Variable
	Adoption of modern technology	Other supporting variables remaining favorable (2,3,4,5, of Figure 1)		Income
Village's hypothesized position after harvest	+	+	⟶	+

Figure 2. Reinforcing cycle after the harvest.

nology. Similarly, markets also depended on the truckers, price incentives depended on the government, and the price of agricultural inputs depended on other factors not really mentioned in your study. To be sure, each of these independent variables, in turn, could be specified as a "dependent" variable and worked into a graphic formula similar to those in Figure 1. But then it would have its own list of one or more independent variables that would explain a village's high or low position on it. This was what occurred with your second dependent variable (income) which, in turn, depended mainly on adoption, incentives, and inputs (credit problems could be bypassed with increased income, as also could the middlemen).

There are hundreds of dependent variables that have captured the interest of students of modernization. We shall have occasion to investigate a number of them. We also shall look for relevant independent variables (and "intervening variables," a point taken up later) for purposes of explanation. These may be drawn from social, economic, psychological, cultural, and perhaps other data.

In commenting several years ago on political science studies in Latin America, Merle Kling noted advantages to, at least, specifying concrete dependent variables:

"Adherence to the research convention of specifying the dependent political variables is a relatively simple device for improving the symmetry of research, but heretofore it has not been absorbed into the main currents of political research on Latin America. Yet the regular application of this convention would facilitate comparison between one study and another, circumvent the limitations of a purely descriptive report, possibly introduce a much-desired element of cumulativeness into Latin American studies, and perhaps add to the durability of each separate research effort."[4]

Current trends in the social sciences suggest that it also is important to be as rigorous as possible with independent variables. At the very best our disciplines remain vague, inconclusive, and frequently inconsistent. Specifying the variables, both dependent and independent, is one way to avoid some of the pitfalls.

LONGITUDINAL VERSUS CROSS-SECTIONAL ANALYSES

The usage you have given the variables thus far may be termed "cross-sectional." Selecting the facts relevant to an explanation of the adoption variable, you have sought to explain your village's position on it for a particular moment in time. Variables may be used in other ways, of course, and one way is termed "longitudinal." Generally, when one uses a variable "longitudinally," he is interested in describing and perhaps explaining a village's (or some other unit of analysis) pattern of change through time. This is a "change process" focus which also may be made more rigorous by the use of appropriate variables. Suppose, again for illustration, that in addition to explaining the adoption-of-modern-agricultural-technology variable in your village, you also had acquired an interest in investigating and explaining the growth of its organized group activities during the past 10 years. You observed some growth, and you were told that there had been considerable more before your arrival. Is there some way in which you could trace out the change from year to year and closely compare, in the respective time periods, the village's organizational condition? If so, you might then be able to move an additional step and, as previously, explain the "whys" of this growth.

One of the ways social scientists attempt to do this, particularly if their data is primarily qualitative, is to employ the use of "ideal-type" variables. Frequently they will form these variables by placing opposite-meaning "ideal" abstractions at each end of a "continuum," as in Figure 3. Several well-known classic ideal-type formulations, in addition to the "traditional" and "modern" ones shown, are Fred Rigg's "agraria-industria," Robert Redfield's "folk-urban," Emile Durkheim's "mechanical-organic," and Ferdinand Toennies' "gemeinschaft-gesellschaft."

Polar-opposite types, such as the above, are ideal in the sense that they represent only an idea. Max Weber, one of the first to exploit their analytical power, viewed them as one-sided accentuations of concrete individual features of a society so arranged that they formed an "analytical construct." Of course, in its conceptual purity the mental construct cannot be found anywhere in reality. The purpose of the ideal types, therefore, is not to represent reality so much as it is to synthesize an ideal set of conditions that societies (or any

Figure 3. A variable composed of ideal-type polar opposites.

other unit of analysis) may more or less approximate. Thus the ideal types form the "ends" of a variable on which any relevant units can be compared. The "continuum" represents the real world in between.

Try your hand at an ideal-type formulation. Think up an ideal rock festival. Consider the concrete individual features you see in that festival—participants, listeners, location, degree of originality, expertise, and so forth. If you make your "analytical construct" complex enough you very well may have an ideal type on your hands. Now do likewise for the ideal Bach concert. Again, you may end up with an ideal type. Whether these are polar opposites or not may be problematical, but some music festivals and concerts may, indeed, approximate—some more so than others—the features you have included in your Rock-Bach ideal types.

Back to your village again. There you also could create polar opposites that would facilitate a study of the village's organizational growth, which you are investigating. A couple of tags you might consider would be "atomization" and "organization," each respectively indicating those ideal conditions where no group activity exists, on the one hand, and no unorganized individual activity, on the other.

By devising a way to measure the relative levels of atomization and organization in your village at successive periods of time during the past 10 years, you could plot the growth (or decay) of organized activity and then compare the village to itself at different points in time. At each point of comparison, you could look for independent variables that might explain what you had observed and measured.

Suppose you found that 10 years ago the village was at point A on Figure 4. Right now, however, you find that it is at point D. The trend is obvious. The village, for reasons you would try to explain through the use of independent variables, has been losing characteristics of the "atomized" ideal type and has been acquiring those of the "organized" type. The intermediate points of B and C indicate the village's respective position on the variable at, perhaps, seven and three years ago.

In reality, a village, or any other unit for that matter, can move "backward" as well as "forward" on this or almost any other variable. If it is moving

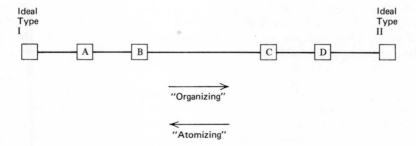

Figure 4. Processes of change in organized behavior.

forward on this variable then interpersonal mistrust is being replaced by trust, and organizations are being formed to attack village problems. If it is moving backward, then organizations are decaying, the level of interpersonal trust is falling, "traditional man" is taking over in the system, and the influence of "modern man" is on the wane.

The usage of dependent and independent variables, whether the focus is cross-sectional or longitudinal, is one way to sharpen our thinking and research. There are other advantages deriving from their use as well. By thinking in terms of explicit variables we are more readily adapted to assimilating the powerful insights that empirical and analytical theory can give us. Let us turn to these considerations.

THEORY, VARIABLES, AND GENERALIZATIONS

One goal of social science is to reach and refine general explanations and predictions about an increasingly wider and more complex variety of human behavior. A social-science approach, therefore, must separate itself from purely historical or journalistic approaches, which look respectively at the past or present with an eye to determining the minutiae of some particular event or series of events within historical or contemporary contexts.

In refining general explanations and predictions, the "exact" sciences, as well as our own trial-and-error endeavors, have taught us that explanation and research divorced from theory are often unproductive. Accordingly, social scientists today have begun to place a great deal of emphasis on theory and are now working out of one or more models or theoretical "paradigms." However, whereas the physical scientists in many instances are in general agreement on their theories (the Einsteinian one, for example, as opposed to the earlier ones elaborated by Galileo or Newton) the social scientists are not. When you hear or see the terms *functionalism, structural-functionalism, conflict theory, historical materialism, diffusionism, cybernetics, communication* and *information processing theory,* and *systems theory* in any of their numerous individual varieties, you will be aware that reference probably is being made to a social-science paradigm—a kind of selective theory, a way of looking at the world.

At present there is little likelihood that social scientists will agree on the superiority of any one of these or additional unmentioned paradigms, partly because each frequently has legitimate claims to relative superiority depending on the variables selected for study. Some paradigms or models are strong in their explanation of stability, maintenance, and control; others in explaining the impact of intervention; others in explaining revolution, and so on.

Nevertheless, in each instance where a respective paradigm is most powerful, an interesting consequence derives from its use. The user is alerted to more aspects of reality than he already knows; he is sensitized to relationships among variables that he might otherwise miss; and he also is made aware of the potential bounds of the empirical data relevant to his dependent variables. The influence of theory and the potential value deriving from it, therefore, is enormous.

This implies, of course, that the theory—at least, some parts of it—is amenable to "testing" in the world of reality. The key concepts and relationships of which it speaks must be suitable to some kind of "measurement." And the relationships themselves must be specified in such a way that testable hypotheses emerge. One does not have to have a theory to create a hypothesis, of course; for you have already advanced one dealing with your adoption and income variables (line B, Figure 1; and Figure 2) that has little theoretical underpinning. But a working theory gives one much more analytical leverage.

Later we shall examine a "middle-range" theory that illustrates the points made in this section. For the moment, however, let's turn to a discussion of some additional basic modernization concepts.

BIBLIOGRAPHICAL ESSAY

Your "field research" touched on many theoretical and methodological points that were well beyond the scope of Chapter 1. It is useful to be aware of some of them, however. A standard introduction and general reference to research methodology is Claire Selltiz, and others, *Research Methods in Social Relations*. This work should be supplemented by a basic introduction to the philosophy of explanation. A good one to begin with is Richard S. Rudner, *Philosophy of Social Science*. A more rigorous, but still basic, treatment of philosophical considerations in explanation is Robert Brown's *Explanations in Social Science*. (For complete references see the bibliography.)

Explanation and theory-building are not identical, as Chapter 1 has attempted to show. A very good essay that treats this relationship in depth but still at a level open to an introductory student is David V. Edward's *International Political Analysis*, Parts III and IV. Additional and more sophisticated works are: Llewellyn Gross, *Sociological Theory: Inquiries and Paradigms;* James C. Charlesworth, *Contemporary Political Analysis;* Walter Buckley, *Modern Systems Research for the Behavioral Scientist;* and Carl G. Hempel, *Aspects of Scientific Explanation.*

Interestingly, social scientists in the United States are not the only ones concerned with explanatory and predictive theories. Among students in the socialist countries also there is an incipient movement in this direction. (They had been taught that a Marxian framework could answer nearly all the questions; now, however, they realize that such a monistic approach is grossly inadequate.) I refer specifically to the discussion of Jan F. Triska, "The Socialist World System in Search of a Theory," in Jacobs, editor, *The New Communisms*.

The current conflicts among models or paradigms in the social sciences are not peculiar to those fields. Similar disturbances have occurred in the physical sciences. At the present time, it appears that the intensity of these conflicts is greatly attenuated because of the general acceptance since Einstein of a relatively small number of general theories. Nevertheless, today's situation did not come about peaceably. Anyone interested in this phenomenon must read Thomas S. Kuhn, *The Structure of Scientific Revolutions*, second edition, enlarged. Kuhn has made a brilliant and original analysis of the major causes and consequences of revolutions in basic scientific concepts. He even has a word or two to say about the social sciences.

Of course, considerable contemporary writing, although not necessarily related to a paradigm or theory, is nevertheless rigorous and deals with variables. Popularly known as "correlational analysis," some recent examples have introduced a new statistical technique (causal path analysis) that permits one to impute causation among several factors or variables. A good example is Robert D. Putnam, "Toward Explaining Military Intervention in Latin American Politics."

The world of the peasant has just begun to be opened to social scientists (with the exception of the anthropologists who have had a continuing interest in "primitive" peoples). The best general introduction along lines implied by the account of "field work" in Chapter 1 is Eric Wolf, *Peasants*. In considering peasants within the context of technological change and economic development, two works should be consulted: the first is the highly readable book by George M. Foster, *Traditional Cultures and the Impact of Technological Change,* and the second, a bibliographical essay that makes available hundreds of references, is Joel M. Halpern and John Brode, *Peasant Society: Economic Changes and Revolutionary Transformation*. A general treatment also of interest and worth is Jack M. Potter, and others, *Peasant Society: A Reader*. For Latin Americanists, Rodolfo Stavenhagen's *Agrarian Problems and Peasant Movements in Latin America* is a must. Then, to capture the new phenomena of migration and rural-urban peasant linkages, see William Mangin, editor, *Peasants in Cities.*

Numerous technical considerations in transforming traditional agriculture, including the problem of motivation, are treated by Theodore W. Schultz, *Transforming Traditional Agriculture*. Following this, and in order to gain a better insight into the relationship of agriculture to national economic goals and priorities, consult Carl K. Eicher and Lawrence W. Witt, *Agriculture in Economic Development.*

The use of ideal types as an analytical tool—a very old device, in fact—has increased in recent years. The most powerful contribution to studies of modernization that ideal types make seems to be when they are cast as variables within the context of some abstract theory of change. Specifically, the "traditional-modern" continuum was popularized by Daniel Lerner in his seminal and trailblazing work on the Middle East (*The Passing of Traditional Society*) and has been taken up in one or another variety by many social scientists. There is now a growing feeling that the "traditional-modern" categories are too "loose," however, and more rigorous specifications are being developed. These as well as earlier ones are employed as much for understanding and describing psychological change as for economic and social change.

The "agraria-industria" ideal-types come from Fred Rigg's "Agraria and Industria: Toward a Typology of Comparative Administration." The "folk-urban" formulations derive from Robert Redfield's *The Folk Culture of Yucatan*. Emile Durkheim, approximately 75 years ago, developed his "mechanical-organic" continuum while trying to explain the various types of community solidarity that he encountered. And the gemeinschaft-gesellschaft variety originated from Toennies' very old study of community types. For a comprehensive discussion on the use of ideal types in modern social science, see John C. McKinney, *Constructive Typology and Social Theory.*

CHAPTER 2

Modernity and Modernization

Modernity is both a state of mind and a state of being. It deals as much with people's attitudes and values as with their physical and social world. *Modernization,* on the other hand, is the process by which modernity is reached. As that process unfolds, attitudes and values, along with the physical and social environment, undergo change. A traditional-modern ideal-type continuum is frequently used to describe that change.

There are obvious problems with these terms. For instance, contemporary definitions are as time-bound as were those that preceded them decades or centuries ago. It is to be expected, therefore, that "modernization" and "modernity" today do not carry the same meanings as they did even as late as 1850. Nor is it likely that contemporary definitions will be any more durable. Indeed, at the present time we can only hazard an educated guess about what the meanings in the twenty-fifth century—only 500 years from now— will be.

In the nineteenth and early twentieth centuries, "modernization" referred primarily to the growth of rationality (with a corresponding decline in mysticism and magic), to secular ways of thinking and behaving (as opposed to sacred or theological ways), and to associated patterns of action that released men from the chains of superstition and the tyrannical bonds of despots. The really modern man was a cool philosopher, a natural or physical scientist, or perhaps even a successful entrepreneur. His world was one of secular books, test tubes, experiments, and real-world observations; not one of superstitions, magic, and doctrinal explanations of the world and all it contained. Moreover, in those days the man of modernity considered himself to be a free man, or at least one who ought to be free, unbound not only by fetishes, rituals, and ceremonies but by despotic political systems as well. A modern nation was one wherein all these conditions largely prevailed.

In the world of the 1970's, however, rationality, secularism, and political freedom are not considered to constitute a sufficient definition of modernity. New symbols have been added. Moreover, there has been some rethinking about the meaning of "freedom." Consequently, modernity has been redefined, at least, in part. To be considered modern according to prevailing contemporary thinking, therefore, an individual (or a nation) must not only be rational and secular but must apply those attributes to a specific developmental task— and all this with *or* without political freedom. That task is a successful

24

economic conquest of the environment. Thus, today, the single most important popular symbol of national modernity is a country's relative state of economic development.

There are underlying considerations of even prior importance, however. One of them deals with a nation's innovative capacity. First, if people are to constantly develop economically (to enhance their productive capacity) they must, as David Apter insists, have a capacity to innovate without falling apart —to alter their beliefs and to accept change so that new roles relating to the productive use of technology can surface. Second, the respective nation must produce the kind of social framework that will provide, and pass on to successive generations, the skills and knowledge that living in a technologically advanced world requires.[1] A modern nation is one that not only can handle change but also can appropriate it to good advantage—economic development. Modernization subsumes the processes by which a nation and its people approximate that goal.

One way of improving a nation's productive capacity—to become more modern—is to industrialize. There may be alternative ways to develop economically. But, strikingly, most political leaders in the Third World do not seem to think so. Regardless of their resources, markets, population size, and so forth, they all want to industrialize. They believe—and maybe correctly— that it is only through industrialization that sustained higher productive capacity, and therefore economic development, can occur.

In their minds this is modernity, a condition which, in its "finest hours," presumably is something akin to what Walt Rostow once called the "age of high-mass consumption."[2]

Modernization—the progressive move from nonmodernity to modernity, or from traditionalism to modernism—denotes the process whereby men adjust themselves in terms of politics, society, and culture so that they can develop their environment economically. Today the really modern man is one who can energetically participate in the creation and consumption of material wealth. The changes required in his attitudes and values are those that will allow him to function in the elaborate organizations necessary to progressively widen control over nature and to distribute the resulting material benefits. In relation to the values of a century or so ago, such behavior implies changes in man's perception of himself, of his fellowman, of his material environment, and of time itself. Of course, not everyone agrees that these changes are "good." They take place, nevertheless, as modernization advances.

A pervasive value of economic growth exists in nearly all the countries of the world. People want to be not only modern but ultramodern if they can. Of course, in terms of the new economic symbols, many countries have not achieved even a minimal state of modernity. Indeed, actually, several have scarcely incorporated the old symbols of rationality and secularism. But no country seems to be immune from the desire to develop economically. Thus the spirit of nationalism that has fired hopes and imaginations in so much of the developing world also presents a kind of "ideology of development." It presumably illuminates a way by which rapid economic progress may be achieved. Yet, while the goal is clear, the exact process by which one gets to it occasions great argument. Nevertheless, the search goes on.

The enormous impact of these developmentalist ideologies caught many scholars unprepared. Wilber Moore has observed:

"The magnitude of the ideological commitment to economic growth was not predicted by anthropologists and sociologists, who emphasized and exaggerated the integrity of the traditional social systems and the diversity among them, or by economists, whose motivational assumptions were more nearly right but who understated the availability of entrepreneurs as agents of change and overstated the restrictions of resources and technology."[3]

What will modernization and modernity mean in the twenty-fifth century? *More* "high mass-consumption"? Most unlikely, I think. Perhaps the symbols of modernity 500 years hence will be associated with man's ability to transcend time and space intellectually—or perhaps even to do so materially. Modernization would then imply the process through which men and nations acquire these abilities and all the related symbols. Who knows? The spectacular prognostications of new symbols for the America of the 1980's are sufficient to fill one with considerable awe. Indeed, we may find the symbols of modernity in 1985 to be associated with the consequences of economic development rather than with the creation of more of it—with the handling of wastes and pollution to prevent this planet from becoming uninhabitable. In any event, no one appears capable of conceiving what five centuries of accelerated change —of the geometric variety we have known in the last quarter century—will bring to our descendants. In fact, we can only guess what this change may bring to the descendants of the people in the Third World of today who are still groping for the economic symbols of modernity—and sometimes even for the earlier ones of rationality and secularism. Whatever the outcome, no doubt it will include a high degree of diversity.

ATTITUDES AND VALUES

For "non-modern" people to successfully pursue the late twentieth-century symbols of modernity, some people have argued that a number of well-ordered attitudes and values handed down from previous generations must undergo change. Change of this kind is both difficult and disruptive because many traditional points of view have the sanction of centuries of use, have been purified by ritual and magic (or their equivalent in religious doctrine), and may have maintained stability and order very well in a mainly premodernizing environment. But once a society or a nation alters its goals—from traditional stability to modernizing change—many traditional ideas about self, fellowman, and the world must also change if achievement of the new goals is to be even remotely possible.

We are not by any means talking about a wholesale discarding of the past. Indeed, we are impressed, as Apter has noted, "with what appears to be the infinite malleability of culture, its persistence and toughness and capacity to perform many functions and serve many masters."[4] What generally occurs is a selective replacement of attitudes and values in such a way that man can live and function in a changing environment and can pursue the new materialistic goals without suffering psychic breakdown. Many old values and attitudes remain and will continue to do so as long as they seem in any way useful for, or at least not a hindrance to, modernizing change.[4a]

If you think of "attitudes and values" as being associated with ideal types which one might employ to describe traditional or modern man (rather than reacting to their "goodness" or "badness" at this point), the exposition will be considerably facilitated. This is necessary if one is ever to "come to grips" intellectually with the disruptive implications of a rapidly changing environment, particularly if the changes have already placed a country in the age of "high mass-consumption." Indeed, social scientists of our fictional twenty-fifth century probably will not view America's values as ever having approached the pinnacle of virtue that we frequently believe they have attained. From their vantage, many of our present ideas will appear frighteningly archaic. Yet they are functional for our time. They facilitate the specification of a modern nation as modernity is currently defined. But if new conditions arise that occasion a redefinition of modernity, we shall find it necessary to alter many of these time-honored attitudes. In a world of change, few values and attitudes appear immune to alteration or redefinition. We may consider this a most undesirable turn of events. It nevertheless happens.

With respect to the contemporary scene, one writer, Everett M. Rogers, has developed 10 independent variables that describe a subculture of peasantry[5] or, in our terminology, the world of traditional attitudes and beliefs largely incompatible with the modernity of the 1970's. Accordingly, to the extent that people in such a subculture modernize—and much of the world is modernizing these days—they change their positions on a progressively expanding number of the variables. These are not the only useful variables, of course, but they do illustrate the points that have been raised.

One of the variables is "mutual distrust in interpersonal relations." A highly distrusting society would be composed of arch-individualists, men fearful of trusting their neighbors under nearly all circumstances. Obviously with such a high degree of distrust little organized activity of the kind needed for increased productive capacity could be possible. There could be no banks, no cooperatives, no stocks, and no effective bureaucracies, interest groups, or political parties. In the traditional world of subsistence agriculture where each family must be largely self-reliant, such distrust functions to protect the family from exploitative "friends" or experiences where one simple miscalculation could prove disastrous for survival. But this attitude is incompatible with modernity. Therefore, as modernization proceeds, the bearer of such an attitude must modify it if he cares to participate very actively in the process itself.

Another of the variables is "fatalism," that is, a state of mind wherein man, if he is highly fatalistic, considers himself totally dominated by nature and the circumstances that surround him. "Whatever will be will be." Or, more likely, "whatever *is* will be." Such a person believes that there is nothing he can do to alter his station in life or master his environment. If he is not a victim of the demons, then certainly he must be one of a vengeful god or an enraged saint. With a psychology of this kind one would not be too encouraged to harness rivers, reclaim lands, or rationally fight disease. Such attitudes must and do change as people modernize.

Still another attitude is abstracted by the variable "empathy" (or lack of it). If one has low empathy he greatly lacks an ability to think of himself as engaged in roles different from those to which he is accustomed. How could a peasant of your village ever begin to use insecticides, to drive a tractor, to be president of a cooperative, or to do any other out-of-the-ordinary activity if he has no capacity to see himself as doing anything outside the established roles of traditional life? Indeed, empathy is such an important variable that Daniel Lerner, in his pioneering study of the Middle East, considered it to be one of the most important hallmarks of man's capacity to modernize. Many men simply do not have that capacity. When asked what he would do if he were president of Turkey, a low-empathy peasant declared to Lerner's researchers: "My God! How can I . . . I cannot . . . President of Turkey . . . master of the whole world?"[6] The man obviously could not see himself in a presidential role; he probably could not think of himself as acting in a good number of lesser caliber roles either.

Rogers' remaining variables similarly useful in demonstrating the incompatibility of some attitudes and values with modernity are: limited view of the world, lack of an ability to defer personal gratification, limited aspirations, lack of innovativeness, familism, perceived limited good, and dependence on and hostility toward government authority.

If Rogers' "subculture of peasantry" isolates the *traditional* attitudes and values that are inimical to a modern environment, what, then, is the *modern* state of mind that allows man to produce and handle this environment? Let's start looking for the answer to this question by examining the other side of empathy.

Most readers of this book are students—and they have been playing that role for 12 or more years. No doubt there are scores of other roles that they play quite well during summer vacation months; and, perhaps, many can think of themselves as eventually becoming anything from technical or professional experts to corporate executives, social workers, or politicians. University students tend to be highly empathic. They probably are more so than their parents, and probably much more so than their grandparents. In part, it is through their empathy that a modernizing world will become more modern. Thus simply the possession of high empathy places them literally a world apart from Rogers' peasants on many of the "subculture" variables.

Aside from high empathy, there are several additional attitudinal and valuational features of modern man that add to a definition of his psychic modernity. In fact, Alex Inkeles argues that modern man presents a general syndrome of variables that all hang together. He indicates that some of the more important ones are,

"(1) Openness to new experience, both with people and with new ways of doing things such as attempting to control birth; (2) the assertion of increasing independence from the authority of traditional figures like parents and priests and a shift of allegiance to leaders of government, public affairs, trade unions, cooperatives, and the like; (3) belief in the efficacy of science and medicine and a general abandonment of passivity and fatalism in face of life's difficulties; and (4) ambition for oneself and one's children to achieve high occupational and educational goals."[7]

Other features of the syndrome are equally important. One is "achievement" as opposed to "ascriptive" norms. Modern man thinks that one should be rewarded according to his contribution and not according to whim, special hereditary and racial principles, or political ties. Yet an additional feature is an attitude of inquiry and questioning about how men make choices—moral, social, and personal. It is frequently noted that, in a world of change, choices become available as never before. Modern man's self-conscious concern with choice and its practical availability in his modern world have led to an attitude of experiment and invention. Accordingly, progressively more of the world becomes explicable in rational and scientific terms even if the problem of moral choice is never satisfactorily resolved.

Besides these features, various authorities of change have noted that as man becomes more modern he develops an increasing concern for carefully planning affairs in advance. He progressively becomes more interested in the news, preferring news of national and international import over news that deals merely with sports, religion, or purely local affairs. Moreover, such a man begins to distinguish between personal and political relationships; he builds a strong ego; and he develops opinions related to a widening variety of contemporary topics about which he increasingly becomes better informed. He develops faith in other people and is concerned with the need to affiliate with them in an organized way.

As man modernizes, he gradually eliminates from his psychology the attitudes and values incompatible with modernity, and he acquires those that support it. Obviously, of course, no man is *purely* modern. In many respects we are dealing here with ideal types. Nevertheless, some men are more modern than others. And those who are, demonstrate a higher capability to participate in and produce more of the symbols that are associated with a modern society and economy.

INSTITUTIONS AND ENVIRONMENT

To say that a nation is favored with a psychologically modern citizenry does not, in itself, define that nation's modernity. Quite aside from people's attitudes and values, one must also reflect on the social, political, and economic institutions that permeate any country. We have already indicated the pervasive position that economic development holds in all contemporary definitions of modernity. Yet, in addition to this environmental feature, there are many others that relate to a country's whole institutional fabric. Therefore, having touched on the attitudes and values that deal with the *psychological* features of modernity, we must also examine the *structural* ones.

Every nation has some kind of economic structure. It has a more or less coherent pattern of activities that facilitate the production, marketing, and consumption of products. An economic structure may be simple (like that associated with small-scale agriculture or near-subsistence farming) or complex (like that related to industrial, commercial, and service activities). The more complex the structure the more specialized are the roles (the jobs, occupations, and the like) that make it up.

Likewise, all nations (except, perhaps, those in a state of revolution) have some kind of social structure. They are characterized by an ordered interaction of people who play out various social roles. Lords, servants, farmers, shoeshine boys, and entrepreneurs are but several of hundreds.

In an analogous way one can also speak of a family structure, a bureaucratic structure, a political structure, an occupational structure, and so on for considerable length. Thus numerous structures may be specified. Some have to do with institutions that produce and disseminate goods and information, others with the integration of geo-human life patterns (city-town-village), others with formal government and politics (courts, legislatures, executives, voting) and informal modes of political participation (through interest groups, propaganda, and small-group persuasion), and so on.

Some of the structural features of the modern nation include high levels of productive capacity, predominantly urban living, high levels of education, a widespread use of mass communication, a rationalized bureaucracy, and orderly institutions for political participation. Hence, a modern country is not only full of modern people but it is also highly developed economically, highly urbanized, and highly literate. It demonstrates high levels of media participation (television, radio, newspapers, periodicals) as well as a complex network of rapid communications (telephones, roads, rails, and air). It is administered by a bureaucracy operating under general rules equally applicable to all men, and it is composed of citizens who actively participate one way or another (through voting, interest groups, political parties) in governmental and political affairs. A traditional society ranks extremely low on these variables, although in some countries, especially in Latin America, it is not uncommon for large urban centers to exist in an otherwise relatively traditional environment.

There is, of course, a relationship between men's values and attitudes, the environment in which they live, and the society to which they belong. It is a difficult relationship to determine at times. Some of the reasons for this are discussed in a following section. For the moment, however, we must emphasize that the structural features of a country, considered alone, do not explain its modernity any more than do the psychological attributes of its citizens. Some men having modern values and attitudes do at times live in a traditional environment. Likewise, we are apt to find that some of the most densely populated urban centers shelter people who possess nearly all the attributes of Rogers' "subculture of peasantry." By this we do not mean to imply that the structural features of modernity are not important. Quite the opposite. In terms of its current definition, modernity could not exist without them.

Processes of Structural Change

We have considered some of the attitudes and values that undergo change as men move from traditional ways of thinking *toward* modern ones. In an analogous manner we may also consider some of the processes of structural change that occur as a nation shifts from a traditional environmental setting toward a modern one. One widely accepted explanation of what happens derives from the "structural-functional" school of analysis. The keys are the concepts of "differentiation" and "specialization." These relate, among other things, to the creation of new structures and to a "dividing up" of the old roles into more specialized groupings. For example, the family is a structural feature of almost every society, traditional or modern. And, in most traditional societies, it carries out not only economic functions but educational, occupational training, and policing ones as well. Thus in a traditional society any given role structure (the family, for example, with various roles played by the parents, the children, and the relatives) carries out numerous social functions. In a modern society, however, many of these functions are taken over by specialized role structures such as school systems and police departments. Accordingly, when sociologists speak of differentiation and specialization as endemic characteristics of modernization, they generally refer to social institutions such as the family which begin to share some of their historical functions with new and more specialized agencies or institutions as the processes of modernization move along. The family remains, to be sure, but in the modern society the number of its functions has greatly decreased. The same process of specialization and differentiation goes on in occupations, bureaucracies, and the like.

Neil J. Smelser has made one of the best presentations of differentiation and specialization as they relate to modernization. He focuses on the kinds of social change that accompany a growth in the economic symbols of modernity, that is, "growth of output per head of population." His main structural variables deal with technology, agriculture, industry, and human ecology. Differentiation and specialization are seen to occur as a society moves on each variable from conditions specified by one ideal-type toward those indicated by the other. These are: (1) in technology, from simple traditional techniques toward application of scientific knowledge, (2) in agriculture, from subsistence farming toward commercial production of agricultural goods (specialization in cash crops, agricultural wage labor), (3) in industry, the transition from human and animal power toward industrialization, and (4) in ecological arrangements, the movement from the farm and village toward urban centers. He argues that, although it is not mandatory, these several processes often occur simultaneously.[8]

The institutional and environmental features of the *modern* society or nation are fairly well established in terms of current definitions. Such a society is more urbanized than not, more literate than not, more industrialized, scientific, and communicative than not. Moreover, the *modernizing* society continues structurally to differentiate its institutional fabric and to specialize in functions that contribute to a realization of the features of modernity.

THE CRITICAL MIX: HOW DO MEN AND SOCIETIES MODERNIZE?

Given that *both* men and societies modernize as a nation enhances its productive capacity, which modernizes first? Is economic development dependent first on modern attitudes and values and only second on modern structures and institutions? Could it be the reverse? Or, could it be that economic development precedes them both? Solid answers may appear facile; however, the relation, whatever it is, is undoubtedly more complex than one might at first imagine. As economic advances are made, some observers are able to see only "a complex interaction between changing institutions and environment on the one hand, and evolving attitudes and values on the other." Indeed, many experts are hesitant to posit causal linkages between the psychological and structural features of modernization (or between both of these and economic development) because in many instances of rapid change the direction of causality may be impossible to determine. In the "very beginning" of the development of current symbols of modernity, some individuals, no doubt, had to be innovative and empathic for the first time, and had to produce the psychological makeup that allowed them to create and glory in environmental change. There had to be a psychological drive originating somewhere that mobilized some men to modernize. Max Weber thought he found it in "The Protestant Ethic." Yet non-Protestant, in fact non-Christian, attitudes and values have also been associated with modernity (for example, Japan). In any event, once the symbols were established they in turn influenced the attitudes and values of many traditionalists who later came into contact with them. Thus one might argue that attitudes and values changed first and were followed thereafter by the development of the structural symbols of modernity, including those related to economic development. But someone else might easily argue that the value change itself resulted from striking antecedent structural events (such as a breakdown in a traditional economy, an invention that totally altered the relation of man to his work, or the appearance of a Calvinistic religion).

The question of what happened "first" in the history of technological and economic advances is, of course, an interesting one. It may also be unresolvable and one that we shall do well to leave mostly to the pursuit of others. In any event, except for some peripheral comments that follow, it is beyond the scope of this book. Instead, let us look at the difficult relation of modernizing men to modernizing societies in the contemporary world where economic development, or the desire for it, already is a fact of life.

At the present time the processes of modernization, no matter how lacking in apparent significance, are at work virtually everywhere—from tiny Kuwait to giant India, from Russia to the United States. In the contemporary (as opposed to the historical) world, what are the forces behind the change? Given any state of modernity, where does more of it come from? Does the dynamic force, the "energy," lie in the institutions and structures of the society, in the attitudes and values of the people, or in some complex and intricate combination of both? These are important questions not only for understanding modernization but also for understanding the "energy sources" of change—the causal dynamics behind the whole business. Currently there are, at least, three general approaches to answering these questions.

The Institutional Perspective

The first answer is that the psychological processes of modernization (the development of interpersonal trust, empathy, faith in the future and the other modern psychological features already noted) are dependent variables explained by larger institutional and structural processes occurring in the society as a whole. This argument is very compatible with the old "diffusionist" school of thought, although diffusionism certainly is not the only way that such change may occur. But applied to modernization, the diffusionist assertions are that while the dynamics for modernization somehow originated in the West (as part and parcel of the Industrial Revolution), their consequences (a modern psychology, urbanization, literacy, differentiation and specialization) later "diffused" throughout the world because of the overwhelming expansive influence of the early industrial nations. From this point of view, the colonial powers themselves sowed the seeds of modernization in Africa, Asia, and the Middle East by transferring to those areas all the structural paraphernalia of a modern commercial city. Similar influences, it is argued, were at work in Latin America. Indeed, it is from this thrust that the large primate cities so characteristic of many Third World countries are said to have originated.

Once colonial peoples become habituated to the transplanted structures and institutions, some of them began to acquire the ideas, values and attitudes necessary to sustain the transplants—or, at least, to desire to sustain them. The question as to why some traditional people in the modernizing world were, and still are, infected sooner than others by modernizing values is not answered very well, if at all, by this argument. Clearly, however, the "institution-first" perspective views the dynamic cities as being the "energy of change" for the further differentiation, specialization, and development of modern values and attitudes.

All this suggests that man's attitudes and values are somehow "captives" of his environment, that values change only insofar as the environment changes first—that a modern psychology is preceded by differentiation and specialization. Thus in the developing world of today a modernizing psychology does not surface, the argument goes, unless large structural events involving significant portions of the society are in progress or have already occurred. This institutional perspective considers attitudinal change as a by-product of the "great lumbering social processes" that already have an engine of change somehow built into them. For the contemporary period that dynamic engine clearly is seen to be the world that is already modern. This includes the "Western World," loosely taken as a whole, as well as modern cities elsewhere (there are a great number of them) that originated as a product of earlier contact with the West. Many contemporary theorists in sociology, political science, and economics pay strong credence to this point of view in one or another of its elaborate versions. In short, modern symbols exist (associated primarily with the cities), and when people make contact with them, they frequently desire to acquire or participate in the benefits they represent. In the process the participants' traditional attitudes and values undergo modernizing change.

Certainly there are impelling examples of the dependence of modern attitudes on a supporting modern environment. Where would you say your own "need" to achieve and excel came from? Would that need be the same had you been born and reared among the head-hunting Jivaros of southern Panama, the white-skinned Hairy Ainus of Japan or, for that matter, the peasants of your village? The odds are infinitely high that they would not be the same. Many social scientists would argue that you really acquired those values from your parents or early acquaintances, and subsequently found them reinforced by the modern institutions of your society. You have been *socialized* to "need."

The peasants of the village that you studied, following this argument, acquired values and attitudes amenable to the adoption of modern agricultural technology not out of a vacuum but, instead, from large on-going changes in their environment. Specifically, their acquisitive values, in terms of modern symbols, developed through increasing participation in the market system of their modernizing country. Subsequently, they perceived better ways to play the market game contingent on their adopting a more productive agricultural technology. The fact that they knew of the technology at all was due to the agricultural experiment station set up by the national government. *Had it not been for adverse structural conditions (credit, transport, and the like) the peasants would have put the "diffused" ideas into practice.*

One branch of a theory known as "cognitive dissonance" illustrates this general relationship of attitudes to environment. As interpreted by Albert O. Hirschman in a nontechnical language the theory holds that a person who commits himself to some kind of modernizing behavior contrary to his beliefs or values is in a state of *dissonance*. (As, for example, when a peasant is forced, out of economic necessity, to leave his yoked oxen in the country and take a menial city factory job.) "Such a state is unpleasant, and the person will attempt to reduce the dissonance. Since the 'discrepant behavior' has already taken place and cannot be undone, while the belief can be changed, reduction of dissonance can be achieved principally by changing one's beliefs in the direction of greater harmony with the action."[9]

Roughly, the thrust of the point is this: if political leaders desire that people's values and attitudes should modernize so that economic development may occur (or increase), then they should set up structural or institutional mechanisms that encourage people to change to a modernizing behavior. The appropriate modernizing attitudes, it is argued, will then have an automatic tendency to fall in line as the individuals attempt to reduce the dissonance between their values and their new roles.

Notice, however, that Hirschman's cognitive dissonance argument presupposes that some modern institutions and symbols already exist in the country. Otherwise, how would it set up appropriate inducements for modernizing behavior? Similarly, one also must suppose that the country has, at least, a few modern men.

If one accepts the premises of the institutional argument, what conclusions does he draw for the developing world? A nation that has already begun to modernize can make itself more modern more quickly by inducing its people into situations in which they must "act" modern, regardless of their existing values, attitudes, or beliefs. In due time they will begin to "think" modern as well.

One institutional device frequently employed for this purpose is compulsory education. To make men modern—or more modern—one puts them or their children into the classroom. Literacy not only is a universal symbol of modernity but it also creates "favorable" conditions of dissonance. From this experience come men whose values have presumably modernized—at least, a little.

Throughout the developing world a great emphasis has been placed on educational systems that are capable of introducing the masses to modern symbols. Sometimes the effort is pushed with such enthusiasm that it creates enormous political tensions and strain. A system may produce considerably more people educated in modern ways of doing and thinking than it can absorb into its infant modernizing economy and society. Perhaps the economy is sluggish. Or perhaps the society is so rigid that structural change is greatly resisted, thus preventing the integration and absorption of the newly educated. Typically, such a "surplus population" becomes very upset and may indeed become subversive. A president of an African country declared, when caught in a situation of this kind several years after the United Nations had set up an impressive mass literacy program in his country, that education before employment was an unproductive social experience.

The other structural or institutional devices often cited as frequently having a modernizing effect are: (1) the development of the nation state with its bureaucratic apparatus capable of penetrating to the very core of a traditional man's life; and (2) the industrial enterprise, especially the factory, which has such a pervasive influence on its workers in terms of how they relate to each other (organization) and their work (specialization, new product lines, time demands and requirements, consistency, speed, and the like). All these features are structural and institutional characteristics of the environment. They are seen to harbor modern symbols that, once diffused among the people, will cause their attitudes and values to begin to modernize as well.

We frequently see the conclusions of this argument reflected in public and private policy in the United States as well as in other countries. The United States government's Headstart Program, for example, was based on the assumption that one could take preschool children from a "traditional" home, put them in a modern institutional environment, and thereby influence their values and attitudes to "modernize." We see similar concepts at work in the

"Indian Programs" at various universities in the United States. It is thought that taking college-age Indian youth off the reservations and placing them in a modern environment for the school year (preferably having them live with a "modern" family while they attend school) will enable them to acquire the attitudes, values, and skills necessary to rise above the poverty and backwardness of their native tribes and to be able to handle the white man's world on the white man's terms. If the contemporary symbols of modernity were different from what they are, the tables might be turned—a sobering thought one ought to consider from time to time.

Daniel Lerner, one of the first to produce a significant empirical work on contemporary modernization, has some thoughts that relate to these points. As mentioned in a previous section, he views the hallmark of modern man as being "psychic mobility," that is, an inner psychological dimension that allows him to operate efficiently in a changing world. The significant point for this discussion is that Lerner sees psychic mobility (empathy) increasing as a product of man's association with progressively modernizing structures and institutions in his environment. First comes urbanization with its assimilation and creation of modern symbols. The cities are first in influence, he argues, because only in them have there developed the complex skills and resources that characterize the modern industrial economy as we now know it. Then, "within this urban matrix develop both of the attributes which distinguish the next two phases—literacy and media growth."[10]

In the literacy and media growth stages, both of which are directed largely by the modern institutions of the society, an interaction occurs which accelerates the development of each. That is, literacy demands media growth to satisfy it and media growth in turn encourages the growth of more literacy. The elaborate technology of industry is fairly well advanced in the cities, sufficient, at least, for it to be producing newspapers, creating radio networks, and showing motion pictures on a massive scale. All of these are indicators of media growth, and they in turn accelerate the spread of literacy. Out of this, Lerner sees a fourth developmental stage emerging, one defined as a kind of participation in the society (voting, for example) that welds man to the larger nation in terms of interest and psychological commitment.

In all the institutional cases one of the assumptions is that as people come into contact with a changed environment they will also develop a changed pattern of attitudes and values. However, except for the theory of cognitive dissonance or the concept of "psychic mobility," there is very little to demonstrate how a nation moves from one modernization phase to the next, or why an urban person more frequently than not becomes literate, listens to radio, and develops a coherent pattern of modern values and attitudes.

The Psychological Argument

The second answer to the major question about whether the energy source of modernization derives from psychological or institutional factors is essentially the antithesis of the first. This one holds that massive changes in institutions and environment, such as those exhibited by the processes of structural modernization and economic development, are simply another way of talking about the visible results of large aggregations of social-psychological events that are now in process or have already taken place. In other words, attitudes and values of large groups of people somehow modernize; the people organize themselves and then go about the task of modernizing their environment. In the case of the man who abandons the country for the city, the psychological argument holds that he does so not only because he no longer values the country and its backward institutions but because he *already* aspires to participate in the modernity of the city. His attitudes and values changed *prior* to a change in his behavior. He was able to relieve the dissonance problem by altering the behavior to conform to new values. This, therefore, is an alternative tack on the cognitive dissonance theme.

The natural effect of the new modernizing behavior is to cause social and political structures to differentiate and to become more specialized, and to make the economy grow. As a case in point, the psychology-first view is reinforced by examples of school desegregation in the United States. Desegregation, some people say, occurred in practice because a majority of people had *previously* acquired values and attitudes harmonious with a new desegregation law or the enforcement of an old one. The law functions because of the values of those people in a position to enforce it. But the values themselves are not necessarily created by the passing of the law. Accordingly, it supposes that the strength of democracy derives primarily from the beliefs and values of the people, and only secondarily from the structures or institutions of their society. It is argued, therefore, that it would be futile for anyone to transplant the *institutions* of American democracy to the Third World and expect them to work at all—unless, that is, *values and attitudes* supportive of democracy already existed there.

In light of the above argument, and in an attempt to get at the basic dynamics behind modernization, some authorities have said that it is better to abandon the notion of institutions and structures and to go directly to the new attitudes and values of people. Thus, in responding to the question of how men develop modern skills and attitudes and how a society, an economy, and a polity become modern, the answer is clear: there is a "mental virus"[11] of some sort, to use David McClelland's term, that must first exist in the minds of the people. To the extent that people have that virus they will be psychologically equipped to modernize. If favorable conditions exist, the society will become activated, and people will push ahead with the task of modernizing their structures, their institutions, and their general environment.

The answer as to *why* a society chooses a particular time rather than some other to modernize is not treated very well by the psychology-first perspective. Nevertheless, the preconditions of modernity are seen to exist in the psychology of the people, not in the structural symbols of modern cities. Therefore, one cannot be fatalistic, lazy, and have a preference for leisure over work (no matter what the structural symbols of his environment are) and hope to become modern very soon—or to keep an already modern society up on its modernity.

Myron Weiner asks an appropriate question of this school—and offers his own response: Do some traditional societies have within them, then, the mental seeds of modernity—the Max Weber thesis?[12] While Weiner buys some facets of the psychology-first argument, he clearly is not willing to concede that any specific psychological factor has a claim to "historical necessity." He prefers the concept of "substitutability," that is, the idea that among the great number of value systems that exist in the modernizing world of today it is possible that several, or even many, will be compatible with modernization. Indeed, in the contemporary world some value systems may actually encourage the process whereas a century ago they would have impeded it. All men of today, in other words, do not have to acquire the "Protestant Ethic" to file a claim on modernity. They may already have their own peculiar "virus" that simply needs to be activated.

Some research in social-psychology is motivated by this second point of view, that is, that people may modernize their attitudes and values independently of the traditional institutions and structures of their society. For various social scientists, modernization dynamics, therefore, become meaningful only when interpreted basically as a reflection of attitudes and values. If the modern attitudes are there, then in due time the institutions and environment will have a tendency to harmonize with them.

"Adaptive Inventionism"

There is still a third answer. This one accepts many of the perspectives of the institution-first *and* the psychology-first arguments. But it nevertheless holds that the processes of modernization are too complex to allow rigid causal categories to be established. At times the "energy of change" may derive more from the structural ingredients of modernization whereas at other times it may derive more from the psychological ones. More likely there is always a mutual reinforcement wherein modernizing institutions impinge on and change traditional values, and modernizing values work to undermine traditional institutions and to encourage the elaboration of modern replacements.

One important point here is that attitudes and values are seen as being especially causally important in mediating the effect of environmental change and in integrating new role structures that arise out of the modernization process. Structural differentiation and specialization are incredibly divisive of established society. This divisiveness may be overcome if attitudes exist that provide a more or less common ground for "nationhood," helping therefore to keep the society of a modernizing country from being completely torn apart. Social disturbances are frequent in countries where the process of institutional modernization (differentiation and specialization) proceeds at a much more rapid pace than does the development of modern values and attitudes among groups in the society. There is another side to this coin, of course. Social disturbances also arise, and frequently more often, when attitudes and values undergo modernizing change but the structures and institutions suffer from archaic rigidity; when the elite who preside over them feel threatened by change and employ whatever means are at their disposal to prevent it.

Much of the important "macro" research going on in the field of modernization resides very comfortably in the "adaptive invention" framework. Accordingly, the notion of a "single path" to modernization, such as that advanced by Marx and others both in and out of his school, is rejected. Indeed, modernization is not considered to be amendable to unilinear explanations of either the psychological or structural variety. The force behind the process may be psychologically derived, structurally derived, or derived from a combination of the two, depending on the circumstances. Moreover, in the same country it may be different at differing times because of the complex ways that "backward" and "progressive" sectors affect each other and the degree to which the society may be suffering profound social cleavages.

Discussions of the above-mentioned ideas on *institutions* and *values,* and the processes of change that may cause alterations in their nature and structure, frequently do not include a treatment of the antagonisms created in societies that undergo rapid change in either one or both of these dimensions. And it is precisely here that a new and rapidly expanding group of political economists, some with a "neo-Marxian" bent, have entered the intellectual foray, decrying not only the current lack of attention on the part of many American social scientists to the subjects of class, conflict, and power, but the "colonial" and "imperial" policy consequences that sometimes have followed from their manipulative "functionalist" studies.

These are two entirely different approaches to an understanding of development, each of which operates under equally differing assumptions about reality. Thus the functionalists emphasize common interests and values that presumably are shared by members of the society, while the conflict theorists, on the other hand, emphasize those values and attitudes that divide the society. And

"where functionalists stress the common advantages which accrue from social relationships, conflict theorists emphasize the element of domination and exploitation. Where functionalists emphasize consensus as the basis of social unity, conflict theorists emphasize coercion. Where functionalists see human societies as social systems, conflict theorists see them as stages on which struggles for power and privilege take place."[13]

Let us consider some of the policy and analytical conclusions that derive from the differing perspectives. With respect to the peasant, the conflict school would look not for fatalistic attitudes and a limited world view as variables explaining his poverty and backwardness but, instead, for the society's structural arrangements (land-tenure system, elite-peasant class relations, and the like) that prohibit him from participating in the country's political economy on other than highly disadvantageous terms. In our example (presented in Chapter One) this, indeed, was the case. However, in other instances—perhaps a decreasing number of them now—it is also apparent that answers to the peasantry's economic backwardness may be found, partially at least, in some combination of Rogers' "subculture of peasantry" variables,[14] or what George Foster has called "psychological barriers to change,"[15] or what Oscar Lewis has termed the "culture of poverty."[16] That these latter explanations have recently come under increasing attack reflects, no doubt, the changing conditions in which the peasantry and other political, social, and economically marginal people live. We are led to conclude that, as time passes, peasants and other "un-modern" people will be increasingly less out of gear psychologically vis-à-vis modernization than they are structurally—artificially blocked, as it were, from participation in a world they desire.

With respect to policy analysis, conflict approaches would seem to have greatest insights in countries like those in Latin America (for instance, Argentina, Brazil, Peru, Guatemala) where profound social cleavages exist and huge squatter and peasant populations are victimized by ruthless exploitation, corruption, and political helplessness. Functionalist approaches to development no doubt would operate superbly in more benign social circumstances. One of the problems now, however, is that the more that either psychological or structural modernization advances in the Third World, the more the resulting social and political situation will change from benign apathy to malignant tension. This we shall examine in the next chapter.

It may now seem apparent that, while the processes of modernization are very difficult, there is nearly as much difficulty in their study. There is some truth here, and the traditional rigidity of the academic disciplines has been one contributing factor. As each academic field specialized in its study of modern countries it was natural that it should focus on specialized aspects of modernization in the developing countries. Specialization, of course, is all right and necessary, but hardly fruitful for "ecological" understanding if important "cross-disciplinary" variables are either ignored or judged to be unimportant simply because they happen to reside in the other guy's discipline.

Specialization has encouraged the economists to focus on man's application of technology for the control of his environment, especially in terms of raising a country's gross national product. But many economists have been notorious for their ignorance of the social, psychological, and political variables that affect the *ability, capability* or *desire* of men to apply technology. Only in the closing years of the 1960's did significant numbers of important economists begin to change their outlook.

Sociologists and social anthropologists, on the other hand, have concentrated on differentiation and specialization, and on ways in which technology may be applied through different institutional or structural devices. They have, however, only glanced at the questions of economic resources and political capability.

Social psychologists have been concerned with important "mental viruses." Political scientists have focused on the problems of nation building, and on ways to increase the capacity of the government to innovate and to assimilate newly mobilized groups without suffering institutional breakdown. And it is true that all of these disciplines, including that of the economists, have developed an increased interest in the disruptive features of modernization: inflation, rising social tensions, mental illness, violence, delinquency, and racial, religious, and class conflict. But as long as the disciplines remain academically isolated from each other none, in and of itself, will bring us much closer to an understanding of what modernization is all about. None is sufficiently general to encompass the interrelated impacts of a modernizing economy, society, polity, and psychology without making an explicit effort to move outside its own specialized territory.

BIBLIOGRAPHICAL ESSAY

The contemporary proliferation of publications dealing with various aspects of modernization has been staggering indeed. A slowdown is nowhere in sight. It is therefore obviously beyond the scope of this chapter, not to mention my own capacity, to give a definitive up-to-the-moment reference for all the general points that have been raised. Nevertheless, the works I have selected are well recognized in their respective fields and provide in-depth treatment or illustrations of the points to which they refer. In addition to the usual bibliographies included in each cited book, a number of books also provide specialized bibliographical essays.

I have mentioned some of the differing value definitions associated with modernity and modernization. Some important works placing current symbols in comparative historical analytical perspective should be consulted for the important insights they provide. One of the first serious contributions in the historic-comparative area is "Economic Backwardness in Historical Perspective" by the economist Alexander Gerschenkron. Several years later a sociologist, Neil Smelser, put his structural-functional paradigm to work in *Social Change in the Industrial Revolution*. Here he explored in detail some of the themes that were later crystalized in his "Toward a Theory of Modernization," a work meant not only to clarify the processes of structural change in the contemporary world but also to move away from the static biases frequently attributed to any form of functional theory. A subsequent (1963) important contribution to this topic was made by the political sociologist Seymour Martin Lipset in *The First New Nation: The United States in Historical and Comparative Perspective*. Then in 1966 appeared two general volumes by long-time students of the field: C. E. Black, *The Dynamics of Modernization*, and S. N. Eisenstadt, *Modernization: Protest and Change*. Major comparative works from political scientists published shortly afterward are Dankwart A. Rustow, *A World of Nations* (1967), and Samuel P. Huntington, *Political Order in Changing Societies* (1968).

Important contributions have also been made by economists. The authors of two important works are Brazilians. Roberto Campos, in *Reflections on Latin American Development*, not only traces out some of the historical development problems but also points out quite convincingly the many psychological, political, and social factors that bear on economic development—or nondevelopment. Celso Furtado deals explicitly with Brazil but also picks up themes of general application to many developing countries in *The Economic Growth of Brazil*. Of course, the economists generally have been more interested in the present and the future than in the past and, hence, most of their contributions lie in areas other than historical analysis. An important early volume that has set the stage for much later research for the present and the future is Albert O. Hirschman's *The Strategy of Economic Development.*

Probably the most impressive work in social psychology, in terms of historical analysis, comes from David C. McClelland. He has investigated the history of the great nations that have risen economically and has demonstrated that in nearly every case a "need-achievement virus" was present in the society at least one generation before economic growth began. I refer specifically to his *The Achieving Society,* and also to his "The Impulse to Modernization."

An additional contribution which alerts one to the social-psychological preconditions for economic development comes from an economist who concluded that traditional economic approaches left too many questions unanswered. See Everett E. Hagen, *On the Theory of Social Change: How Economic Growth Begins.*

In spite of the ambiguities associated with past or future meanings of modernization and modernity, current specifications and usages are well treated, with a considerable review of the literature, in Allan Schnaiberg, "Measuring Modernism: Theoretical and Empirical Explorations"; Reinhard Bendix, "Tradition and Modernity Reconsidered"; Joseph Gusfield, "Tradition and Modernity: Misplaced Polarities in the Study of Social Change"; Alex Inkeles, "Making Men Modern"; Kenneth S. Sherrill, "The Attitudes of Modernity"; and Myron Weiner, ed., *Modernization.* In addition, an inspection of Everett M. Rogers, *Modernization Among Peasants,* and David E. Apter, *Some Conceptual Approaches to the Study of Modernization* is useful. In all of these works the general themes of industrialization and economic growth, and the prerequisites for and consequences of that growth in politics, society, and culture are treated in detail in both structural and psychological terms.

Neil Smelser, one of the best representatives of the "institutional change" orientation to modernization, has made his points in "Toward a Theory of Modernization." His work is included in the extremely influential structural-functional paradigm largely crystalized in its early versions by Talcott Parsons, *The Social System.* Seymour Martin Lipset's works are oriented to that paradigm as is also one of the important early works on politics associated with modernizing societies, the Almond and Coleman volume of *The Politics of the Developing Areas.* As regards modernization among the peasantry, an important article, also out of the structural-functional paradigm, is by Henry A. Landsberger, "The Role of Peasant Movements and Revolts in Development."

The diffusionist school of modernization is one of the two oldest that currently deal with social change. The other one is, of course, the Marxist. Diffusionism, although greatly modified and qualified when compared with its earlier versions, is still a popular interpretation of the energy force behind modernization. It is unlikely that one could pick any given author in the literature today and fit him neatly into this or any other category. However, some authors tend implicitly or explicitly to emphasize one perspective over another, although they frequently do take multidimensional approaches. Among those who accept one or more aspects of the "diffusionist school" are Gabriel A.

Almond and Sydney Verba, *The Civic Culture;* Karl W. Deutsch, *The Nerves of Government;* Seymour Martin Lipset, *Political Man;* Frederick Harbison and Charles Myers, *Education, Manpower, and Economic Growth;* Archibald O. Haller, *Urban Economic Growth and Changes in Rural Stratification;* Harold Lasswell, *The Emerging Internation Culture;* and Daniel Lerner, *The Passing of Traditional Society.* Finally, for specific works on the effects of the cities, consult Gerald Breese, ed., *The City in Newly Developing Countries: Readings on Urbanism and Urbanization.*

In regard to the notes on cognitive dissonance, one should be aware that the points raised in this chapter may be considered somewhat aberrational. The theory was first advanced in 1957 by Leon Festinger, *Cognitive Dissonance.* Since then the approach has been widely investigated and empirically tested. A summary of much of the empirical evidence, together with a chapter on applications to problems of social change, is in a volume by Jack W. Brehm and Arthur R. Cohen, *Explorations in Cognitive Dissonance.* The theory by no means is universally accepted. It has been given a highly critical appraisal by N. P. Chapanis and A. Chapanis, "Cognitive Dissonance: Five Years Later."

An excellent treatise relating to one aspect of the cognitive dissonance theme is John H. Kunkel, *Society and Economic Growth: A Behavioral Perspective of Social Change.* In it he presents a "behavioral model of man" and shows how attitudes and values can be changed by sanctions and reinforcements so that predictable or wanted behavior is attained. He then shifts all this into the question of economic development, demonstrating how attitudes and values compatible with this development may be fostered. "It may be hypothesized, then, that the major problem of economic development is not the alteration of character, values, or attitudes, but the change of those selected aspects of man's social environment which are relevant to the learning of new behavior patterns" (p. 76). Kunkel, therefore, largely rejects values, attitudes, and personalities as important causal factors.

A rich sociological tradition exists based on "class conflict" with economics as the independent variable. Many who subscribe to this tradition would, of course, dislike the idea of being linked up with Marxism in any way. A distinction must be made, therefore, between the ideological tradition associated with Marx but mainly created by Lenin, and some of the very meaningful themes Marx spawned for later social scientists. A very good treatment of some of the issues along this line may be found in W. G. Runciman, *Social Science and Political Theory;* Reinhard Bendix and Seymour Martin Lipset, "Karl Marx's Theory of Social Classes"; Glaucio A. D. Soares, "Economic Development and Class Structures"; and Herbert H. Hyman, "The Value Systems of Different Classes."

Much of the "new sociology" and "new political science" implicitly rests on class conflict and economic determinism—or near economic determinism—as basic assumptions. An exemplary volume is by Irving Louis Horowitz, Josué de Castro, and John Gerassi, *Latin American Radicalism: A Documentary Report on Left and Nationalist Movements.*

Two works that bring out the relation of psychology to society and the social meaning of economic growth are Lambert and Lambert, *Social Psychology,* and Whyte and Williams, *Toward an Integrated Theory of Development.*

Occasionally an excellent annotated bibliography appears on the subject of modernization and development. One, dealing with the social and cultural aspects of modernization and particularly worth recommending is by John Brode, *The Process of Modernization: An Annotated Bibliography on the Socio-cultural Aspects of Development.* Its categories include general descriptions of social change, industrialization (including works specifically on its social impact), urbanization, and rural modernization. Another, which includes additional categories, is Karl W. Deutsch and Richard L. Merritt, *Nationalism and National Development: An Interdisciplinary Bibliography.*

PART II

Social Forces and Political Institutions

Part I considered two of the general underpinnings of modernization studies: (1) the basic tools of analysis that social scientists employ—variables, hypotheses, and theories, and (2) some of the underlying concepts dealing with modernization—what it is, its general features, some of the processes of change that may be associated with it, and how all of these factors relate both to people and to the institutions under which they live.

There is a multitude of interesting economic, social, political, psychological, and cultural topics directly related to modernization that could now legitimately attract our attention. We could, for example, look into the function of markets in a developing economy. We could trace out the effect on a traditional economic system of changing supply and demand. We might also look into the economies of scale of infant industries. Likewise, we could investigate the whole psychological realm of resistance to change, of psychic breakdown and trauma, and of value adaptation, all of which have some effect on, and are affected by, the existing culture.

Or we could deal more explicitly with the sociology of economic development. We might look further into theories of development. We could study the relation of population growth to development. We might even trace out some of the bureaucratic aspects of modern development with their accompanying role changes, specialization, and differentiation.

Of course, we cannot investigate all of these and the many other topics of related interest. We must be selective. The choice here is determined by my own interests and professional competence. Thus we now move to a consideration of those aspects of the sociology of economic development—social mobilization, or the rise of new social forces—that relate directly to political institutions and to what we might call the "politics of modernization." These two modernization-related phenomena—social mobilization and the politics surrounding it—are intrinsically interesting. The way in which they relate to one another is also crucially important. Nations that attempt to modernize but cannot handle the political tensions that modernization produces have scant hope to stay abreast. They become the victims of change rather than productive participants in it.

CHAPTER 3

Development and Decay—Protest, Reaction, and Revolution

Rapid environmental changes (industrialization, urbanization, increases in literacy and communications, and the like) and the value changes that tend to accompany, precede, or follow them produce what Karl Deutsch has termed "social mobilization." It is a process by which "major clusters of old social, economic and psychological commitments are eroded or broken and people become available for new patterns of socialization and behavior."[1] The capacities, wants, needs, and expectations of those involved expand at an alarming pace. A natural consequence is that people so mobilized desire participation in their country's politics, economics, and society in ways that may not be governed or sanctioned by traditional norms or procedures. The peasants want to vote and acquire economic benefits and personal freedoms; the students want to make public policy; and the economic middle class wants to do—and enjoy —everything, while the traditional aristocracy wants to hang on to its privileges and unshared power.

Usually the wants and expectations of newly mobilized people rise considerably faster than the existing capacity or willingness of a nation's traditional elite and traditional institutions to respond satisfactorily to them. The resulting gap between the expectations and psychic availability of socially mobilized people for new commitments, on the one hand, and their opportunities to realize those expectations and engage in the new commitments, on the other, helps to produce political instability; it may also set the stage for serious civil disorders.

Countries in what has been termed the Third World generally have a low institutional capacity to bridge the rapidly rising expectations-opportunity gaps. They may have too few (or unknown) resources to exploit, an insufficient income to distribute, or less than a realistic vision of how to make investments and reap profits. They may be plagued with corrupt businessmen and conniving politicians, ruled by traditional leaders unwilling to make a commitment to change, or may be overwhelmed with clerics who perceive all environmental and value change as a threat to the holy sanctity of the world. They may be controlled by an oligarchy that fosters economic development but, being fearful of the social and political consequences, clamps down hard to maintain the status quo in areas of power, privilege, and prestige. Traditional authority suffers. It no longer answers the questions or provides the answers. People begin to look elsewhere.

In the wake of these unsatisfactions, the traditional political arrangements tend to lose their legitimacy among the more mobilized but less satisfied groups in the society. But new patterns of authority—approaching what Max Weber once called "rational-legal" authority—embodying complex bureaucratic and legal norms in institutions that have both the capacity and the will to react adequately to the situation, are slow to emerge. In the resulting wasteland operate military coups, frightened authoritarian despots, revolutionary and charismatic leaders, and social chaos.

Rapid economic and social change, whether primarily psychological or structural, does not impinge on all groups in a country at the same time. It tends to begin in the large cities. Even there, in the early stages, change drastically affects only selected groups. However, as more individuals become involved, the expectations-opportunity gaps loom ever more pervasive, frustrating, and even frightening. The political effect of rapid economic change is not unlike a fire under a teakettle. Unless the flames are dampened or the teakettle cooled with additional water, the molecules, as people, eventually begin to jump.

Most individuals who suffer expectations-opportunity gaps would, of course, like to see the gaps closed. Realistically, this can happen in only one way—by increasng the economic, social, and political opportunities that they seek. Contemporary "gap people" fully realize this; they frequently organize, form alliances with groups of like persuasion, and attempt to do something about their peculiarly modern problem. If the established elite feel threatened by such activity (as frequently happens), they will resist many, or all, of the changes that their socially mobilized subjects seek. Under these conditions, and in direct proportion to the unwillingness or inability of the establishment to meet the gap problem, the society progressively becomes politically "bifurcated." The socially mobilized and those whom they threaten "choose up sides," joining groups dedicated either to preserve the status quo or to destroy it.

If a country's political authorities do not respond favorably to the social tearing (in fact, they may not be able to even if they want to), the forces for change, given sufficient time, tend to overwhelm the old elite, weaken their means of resistance and coercion, and eventually remove them from power either through coups, revolutions, or assassinations. Such gross acts do not resolve gap problems, of course. Sometimes they make them worse. Accordingly, there frequently emerges from the tensions of social bifurcation yet another characteristic of rapid environmental and value change. We shall call it "amoral groupism,"[2] a condition in which victorious modernizers end up fighting among themselves just as previously, together, they had fought against the entrenched elite establishment.

It is the rise of new social forces which cannot be assimilated or satisfied by traditional political arrangements that leads to the decay of the institutions which underpin them—to an undermining of the old political order, and to a discrediting of the institutional bases of traditional authority and legitimacy on which it stood. Values and attitudes have changed. The old monarchy, clerics, traditional tribal chiefs, caudillos, military warlords, and authoritarian despots are perceived as standing in the way of progress. Socially mobilized "gap people" frequently withdraw their allegiance from traditional leaders; they establish new associations and create new social linkages that bypass them; they make new commitments that are directed toward eliminating them; and they seek a new world that they perceive can very well exist without them. It is to be expected, therefore, that when the social energy of the newly mobilized members of the society expands (and the visibility of the political decay in traditional institutions becomes progressively apparent), there is also witnessed the drawing of conflicting reactionary and revolutionary forces.

Mobilized gap-people begin their antagonistic course by demanding social and political reforms to achieve a realization of their newly acquired expectations and thereby participate in the new world that they have come to desire. Why are the traditional elite so resistive? For one thing, any change that accommodates the desires of the new groups or classes also frequently strikes at the very heart of the statuses and time-honored privileges that the old elite have long enjoyed. Therefore, reforms that close the gaps for some people quite often create new ones for others. As far as the traditional elite are concerned, therefore, modernization (as opposed to just "economic development") is more a disease than a blessing. It occasions a decay in the institutional underpinnings that support their values, their statuses, and their privileges.

The more reactionary traditionalists sometimes attempt to board up all doors leading to social and political—if not economic—change. At the very least, the older established groups—clergy, landowners, old politicians, and those who benefit from them—try to minimize its effects, especially its tendency to destroy the social values on which traditional status and privilege have rested. Nearly always, however, at least in contemporary Asia, Africa, Latin America, and the Middle East, the rear-action effort comes too late. The mobilization of new groups tends to carry its own momentum. It is only with extreme coercion and repression that the process, once substantially begun, can be stopped. Most traditional political systems lack the power to do that stopping. They may not even be able to implement a successful blockade for sustained periods of time. Thus the traditional elite, though perhaps having no argument against economic development and technology, are nevertheless eventually forced into some kind of an accommodation with political and social change.

Mobilization, expectations-opportunity gaps, antagonisms, and political decay are not the only salient social and political effects of rapid environmental and value change. There is still another. This one deals with the difficulty of developing an institutional replacement for the old politics, that is, "rational-legal" political and bureaucratic institutions. More than any other aspect of change in the contemporary world, "political development" is significant more for its empirical absence than for its modernizing presence. This is not surprising. The very fact that expectations-opportunity gaps generally arise in conjunction with political decay greatly complicates the whole enterprise. Any elaboration of new patterns of authority capable not only of maintaining order but also of absorbing the new groups or classes is thereby made difficult if not hazardous.

If out of the "natural" processes of modernization a new economy and a new society tend to arise, the same certainly cannot be said of the polity. No easy solutions are offered for the replacement of political institutions when values and environment rapidly change. Thus the political instability associated with the whole modernization process frequently extends well beyond the days after economic development becomes a booming reality. The gap between wants and their fulfillment, expectations and their achievement, and capabilities and the opportunity to exercise them continues. The failures of the traditional order to respond effectively to the gap dilemma has undermined its legitimacy. Yet, throughout, little purposeful groundwork is laid for an institutional replacement capable of amelioration and resolution. The gaps remain, frequently becoming worse. Instability therefore continues. It is this threatening instability that charismatic leaders appropriate to their advantage, and that military officers attempt to control for theirs.

Curiously, until about 1964 there was widespread belief that "modern politics," that is, stability and perhaps even democracy, were part and parcel of the great ongoing economic-development process. A modern society, a modern polity, and a modern economy were all thought to hang together somehow. People's psychology would become modernized, their environment more complex, differentiated, and specialized. Their political institutions would become capable of handling modernization's tensions. They would absorb the new social forces and classes and make a satisfactory spot for them in the promised land. Yet stability, let alone democracy, has not occurred with any impressive frequency. The old political institutions decay, but chaos, not order, results. "Modernity breeds stability, but modernization instability," has now become a famous dictum.[3] Thus when the gaps between aspirations and achievement, expectations and their fulfillment, mobilization and political development are high, watch out not only for charismatic leaders and military coups but also for socialist ideologies and political religions. They all tend to thrive on the same kind of underlying circumstances. In the contemporary Third World they are all in plentiful supply.

Economic development, in part, at least, and certainly for sustained periods of time, is now seen to hinge on political stability. The economists have invested no little effort in pointing out economic development failures that derive from political impediments to progress. Instability is one of these impediments. Yet if one wants the kind of lasting stability that holds up under the strain and tensions of modernization—that is, stability that derives from "a closing of the gap" for large groups in the society rather than from purges and coercion—he must speak of the need to develop political organizations and procedures that can integrate the disparate parts of the new society, can ameliorate the conflicts among new groups and new classes, and can aid in the building of political legitimacy. The struggle to do so might take more than all the king's horses and all the king's men, but it is a serious need—and the only means by which orderly government can develop.[4] Yet, we must frankly admit that although economic development seems to be a Herculean task, the development of new, powerful, and legitimate political institutions may be an even greater one.

POLITICAL MODERNIZATION AND POLITICAL DEVELOPMENT

One knows what political decay is, for he can "see" and describe the traditional institutions that are losing their legitimacy. But what is "political modernization," or "political development"? Definitions are as varied as they are numerous. However, major themes are now emerging that no doubt will be with us for a long time. A short historical review will help us to sort them out.

Probably 90 percent of all publications on political modernization and political development date since 1960. The field is expanding rapidly. Yet, in reviewing the literature up to about 1966, Fred Riggs remarked that not only had no adequate political-development theory been elaborated but no consensus had even arisen as to what political development was. He announced he would make his own rather excellent foray "in the confident hope with which one embarks on a treasure hunt—perhaps better, on a 'fishing expedition. . . .' "[5]

In the early 1970's there still is disagreement, but it is perhaps not so great. Political development concepts are not as murky or "culture bound" as they once were; scholars have continually attempted to refine their thinking about, and observations of, the political phenomena associated with modernization. One very important clarification came in 1965 from Samuel P. Huntington.[6] In retrospect his observations seem elementary, yet failure of an earlier realization contributed much to the inadequency and ambiguity of the day's political-development studies. Huntington persuaded his colleagues of the need to place "political modernization" and "political development" (which had been used interchangeably to that time) on separate, if not equal, conceptual planes. *Political modernization* is something that may be but is not necessarily associated with a modernizing people, a modernizing society, and a modernizing economy. On the other hand, *political development,* as a concept, must apply equally to nonmodern as to modern situations. Can one meaningfully conclude that tribal authorities, city states, feudal monarchies, or bureaucratic empires cannot, under some conditions, be politically developed? Political science, of all the disciplines, ought not to cut itself off from fifth-century Athens, the third-century B.C. Roman Republic, the second-century A.D. Roman Empire, or eighteenth-century China.

Huntington views *political modernization* (as opposed to political development) involving several discrete variables.[7] One of them he terms *rationalization of authority*—"the replacement of a large number of traditional, religious, familial, and ethnic political authorities by a single secular, national, political authority." This rationalization entails the application of modern methods of efficiency to political rule and governance, and it deals as much with the psychology of people as with the institutions under which they live. Psychologically, it implies that men have come to realize that government is within their province and is not exclusively tied up with nature or God. Moreover, people's values tell them that "a well-ordered society must have a determinate human source of final authority, obedience to whose positive law takes precedence over other obligations." At the institutional level, and this is Huntington's second variable, political modernization "involves the *differentiation* of new political functions and the development of *specialized* structures to perform those functions." As these structural or institutional changes occur, bureaucracies as well as political organizations become more complex and more disciplined. Likewise, office and power are increasingly allocated according to merit rather than by inherited status or some other pattern of ascription.

Political participation is Huntington's third political modernization variable. As general modernization occurs, more social groups and more mobilized individuals increase their participation in political activities. "Broadened participation in politics may enhance control of the people by the government, as in totalitarian states, or it may enhance control of the government by the people, as in some democratic ones. But in all modern states the citizens become directly involved in and affected by governmental affairs."

Yet, and the point must be made again, Huntington emphasizes that it is nonsense to assume that the rationalization of authority, the differentiation and specialization of political structures and functions, and the expansion of political participation automatically accompany other social and economic indicators of modernization. Modernization is always disjointed. Economic and social change occur in the absence of a complementing political change. Instability is one result. The alternative course is for the political leadership of a country to make a conscious effort to institute and develop the political modernization variables —hence, *political development*. This is a process that just does not happen by itself.

If we think of political modernization as a dependent variable we can readily see that Huntington has selected three main sets of independent variables to explain it: (1) rationalization of authority, (2) differentiation and specialization, and (3) political participation. He has also given us various clues as to how to relate these variables to ongoing events in the world of reality.

Huntington sees a positive temporal correlation among the three independent variables. That is, there is a tendency for them to "hang together." When rationalization of authority increases, differentiation and specialization, along with political participation, tend to increase also. Whether a rise on one independent variable occasions a corresponding change on the others, or whether all of them are simply independently influenced by other environmental or value changes, we are not told. Indeed, it may be that one has to speak of a complex reciprocating relationship among all the variables. The exact nature of the temporal or typological relationship, therefore, may be determinable only through empirical investigation.

Perhaps an exemplary "graphout" will help (Figure 5). Notice that the broken lines which join the independent variables to each other signify that the relationship, whatever it may be, is open to theoretical speculation or is determinable only by empirical verification.

We may also look at the temporal relationship of the variables by means of a "formula." Thus,

Political development, though related to political modernization, nevertheless is a concept that may be associated with any regime, modern or traditional.

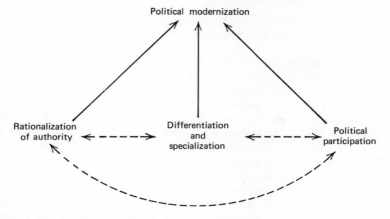

Figure 5. Huntington's political modernization variables.

Huntington explains his thoughts on the matter with two independent variables: *scope of support* and *level of institutionalization.* "Scope of support" relates to the degree to which people are willing not only to abide by their class, tribe, or nation's laws and political procedures but to support them as well. "Level of institutionalization" deals with the processes by which political organizations and procedures come to be valued in the group or society *and are capable of meeting political expectations.* In the Third World the variable relates to the capability of these organizations and procedures to enhance stability by ameliorating the tensions that modernization produces and by facilitating a realization of the expectations that it inherently promises. These are made possible only if there is a wide scope of support for, and an institutionalization of, the organization and procedures that are modernizing.

There is a relationship, of course, between political modernization, political development, and the kind of social mobilization discussed in the first pages of this chapter. We have noted, for example, the instability that results when social mobilization rapidly advances but modern and developed political institutions do not. One also could speak of cases of a "dynamic stability" arising where modern and institutionalized political organizations and procedures do indeed

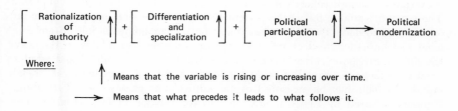

arise. By using countries that you know something about, try out the following symbolic propositions and their associated concepts:

1. $(SM\uparrow) + (PM\uparrow) + (PD-) \longrightarrow PI$
2. $(SM\uparrow) + (PM\uparrow) + (PD+) \longrightarrow PS$

Where:

$(SM\uparrow)$	=	social mobilization rapidly increasing.
$(PM\uparrow)$	=	political modernization increasing.
$(PD-)$	=	low level of support and low level of institutionalization of the modern political organizations and procedures (lack of political development).
$(PD+)$	=	presence of high levels of political development.
PI	=	political instability (indicated by a lack of general agreement on the rules of the political game and characterized by mass protest or its containment by the use of, or threatened use of, massive coercion.
PS	=	political stability.
$\longrightarrow$	=	what precedes it has a high probability of leading to what follows it.

Fred Riggs has also made an important contribution to the political development literature. He especially helps us to understand some of the conflicting goals that arise during periods of rapid modernization.[8] (The Riggs and Huntington formulations, taken together, subsume many of the political development variables advanced by others.[9] It is therefore helpful to become at least casually acquainted with both their views. Selected notes on other important contributors will be found in the bibliographical essay.)

Riggs, as does Huntington, utilizes the concepts of "differentiation" and "specialization," but he does so with a specific concentration on "key governmental technologies." Relating these to two additional political-development variables—*equality* and *capacity*—he puts them all together in a provocative typology of dialectical developmental stages.

Riggs' *differentiation* variable relates to the creation of what he terms "political technologies" (bureaucracies, parties, legislatures, and the like) in a modernizing country, and to the manner in which these technologies specialize and divide up their functions. The *capacity* variable refers to the ability of a political and administrative system, by the support it receives and the authority it exercises, to adopt collectively authorized goals and then to implement them. The *equality* variable reflects the extent to which those who are ruled have an opportunity to make their voice heard and have their influence felt on government and bureaucratic decision making. This variable also relates to the way the ruled participate in the benefits that derive from governmental and administrative functions. Equality, thus understood, is not the same as social equality, which may be measured by the equivalence of one's social standing. Equality, as used by Riggs, relates only to the relation of individuals to the inputs and outputs of their government. Following Riggs' argument, a political system is highly developed to the extent that it is highly differentiated, has high capacity, and affords a wide participation in its decision making and in the benefits that it produces.

But let us return to the central theme. The major technological inventions in government, Riggs argues, are basically three: bureaucratic organization, representative assemblies or legislatures, and political parties. Of course, Riggs adds, there are a host of minor technologies that are of supporting relevance, and some of these are the use of examinations as a test for recruitment, the use of voting as a vehicle for decision making, judicial procedures for the settling of disputes or violations of law, and the creation of private associations and corporations as more or less permanent legal entities (judicial persons), such as, labor unions, peasant leagues, manufacturers' associations, business corporations, incorporated towns and cities, and so on.

Riggs stresses that these, as all technologies, are subject to sudden qualitative jumps. When they are introduced into an environment that is already characterized by rapid social and economic change (where conflicting values exist and supporting institutions frequently do not), the result is a "dialectic" in which political development, to the extent that it occurs at all, does so in qualitative leaps—in stages. At each stage a considerable amount of "give and take" frequently occurs as opposing social forces jockey for position and advantage.

The introduction of any or all of these technologies primarily affects the political differentiation variable. New technologies increase the complexity of the political system, the number of functions it performs, and the specialized manner in which it carries them out. Riggs agrees with Huntington, however, that this is not the same as "political development." The introduction of a new technology (a legislature, for example) by no means guarantees the solutions of political problems, or even its own existence over time. Yet to the extent that the new specialized roles are accompanied by an increase in "scope of support," to use one of Huntington's phrases, it enhances the *capacity* of government to govern and implies a widening participation ("equality") in government "inputs" and "outputs." Political development therefore takes place.

Riggs makes the interesting point that the less modern the society is, the less differentiated (fewer political technologies) its political system needs to be. Likewise, the less relevant are the goals of capacity and equality. A traditional society has less need for governmental services. Governmental influence also is relatively less. Moreover, premobilized people usually make few demands for political equality.

The more modern and complex the society, however, the greater are the demands both for governmental capacity and participant equality. The demands can be satisfied only through increasing the differentiation and specialization in political technologies. In a complex society an undifferentiated political system is simply not able to satisfy either of the goals.

Riggs notes that in the transitional period of modernization not only does differentiation of the political system tend to lag behind the processes of modernization in other sectors but also great conflicts between the goals of equality and capacity occur among competing groups in the society. The traditional landlords, for example, may argue for greater government *capacity* to control the mobilized masses. Accordingly, they will push for the creation of a more highly specialized and differentiated police force, army, and investigative bureaucracy. The mobilized masses, on the other hand, generally want greater political *equality*. They demand that the differentiation and specialization of the political system occur in areas where that goal will be enhanced—by the creation of responsible representative legislatures, autonomous judicial systems, and a citizen's "Bill of Rights" with mechanisms for enforcement.

For illustration, assume that some country in the Third World has a fairly low differentiated political system and, therefore, finds it impossible, at its particular level of political technology, to provide either equality or capacity to any substantial degree. But suppose that the country nevertheless is in a position to produce either one or the other of these goals in some degree of abundance. In this case, an inverse relationship exists between the capacity and equality variables. Conflicting groups will bring great pressures on the political system to differentiate (to improve its level of political technology), but in the areas that it selectively values. Thus any success by one competing group will be at the expense of another. As long as this kind of struggle must be enacted, Rightists and Leftists, or Conservatives and Liberals will view their own respective values of capacity and equality as being synonymous with political development. But as long as the political system does not further differentiate, the conflict, short of a revolution, will never be ameliorated. The demands of one group can be met only at the expense of the others. The term, "Zero-sum game" has been coined to describe this dilemma.

In summary, Riggs views political development as comprising mostly a growth in governmental capacity and participant political equality, with the differentiation of governmental structures and specialization of functions (facilitated by the introduction of key technologies) as the way to achieve the capacity and equality goals. The higher the level of governmental differentiation, the higher the nation's potential to achieve equality or capacity, and perhaps both of them together.

When Riggs' notions are combined with Huntington's ideas about political modernization and political development, on scope of support and social mobilization, it becomes clear that if a country is to enjoy a modicum of stability, or perhaps even to survive during the period of modernization, not only must it continually differentiate the modern technologies in its political system but it must also increase its capacity to absorb, to reform, to innovate, and to satisfy. Is it small wonder that most modernizing countries find their political institutions a little deficient for the task?

Superpower Constraints on Political Development

Small states may live in social, political, and economic isolation from one another, but nevertheless they all share a common horizon: superpower interest in their external alliances. There follows, naturally, a superpower concern in the domestic affairs of Third World countries, especially when these countries begin to flux and change rapidly, threatening, as they frequently do, to crack some big power's "sphere of influence."

For a quarter of a century the United States and the Soviet Union have been making heavy investments in the Third World to gain ideological influence if not geographical security. However, both powers have been much more successful in undermining national governments than they have been successful in fostering a growth of autonomous political institutions strong enough not only to govern with United States guns or Soviet tanks but also to reform societies, heal social wounds, absorb new groups, process demands and, while doing it, gain a wide scope of support from within the society. If in theory the big powers could foster political development, in practice, they have not.

For a number of years the Soviets seem to have had a better track record than the Americans as far as offense strategies are concerned. But the present situation is increasingly discouraging for them. If we Americans have China, Egypt, Cuba, and India, and to a lesser degree Chile and Peru as examples of frustrated ambitions for a stable influence in the Third World, the Soviets have not only China, Egypt, and the Sudan, from which they have been largely if not totally expelled, but Libya and Indonesia as well to think about. In many ways the dynamic events of rapid social and political change in these nations have produced consequences more commensurate with Third-World interests than with any which the superpowers have canonized. As the pace of modernization quickens, no doubt this trend will also. Continued attempts to produce results to match superpower interests have frequently only deepened the quagmire (for example, Vietnam for the Americans; China and Egypt for the Soviets).

First-generation academic models of political development made little or no provision for analyzing the influence of great powers over internal decision making in the Third World. This is curious, because political development, of all forms of development, tends to require a series of purposeful development acts on the part of major elite in the country. Insofar as the great powers make alliances with an elite segment, which in turn relinquishes a portion of its own decision-making power for security or ambition, there results more, not less, domestic social tearing; more, not less, need for coercive powers; and greater, not lower, probabilities that a country's ruling elite will remain indebted to the international interests of a superpower more than to the domestic developmental requirements of their own country. Such an elite cannot foster political development because, to all other domestic groups, they have become "sellouts."

Thus, quite aside from consciously engaging in the Herculean task of trying to develop a nation politically and of handling the internal tensions of so doing, the influence of superpowers, especially that of the United States, discourages efforts to develop politically or reduces the motivation even to try. Elite who wish to make the effort must also expend huge amounts of energy just to control (although they may, on occasion, also take advantage of it) the corrupting influence of a superpower in their country—the Americans who are trying to prevent revolution and the Soviets who are trying to assure that more of its occurs.

Robert B. Stauffer has made a classification of the areas in which great powers apply constraints on political development in Third World countries.[9a] These include both *political* and *economic* constraints. In the political area, Stauffer notes that ideological capitulation to the United States in alliance systems tends to bring with it economic and military support for "right-wing" domestic elite groups. The result is to increase the capacity of government to maintain stability—primarily on the basis of coercion—but also to reduce the motivation of that same government to make improvements on Rigg's "equality" variable. The possible level of differentiation in political technologies is therefore reduced and the probability that any modern political institutions will become both institutionalized and receive a wide scope of domestic support is commensurately lessened.

A second political area deals with the way in which great powers attempt to place restrictions on sources of external help other than from their own bloc. One of the main arguments advanced to justify American intervention in Guatemala in 1954, and to raise the threat of intervention in Cuba nearly a decade later, related to those countries' receiving arms from the Soviet bloc. Frequently serious domestic political decisions concerning foreign aid and trade cannot therefore be made without considering the reaction of one or another superpower whose heavy influence may be close at hand. Superpower "vetoes" do not help domestic political development. On the contrary, they frequently hinder it.

With respect to economic constraints on political development, the influence of certain kinds of foreign private and public investments (business enterprise and foreign aid) is frequently mentioned. Americans have long argued that their business investments in Third World countries help these countries to develop economically. Domestic nationals counter by observing that in time those investments (especially those in extractive industries and basic infrastructure) tend to be counter productive as the repatriation of profits in time begins to exceed the investment originally made. But the crux of the situation, from the modernizing nationals perspective, is that foreign investors, in collusion with their favorite political friends back home, frequently attempt to create a business climate that maximizes their own interests regardless of the resulting impact on sectors in the country in which their operations are located. Indeed, at times the businessman and his politician or bureaucratic friends combine to try to manipulate not only national economic and political decisions but the country's choice of leadership as well. In March of 1972, for example, Washington columnist Jack Anderson disclosed documents alleging a collusion between the International Telephone and Telegraph Company and the CIA to cause a collapse in the economy of Chile and thereby provoke the Chilean military into staging a coup. This would, presumably, have prevented Marxist Salvador Allende, who had threatened to nationalize IT&T's Chilean investments if he became president, from being elected. The efforts, if they were ever attempted, failed. But the allegations are believed in nearly every Third World country where such corrupting pressures are part of daily living, practiced as much by the Americans as by the Soviets.

The same charges are frequently leveled at the foreign-aid program of the United States. Being "security conscious," American aid is tendered (in grants, loans, and military assistance) primarily to enhance security, at least, this has been true to date. Assistance, therefore, goes to our anti-communist "friends." Accordingly, right-wing dictators as well as reformers who are thought to be politically "safe" receive aid and project support while the other kind do not (or receive it in reduced amounts) unless, of course, they happen to be fighting their own battle with the Soviets (Yugoslavia) or, perhaps, just successfully playing off one superpower against another (as some African states have done from time to time).

Thus America becomes an extension of the political conflict of modernization because it takes domestic political sides and, for good or ill regarding political development, does not hesitate to support its security choice (for example, Vietnam, the Dominican Republic, Cambodia, Thailand, Laos). The results may foster political development, but usually they do not because, to paraphrase Huntington,[9b] our CIA has been more skilled in subverting regimes we do not like than it has been skillful in building politically developed governments that we might be able to stomach ideologically. Our dilemma has been one of trying to stabilize political institutions of the kind that exclude the participation of highly mobilized political groups at the very time when, to develop politically, a nation's institutions must be forged in such a way as to assimilate them.

It is for great-power interests and those, usually, of an "enclave elite"—not necessarily for the interests of political development in Third World countries— that big-power-small-country alliances are forged, aid given, and security missions launched. Economic development may result. But whatever political development may occur is highly accidental.

MODERNIZATION AND REVOLUTION

Insurrections, rebellions, revolts, coups, and wars of independence may, at times, arise from conditions similar to those that encourage revolutions. Later we shall deal with some of these kinds of events in detail. Nevertheless, revolutions, because they are so different from other acts of violent dissent in their social consequences, are distinct. "A revolution," Huntington says, "is a rapid, fundamental, and violent domestic change in the dominant values and myths of a society, in its political institutions, social structure, leadership, and government activity and policies."[10] Sigmund Neumann's well-known characterization concurs: A revolution is "a sweeping, fundamental change in political organization, social structure, economic property control and predominant myth of a social order, thus indicating a major break in the continuity of development."[11]

If the above observations define the consequences of a revolution, they also suggest why revolutions are so rare. Most countries have never had one. Why, therefore, do they occur? For a starter I suggest that revolutions occur (1) because the values and attitudes of great masses of people become seriously "dysynchronized" with the structures and institutions under which they live, and (2) because the mobilizing effects deriving from value and attitudinal change under these circumstances have been suppressed by entrenched and intransigent elite who nevertheless suddenly lose their capability for coercive deterrence.

The frenzied social activity required to overcome entrenched resistance to structural and institutional change necessitates long-term fueling. Revolutions do not occur "out of the blue," therefore, but only when less violent forms of synchronizing types of social change have been prevented. Revolutions are associated with desperate "gap people," with decayed traditional authority, and with weak and undeveloped modern political institutions. They are but one of the many possible manifestations of the tensions of modernization. Only modernizing "gap" countries can have them.

"Revolution of rising expectations" was a popular explanation in the early 1960's for the radical (revolutionary) politics of mobilized groups in many countries of the world. And one can see a kind of common-sense logic to it. As people became socially mobilized, their aspirations and expectations for material progress, social well-being, and political participation increased. These are interesting observations. They do not, however, account for revolutionary behavior. While the journalists had correctly pointed to the evidence of rising expectations, it was not the existence of these expectations but, instead, the bitter personal frustration of their nonrealization that was at the core of much of the radical protest and revolutionary activity. Thus eventually, "revolution of rising *frustrations*" was coined to allow, again in a common-sense way, a better explanation.

If revolutionary behavior has social origins, as we have argued, and is primarily fueled by rising frustrations among socially mobilized "gap" people, then we must look beyond the "riff-raff" theory (revolutions are *caused* by long-haired radicals, for example) or the "conspiracy" theory (revolutions are *caused* by a few plotters) for adequate explanations. Thus, we would argue, a large percentage of present-day protestors and would-be revolutionaries cannot be characterized simply as endemic riff-raff or conspiratorial militants—although some of them may indeed be. But frequently those most agitated are the heretofore "dormant" peoples of the world, those who at the present moment are being socially mobilized by the effects of modernization while also suffering a revolution of rising frustrations in their own lives as a consequence of it. If the parameters of revolutionary activity have increased in recent years, it is because peasants along with ethnic, racial, and tribal groups and other low-status or minority peoples are now vigorously searching, as never before, for self-identity, self-determination, and material progress. They seek to satisfy their new expectations. Thus contemporary protest agitation and revolutionary behavior has now moved beyond students, intellectuals, and middle-class radicals—who somehow have always been malcontented—to include, perhaps, a majority of "low-status" but nevertheless mobility-searching peoples.

In the Third World any upward mobility or opportunity-success such people attain frequently requires that they turn to aggression. In spite of their rising expectations and changing values, they frequently find themselves living in a more or less "opportunityless" environment, compelled to seek new rewards and satisfactions from powerful yet unsympathetic if not openly hostile and intransigent religious, economic, and political groups which historically have dominated them. Under these conditions concessions are not gifts but, instead, hard-won fruits of conflict. When they are faced with blocks to their opportunities, we should not be surprised if such highly mobilized people attempt a radical solution to their modernizing problem. Revolution is only the most extreme option of several that may be open to them.

No country now seems to be immune to environmental change, nor its people to the accelerating aspirations and value transformations that tend to accompany it. Indeed, in this regard even the United States has not escaped chastening experiences. Many of America's blacks, Chicanos, and Indians are now demanding a reorientation of their relationship with the larger society. Black Power, Brown Power, and Red Power, therefore, are to be noted not so much for their curious peculiarity as for their monumental generic significance. They, too, are a product of "modernization."

Frustration of the achievement of anticipated goals was seen as a basic cause in the social disturbances of the early 1960's. Perhaps it was no coincidence that about this time a revival and reinterpretation of some old "frustration-aggression" theory began to emerge. Started on a clinical and experimental basis at Yale University in the 1930's, it has been picked up by social and political psychologists, reelaborated and refined, and advanced as an explanation of the kinds of broad classes of events that can lead to revolution. Indeed, frustration-aggression theory, in one or another of its present-day versions, has now become one of the most widely accepted academic explanations of the basic causes of revolution. Its premises and assumptions are, we shall learn, intrinsically related to the preceding discussion on revolution and modernization.

Much of the frustration-aggression literature singles out two main categories of independent variables for purposes of explaining the frustration and, therefore, the rebellious behavior that frequently is associated with it. These are (1) preconditioning or stage-setting variables, and (2) contributing or facilitating variables. The first category is associated with environmental and psychological changes that occur over a fairly long period of time, say 10 to 30 years. The second identifies independent variables of a more proximate time reference. These tend either to aggravate or mitigate situational factors, facilitate or impede the protestors' organizational efforts, or encourage or discourage the psychological commitment to collective protest.

The Preconditioning Variables

Almost invariably the preconditioning variables are cast in terms of "gap" hypotheses, a point highly consistent with our observations up to this point. Thus if *social aspirations* are high but *social achievements* low, to use the terminology of Feierabend, Feierabend, and Nesvold, the basic gap preconditions are set.[12] The source of social protest energy has been born. Then if "hope" of ameliorating the gaps rather than despair of any solution characterizes the collective psychology of those involved, the motivation for social protest and perhaps revolution is enhanced.[13] Such a combined structural-psychological approach rejects strictly psychological theories which hold that collective aggression, protest, or revolution is (a) solely instinctive, or (b) solely learned. Such an approach also rejects exclusively structural theories which consider such *single* variables as poverty, class conflict (in the Marxian sense), conspiracy, or solidarity, taken alone, to be sufficiently explanatory.

This still leaves unsaid, however, anything about the actual motivational link between the environmental or psychological factors that are responsible for the "gaps," and the aggression, protest, or revolutionary behavior that *may* flow from them. This is one aspect of the problem about which we must make some considered theoretical assumptions and must proceed without proof, at least, for the present time.[14] It is at this point that some social scientists place frustration as a key link. Yet it is also true that others have demonstrated that protest and aggression are related to "threats" made against a group by some outside agent in possession of a considerable degree of power credibility.[15] Still others have been persuaded that aggression and, therefore, protest are a product of some *combination* of frustration and threat. There are other motivational links, of course, but for now we shall use frustration-aggression, or perhaps frustration-threat-aggression sequence.

One of the best contemporary exponents is Ted Robert Gurr.[16] Gurr maintains that frustration, and the aggravation to it that threat imposes (police or military coercion, mainly) can be linked to the environment by a gap hypothesis that lays claim to "relative deprivation" as its key concept. Relative deprivation exists when the values to which people collectively aspire are unrealizable— and yet selfishly enjoyed by others around them—under the conditions of life that prevail. When collective "value expectations" (one of Gurr's independent variables) are higher, or particularly if they are *rising faster* than a group's "value capabilities" (Gurr's second independent variable, defined as a group's capability of actually securing participation in values for which it has developed certain collective expectations), then relative deprivation will be felt not only by individuals but by an entire group. This produces collective frustration. Such frustration may lead to collective protest, and perhaps to revolution. Under conditions of threat it may lead to violence. Thus, "Why Men Rebel" has its origins in the social system, not simply in psychodynamics, external conspiracies, and the like.

If the existence of "gaps" (in this case those identified by "relative deprivation") sets the stage for protest, how do the gaps arise in the first place? What processes of change are to be noted? In the specific example at hand, why do *value expectations* rise while *value capabilities* lag behind? The answers to these questions, Gurr holds, are to be found in the environment. Changing *value expectations* have social origins in exposure to new modes of life, new ideologies, or value disequilibrating experiences. On the other hand, *value capabilities*—Gurr's second main independent variable—are not so easily influenced. If they were, and were to rise proportionately to the rise in new value expectations, no frustration would result and, hence, no collective protest would likely occur. But value capabilities are notorious not for their presence but for their frustration-producing "almost-touchable" absence. Even at best they belong to a world of long-range change—and therefore to dreams of a land of promise rather than to the possibilities of present enjoyment.

Thus under conditions of rapid environmental and demographic change— urbanization, accelerated literacy, industrialization, for example—*value capabilities* frequently lag behind rises in *value expectations.* The lag is not to be explained by the effect of new demonstrations and experiences, however, but by the stringencies of an environment that tends to produce more mirages than tangible improvements. Perhaps in the absence of protest the newly aspiring group lacks political power, economic clout, or pressure-group persuasiveness of a degree that would encourage the society to make an urgent accommodation to its felt needs. It is thus easy to see why politically, socially, economically, or religiously excluded yet modernizing (and therefore value-changing) people in the world today should find themselves both frustrated *and* at the forefront of so much protest. Fired by the demonstration effect, or whatever else, they not only aspire but expect to participate in values of which they have long been deprived. The larger society or imperial world has historically excluded them from political participation, economic benefits, and social status. The structure of their society has made the enjoyment of new values difficult. Entrance has required not only protest but sometimes violence. New opportunities frequently have not been available otherwise.

The idea that collective aggression derives from group frustration (or a combination of frustration and threat), and that the frustration itself has origins in the real world of gap-producing experiences and environmental change, is one way of conceptualizing a causal sequence with protest as one of its ends. Much empirical evidence supports this type of theory. Nevertheless, while contemporary versions of frustration-aggression theory are among the more generally known, they are not the only ones purporting to establish motivational links between the environment and protest. Other approaches link protest to solidarity-producing aspirations or changing structural binds,[17] to status incongruency or discrepancy,[18] and to the breakdown of "homeostatic equilibrium."[19] All of these approaches advance insights worthy of attention.

Regardless of the various motivational assumptions, the notion of "gaps" as the basic origin of collective protest and, therefore, revolution prevails. Thus while Ted Gurr has his gap arising from a discrepancy between *value expectations* and *value capabilities,* and Ivo Feierabend and his associates between *social expectations* and *social achievements,* Chalmers Johnson has his deriving from *value* or *environmental* change that produces a disequilibrated social system.[20] Samuel P. Huntington, as we have seen, demonstrates that rising gaps or discrepancies between *social mobilization* and *political development* are also associated with various types of protest movements.[21] Frank W. Young posits a discrepancy between *differentiation* and *relative centrality* to be a key gap-related explanation of "solidarity movements" and, therefore, the capacity to protest.[22] And elsewhere I have explored the utility of *capacity* and *opportunity* as meaningful variables for gap hypotheses.[23]

Contributing or Facilitating Variables

If widely shared "gaps" produce frustration, solidarity, or the like, and thereby foster a kind of kinetic social energy that may be directed toward aggression and perhaps revolution, what are some of the "contributing" or "facilitating" variables that may shift this energy potential into some form of dynamic protest? Not all people find frustration or "gaps" a sufficient motivation for aggression or protest. What is it, then, that tips the scale? On the other hand, given the existence of some form of potential protest energy that the "gaps" are thought to produce, what impedes the triggering of an energy potential into protest activity? Answers to these questions can be approached by a consideration of the categories of independent variables that aggravate or mitigate situational factors (the gaps themselves), facilitate or impede organizational efforts among the protestors, or encourage or discourage a psychological commitment to collective protest.

Mobility Perceptions

A category of variables frequently raised for consideration is one that we have called mobility perception variables. They deal with the mental images that "gap people" have regarding future alleviation of their currently felt frustrations (considered in a goal-blocking rather than in a clinical definition). If there is reason to believe that frustration-relieving opportunities will be opening up in the acceptably distant future, there will be little motivation to stage a collective, and certainly not a sustained protest effort. There may still exist a tremendous commitment to organizational effort, but the result, in this case, will not be protest so much as gradual progress within the system toward the realization of collective goals. On the other hand, of course, a sudden awareness of a bleakly satisfying future tends to increase the gravity of presently felt frustrations.[24] These "negative" mental images enhance the short-run motivation to protest. They encourage people to fight against the alleged causes of their relative deprivation and to strike out against those who have allegedly denied them opportunities and frustrated the achievement of their expected satisfactions. Of course if, for one reason or another, "hope" of goal attainment is totally lost, then despair and resignation to a life that is "poor, brutish, mean, and short" may result. Under these conditions slaves choose not to protest publicly their slavery, nor "gap people" to protest their relative deprivations.

Just as the motivation to protest is affected by perceptions of upward mobility in one's home environment, so also is it affected by perceptions of what we might call "horizontal mobility" elsewhere, that is, the acquisition of goal-oriented opportunities in another city, region, or country. Generally, when perceptions of upward mobility appear unsatisfactory in a group's usual environment, the most highly frustrated among them, the "cream" of the potential protest, skims itself off and migrates—if it can. The net effect is a reduction in the collective potential to protest at the point of origin.[25] On the other hand, blocks placed on emigration will enhance the probability of a collective protest movement emerging at home if "gap" conditions prevail. Thus the following hypothesis, which assumes the existence of a "preconditioning gap," emerges.

HYPOTHESIS 3:1

The motivation to protest, at least in the short run, is enhanced when mobility opportunities are perceived not to exist.

COROLLARY 3:1:1. The motivation to protest, in the very short run, at least, is reduced when mobility opportunities are perceived to exist.

COROLLARY 3:1:2. The motivation to protest is sharply reduced when objective mobility opportunities do exist.

Societal Responses

If a frustrated group's perceptions of future value satisfactions or opportunities influence its motivation to engage in revolutionary behavior, it is equally certain that future perceptions themselves are in many ways influenced by the social, economic, and political environment. So that we can explore this relationship, two sets of variables are brought forward for consideration. One we have labeled *social absorption,* the other *social coercion.*

If a moderate protest movement or incipient revolutionary activity arises, and the larger society, or the relevant governing elite in it, choose to listen to the grievances of the rank-and-file protestor, if not the revolutionary himself, and to act on them in an "absorptive" way, the likely effect will be an amelioration of the gaps, a more satisfying perception of future goal-oriented opportunities and, therefore, a reduction in frustration and the potential for collective protest. Absorption generally has concrete indicators, such as land reform, tax reform, programs to enhance occupational mobility, and the assurance of voting or other political participation rights.

But the larger society rarely acts so benignly, at least, in the beginning stages of a protest movement. As revolutionaries call for a redistribution of some if not all of the society's values—wealth, status, prestige, or political power, it is not surprising that those who are challenged should resist the demands, alert the police, and attempt to clamp down hard on "law and order." "People want too much too soon." Thus some members of the larger society are prone to activate the *social coercion* variable even if others are flexible enough to render considerations on *social absorption.*

The evidence suggests that a preponderance of "coercion" over "absorption" initially has an inverse and, eventually, a curvilinear effect on both a group's motivation to protest and the intensity of their protest.[26] Nuisance coercion is expected, of course. To a point beyond that, however, coercion simply angers (threatens) and thereby radicalizes protestors. If moderate amounts of coercion are inconsistently applied, the stimulation to protest by violence probably increases. If enough coercion is consistently applied, however (assuming an institutional capability and willingness to do so), it will render the revolutionary leadership ineffectual (by detention or extermination), cow the participants (by "legal" terror and abuse), and thus throw the militants into organizational disarray. The motivation to protest, and the capability to do so, will be accordingly reduced. The underlying frustrations or bind-producing gaps are never resolved, however, but only made worse. The society therefore finds it necessary progressively to move toward police-state status, becoming in the process more amoral and polarized. Frequently only a military dictatorship can keep such a society from flying apart. The alternative is civil war—which may occur anyway. The following hypotheses synthesize these observations.

HYPOTHESIS 3:2

Social reforms, or the credible promise of such reforms, which the protestors perceive as collectively enhancing their opportunities and value satisfactions to a point somewhat near their value expectations will tend to reduce motivations to protest.

HYPOTHESIS 3:3

A curvilinear relationship between coercion and the intensity of revolutionary activity tends to exist, with protest intensity smallest at low and extreme levels of coercion, and highest at medium levels of coercion.

Accelerators

An additional set of factors that has some bearing on the intensity and inclusiveness of revolutionary behavior once structural and psychological binds are set is frequently termed "accelerators."[27] Accelerators shift the energy of moderate collective protests to a level of greater intensity. No doubt many real-life factors potentially could serve an accelerator function. An important one that seems to crop up in most Third World countries at one time or another relates to unfulfilled promises. There is an old saying that "unkept promises make enemies of friends." Bureaucratic and political promises to frustrated and potentially aggressive low-status or "out" groups may not be made between friends, but if unfulfilled, they nevertheless exacerbate the sense of frustration that the promises were meant to alleviate. The probability of intense protest therefore increases. This "mirage effect" is all the more intolerable because it is believed to have been perpetrated not only hypocritically but cynically.

HYPOTHESIS 3:4

Bureaucratic or political promises of measures intended to enhance value capabilities or satisfactions of protestors tend to radicalize them if the promises are not kept.

Energy Facilitators

Another set of independent variables that acts on "gap people" and affects their commitment to protest and, perhaps, to engage in revolutionary activity is one that we have called *energy facilitators*. Their most dramatic impact is under conditions of intense structural and psychological binds or gaps where frustration and rage are keenly felt. The functional impact of the energy facilitators is to neutralize or negate the normal deterrent effect of coercion on civil disobedience or violence. The variables thereby facilitate the shifting of pent-up social-protest energy into any one of a number of forms of dramatic protest.[28] Two energy-facilitating subgroups are discussed: *group resources* and *group linkages*.

Group Resources. Concrete factors of importance in this category relate to organizational strength, leadership competency, relative extensiveness of followership, attractiveness of the doctrines or ideologies that articulate the protests, and adequate materiel. A favorable existence of a combination of these resources facilitates organizational solidarity and the pursuit of collective goals and, therefore, the efficacy of protest. It also helps to create a "countervailing power" situation vis-à-vis opposing groups, thereby encouraging them either to moderate (or increase) their coercive attacks. In any event, when a protesting group is in possession of substantial resources it frequently perceives the benefits potentially derived from protest to be higher and the costs lower. The psychological commitment to protest is therefore enhanced.

Group Linkages. The second subgroup of energy facilitators which has a dramatic effect when intense frustration and anger is felt deals with linkups between frustrated groups and well placed elite in the national culture, or a counter-elite that has demonstrated a great deal of influence (revolutionaries, foreign governments). The linkages enhance the probability of protest intensification because they directly inhibit, or the protestors think that they will inhibit, the establishment's coercive capability. The linkages may also provide effective channels for building up the resources noted above which later may be used to protect the protestors and help them to assert their demands. Thus the elaboration of protective linkages is considered to be a very desirable insurance policy. The existence of such linkages creates incentives for protest under conditions where the appropriate motivation is already high.

Catalysts

Our final category of independent variables that reflect on the emergence and intensity of collective protest and revolutionary behavior *of the masses* is termed *catalysts*. Frequently they constitute the final "spark" in a long chain of events that leads to riots, revolutions, and other forms of dramatic protest. Usually they are one-time happenings that dramatically focus collective attention on the presumed causes of a group's problems, providing the participants with a feeling that violent response is called for. Or, catalysts may also expose the inability of the elite to maintain its monopoly of force. Chalmers Johnson has argued that "these are not sets of conditions but single events—events that rupture a system's pseudo-integration based on deterrence."[29] The spark may be an arrest, an assassination, or even the appearance of a charismatic leader, particularly if he is in a position to convince potential protestors that the power of the dominant elite has evaporated or, somehow, can be negated by forceful action. A catalyst does not *cause* a dramatic protest in the strictest sense so much as it inflames a sense of rage regarding the underlying gap conditions already present. Catalysts push the sufferers to a point of psychological boiling, making life as it is presently experienced intolerable, and dulling the perception of the personal consequences of probable retribution.

By combining our description of the facilitating variables and the idea of catalysts with our previous discussions, we have the following assumptions, hypotheses, and corollaries.

HYPOTHESIS 3:5 AND ASSOCIATED ASSUMPTIONS

ASSUMPTIONS. Relative deprivation exists, perceptions of its future alleviation have recently taken a bleak downturn (perhaps because the state has elected coercion over absorption as a means of controlling the protestors), and possibilities of escaping the resulting frustration through emigration are not perceived to be attractive.

HYPOTHESIS 3:5. *A successful elaboration of energy facilitators, such as group resources and linkages, heightens the probability of intense protest.*

COROLLARY 3:5:1. The motivation to elaborate energy facilitators correlates with the existence of "gaps" (intensity of frustration) and threats (coercion).

COROLLARY 3:5:2. The existence of energy facilitators increases the realm of potential catalysts.

COROLLARY 3:5:3. The continued presence of accelerators, such as unkept official promises of reform, motivates frustrated groups to elaborate energy facilitators and therefore to be even more susceptible to organizational overtures, charismatic leaders, revolutionary ideologies, and the like.

Since revolution is simply an extreme manifestation* of the tensions endemic to modernization, people who live through a revolution quickly realize that their problems are far from solved. Such violent protest may preside over the final destruction of old and decayed traditional institutions, but the political actors who surface during such times have a great difficulty fabricating any modern replacements. Although the resistance to social reform is considerably reduced because that resistance is partially if not wholly eliminated, this does not automatically create for the victorious either the will or the capability of living harmoniously with constant change. Change does not cease when the revolution has ended.

THE PROBLEM. It is easier for people to unite in their hate for something than it is for them to join together in building a new world of values and institutions in which they can commonly agree. Thus, like all other facets of institution building, creating a new society after a revolution—a society in which there is a possibility of reducing gaps between peoples' expectations and the opportunities of their being fulfilled—requires a special kind of leadership as well as special environmental characteristics. We shall consider some of these in the next chapter.

BIBLIOGRAPHICAL ESSAY

"Social mobilization," a concept applied to the selected processes of change that motivate people to aspire to a new world, is now well established in the modernization literature. Karl W. Deutsch, in "Social Mobilization and Political Development," established the basis for its current but varied usage. Playing on similar themes, he subsequently created a cybernetics model of change in *The Nerves of Government: Models of Political Communication and Control.* Most studies which in any way deal with social mobilization pay deference to Deutsch's pioneering work. Indeed, taking Deutsch as a point of departure, J. P. Nettl has written an entire book on the subject: *Political Mobilization: A Sociological Analysis of Methods and Concepts.*

In this chapter we discussed in some detail the concepts of "political decay" and "breakdowns in modernization." Although they are now widely used, significant analytical work on them dates only from about 1964. For a long time there was a kind of eighteenth-century bellicose optimism regarding modernization. Only when the evidence forcefully demonstrated that the political capabilities of many developing countries simply would not allow the "onward and upward" syndrome to go unchallenged, did scholars begin to search for better explanations. In 1964, S. N. Eisenstadt appeared with his "breakdowns of Modernization" and, in 1965, Samuel P. Huntington published "Political Development and Political Decay." Both scholars have continued their arguments in subsequent publications—an indication of the theme's enduring relevance. In 1966, for example, Eisenstadt's *Modernization: Protest and Change* appeared, a difficult but perceptive work. In 1968, Huntington published his stimulating study, *Political Order in Changing Societies.* Nearly every writer on the subject of modernization now pays tribute to the insights of these two important scholars.

The points on social conflict, cleavage of interests, and challenge of new generations are effectively treated by Huntington and Eisenstadt in the works mentioned above. Also, one should consider the excellent volume edited by James C. Davies, *When Men Revolt and Why.* In addition, there is an excellent and innovative study by Nathan Leites and Charles Wolf, Jr., *Rebellion and Authority: An Analytic Essay on Insurgent Conflicts.* But perhaps the most readable on these points, at least, for introductory students, has been written by an economist, Robert L. Heilbroner, *The Great Ascent.* Excellent case studies that portray the conflict dimensions are also available, and Albert O. Hirschman's *Journeys Toward Progress* is one of the best.

In attempting to conceptualize what happens to a modernizing society when its members approach nearly irresolvable differences of opinion, the term "social bifurcation" has been advanced. It is a concept sometimes used in macro sociology and frequently employed in political science. Chalmers Johnson

71

(*Revolutionary Change*, 81–87) deals with it. However, the most articulate presentation that I have found is in Samuel P. Huntington's essay on "Social and Institutional Dynamics of One-Party Systems." A society may exhibit other than socially bifurcated forms, of course, and some of these we shall explore in subsequent chapters.

Rapid modernization increases conflict and lowers consensus. In so doing, it threatens the stability of the state. Experience has shown that a modernizing society held together solely on the basis of coercion does not leave its leaders in power indefinitely, nor does it achieve the goals of capacity and equality it presumably seeks. Thus one of the great tasks of nation building is to reverse the consensus to conflict tendency. Some important contributions on this whole question have been made by Myron Weiner, "Political Integration and Political Development," and Claude Ake, *A Theory of Political Integration*.

The modernizing countries' difficulty in elaborating new political institutions capable of initiating and carrying out the social and political reforms necessary to absorb mobilized masses and enhance political stability has captured the interest not only of academia but of social technicians and engineers as well. The United States Agency for International Development, for example, has been supporting conferences on "institution building" in which the participants, who come from many countries and all relevant walks of life, attempt to grapple with the problems in both a theoretical and practical way. Among writers in the academic field, some of the more important "nation building" and "institution building" insights are found in Deutsch's *The Nerves of Government*, Huntington's *Political Order in Changing Societies*, and Dankwart Rustow's *A World of Nations*. One also should review the excellent "bridge work" (between theory and its practical application) being done by Milton J. Esman. Much of Esman's work is now circulating in mimeographed form, but an early published essay is "The Politics of Development Administration."

The literature on political modernization and political development not only is legion but confusing. In this chapter I have attempted to indicate some of the most paramount conceptual themes. The most significant early work began with the Social Science Research Council's *Committee on Comparative Politics*. The Committee's series of conferences has led to the publication of a set of exploratory volumes. A sample includes: Lucian W. Pye, ed., *Communications and Political Development;* Joseph LaPalombara, ed., *Bureaucracy and Political Development;* James S. Coleman, ed., *Education and Political Development;* Lucian W. Pye and Sidney Verba, eds., *Political Culture and Political Development;* and Joseph LaPalombara and Myron Weiner, eds., *Political Parties and Political Development;* and *Crises and Sequences in Political Development*, by Leonard Binder, James S. Coleman, Joseph LaPalombara, Lucian W. Pye, Sidney Verba, and Myron Weiner.

Many other works, of course, have been considered important. Among those of continuing interest are: Gabriel A. Almond and Sidney Verba, *The Civic Culture;* Seymour Martin Lipset, *The First New Nation* (as well as Lipset's *Political Man*); David Apter, *The Politics of Modernization;* Gabriel

Almond and Bingham Powell, Jr., *Comparative Politics: A Developmental Approach*; Lucian W. Pye, *Aspects of Political Development*; and John H. Kautsky, *The Political Consequences of Modernization*. In addition to all these, one should sample the more recent theoretical articles dealing with one or another specialized aspect of political development or political modernization. Two good ones are "Growth, Development, and Political Modernization," by Karl D. Schweinitz, Jr., and "Political Development and Strategies for Change" by Egil Fossum.

Efforts have been made to apply many political development and political modernization concepts to case studies of specific countries. One ought, in particular, to look at the pioneering works of Robert E. Ward and Dankwart Rustow, *Political Modernization in Japan and Turkey*; David Apter, *Ghana in Transition*; Myron Weiner, *The Politics of Scarcity: Public Pressure and Political Response in India*; Frederick W. Frey, *The Turkish Political Elite*; and F. LaMond Tullis, *Lord and Peasant in Peru*.

Considerably more has been written in the field of political development and political modernization than one can possibly mention in the short space alotted here, but excellent review summaries are readily at hand. I am referring in particular to those by Fred Riggs, "The Theory of Political Development;" Chong-do Hah and Jeanne Schneider, "A Critique of Current Studies of Political Development and Modernization," and Gabriel A. Almond, "Political Development: Analytical and Normative Perspectives."

Edited volumes containing one or more articles relating to themes raised in this chapter include: Kebschull, *Politics in Transitional Societies*; Finkle and Gable, *Political Development and Social Change*; Welch, *Political Modernization*; and Ness, *The Sociology of Economic Development*.

In the discussion of frustration-aggression theory and related considerations it was advisable to include considerable bibliographical discussion of specific textual references. The chapter notes, therefore, should be followed with care. John Dollard and his colleagues (*Frustration and aggression*) gave this theory some experimental basis at Yale in the 1930's, and Leonard Berkowitz has since followed with some tightly reasoned arguments (refer to entries under his name in the bibliography).

As with all theories, that of frustration-aggression has its weaknesses as well as its strengths. Thus Peter Lupsha ["Explanation of Political Violence: Some Psychological Theories versus Indignation," *Politics and Society*, 2, No. 1 (Fall 1971), 90.] can observe that "While psychological conceptions such as frustration-aggression may be sufficient to explain some forms of violence, frustration is not necessary for the occurrence of violence." After making a fairly competent critique of psychological theories, Lupsha concludes that as much explanatory power is to be found in the idea of "indignation." "Does it [the root of violence] really lie in rising expectations on relative deprivation, or is it rooted in indignation over the wrongfulness of actions which violate the norms and values that people believe are right and proper? It is rational for citizens to engage in violence to redress grievance when other measures fail, and it appears that any frustrations that are involved have more to do with political indignation and system legitimacy than with psychological deprivations or expectations" (p. 103).

Where the explanatory power of "relative deprivation" and "frustration" win out over "indignation," however, is under conditions in which rapid environmental and value change are occurring—such as during periods of rapid modernization. Perhaps the idea of "indignation" could be better used as an explanation in stable societies that are suffering a little aberrant behavior from a deviant sector.

CHAPTER 4

Ideology and Leadership

People enmeshed in a rapidly changing social and economic environment frequently disagree about the goals their country should pursue and the priorities that it ought to meet. This is as true among modernizers as it is between modernizers and the traditional elite. Different groups have differing and sometimes incompatible goals and interests. Unless there is some agreed-on "ogre" (such as a colonial power) against which the modernizing groups can vent their frustration and anger, they are likely to identify more strongly with, and give greater allegiance to, their tribe, region, class, or small group than with what outsiders may call their fatherland. Indeed, on occasion it is in name only that one even speaks of a geographically recognizable country as a "nation."

This problem of national self-identity is further compounded by the tendency of people to see in the processes of development and modernization a kind of "zero-sum" distribution of desired goods and values. As a result, the term "amoral groupism" has been coined to describe the resulting phenomenon. Whether based on fact or fantasy, a "you win, I lose" mentality arises. Thus as one pursues the fulfillment of his new aspirations (which may imply that he prevent others from fulfilling theirs) he is morally restrained from predatory behavior only when he deals with members of his own group or class. Some observers call the resulting behavior not only amoral but corrupt. Depending on one's point of view it may be both.

DEVELOPMENTALIST IDEOLOGIES

Modernizing national leaders may overcome these "anti-nationhood" pressures —partially at least—if they elaborate for their countrymen a selective "world view," one that provides the kind of doctrine and slogans which simplify an interpretation of the past, explain the present, and chart a common course for the future. If the sloganizing strikes receptive chords, the followers may actually come to believe they have acquired a passport to the promised land. It does not seem to matter that the rhetoric may be absurd, the doctrines false, the slogans cheap, or the aspirations unreachable. "Belief" is sufficient. To the extent that such belief and faith are broadly shared, national identity and a working dedication for the perceived common good are greatly enhanced. Those who cannot be neutralized or persauded to join the cause are judged to be "expendable." They frequently find themselves thrown onto the trash heap of history.

Formulations of doctrines and slogans, along with their associated explanations of the human condition, are sometimes referred to as "ideologies." From time to time national leaders have been able to weld them into a kind of political religion. Thus Marxism or communism, ideologies that have been made into political religions of one or another variety, are only extreme variations of a general pattern. In Third World countries these and other ideologies have flourished most widely and successfully when the development of modern social and political institutions has lagged behind the pace of social mobilization, and environmental and value change. Ideologies thus tend to thrive on instability and uncertainty, particularly when the institutions of the past have become bankrupt and the fabrication of replacements has not yet occurred.

Most ideologies in the countries under study here are "developmentalist." That is, while they thrive on gaps, their continuing credibility rests on their promise of progress—of a "catching up" with the industrialized nations. The resulting spectrum extends all the way from Maoism and Marxist-Leninism through African Socialism, Pan Arabism, and Christian Democracy. In each case, and one can certainly see why, they are buttressed with slogans of self-sacrifice for the good of the community, of national destiny, and of glory to the fatherland. They are also "socialist" in orientation. For many American observers this invariably brings up a "conspiracy syndrome."

When a leader of a developing country says, "we are socialist, nationalist, and developmentalist," most Americans may not know exactly what he means, but many are sure that he has definitely sold out to the Communists. On the other hand, if the leader claims to be a pro-Western, anti-Communist monarch or dictator, that is something else. "We may not condone his politics," we are told, "but he is our friend." Such leaders support many of our foreign policies and, until recently, have predictably voted with us in the United Nations. In the past they have also received congressional medals and presidential awards.

There is something faintly perverse about American history and culture which allows us to sidle up to small-time tyrants and call them friends of democracy but causes us to become terrified when an authoritarian developmentalist speaks of his socialist economy. If for no other reason this characteristic is unfortunate because it tends to leave in a decreasing circle of international "friends"—and soon those remaining few in the developing world will all be gone. With or without us the mobilized peoples of Asia, Africa, Latin America, and the Middle East will continue to attempt to develop their societies and their economies. In the process, they frequently send our traditional friends out to pasture—if not to the grave.

There is another dimension that upsets our State Department as well as United States foreign investors. For a variety of reasons the new nationalist leaders have rejected "capitalism" as an economic model of development (even though they may accept democracy as a political ideal). In its place, or perhaps because of capitalism's perceived failure in their particular environment, they have their socialist rhetoric and maybe even their socialist economy, although the latter will likely have a mixed socialist private-enterprise orientation. "The true African Socialist," President Julius Nyerere of Tanzania once said, "does not look on one class of men as his brethren and another as his natural enemies. The foundation and the objective of African Socialism is the extended family. . . . It is opposed to Capitalism, which seeks to build a happy society on the basis of the exploitation of man by man; and it is equally opposed to doctrinaire Socialism, which seeks to build its happy society on a philosophy of inevitable conflict between man and man."

Socialist ideologies in the Third World contain a bewildering variety of beliefs, theories, and doctrines—too many, in fact, for any foreign observer to have much success in predicting what any given socialist leader's exact alliances and specific programs will be. The general developmental tasks which, once accomplished, will lead, they say, to the promised success of higher productivity are reasonably clear-cut, however. Nearly all the socialist leaders somehow must reorganize the social and economic features of their country's agricultural sector. They must achieve a surplus of food which then may be transferred to workers trained in the ways and wiles of factory jobs and city life. Moreover, relentlessly they must create conditions in which all workers can contribute to the accumulation of investment capital: a nation cannot consume all it produces and grow economically. Some brand of socialism, although they do not know which, must contain the magic key. Or so they believe.

The tasks of development are so great that communism (a variant of socialist ideology and practice) is believed by some to be the only solution. "Where land is needed, it is taken," says Robert Heilbroner, who describes this point of view. "Where workers are needed, they are moved; where opposition occurs, it is liquidated; where dissent arises, it is suppressed. In place of entrepreneurs who may hesitate for fear of losses, it provides factory managers who are given orders to build. In lieu of a government which must accommodate the claims of the old order against those of the new, it establishes a government whose only orientation is to the future."[1] The denial of personal freedoms is a scant price to pay, it is said, for the promised development of a new order in which man's economic and social aspirations can be realized.

Many mobilized and on-the-go people in the modernizing world are likely to see communism, or even lesser authoritarian brands of socialism, in a much different light than do many of us. As expressed by Heilbroner:

"Never having known political freedom, the hungry peasant and city laborer do not regret its absence. Accustomed to brutality and indifference from the upper classes, the common man submits to the whip of new masters with resignation. Already bent under a heavy yoke, he will bear the still heavier burdens of communism . . . if he sees a chance of lifting the incubus of the past from the shoulders of his children and grandchildren. Even the economic realities of the present communist nations, with their drab living standards, are apt to appear more 'real,' much closer to imaginable achievement, even more psychologically appealing, to the common man of the backward areas than the gaudy and fantastically removed way of life in the West."[2]

Yet, while communism has its presumed attractions, it also has enough obvious drawbacks to prevent any wholesale rush to accept it. The nationalists, in most instances, have instead set out to forge their own brand of socialism—a kind presumably adapted to their own temperament, times, and environmental conditions. In Africa, for example, Ndabaningi Sithole speaks of an ideal socialism that orders the relationships between people and their economy "so that maximum economic benefit accrues to the maximum number." His is a socialism that is "people-centered." It is also based on their willing cooperation. He shows how all the great African modernizers have picked up these themes and why, therefore, they have been more concerned about "helping hands" than with "ideological sources."[3] By alternately playing the Russians and Americans against each other, some African leaders have been able to derive economic benefits from both. "We accept your help but not your 'isms.' " Thus the more reasoned African leaders are unwilling to run headlong into the arms of anyone else's ideology. They want socialism, but they want it to be one of their own creation. It is not unexpected, therefore, that African socialist models should be quite unlike socialism elsewhere. Accordingly, while nationalist doctrines and slogans in Africa focus on development, their orientation nevertheless is related more to the communitarian traditions of African society than to the economic problems suggested by European socialist ideas. Through state planning, stimulation, and mobilization of human and physical resources, the African socialists are equally as intent on preventing the emergence of class divisiveness as they are in fostering economic development. As usual, however, idealism and reality are frequently far apart.

In Asia, socialist ideals among the national modernizers range all the way from Marxist-Leninist brands to moderate social reformism. In Latin America they extend from the Marxist wing to the new wave of "Christian Democracy." The latter has received considerable impetus from Pope John's encyclicals on social reform. In the Arab world, Charles Anderson and his colleagues speak of at least four distinctive variations: The United Arab Republic's military socialism, or "Nassarism," which is characterized by a search for rapid economic development; the Algerian brand of peasant socialism in which it is believed the peasants will emerge as the supreme power in the society; the Destourian socialism of Tunisia, the main features of which seem to be state intervention in the planning and execution of practically everything, including leading the country back to the symbolic imagery and strength of self-sacrifice and struggle of early Islam. Then, there are the "Ba'ath" socialists for whom nationalism and socialism are two sides of the same coin. "Socialism [for them] is much more than a matter of economic organization; it is a way of life, a key to comprehension of the whole cultural universe."[4]

In each case the leaders thrust their country into the future and hope to usher in the promised era as quickly as possible. As long as they are able to command the faith and imagination of most of their subjects, and as long as large gaps exist between people's aspirations and the fulfillment of their hopes, socialist ideology and considerable socialist practice will be evident in the contemporary Third World.

LEADERSHIP AND THE BIG GAP: THE EMERGENCE OF CHARISMA

Many social scientists are prone to think of political leadership as a dependent variable. That is, the possible leadership forms and styles of any given time and place are believed to be dependent on social, economic, and cultural conditions. In part these observers are right. But their argument, if taken literally, clouds an understanding of important political processes. Under certain conditions political leadership may become one of the great independent variables of modernizing times. It may forge the kind of economic, social, and political destiny that in all likelihood would not be produced in its absence. Thus, although similar social and economic circumstances may encourage the rise of a Gandhi or a Ho Chi Minh, for the subsequent evolution of the nation it makes a great deal of difference exactly whose leadership values and ideologies emerge victorious. One should realize that there is no little ideological conflict among the modernizing elite—let alone between modernizers and the traditionalists.[5]

An understanding of the nature of political leadership in modernizing countries, and a specification of the social conditions that affect that leadership are helped by concepts developed many years ago by Max Weber, one of the fathers of modern social science. Having delved into the history of nations and their political institutions, Weber thought he discovered that some men *willingly* obeyed political authority out of habit, others out of devotion to a particular person, and still others because political authority facilitated a pursuit of their private or public interests. Whereas some combination of the three authority patterns would probably always be present in a country at any given time, Weber recognized that one or another of them might predominate in concrete situations. There also could be, and most likely is, differing combinations of authority patterns among various groups or classes in any given society.

With Weber in mind, we could argue that among those who willingly submit to authority (as opposed to being primarily coerced), some do so primarily because they—and perhaps their fathers—have habitually obeyed established laws and abided by traditional customs; others because they have a particular respect or devotion for a political leader and faith in his power to accomplish "miracles"; and still others because they have a broad respect for the utility of and personal benefits deriving from rational-legal political institutions and procedures. (These are "legitimate" *ideal types* of authority where submission derives more from value congruence between the institutions or leaders and the citizenry than from coercion.[6] Political authority exercised primarily by coercion is, by definition, therefore, "illegitimate.")

Weber thus identified three legitimate *ideal* authority types: men who obey out of habit legitimize *traditional* authority; those who obey out of devotion and faith in miraculous "pay offs" legitimize *charismatic* authority; and those who obey out of interest legitimize *rational-legal* authority. In Third World countries the first of these three is exercised primarily by traditional religious leaders, caudillos, monarchs, and similar entities; the second, at one time or another in the modern day at least, by such spectacular personages as Fidel Castro, Juán Perón, Ho Chi Minh, Kwame Nkrumah, Mao Tse-tung, Sukarno, Gandhi and (in the United States) Martin Luther King; and the third is exercised by modern bureaucratic forms of authority such as generally exist in the United States and, to a lesser degree, in the Soviet Union.

We shall now examine charismatic authority in detail, attempting to describe its parts, to explain the conditions under which it is most likely to emerge, and to shed some light on the effect authority of this kind has on national politics. An intrinsic interest in charismatic authority is made all the more relevant because of its contemporary existence in nearly every country of the world. In Latin America and other Third World countries the political and social effects of its presence are most enduring if not unstabilizing.

The Leader and the Led

Cultural variables (for example, traditional personalistic leader-follower identities in Latin America) may facilitate the appearance of charismatic leaders, but they do not, in the strictest sense, provide the "necessary" conditions for their emergence. Such leaders arise in societies where *personalismo* and its related "strongman" attractions do not exist as a dominant cultural trait. Thus if culture does not provide a fundamental explanation of the appearance of charismatic authority, what does? We argue that the necessary conditions are social and political. They occur at a particular juncture in the history of a modernizing nation or society when (1) there is a decrease in the legitimacy of old traditional authority (no longer do men wish to obey out of habit), and a reduction in the relative number of people who willingly subscribe to its power to command; (2) when coercive deterrence of a "despotic" power is weak or declining relatively; and (3) when Weber's "rational-legal" institutions are also weak and underdeveloped. Traditional institutions of authority are dying; modern ones are barely emerging; and forces desiring despotic coercion are relatively underpowered vis-à-vis newly socially mobilized, frustrated, and angry groups or classes. It is into this gap, into this climate of uncertainty, yet cautious hope, that the charismatic leader steps with rhetoric, ideology, and a code book for the future to capture the hearts and minds of angry, frustrated, and mobilized people. Such a leader may even raise military forces and preside over a crushing of the old order (for example, Castro in Cuba, and Mao in China). When such social revolutions do occur, therefore, nearly always it is to the accompaniment of a charismatic leader's artful rhetoric and skillful political command. Thus if social revolution is a function of "modernization," as we argued in the previous chapter, so also, to a great extent, is the rise of charismatic leaders.

Before we proceed to an exposition of the conditions for the emergence of charismatic leadership that are mentioned above, however, we must first describe in more detail the nature of this leadership. A charismatic leader's power to command lies as much in the eyes of his followers as in the drums he plays or in the personal attributes that he may possess. If a biblical Moses walked in, one so tongue-tied that he required the services not only of a speech writer but a speech maker, would we hail him as our leader, pick up our belongings, and follow him into the wilderness? Several thousand did and continued to do so for 40 years. For his time and his place, he had the "charisma." In the modern day this attribute seems to require a different kind of embodiment. And that is the rub. Charismatic leadership is a relationship, not an isolated entity.

What is a charismatic leader's special relationship with the masses that makes his whole operation so convincing? From Weber we have the following insight.

". . . The term 'charisma' shall be understood to refer to an *extraordinary* quality of a person, regardless of whether this quality is actual, alleged, or presumed. 'Charismatic authority,' hence, shall refer to a rule over men . . . to which the governed submit because of their belief in the extraordinary quality of the specific *person*. . . . The legitimacy of the charismatic rule . . . rests upon the belief in magical powers, revelations and hero worship. The source of those beliefs is the 'proving' of the charismatic quality through miracles, through victories and other successes, that is, through the welfare of the governed. Such beliefs and the claimed authority resting on them therefore disappear, or threaten to disappear, as soon as proof is lacking and as soon as the charismatically qualified person appears to be devoid of his magical power or forsaken by his god. Charismatic rule is not managed according to general norms, either traditional or rational, but, in principle, according to concrete revelations and inspirations, and, in this sense, charismatic authority is 'irrational.' It is 'revolutionary' in the sense of not being bound to the existing order: 'It is written—but I say unto you. . . .' "[7]

The fact that such personal authority can exist at all derives from the failure of traditional authority to maintain its legitimacy or of rational-legal authority to command respect. Yet Weber also makes it quite clear that charismatic authority commands allegiance only because people believe that it will lead them, quite realistically, into the "promised land." In the present context that means into a world of modernity. Thus the leader maintains charisma only as long as his followers continue to believe that he will not only show the way but will produce the goods.

Processes of Change and Charismatic Leadership

We have argued that, in general, there are three categories of necessary conditions that help to explain the emergence of charismatic leaders: (1) a decrease in the legitimacy of old traditional patterns of authority, (2) a relative decline in the power (but not necessarily the desire) of those in authority to maintain their position by coercion, and (3) the relative absence of developed "rational-legal" political institutions. In the contemporary period the appropriate fixing of each of these conditions is inexorably linked with the rapid environmental changes (industrialization, urbanization, an increase in literacy and communications, and the like) that are associated with modernization and the value changes that tend to accompany, precede, or follow them. How does it happen?

The previous chapters have given us a clue. There we saw that as social mobilization increases, the process tends to break down or erode major clusters of old social, economic, and psychological commitments. People involved not only become available for new patterns of socialization and behavior but they begin to demand the opportunities to experience them. Traditional authority suffers because habitually it cannot, or will not, rise satisfactorily to meet the challenge. Frequently it attempts to contain the resulting tensions by police power and other forms of coercion.

But the peasants, contained and silent for generations, begin to demand the right to vote and to acquire economic benefits and personal freedoms. Students become more vocal than ever, demanding participation in the elaboration of public policy and pushing for substantial reforms in the society. Among the new classes that are born, the economic middlers no less than others want their share of benefits—political, social, and economic. And workers want the right to bargain collectively—and to strike if necessary—to improve their working conditions and economic well-being. Expectations rise rapidly. Opportunities for their realization tend not to rise commensurately. The result, we have argued, is psychic dislocations, frustration, anger, and sometimes despair.

Traditional authority suffers. It no longer answers the questions or provides the answers. Indeed, sometimes it does not even know the kinds of questions to ask, let alone the answers to propose. Its relative power declines also in direct proportion to the rise of new groups who withdraw their allegiance and begin looking elsewhere for political authority. Modern rational-legal forms of authority are relatively underdeveloped because it takes longer for authority to become institutionalized than it does for allegiance to be withdrawn from it. Hence the "gaps" result. Perhaps, the attention of those involved focuses on a new political personality. Is he convincing? Can he work miracles? Can he really say it like it is? Does he carry a mystique, or can he be made to have one? If so, he might turn out to be the new "prophet" who has come to usher in the promised land.

Ancient societies as well as modern ones have had their prophets, of course, both political and religious. Yet they have all tended to emerge out of conditions characterized by massive dislocation, frustration, coercion, and anxiety. Modernization simply creates more of those conditions and, therefore, increases the probability that charismatic authority will appear more frequently. This is one of the basic reasons why the world has experienced such a large number of these leadership styles in recent years, particularly during the 1960's.

In summary, we have the following hypotheses:

HYPOTHESIS 4:1

Charismatic leadership is made possible by a combination of (a) situational factors (characterized by system-wide societal dislocations) affecting large

sectors of the population, and (b) personality or personal-quality factors pos-
sessed by a potential leader. Situational factors include (i) a decrease in the
legitimacy of old traditional patterns of authority, (ii) a relative decline in (but
not absence of) the power or willingness of a state (or international system) in
the presence of declining political legitimacy to maintain domestic stability on
the basis of coercion, and (iii) the existence of relatively underdeveloped
"rational-legal" political institutions capable of absorbing and assimilating new
groups and classes. Personality or personal-quality factors of a leader (i) include
a capability to, in a sense, exercise economic and social "magic" for the welfare
of the governed—or, at least, have them believing that he can, (ii) require an
adeptness or flair for "saying it like it really is" (ideology, doctrines, slogans)
which reinforces a belief in the previous item, and (iii) generally demand an
origin (birth and early rearing, at least) indigenous to the masses.

HYPOTHESIS 4:2

Rapid environmental and value change such as is commonly associated with
"modernization," mobilizes new groups and classes to demand economic, politi-
cal, and social rights and opportunities.

HYPOTHESIS 4:3

The failure, or inability, of traditional political institutions to respond favor-
ably to the demands causes a decline in their legitimacy (political decay), but
in no way insures that a more capable, effective, or legitimate "rational-legal"
set of institutions will replace them.

The Effect of Charismatic Leadership: Crisis and Chaos

The charismatic leader's mission, given the conditions of tension, uncertainty, and unpredictability accompanying his emergence, is somehow to bridge the gap between the decayed past and the yet undeveloped future and, in today's modernizing countries, to provide some economic and social opportunities for his frustrated followers. Most often, however, such a leader is infinitely more successful in erecting the basic truss work than he is in completing construction and moving the cargo. Very quickly he finds that his competency to preside over a destruction of the past, or at least take advantage of the chaos in its wake, is not accompanied with an equal capability to develop the new and promised better order. There are three main interrelated reasons why this is true. One, we might call the "crisis of succession." The other two, equally crisis oriented, relate to the "routinization" of the charismatic leader's authority and the successful continuation of his "payoff" contract with his followers.

In the succession and routinization crises, an essential point to notice is that while the leader may virtually be deified by his followers, his immediate associates are quite aware of his mortality. In the event of his death or loss of charisma, who will succeed him? In the absence of an established succession pattern (and there is none because the old order that provided such things no longer works), who will decide? How will the nearly inevitable infighting among potential successors affect the country? If intense challenges are made and interpersonal elite rivalries are high, then considerable chaos can be expected. Occasionally, civil wars have resulted.

A second point relating to routinization and succession deals with the payoff contract. The "gap" conditions of uncertainty—and yet hope—favorable to the emergence of a charismatic leader do not last forever. If he is successful in his payoffs, he reduces the gaps and, therefore, the conditions on which his authority rests. Followers then tend to want to establish a "rational-legal," predictable, and institutionalized order of authority. If successful with his magic, the charismatic leader literally works himself out of a job. However, if unsuccessful, he also tends to lose his charisma; his followers who once so ardently worshiped him now desire to cast him off for more promising material. They may even prefer a military dictatorship to his continued personal rule. Either by success or failure, therefore, the leader's authority is eventually challenged. How will he handle this? Will he respond with cries of treason and stage a campaign of repression? Will he attempt to compensate by wasting resources on some foreign enemy or domestic scapegoat, not only losing his charisma but becoming a despot as well? Or will he consciously attempt to build new political institutions and organizations that will survive his own political lifetime? Will he gracefully retire from leadership if it becomes apparent that a rational-legal authority is possible, that political development has occurred, and that "routinization" of his charisma has become a fact?[8] There are examples in history both of artful graciousness and clumsy repression. Unfortunately, there are more leaders who cry treason than there are those who step aside to be venerated as the "founding father," all the time knowing they are no longer needed—or wanted—in any other category.

While charismatic leadership may in many ways contribute to the temporary stability of a country that is undergoing rapid environmental and value change, particularly when it stands in a "no-man's land" between the discredited past and uncertain future, such leadership also can delay the institutionalization of new "rational-legal" authority patterns capable of enhancing stability during times of further change. Ruth and Dorothy Willner have described this point very well:

"The charismatic leader may become trapped by his own symbols and substitute symbolic action as ends instead of means. Viewing himself as the indispensible prop of his country's existence and the only one in whose hands its destiny can be trusted, he may treat constructive criticism as treason. Those surrounding him may do little more than echo him and vie for his favor while awaiting his demise and hoping for the mantle to descend on themselves. Charismatic leadership does not provide for orderly succession. In its absence the crisis of succession may undo much that was built up and conserved."[9]

These are some of the reasons why charismatic leadership, although critical and important during times of rapid change and uncertainty, is nevertheless highly unstable. Moreover, because satisfactory "payoffs" over an extended period are unusual, the stage is set for a charismatic leader's frequent replacement by an "illegitimate" authority type—a military dictatorship. We shall consider this possibility shortly.

In summary we have the following propositions.

HYPOTHESIS 4:4

Charismatic leadership is highly unstable. Either by success or failure in achieving his goals such a leader may lose his charisma. The way to preserve charisma seems to be in knowing when to make it a legend, by bowing out of political power (willingly, or by death, martyrdom, or a coup), and moreover by doing so only at the apex of success, not at the depth of failure.

HYPOTHESIS 4:5

Charismatic leaders who do not withdraw at a "charisma preserving" time have a tendency not only to delay the emergence of developed rational-legal authority patterns but also to become despots in their own right.

MILITARY REGIMES

Nearly every country has an established military. In Asia, Africa, Latin America, and the Middle East the expenditure of precious currencies to maintain standing martial forces is justified, it is said, on the need to defend the fatherland as much from internal subversives as from external enemies. In individual countries there may be honest argument about these needs, but seldom is there disagreement about the consequences to which their fulfillment gives rise. The resulting militaries become powerful, sometimes dominant, political forces in their respective country's politics. Whether it be professional axes to grind, personal or institutional reputations to maintain, or private, corporate, or public interests to preserve or pursue, one way or another the officers make their political clout felt. That influence may be indirect (as, indeed, sometimes happens in the United States), or it may be a "behind the scenes" adventure in which the civilian government is little more than a puppet front for the military. Or it may even involve the military's "capturing" the country, cashiering all the civilian political leaders, and abrogating the nation's political institutions.

In the case of a complete military takeover there is at least one additional certainty. Unless the military is able to preside over a transformation of the society as well as one of the economy, and thereby to close the "gaps" which people believe they suffer, its governance tends to become unstable. In this regard military regimes are somewhat like charismatic leaders. If they operate wisely, however, time can temporarily be on their side because while they use force to take power (and although this, by definition, is not "legitimate"), they also can use force to keep power until the wounds are healed, the gaps reduced, and the need for coercion lessened. Thus in the short run, at least, military authority may be made legitimate as well as strong if the officers actually put the society in order and close, or at least begin to close, some of the "gaps." But few officers are sufficiently wise to be this prudent *and* this successful. They may produce strident gains in the economy, but rarely are they able to withdraw from political control and leave in their place political institutions that are any more powerful or legitimate than those they overthrew.

One problem with military rule, therefore, is its political ineffectiveness over time. True, the colonels *may* "stabilize" the country, and they *may* even make it grow economically. But because they have an institutionalized habit of ineffectiveness when it comes to building new political institutions, they usually are able to accomplish the stabilization and growth feats—when they accomplish them at all—only with various forms of martial law and accompanying suppression of divergent political views. In time the military has a tendency to become simply another actor in an amoral society of conflicting social forces —sometimes no better, frequently no worse.

The military plays its part of the game "for keeps," however. In the past decade no less than 32 Third World countries have been, or still are, under its direct rule.[10] For the moment our concern with these regimes and those yet to join them is twofold: we want to understand (1) why the coups occur, and (2) what the social and political impact of the resulting military regimes is on the whole society.

Why the Coups Occur

The first of the two above-mentioned dependent variables (why coups occur) has received considerable attention from social scientists. Their conclusions have been diverse and sometimes conflicting. With the advantages of cumulative evidence and facts, however, a consensus seems to be emerging. Thus it is now fairly well accepted that a search for the causes of coups must begin not with military variables but with societal variables. The critical answers are not to be found in the social origins of the officers (although this might extend a qualifying influence under some conditions), the nature of foreign military training missions, the source of external military aid, or the lack of a tradition of separation of civil and military power. The answers reside in social-system disturbances that neither traditional political institutions nor infant rational-legal ones are capable of handling. The military intervenes in that twilight period when social mobilization has far outstripped political development. There is nothing to stop it. The society is amoral and corrupt. Its modern institutions are weak and relatively underdeveloped. Every mobilized group is in the arena pitching with its own particular forte. The students are striking and rioting; the clerics are reading pastoral letters and leading their flocks into verbal if not physical battle; the intellectuals are hatching plots and maybe even attempting to stage revolutions; the peasants are invading lands and expelling their landlords. "The most important causes of military intervention in politics are not military," Samuel P. Huntington was therefore led to conclude, "but political and reflect not the social and organizational characteristics of the military establishment but the political and institutional structure of the society."[11]

With a few notable exceptions (Cuba, Bolivia, Russia, China, and Mexico), the military, if it has chosen to take a stand, has won the struggle. It has the guns and a near monopoly of force. In the final analysis, however, it is clear that the causes of military intervention deal not so much with the strength of the military as they deal with the weakness of the nation's civilian political institutions and procedures. For lack of political development the nation must pay political and, perhaps, even social and economic deference to the military officer corps.

Not only are the critical explanatory variables societal ones but they also consistently relate to gaps between social mobilization and political development, between the rise of social forces and the development of integrating political institutions. When these discrepancies exist there is likely to be political instability, corruption, and perhaps even violence, all within the context of an amoral society. It is these conditions that sound the clarion of duty to the military. Rhetorically they ask: "Who else can save the fatherland?" As the pace of environmental and value change increases, the military will ask that question with increasing frequency. Already an affirmative response has been received from the militaries of roughly 25 percent of the world's nations.

Yet sometimes a colonel or general himself will take on the aura of a charismatic leader. Thus military authority and charismatic authority—for some people—may be held by the same individual. However, for reasons discussed below, this particular combination tends to occur only in societies with a fairly low, yet rapidly increasing level of social mobilization (for example Libya).

With the preceding arguments regarding the rise of military authority in mind, we make the following summary proposition.

HYPOTHESIS 4:6

As with the rise of charismatic leaders, the existence of unrequited anxieties if not outright societal disturbances occasioned by "gap" conditions precede the manifest intervention of the military in politics. The two forms of leadership—one with transitory political legitimacy, the other usually struggling to obtain it—rise as a result of essentially the same conditions. Depending on other factors to be noted below, there may be a sequential pattern.

We now consider the social and political consequences of military intervention. They are different in differing situations for reasons that, we argue, are at least partially predictable.

Social and Political Effects of Military Regimes

If the causes of military intervention have been systematically explored, it is less certain that the same can be said of the consequences. Some observers maintain that the effect of military intervention is to accelerate the process of social change, to break the country loose from the bonds of tradition and the intransigence of the old elite. They cite supporting cases from Egypt and Peru. Sometimes they even add Libya, Ghana, Indonesia, Syria, and Iraq. Yet other observers hold an opposite perspective; they are equally able to cite illustrative cases—Brazil, Argentina, Vietnam, and Guatemala. If a military intervenes politically because of a disjointed social system, then its goal must be to prevent a further disjointing—to prevent further political decay, or mobilization, or perhaps both. "This is so because the point of the coup is to prevent from happening what, it is assumed, would happen in its absence."[12] On the other hand, the officers may intervene precisely because, unless they do, what they desire in terms of happenings will not be allowed to occur. Corruption may continue to infuriate them, and elite intransigence may continue to keep them, along with other newly mobilized groups, on ice.

Thus as social scientists survey military intervention in contemporary societies undergoing rapid environmental and value change, many of them are much more impressed with their ability to diagnose the causes than they are with their ability to predict the consequences. The problem is that some officers, when they gain control of a country, seek to accelerate political and social change as well as to encourage economic development. Yet others desire not only to thwart such change but to return the country to some kind of *status quo ante*. Depending on one's point of view and the particular position a military junta takes, some officers might be dubbed "reactionary fascists" and others, "military socialists." Hence, it is confusing. Yet there is one certainty: whatever past roles the military may have exercised, the present ones are increasingly affecting more people because they now occur when social mobilization is rapidly increasing and political decay is widespread. The "palace coup" may still occur. But its consequences are potentially more pervasive than ever before.

Yet diagnosing and, perhaps, predicting the consequences of military coups and other types of interventions are not totally without hope. At the present time the most promising areas in which to begin research seem to be associated with a relationship of two sociopolitical variables with which we are already acquainted—social mobilization and political development (increasing rational-legal authority)—and one military variable—the social origins or class identification of the officers or, in the absence of any clear-cut evidence there, the "reference group" to which the officers are emotionally or professionally attached. The evidence suggests that the larger the gap between the two sociopolitical variables (along with increasing numbers of people affected by that gap), the more likely it is that military intervention, when it occurs, will serve the cause of political and social conservatism. The smaller the gap and the fewer the people involved, the more likely it is that military intervention will facilitate further social mobilization and political change. There are obvious negative cases (many of which can be explained by adding the social origin or reference group variables) to these generalizations but the trend seems to hold. Thus in the modern day, "military socialism" or "Nassarism" (after

Egypt's deceased Nassar) seems to surface when the masses are not yet highly mobilized. It is under these conditions that a military officer may take on a charismatic role for the relatively deprived middle class. If, on the other hand, social mobilization has reached the masses when a coup occurs, *and particularly if a civilian* charismatic leader is in the forefront of a mass reform movement (as opposed to simply middle-class agitation), one can expect that military intervention will have a dampening effect on social and political reform, although the officers may still pursue an expansionary economic development policy.

Among the best insights thus far on the sociopolitical variables are those of Samuel P. Huntington.[13] He calls a society "Praetorian" when mobilized forces are politicized but strong rational-legal political institutions have not yet developed. *Praetorianism,* therefore, describes group behavior in "gap" societies where amoral groupism is a daily offering. Through the use of ideal types, Huntington describes the Praetorian societies in relation to their level of social mobilization—"oligarchical," "radical," and "mass." Each respectively reflects increasing orders of mobilization and gaps. In the oligarchical setting only the traditional elite are politically relevant. In the radical situation an economic and professional middle class has become mobilized. In the mass praetorian society even the peasants constitute a force that must be reckoned with.

The military in an oligarchical praetorian society is probably the first institution to begin to modernize. Military personnel, especially the junior officers, are introduced virtually en masse to new ideas, experiences, and value-challenging situations. This is sometimes an unwanted by-product of the training required to turn soldiers into efficient handlers of sophisticated weaponry and communications. The phenomenon has occurred as much in traditional monarchies as in old republics. Initially, the old elite tend to remain impervious to the young officers and their new ideas. The establishment continues to believe that the military will defend the sanctity of the old order against its enemies, foreign and domestic. It is a curious dilemma: the more sophisticated the young officers become the less respectful they are of that old order, much less committed to its defense.

As these changes occur among junior military officers, similar phenomena are at hand in the larger society. New social groups or classes are emerging to handle the new economic functions of a technologically advancing economy. The old elite are by no means against that, since only a few of them are against "development." But the elite tend to prevent the newly mobilized from acquiring the social status, economic rewards, and political influence that is now expected. The oligarchs want "modernization," but only in areas from which they derive benefits yet suffer no loss in traditional status and privilege. Newer social groups or classes do not see it this way at all. They become dissatisfied with the elite on whose whim the governance of the nation rests. Among the young officers the tension may be very serious; they are expected to defend an order which, in their eyes, is becoming bankrupt. Frequently unable or unwilling to contain the tension, they rebel against their senior colleagues and depose the oligarchs whose world they earlier had sworn to defend. Once the coup is consolidated, the junior officers may elect to hold onto the reigns of administrative power, or they may turn these chores over to the new middle groups or classes and the nationalist intelligentsia which, by its own nature under these conditions, also wants substantial economic, social, and political reforms.

As further modernization and mobilization occur, as more people become politicized and demand entrance into a world that promises equality, freedom, and progress, the role taken by an intervening military also changes. It becomes more reluctant to allow political and social changes to occur, let alone to champion them. Indeed, a reactionary coup may occur (politically conservative although it may be economically expansionary) if a civilian government begins to appeal to newly mobilized groups which the military may wish to exclude from power. There is a dilemma of a special quality and magnitude here. For whatever virtues military officers are noted, one of them is not an abundant confidence in the ability of mobilized peasants, blue-collar workers, or laborers to govern themselves "as they should." The military is frequently willing to accommodate politically the middle classes, but seldom do its benevolent instincts dip much deeper into the social pyramid. As conservative or reactionary military vetoes are generally associated with increasing lower-class political participation (or attempts at participation), a civilian government or charismatic leader in a Praetorian society appeals to such a class only at the risk of losing its political job.

It is something of a paradox that the more backward a *rapidly modernizing country* is, the more likely its military will play a reformist political and social role; the more "modern" the same country becomes, the more likely will its military play out a holding function.

One can see some justification for concluding, as does Eric A. Nordlinger and José Nun, that soldiers in the contemporary Third World act in accordance with their middle-class interests and identities.[14] When the political system in which they live acts to exclude them (oligarchical Praetorianism), they become the radical reformers. But when social mobilization extends to the point where the lower classes also demand entrance (as the middle class previously did), the officers develop a conservative posture and, in essence, attempt to fabricate a new kind of "oligarchy of the middle class." In the absence of explanatory qualifiers here, the officers' "reference group" (the values and attitudes held by those with whom the officers professionally identify) seems to account for some of the apparent negative cases.[15] Other factors may also help to refine the analysis.[16]

If these generalizations are valid, there are some serious lessons that ought to be learned. A country already experiencing a substantial gap between political development and social mobilization—one that has dipped deep into its social system—will probably not have a military disposed to wielding much pressure for political and social reforms which produce more equality in the society. American generals and foreign-policy planners who indiscriminately argue that strong military establishments in Latin America and elsewhere are our best hope for long-range stability will most likely be disappointed as often as they are not. As the pace of environmental and value change accelerates, disappointments over successes in all probability will increase. Thus most Latin American societies, which already are highly mobilized, "are beyond the possibilities of Nassarism. They are too complex, too highly articulate, too far advanced economically to be susceptible to [political] salvation by military reform."[17] Such, theoretically at least, is the case with Brazil.

Coalition-Building in the Military and Its Relation to the Political and Social Effects of Military Coups

Aside from the social causes and political consequences of coups, still another military dimension holds continuing interest. This one deals with takeover strategy. Strategy draws our attention not only because it is intrinsically interesting but because different kinds differentially bear on the intensity and style of the military's political role once it has assumed power.

For whatever reason the military intervenes, whether to promote social and political change or to assure that no more of it occurs, rarely does it do so as a monolith. Among the officers, and even among those who form the conspiratorial block, there are varying shades of political beliefs and ideological dedication. Martin Needler has developed a "swing man" concept to explain the political effect. In particular, his idea shows how strategies that relate to conspiratorial coalition-building can affect the military's eventual social and political posture.

Needler's "swing man" is the last important man (or group) to join the plot before a coup is attempted. The swing man's position is, therefore, an interesting one to consider. If the perceived success of the coup derives from an adequate coalition of dissident officers, then it seems clear that the last man or group to join the conspiracy has provided whatever is needed in size and weight to reach the critical intervention threshold. The actual importance of the swing man may derive from one or more of several factors, including his prominent position of command in the military and his favorable contacts in the civilian world. Typically, he is also the man whom the military selects to head the post-coup provisional government that will run the country. The interest for politics lies in the paradoxical situation this creates. "The swing man becomes the leading figure in the new government; yet he is the person who was least committed to the objectives of the coup, whose threshold to intervention was the highest of all the conspirators, and who was, as a last-minute addition to the conspiracy, perhaps out of sympathy with, or not even aware of, the more fundamental aims of the group that hatched the original plan."[18]

If the intent of the original plotters is to intervene on the side of radical reform, the swing man will be less committed than any of them. If their intention is to return to the old days, he will be the least committed to that line. Most likely he will be a "moderate," neither as hard nor as soft as a great many people wish him to be. Thus he will eventually find himself in conflict with many of his fellow officers who will see in him little to appreciate and much to detest. Small wonder, therefore, that one coup frequently is followed by another, and yet another, as the left and the right within the military jockey for position and power. The swing man walks an exceptionally precarious tight-rope. He also frequently falls.

The following propositions relating to the political and social consequences of military regimes emerge.

HYPOTHESIS 4:7

In Praetorian countries where social mobilization has dipped down primarily only to the level of an "economic and professional middle class," the social and political effect of military regimes tends to be "left-wing" reformist. Deviations from this proposition occur if the social origins or reference group of the victorious officers is oligarchical or elitist. In this case, however, "coups-within-coups" can be expected if junior officers are recruited from middle or lower class groups.

HYPOTHESIS 4:8

When coups occur in Praetorian countries experiencing rapid mobilization among blue-collar workers or peasants, the social and political effect of any resulting military regime tends to be "right-wing" reformist in social and political areas, but may be expansionary in economic ones. Deviations occur if junior rather than senior officers gain the upper hand in military infighting, particularly if their social origins or ideological reference groups hold the lower classes in some esteem.

HYPOTHESIS 4:9

In Praetorian countries with low-levels of social mobilization, the military may successfully foster the development of rational-legal political institutions which, after it withdraws from power, might survive it.

HYPOTHESIS 4:10

In Praetorian countries with high levels of social mobilization, the military has little capability of establishing rational-legal political institutions but may be highly successful in areas measured by aggregative economic indices.

The above discussion and associated hypotheses crystalize some of the reasons why military leadership, as charismatic leadership, is sometimes volatile and unstable. One military authority may be replaced by another. It may be destroyed by a revolutionary movement. Or it may just keep the country dangling in limbo for an indefinite period—turning politics back to civilians when complexities become overwhelming only to retrieve them once again when the civilian politicians cannot produce the promised order either.

If either military or charismatic authority is to be replaced by more orderly rational-legal forms of government, the first task is to begin to close the gap between social mobilization and political development. As it is unlikely that anyone will be able to stop social mobilization, the key to stability must therefore lie in political development. Yet to accomplish this entails a conscious act as well as an enormous will. Charismatic leaders, as likewise military officers, frequently have neither.

If charismatic leaders and military regimes have difficulty in closing the institutional and psychological gaps between social mobilization and political development on the one hand, and on the other, those between new expectations and insufficient opportunities to realize them, what about some of the "old leaders," such as traditional monarchs, who may actually wish to modernize their countries rather than to close up all the doors to change as some of their oligarchical friends have done. Are they in any better position to accomplish a developmental feat that seems to be as equally elusive for charismatic leaders as it is for military officers? Let us see.

TRADITIONAL MONARCHIES

The kings of Saudi Arabia, Morocco, and Jordon, the venerable Haile Selassie of Ethiopia, and most other contemporary traditional monarchs who in varying degrees rule as well as reign, are as different in personality as they are in leadership style. Modernization, however, has condemned them all to at least one common dilemma—a low probability of survival. In varying degrees they are being challenged by a frustrated middle class, an angry intelligentsia, and dissident military officers, groups that they have frequently excluded as much from political participation as from the nation's wealth. In time, substantial numbers of military officers and aroused peasants may join the cacophony, in which case the monarchs will probably fall. As occurred with ex-kings Farouk of Egypt and Idris of Libya, and, indeed, the Ottoman Sultan, the Russian Czar, and King Louis Philippe, the social forces that modernization unleashes, if not absorbed, do lash out.

The old nineteenth-century generation of monarchs as well as their twentieth-century grandsons participate in a legacy complete in form if not in purpose. Both generations have felt obliged to modernize (especially their armies) to save their thrones—the grandfathers by thwarting Western imperialism, their grandsons by preventing revolution. If the old monarchs were successful, can the same be said of the new ones? Many of the grandsons have not been, of course, and for those who remain the dilemma is becoming increasingly acute.

Modernization mobilizes people. Although it affects some more than others, in time it nevertheless has a tendency to reach progressively into the lower two thirds of a society's class structure. As a country's institutions differentiate and become more complex, the people whose lives they touch become more educated, urbanized, and skilled; and their values undergo a substantial transformation. There is a geometric increase in social expectations, economic needs, and fermenting desires to participate in the formulation and execution of public policy. Demands, therefore, rise for social, economic, and political reforms, because it is only by reforms that accommodations can be made. Rarely, if ever, however, are the reforms forthcoming in satisfying quantities, if they are forthcoming at all.

The ensuing gaps—structural and psychological binds, we might call them—produce frustration and sometimes even despair among those who feel that they are being forcibly excluded from enjoying all the fruits of modernization. In the event of rapid economic changes, such as frequently occur when a vast new resource is discovered and exploited—oil in the Middle East, for example —the frustration of certain groups is heightened immensely.

The whole process of modernizing change is inherently dangerous for a traditional monarch. As modernization is not something that he is likely to be able to stop (even if he desired), however, he must resign himself to an eventual forced abdication or learn to lead and direct the process of change that threatens him. The latter is his only hope for long-term survival. Yet can he satisfy his subjects' social and economic wants? Can he extend to them a right to participate in the formulation and execution of public policy and still remain their king—one who "reigns *and* rules," either in his own right or in the name of an oligarchy that has already subverted him?

In the long run, accomplishment under such fortuitous circumstances is problematical at best. As new social forces rise, the old order—the traditional monarchy and the bases of support on which it rests—are called into question. Bureaucratic nepotism; oligarchs with their petty quarrels, family cliques and "corrupt" behavior; painful disparities in the distribution of wealth and social privilege; perpetuation of traditional political authoritarianism at both tribal and national levels—all begin to lose their sanction as legitimate forms of elite behavior. In time, such traditionally sanctioned behavior comes to represent corruption and decadence of scandalous proportions. Those who perpetuate the nation's "new" moral bankruptcy are held in contempt by recently mobilized groups that consistently find themselves, like the servants of old, resentful of both the work that they do and the leftovers from the daily oligarchical festivities that they are obliged to accept as pay for it.

Part of the problem is the king. In the sense of national identity and accepted cultural norms, he and, perhaps, his ancestors have given his land a "headstart" over many other underdeveloped countries. But what should he do now that the pressure for change is on him? Can he leave his old friends—the oligarchy and its bureaucratic sycophants, and the tribal and village chiefs and their faithful charges—and exchange them for the mobilized of the cities—the new middle class, intelligentsia, workers, and junior officers in the military? Can he counterbalance everyone by satisfying and allying himself with the peasantry, such as the Shah of Iran has done? Will the oligarchy and chiefs allow him an "exit visa," will the cities extend the golden key of acceptance, will the army stay in line while the switch is made, or will the peasantry provide a countervailing power that protects him? Or, indeed, will the army remain loyal if switches of some kind are *not* made?

As the society becomes more mobilized, characteristically it also becomes more amoral and corrupt. The king, like the experienced fire walker who has long passed the limit of his endurance, flits from ember to ember—from alliance to alliance—attempting to find relief at the very least, and perhaps even a modicum of comfort *with* security. Yet only rarely are those comforts forthcoming. The embers continue to glow; the old alliances char and weaken. Amidst the confusion, the fabrication of new ones is increasingly more difficult. Eventually the king finds that neither efforts to assimilate the masses or, failing that, attempts to control them through police coercion produce the kind of stability he wants. If he is unsupported by a foreign power, or if the solidarity of the army collapses, the king is finished. "To what extent are [traditional] kings simply the doomed relics of a fading historical era?" queries Huntington in the best essay written on the political dilemmas of a modernizing traditional monarch.[19] In the long run, and in spite of the contemporary spectacular success of the Iranian Shah, the dynamics tend more toward doom than anything else. Yet the stability that eludes the monarch, and which presumably is the pretext of his downfall, is rarely improved on by those who replace him— charismatic leaders and military regimes, the subjects of our previous discussion. They are equally vulnerable. They all forget that mobilized, modernizing people want participation, not paternalism, progress along with rhetoric, and achievement more than nepotism.

If the analysis in the previous chapter is correct, political development requires, among other things, the introduction and institutionalization of new political technologies that will enhance the capability of government not only to govern but to assimilate the new groups and classes that modernization helps to create. One technology may be the modern *political party*. And thus it is this subject that we discuss next.

POLITICAL PARTIES

Political parties do not perforce prevent military coups; nor are they always favorable to the "routinization" of charismatic authority; nor can they necessarily make a traditional monarch become a constitutional one. Indeed, a party leader's rhetoric may frighten the military and cause it to intervene with a "veto coup," particularly if it is about to win an election. Likewise, in the absence of a veto, the continuing political strength of charismatic leadership frequently depends as much on the power of a personalized supporting mass party as it does on the leader himself. And middle-class parties in Third World countries—if they are allowed to operate in the open for long—always end up challenging the power of traditional monarchs. Thus while a party has the potential to help a nation develop politically, it also may facilitate coups, encourage the continuation of military regimes, underpin charismatic leaders, and frighten traditional monarchs into a campaign of repression. One reason for this variation is that political parties are not all alike; moreover, they are also differentially affected by the environment in which they happen to be operating.

Rapid social and environmental change frequently have an adverse effect on a party's potential for aiding political development. Again, the problem is one of gaps. In particular, if the gap between social mobilization and the development of integrating political institutions has already become large before the technology of a modern party is allowed to go into operation, the chasm may be overwhelming. A party then may be exploited by charismatic leaders or driven underground by a military regime or a traditional monarch. Thus in most modernizing countries (where large gaps ordinarily do exist) it is a select party, indeed, that is able to contribute substantially toward a reduction of the problem. Yet a modern "gap-closing" party may be one of the best political tools a modernizing country can have. Let's review the environmental conditions in more detail.

Modernization, for all else that it does, mobilizes people and stimulates them to make political demands. However, as the traditional institutions that legitimized social relations in the old days begin to decay—as we have argued that they do—not only do people's demands go largely unmet but they find less to bind them together in a mutual pursuit of possible solutions. In fact, frequently no longer is there even an umbrella of toleration covering intergroup relations and values. In the absence or weakness of modern institutions and new legitimizing values, mobilized groups quickly drift from one another as well as from the old elite. At the very least the phenomenon of amoral groupism is readily apparent. If the drift is far enough, the new and old groups may even engage in a kind of "societal warfare."

It is the task of political development (and this is, of course, a prescriptive observation) to create an organizational and institutional base capable of counteracting this tendency. Something must be done to facilitate a "binding of the wounds," a processing of demands, an integration of the social forces, and an extending to mobilized individuals of a reasonable stake in the future of their country. This does not mean that all individuals must acquire like values. But there must be more shared benefits than costs in a particular societal arrangement if the politically disruptive effects of modernization are to be controlled. This is the challenge of political development. Political parties may help.

Almond and Powell argue that political parties function to "aggregate" and process various social, economic, and political interests.[20] Insofar as parties are successful in this pursuit, one can expect them to reduce some of the instability ordinarily associated with modernization. Yet Huntington observes that if parties are to accomplish this they cannot be coterminous with a single social force or group. Otherwise they would not perform a political-development function at all but, instead, would encourage the continued fragmentation and warring that already exists.[21] If parties in a modernizing country are to have much effect on political development they cannot, therefore, be the personal property of a charismatic leader, a "legitimizing" front for a military dictatorship, the personal whipping boy of traditional monarchs, or the "lares and penates" of labor, students, intellectuals, industrialists, peasants, or landowners. There must be room in them for more than one closed-corporate family. Accordingly, if a party or party system is to be capable of aiding a country to develop politically, it must relate favorably to two crucial independent variables: *breadth of interest coverage* and *scope of public support*. If the party rates high on these variables, it is probably aiding political development and may even be facilitating a reduction of the gaps that we discussed earlier. If the party or party system rates low, the nation's political life may go on as usual and hopefully will not become worse.

Clearly, these two variables also relate directly to the Riggs and Huntington formulas of political development—to the capacity of government to govern, and to the opportunity of mobilized individuals to participate in politics. If we add some of the variables of those two scholars to the above two, we could say that an optimum arrangement is a party or party system that has broad interest coverage, enjoys a wide scope of public support, enhances the power of government to govern, and maintains that coverage and support over time by fostering a meaningful political participation for mobilized individuals.

Of course, it is not surprising that parties or, for that matter, other political development-related institutions, should frequently fail to meet their intended purposes. Yet there is a lesson that cannot be lost. The only country to successfully overcome a period of intense military intervention in its politics—Mexico—did so through a political party that, although founded by military leaders, became increasingly civilianized as well as capable of meeting the criteria of breadth, scope of support, government capacity, and popular participation.

Transferring these "optimum variables" to types of party systems, it seems apparent that the kind most likely to enhance political development is a "dominant party system." Mexico has one of these. It is this type that most likely will approach the political-development criteria of breadth, scope, capacity, and equality. Rustow has impressively shown, however, that most countries obtain these goals sequentially rather than simultaneously.[22]

Multi-party systems, on the other hand, exist because the respective parties are as narrow in their aggregating functions as the parochial social interests that they champion. They thus fail to meet the criteria of scope, breadth, and political equality. Single-party systems, another type frequently appearing in the Third World, are generally, "top-downward" devices put together by an elite who are "concerned with developing a subjective sense of participation while actually preventing the populace from affecting public policy, administration, or the selection of those who will in fact govern."[23] Although such a system may meet the criteria of breadth (by virtue of the fact that it outlaws all other parties), in time it suffers in scope of support because it only pretends to extend participant political equality. The magic-card trick is eventually found out.

A clever charismatic leader or, for that matter, a traditional monarch, will have his mass party, but he will also allow more than token opposition parties to form. They are his political barometer. They keep him honest. They tell him when his charisma is fading. But such a leader will also keep the opposition weak, since it is the task of his own "dominant party" to play the major political development role—if only he will allow it. In time, if the leader remains clever, he will gracefully bow out and with dignity retire before circumstances arise that make it necessary to expel him in disgrace. Some leaders are this clever; a few are this successful. Some leave viable institutions, others leave only the sordid memories of a life that "almost was."

As for the military and political parties, there has been a mutual aversion. Priding itself in being "above politics," the military is hardly capable of fostering political development. Indications are that officers will be guarding constitutions and saving countries as long as political development remains more an academic abstraction than an accomplished fact. It is rather ironic that the military thus aggravates the very condition it sets out to resolve. When coups occur, parties suffer. So does political development.

BIBLIOGRAPHICAL ESSAY

The phenomenon of intensely conflicting goals among various social forces is again investigated in this chapter. Aside from Ake, *A Theory of Political Integration,* and Weiner, "Political Integration and Political Development" (who both treat this aspect of modernization in varying degrees of conceptual success and theoretical specialization), one should examine concrete case studies. For example, a chronology of political events from any modernizing country would demonstrate the great difficulty of political reform (and, therefore of integration and conflict resolution). Also adding to these difficulties is the fact that if modernizing countries have democratic political institutions where people must be persuaded rather than coerced, the avenues of reform are even more confounding. Alan Angell, "Chile: The Difficulties of a Democratic Reform," has documented several of substantial interest.

The "zero-sum game" is an analytical construct that has received much attention in recent social science literature. George M. Foster, "Peasant Society and the Image of the Limited Good," seems to have been the first to give it substantial theoretical development. The players of the game are seen as having a fixed view of economic resources normally available to them. They act as if they believe that the global amount will always remain more or less the same. Hence, the "zero-sum" title. As resources are fixed, there is also a fixed amount available for distribution. People perceive that the resource pie can only be cut up—not enlarged. Whatever one person wins, another must lose. Whether people actually believe in the assumptions of the game is not as important as the fact that sometimes they act *as if* they did. An annotated bibliography of responses to Foster may be found in Joel M. Halpern and John Brody, "Peasant Society: Economic Changes and Revolutionary Transformation," 78–80.

"Corruption" in developing countries, because it is so prevalent, has received wide moralistic as well as academic attention. Huntington argues that much corruption simply derives from traditional behavior that is carried over into a modernizing environment. In many ways economic development, therefore, makes traditional behavior more rewarding, particularly in the area of nepotism (Huntington, *Political Order,* 49–71). In addition, any traditional restraints, normally effective, lose their deterrence because the institutions that provided the sanctions have decayed. Thus the new national minister frequently sees nothing wrong with appointing all his relatives and friends to bureaucratic positions regardless of their qualifications. Nepotism is an accepted, indeed expected, form of traditional behavior. Modernization just makes more of it possible. And so it goes. J. S. Nye has advanced an extraordinarily interesting way to assess the developmental liabilities and benefits of corruption (for there

99

are both) in his "Corruption and Political Development: A Cost-Benefit Analysis." Additional interesting works on this subject are by Ronald Wraith and Edgar Simpkins, *Corruption in Developing Countries,* partially reprinted in Kebschull, *Politics in Transitional Societies,* 246–254; and two articles by James C. Scott: "Corruption, Machine Politics, and Political Change," and "The Analysis of Corruption in Developing Nations."

Ideology and Charismatic Leadership

"Ideology" is a much-used and frequently maligned term. Karl Marx gave it considerable prominence by relating it to what he said were the distorted and selected ideas advanced by the economically well-off to defend the *status quo.* His original usage still generally holds true, although it is overdone by modern Marxists when they speak of "capitalist ideology." I use ideology to describe a different ideational dimension, one that may be more analogous to "doctrines of change" than to "doctrines of the status quo." Thus ideologies or doctrines associated with modern social movements are to be understood as "tunnel-vision" explanations of the world, the participants' condition in it, and the prospects of future deliverance from the pain and frustration it has created. If the ideas associated with any given ideology invoke "article-of-faith" acceptance, it does not matter—as far as any social meaning is concerned—how distorted or unrelated to objective reality such faith may be.

In modernizing countries, ideology, as defined by Marx, and ideology of the kind associated with social-protest movements, frequently exist side by side. Marx's variety is associated with groups who are bitter about social change that has already occurred or has the prospect of occurring; the other variety corresponds to groups who are bitter because the social change that they want has not been forthcoming.

A general treatise on these and other usages of ideology may be found in Edward Shils, "The Concept and Function of Ideology," and Harry M. Johnson, "Ideology and the Social System." For more specialized references, see David Apter, *The Politics of Modernization,* 323–327, 254–274; and Fred R. von der Mehden, *Politics of the Developing Nations,* 117–140. In addition, the longshoreman-philosopher, Eric Hoffer, has some extremely perceptive insights in *The True Believer;* and Paul E. Sigmund, *The Ideologies of the Developing Nations,* has included examples of rhetoric, doctrines, and slogans.

In regard to people's attraction to socialism and their antipathy toward capitalism, one ought to be aware that one reason why nationalist modernizers have looked at capitalism with a jaundiced eye is because for many years the Western countries, vis-à-vis their colonies, did indeed act within the Marxian definition of ideology. The imperial powers justified their economic system not only for a maintenance of the status quo but for the exploitation of colonial peoples as well. Regardless of the economic utility of capitalism's material incentives and private avarice, therefore, many modernizers have an enormous emotional bias against it. Aside from these points, many observers have raised the issue of the appropriateness for developing countries of a system of economics based on profit, demand, and markets where the latter two may be extraordinarily weak or perhaps nonexistent. Robert Heilbroner, *The Great Ascent,* discusses these points, and they also may be found in Charles Anderson, Fred R. von de Mehden, and Crawford Young, *Issues of Political Development,* 199–205.

The above discussion alerts one to the rationale behind scores of socialist ideologies in the developing areas. The many varieties are amply noted by Anderson and his colleagues (*Issues of Political Development,* 175–219). Additional specific references for various geographic areas are: Gordon H. Torrey and John F. Devlin, "Arab Socialism"; Ndabaningi Sithole, *African Nationalism;* and John D. Martz, "Doctrine and Dilemmas of the Latin American 'New Left.'" In Latin America the influence of Pope John's Encyclicals on the ideological postures of the "new church" has also been significant. This area is treated by Thomas G. Sanders, "The Church in Latin America"; Edward J. Williams, "Latin American Catholicism and Political Integration"; and Ivan Vallier, *Catholicism, Social Control, and Modernization in Latin America.*

There are counterarguments, of course, and one is by John H. Kautsky, *Communism and the Politics of Development: Persistent Myths and Changing Behavior,* 172–183. In particular, he argues, the communist brand of socialism has so many liabilities that it does not appeal to the majority in underdeveloped countries: not to the peasantry nor to urban blue-collar workers, because for them it is largely incomprehensible; nor to the traditional elite, because it prescribes their demise. Its greatest attraction is to people who can loosely be described as intellectuals. Yet, we must hasten to add, these frequently constitute the new modernizing elite.

Rhetoric aside, it is very unusual in the developing world that one should run into a pure "socialist" economy. Most often the countries are "mixed," with heavy state economic intervention in areas where private capital (either because of lack of demand or because the investment risks are too high) is not forthcoming. One of the best examples of economic success with such an economy is Mexico. See Raymond Vernon, *The Dilemma of Mexico's Development.*

The fact that any futuristic ideology must be tempered by the conditions at hand (and cannot, therefore, be imported wholesale from an alien environment or an ideal set of ideas) has gained increasing attention among the practical modernizers. In the particular cases of Ghana, Uganda, and India, this point has been documented by David E. Apter, "The Role of Traditionalism in the Political Modernization of Ghana and Uganda," and Lloyd I. Rudolph and Susanne Hoeber Rudolph, "The Political Role of India's Caste Associations."

The usage of "charisma" and "charismatic authority" certainly is not accepted without question by students of modernization, although many writers have considered these concepts useful. At least one dissenter has gone so far as to state that, since they describe an unstable and nonstructured authority type, no criteria can be devised to identify or measure them. Therefore, he argues, the terms are essentially meaningless (K. J. Ratnam, "Charisma and Political Leadership"). Yet whatever terminology one chooses to employ, somehow he must come to grips with the "personal" authority of the kind spoken of by Weber. Whether one tags it with "charisma" or some other term, it is a phenomenon that must be recognized and dealt with. Claude Ake, *A Theory of Political Integration*, prefers to call it "personal authority," and he makes a fairly good case for this approach. More recently R. S. Perinbanayagam ("The Dialectics of Charisma") rejects both those who have denigrated the use of charismatic authority and those who have not, proposing a *social psychological and communicational* theory in their stead.

Important scholars who do relate charisma to the politics of modernization are Dankwart Rustow, *A World of Nations*, 148–169; N. Ruth Willner and Dorothy Willner, "The Rise and Role of Charismatic Leaders"; Carl J. Friedrich, "Political Leadership and the Problem of the Charismatic Power"; J. T. Marcus, "Transcendence and Charisma"; Edward Shils, "The Concentration and Dispersion of Charisma: Their Bearing on Economic Policy in Underdeveloped Countries"; Guenther Roth, "Personal Rulership, Patrimonialism, and Empire-building in the New States," and Robert C. Tucker, "The Theory of Charismatic Leadership."

When studying a subject such as charisma, one should look at original sources as well as recent elaborations. There are good translations of Weber. One in particular is H. H. Gerth and C. Wright Mills, *From Max Weber: Essays in Sociology* (New York: Oxford University Press, 1946). For more specialized excerpts refer to Max Weber, *Charisma and Institution Building*, edited with an introduction by S. N. Eisenstadt.

The Military

One of the best general works on civil-military relations is still Samuel P. Huntington's *The Soldier and the State*. A subsequent book, *Political Order in Changing Societies*, includes an excellent chapter—"Praetorianism and Political Decay"—devoted to the specific kind of modernization-military-civilian relations discussed in this chapter. Closely following in order of importance are Morris Janowitz, *The Military in the Political Development of New Nations;* Eric A. Nordlinger, "Soldiers in Mufti: The Impact of Military Rule Upon Economic and Social Change in the Non-western States"; Amos Perlmutter, "The Praetorian State and the Praetorian Army: Toward a Taxonomy of Civil-Military Relations in Developing Politics"; José Nun, "A Latin American Phenomenon, The Middle Class Military Coup," and Dankwart Rustow, "Military Regimes," in his *A World of Nations*. In varying degrees these excellent works treat the causes of military intervention, the strategies employed, and the political, economic, and social consequences.

In reference to more specialized areas of research, Robert D. Putnam is the author of a good work that attempts to explain *why* the military intervenes ("Toward Explaining Military Intervention in Latin American Politics"). He reviews much of the literature up to 1966 and also advances a new methodology, "causal path analysis." Putnam shows that his "social mobilization" and "economic development" variables account for about 33 percent of the variance in the military intervention index. He also attempts to relate the index to a third variable, "political development," but his definition and usage here are so inconclusive, or elusive, that he neither confirms nor refutes the generalizations advanced in this chapter.

Latin America, because of the pervasiveness of military intervention there, has been the object of much academic interest. Thus, in addition to Putnam's article, there is Martin C. Needler's "Political Development and Military Intervention in Latin America," a study that he has revised and reworked for a chapter in *Political Development in Latin America: Instability, Violence and Revolutionary Change.* Also, Edwin Lieuwen has written several works on the Latin American military, the most recent being his "Survey of the Alliance for Progress: The Latin American Military."

As the frequency of coups in other areas of the world has increased, they have also begun to capture academic interest along the lines outlined in the chapter. One of the best articles is James Bill's "The Military and Modernization in the Middle East." An additional one related to the Middle East, which includes some excellent case studies, is J. C. Hurewitz', *Middle East Politics: The Military Dimension.* Then, for Africa, Edward Feit has published his "Military Coups and Political Development: Some Lessons from Ghana and Nigeria." One also ought to investigate several of the excellent articles in Claude E. Welch, Jr., ed., *Soldier and State in Africa: A Comparative Analysis of Military Intervention and Political Change.*

For a discussion of coup strategies and techniques, see Rustow, *A World of Nations,* Chapter 4. He has elaborated some interesting typologies there. In addition, five excellent case studies may be found in William G. Andrews and Uri Ra'anan, *The Politics of the Coup d'etat: Five Case Studies.*

Earlier attempts to explain military intervention seemed to concentrate more on military variables (social origins of officers, effect of military training missions, and the like) rather than societal variables, although this generalization is not totally rigid. See John J. Johnson, ed., *The Role of the Military in Underdeveloped Countries,* and Johnson's *The Military and Society in Latin America.* On the other hand, Samuel P. Huntington, ed., *Changing Patterns of Military Politics,* and Samuel E. Finer, *The Man on Horseback: The Role of the Military in Politics* include for discussion both military and societal variables.

Lyle N. McAlister made a comprehensive review of the literature up to about 1966 in his "Recent Research and Writings on the Role of the Military in Latin America," *Latin American Research Review,* 11 (Fall 1966), 5–36; and Alfred Stepan reviewed the works of John J. Johnson, Edwin Lieuwen, and Robert Gilmore in "The Military's Role in Latin American Political Systems," *Review of Politics,* 28 (October 1965), 564–568. Much of the older literature, and now, increasingly, some of the newest, has considered the military as an alien if not demonic force in the society, which tended to act against other groups in its own interest more than in alliance with groups for the interest of the nation. A newer "developmental" literature posits the opposite, that precisely because the military is a somewhat isolated institution, with modern organizational characteristics, it can move in to administer the development of a country in ways that other organizations cannot. The latter group, therefore, perceives the military as being especially suited to act as a nation-building, modernizing bureaucratic force. Both of these orientations are reviewed with references to the literature by Lyle N. McAlister, "Changing Concepts of the Role of the Military in Latin America," *Annals of the American Academy of Political and Social Science,* **360** (July 1965), and McAlister's "Recent Research and Writings on the Role of the Military in Latin America," *Latin American Research Review,* **11** (Fall 1966), 5–36. McAlister also outlines the major opposing propositions found in the literature in "The Military," in John J. Johnson, ed., *Continuity and Change in Latin America* (Stanford: Stanford University Press, 1964), 136–160.

Political Parties

The literature on "comparative political parties" is expansive, but only recently have scholars done research on the functions of parties within the context of modernization. I found four of these recent works to be particularly helpful in the preparation of this chapter: Samuel P. Huntington, *Political Order in Changing Societies,* 397–460; Samuel P. Huntington and Clement H. Moore, ed., *Authoritarian Politics in Modern Society: The Dynamics of Established One-Party Systems;* Dankwart A. Rustow, *A World of Nations,* 207–236; and Joseph LaPalombara and Myron Weiner, eds., *Political Parties and Political Development,* 399–435. The LaPalombara-Weiner volume, in particular, has an excellent selected bibliography.

In addition to the above studies, Lucian W. Pye has an excellent treatise in *Politics, Personality and Nation Building,* 15–31, in which he presents an analytical model of the nature of transitional politics and their relation to party systems. For specific geographical areas, Robert E. Scott's "Political Parties and Policy-Making in Latin America" should be consulted, as also should Lucian W. Pye's "Party Systems and National Development in Asia." For a general treatment of the relation of political parties to modernization in Africa, see James S. Coleman and Carl G. Rosberg, Jr., eds., *Political Parties and National Integration in Tropical Africa.* A good volume containing selections from many contemporary works which, in one way or another, deal with African parties is Irving Leonard Markovitz, ed., *African Politics and Society.*

An interesting discussion on the "commitment" and "change" functions of elections in developing countries is found in R. S. Milne, "Elections in Developing Countries." He also has a very good bibliography. A theoretical volume that has set the stage for a number of country studies is the Almond-Powell *Comparative Politics: A Developmental Approach,* particularly pages 98 to 127.

Fred R. von der Mehden, *Politics of the Developing Nations,* 53–76, presents an interesting typology on the degree of competitiveness of political parties and the systems in which they operate. He also includes a selective bibliography.

The entire issue of *Comparative Political Studies,* **2**, No. 1 (April 1969), is devoted to social structure, party systems, and voting behavior. Although the geographic focus of the various authors is not on the developing world, their research methodology certainly is applicable and should be studied by anyone who is interested in comparative party systems. For more sophisticated theoretical and empirical works of general relevance to parties and party systems, see Seymour Martin Lipset and Stein Rokkan, ed., *Party Systems and Voter Alignments: Cross-National Perspectives,* and also the review essay by Peter H. Merkl, "Political Cleavages and Party Systems."

Traditional Monarchies

The best treatment of the issues raised in this section is by Samuel P. Huntington. See his "Political Change in Traditional Polities," Chapter 3 of *Political Order in Changing Societies;* and "The Political Modernization of Traditional Monarchies." A case study illustration of the themes is presented in the study on Libya appearing in this volume.

PART III

Modernization in Brazil or the Story of Political Dueling Among Politicians, Charismatic Leaders, and Military Guardians

"Everything has been tried," Victor Alba once observed about politics in Latin America: "Efficient dictatorship and corrupt dictatorship, the militarism of animals in uniform and the militarism of intelligent men . . . false revolution and authentic revolution. . . . The only thing that has not been tried is democracy, real democracy, democracy that is at once political, social, and economic, that is government of, by, and for the people."[1]

If dictatorship, militarism, and revolution (except perhaps in Mexico) have failed to produce institutionalized political systems in Latin America that are both predictable (in the sense of functioning under general rules) and participatory (by allowing the masses an orderly way to influence the selection of and decisions taken by political leaders) so have the region's anticlerical liberalism, its demagogic populism, and certainly its paternalistic and clerical conservatism. There have been governments of, by, and for *some* people, of course, but only rarely governments of, by, and for *the* people. Thus most Latin Americans are more used to government by coercion than they are used to government by consent, now as much as in earlier times.

Contrary to earlier predictions, rapid economic development in the last 15 years has not made institutionalized democracy or orderly government by consent in Latin America any more apparent. In fact, rapid environmental change has made the achievement of stable democracy less, not more likely. These are the predictions for the next one or two decades at least. Industrialization, urbanization, and rising literacy, and the changes in people's values and attitudes (including the development of empathy and psychic mobility) that tend either to precede, accompany, or closely follow those changes, have heightened the *desires* of the Latin American masses to participate effectively in politics but have opened insufficient channels for them to do so. Also, these substantial environmental and psychological changes have made many—including growing numbers of the heretofore "politically dormant" peasants—more conscious of their relatively deprived conditions and more critical of the political regimes that they believe help to perpetuate them.

There is yet another ingredient in this potentially volatile situation: the environmental and psychological changes have also heightened the capacity of the masses to protest coercive authority, real or perceived, and to counter those who would wish to protect it. Thus while Latin America is characterized by its nondemocracy now as much as ever before, it is also a region notorious for heightened social protest, violence, police power and counter-insurgency, and inflammatory rhetoric that calls for social and economic revolution.

The political patterns in Latin America, we are led to conclude, are not as different from their historical consistency as they are aggravated. More people are now in the arena pitching with greater intensity than ever before. The effect is to produce more frequent or prolonged appearances of what we would call "crisis leadership" forms: (1) governance by the military, and (2) leadership by charismatic authority. °

In Brazil the economy has modernized and the society is struggling to do so; but the political system is hung up and, for some Brazilians, has proved incapable either of governing or of ameliorating the structural and psychological binds that are associated with modernization. It was into this dilemma of a decaying political past and a yet undeveloped political present that João Goulart entered and from which the military ushered him out. Let us see how it all happened and what some of the social and political consequences have been.[2]

° This is not to be considered as being necessarily synonymous with traditional *personalismo, caudillismo, caciquismo,* or *coronelismo,* which also remain, probably suggesting a cultural variable predispositioning Latin Americans either to a ready attraction to a "strong man on horseback" or a desire to be one. Regardless of the influence of this cultural variable, however, we argue that necessary conditions for the emergence of charismatic authority lie in certain kinds of broadly shared social, economic, and political events.

CHAPTER 5

The Rise and Fall of a Populist Leader

Figure 6. Brazil.

One of the most enigmatic presidents of Brazil is now in exile. Little wonder. His military successor accused him of treason, stripped him of all political rights, officially discredited his regime, and suppressed his followers. He is João "Jango" Goulart, a man of considerable political skill and some charismatic appeal to Brazil's lower urban classes. Depending on one's own point of view, he may be a saint, an opportunist, a communist, or simply a political hack who overplayed his hand. Whatever the truth may be, he certainly is a man who attempted to make political capital with some of the social forces that modernization has unleashed. His fatal mistake, however, was to identify exclusively with the highly mobilized lower classes and to divorce himself from nearly everyone else. Indeed, at times it seemed he was carrying out a "vendetta" against the older more prestigious groups in Brazilian society. Among those that he consistently offended was the military.

The background to Goulart's ascension to the presidency, which runs from approximately 1930 to the crisis that put him in power in 1961, and the events surrounding his removal in 1964, relate a story of power and intrigue typical of much of the developing world. The names and places change; the general dynamics remain. A detailed description of those associated with Brazil will aid our understanding of these frequent dramas and occasional duels between charismatic leaders and military officers and the respective social forces that they represent.

THE BACKDROP

After the breakup of the Brazilian monarchy in 1889 the leading pro-Republican politicians forged a loosely structured federation of states. "Loosely structured," we have to say, because there were always strong regional and state loyalties pulling at and, therefore, weakening the strength and effectiveness of the infant republican federal government. To be sure, strong regional ties and rivalries had existed for a long time. But suddenly the enormous "moderating power" of Brazil's monarch was no longer present. The political dissidents had sent Dom Pedro, one of the most illustrious and intelligent monarchs of all time, into exile. Now the victorious rebels had to make Brazil's patchwork politics work on their own. The experience, they found, was much more difficult than they had supposed.

In many respects the new Brazil resembled the federal system of the United States of America in an earlier period, at least, in the sense that "states rights" over "federal encroachment" was a fact rather than an idea. But in due time Brazil's modernizing thrust into the twentieth century set into motion social and economic pressures that (as in the United States) the old decentralized political arrangements were not prepared to handle. Thus while rapid change created problems that literally cried for a more rationalized and centralized form of modern government, the newly emerging social forces in the states also became more powerful and less amenable to traditional political control and manipulation.

Certainly by the time of the elections of 1930 there was strong evidence that the old political arrangements and understandings were in a state of serious decay. Growth in the cities and the increased political awareness of much of the population there (as well as in the countryside) had struck hard at the political hacks and machine bosses of the backlands. No longer could they deliver votes with a near 100-percent degree of confidence. Nor could they continue to manipulate the political system at their will. The cities were growing in power and prestige. They were resisting, and sometimes striking back. The regime of *coronelismo,* a system of regional politics quite akin to the machine politics of Tammany Hall in the old days of George Washington Plunkit, was experiencing serious disorder.[3]

But for a peculiar device of "electoral stabilization," the political disorders deriving from this decay in the old institutional arrangements might well have appeared long before social pressures actually brought the regime's inadequacies into sharp relief. The time-buying device was the practice of rotating the federal presidency among the political machines of the most powerful states, particularly those of São Paulo, Minas Gerais, and Rio Grande do Sul. The rural political bosses were agreed that the presidency, the one big plum in the Brazilian federal government—and one from which considerable largesse flowed—should be "spread around" so that the benefits of national government would be shared in a predictable fashion. In particular, the device assured that no machine politician of any importance would be excluded from the federal pipeline—at least, all the time. Many politicians from small states were systematically excluded by this arrangement, of course. But by appropriately handling their own votes they could assure themselves of some participation in the bounties. Accordingly, it was the incumbent government and the machine bosses who generally selected the next president. Their nominee nearly always won. And he nearly always assumed the presidency—except in the elections of 1930.

One of the problems in 1930 was that Washington Luis, the incumbent president, broke the rotating principle and attempted to secure agreement from the bosses that his friend and fellow politician from São Paulo, Julio Prestes, would be elected to succeed him in the presidency. The official election returns seemed to confirm the credibility of the president's strategy. Prestes received 1,091,709 out of the 1,890,524 votes cast. But this time the opposition was much more vociferous than ever before. Angrily rejecting the official returns, the losers accused the government of a clumsy electoral fraud.

It is of no curiosity that the political leaders of Minas Gerais and Rio Grande do Sul were in the forefront of the opposition. Following the principle of rotation, the presidency would ordinarily have gone to one of them. In particular, they resented Luis' attempt to install in the presidency yet another *Paulista* (one from the state of São Paulo). It was true, of course, that in past elections losers had always claimed fraud. But they also had abided by election results. This time, however, the reported fraud was so great, the disenchanted so numerous, and the attempt by Washington Luis to keep the presidency within the rubric of his own political machine such a breach of traditional arrangements that the opposition was not content simply with anti-government rhetoric. Thus Minas Gerais leaders shifted their support to the "Liberal Alliance" slate headed by Getúlio Vargas, governor of Rio Grande do Sul. Together they plotted a revolt.

Luis might have been able to pull off his little maneuver had it not been for the disaster of the worldwide economic depression that catastrophically hit the main sectors in industry, commerce, finance, and their friends in Minas Gerais and Rio Grande do Sul, and especially the coffee growers, who had a bumper crop and no market. We can say that there *may* have been a saving possibility because, as events unfolded, it was these disaster-stricken elements who sided with the rebellious *tenentes* (young, nationalistic, development-minded army officers who had been pushing for political and social reforms since the 1920's) to pull the political machines of Minas and Rio into an incipient anti-Luis conspiracy. The old political bosses were cautious at first, however. Since none wanted to initiate a revolt, all waited for the others to make a move.

A catalyst pushed this tense situation over the brink—a political assassination in the state of Paraíba. The assassins belonged to a party that the incumbent president had strongly supported, against the wishes of Paraíba's major political machine. Now a conspiracy, including that state, was quickly hatched; the politicians, the growers, and the *tenentes* made their move. As the rebels and conspirators marched on the capital (Rio de Janeiro) from the three states, Washington Luis found that he lacked support from his military. After more than a month of near bloodless confusion, Getúlio Vargas, a defeated presidential candidate from Rio Grande do Sul, became Brazil's new president. The military, being the "guardian of constitutional order" which had first refused aid to Luis and then had relieved him of power, dutifully presided over Vargas' inauguration.

Rio Grande do Sul had its man in the presidency, all right. But that president was hardly successful in *developing* a new and modern political system. His Machiavellian political style encouraged all mobilized groups to press uncompromising demands. Moreover, his equivocal attitude toward some of his early supporters occasioned their early estrangement. The *tenentes* from his own state soon started an opposition movement. Then in 1932 the whole state of São Paulo erupted in armed revolt. This was not surprising considering Vargas' punitive hand on the old political machine of the former president. But the point of interest is that important groups in Rio Grande do Sul and also Minas Gerais quietly supported the besieged *Paulistas*. São Paulo and its old enemies had become allied in their new-found hatred for the common enemy—Getúlio Vargas.

Vargas eventually did make concessions to São Paulo and other rapidly urbanizing centers, but the more he made, the hotter his problems seemed to become. Deterioration in relations with newly mobilized Brazilians continued right up to 1937. Suddenly, the disenchanted, especially the urban masses associated with the revolutionary wing of the Communist party, erupted in revolutionary fervor. It was an alarmed Vargas who asked for, and a frightened congress that granted, emergency, virtually dictatorial powers. All pretenses to representative democracy were not long in collapsing, for soon the military's authoritarian wing consolidated Vargas' position with a coup. It was under these circumstances that the man from Rio Grande do Sul began the second half of his 15 years as president, a period Brazilians call the *Estado Nôvo* (the New State). It was characterized by a quasi-fascist political style that its supporters said would put Brazil's politics in order. While the Estado Nôvo certainly failed in that objective, it did constitute a kind of holding action that allowed everyone to catch his breath.

Thomas Skidmore has observed that "the Estado Nôvo brought irreversible changes in the institutions of political life and public administration. Most important, Vargas transformed the relationship between federal authority and state authority, and thereby moved Brazil much closer to a truly national government."[4] Thus the president's failure at a "new politics" lay not so much in its modernization as it did in its development. In the wake of a decay in the traditional political order (as the cities gained power and economic changes occurred in the countryside), it was necessary first to build new political institutions and then to develop their capacity to govern, to absorb, and to administer. Vargas' Estado Nôvo centralized authority and established several other features of a modern political state. But the president was unable to develop these features sufficiently well to accommodate the pressures for political participation that new social forces, especially in the cities, demanded.

Part of the problem lay in Vargas' own political style. He had based his New State on the support of "social middle groups" which in time would tend to be displaced, relatively at least, by newer more mobilized groups in the lower half of the social structure. But, in addition, there was the problem of fascism in Europe which, by 1943, appeared not to be viable as much from social as from military perspectives. Vargas knew his own secondhand fascism could not outlive that of Europe.

During the years 1943 to 1945 the president began to change his political style and the social bases of his regime. Anticipating the moment when the political system would be reopened to normal electoral processes, he began to build new linkages with recently mobilized Brazilians that he hoped would preempt the growing influence of the opposing and increasingly vociferous political left, which also had been making capital among them. He began this new phase with a program of extensive social-welfare legislation for the politically mobilized urban masses, compulsory labor unionism (with the government playing a "godfather" role), and the formation of a populist Labor party (Partido Trabalhista Brasileiro—PTB) based on a coalition of government-dominated unions and other newly mobilized groups. Vargas' strategy was to capture and retain these new groups by espousing a program of rapid industrialization for the country and by offering them a favorable place in the process. Obviously, the president was moving away from his traditional supporters and toward hoped-for new ones who would be more representative of the modernizing society and economy that he could see was inevitably coming.

Although in the long run the absorption and integration of new groups is necessary, for Vargas its immediate effect was politically suicidal. The military, already greatly concerned about the growing influence of the political left in the federal government, was incensed with Vargas' alleged tampering with the electoral machinery for the upcoming elections. In October of 1945 the officers, just as they had done to Washington Luis years earlier as "guardians" of the constitution, once again removed a president from power.

Vargas was ousted from the presidency, but he certainly was not finished politically. In the elections several months later the supporters from his home state of Rio Grande do Sul returned him to the capital as their senator. Soon angered by congressional criticism of his late government, however, he quietly returned home and dedicated himself to building and strengthening his new Labor party. Yet so great was his influence nationally that "his ranch at São Borja became a mecca for aspiring politicians; and it was soon clear that the central personality of the period was not the newly elected President, but the recently deposed one."[5] During these years a young neighbor and political activist by the name of *João Goulart* won Vargas' confidence. It was here that Brazil's president-to-be (and citizen-to-be-exiled) began his political career.

Vargas' quiet patience, consummate political skill, and hard organizational labor paid off. Aside from firming up the new social base of his political reservoir, he was actually able to convince many other Brazilians that he was really a democrat, not a dictator. In the national elections of 1950 a highly diverse alliance of his countrymen returned him to the presidency by nearly as many votes as his three opponents combined. Vargas' role as leader of the new Brazilian Labor party had permitted him a platform from which to expound his new political philosophy—a mixture of social welfarism, working-class political activism, and economic nationalism. *Trabalhismo,* as he termed it, almost immediately captured the hearts and minds of many Brazilians who really wanted to go somewhere, and who wanted to create a country that could take its place among the modern nations of the world. At first only a philosophy, in time *trabalhismo* became an ideology and, in turn, part and parcel of a populist political movement. To be sure, the product was not the only movement on the political left (the Communists had one going too), but after 1950 it certainly involved a greater number of people than other leftist movements.

Vargas' new administration was plagued from the start, however. On the one hand a severe drought in 1951 in the already normally dry Northeast pressed him hard. On the other, he was stunned by serious inflationary pressures that angered his blue-collar workers. The political effect of the inflation was most serious because it created agonizing troubles with the labor unions, most of which were affiliated with his PTB party. If this were not enough, the Communists increased their militant activities, even staging an abortive attack on an army munitions dump in Natal. Again the diverse forces which had become allied to put Vargas in power found that with his election their common interests ended.

The president, faced with an obvious erosion of public confidence in his regime, reformed his cabinet in June of 1953 and brought in ministers who could speak for the more militant groups in the society. One of these appointees was his neighbor, his friend, and a Labor party luminary, João "Jango" Goulart.

From the army's point of view (as, indeed, from that of much of the economic middle class), the new labor minister did nothing but aggravate an already delicate problem. He proposed large wage increases for labor unions and opposed a "get tough" policy with strikers. Moreover, Goulart made no secret of his admiration for Argentina's Juán Perón who, at the moment, was busily engaged in pitting his country's labor masses against the entire remainder of the society—including the military. Early in 1954 the consequences surfaced. Eighty-two officers (colonels and lieutenant colonels) of the Brazilian Army, many of them graduates of the prestigious National War College, signed an anti-Goulart memorandum in which they attacked the labor minister on several points. In particular, they excoriated him for his handling of a 1953 national maritime strike. They felt Goulart had played right into the hands of Communist agitators. But, in addition, the officers resented what they felt were undemocratic and anti-constitutional tendencies in the social and economic changes he fostered. They also complained that their own salaries, vis-à-vis the pay of the PTB blue-collar workers who had been making strident gains, were too low. Moreover, as they feared that Goulart was falling under the influence of Perón, they suspected that he might be persuaded to push for an anti-United States coalition with that dictator.

Vargas had experienced military wrath in 1945. It had cost him the presidency. This time he quickly accepted Goulart's resignation and fired his war minister who, he said, had not kept him informed of the military officers' discontentment.

Vargas' sacrifice of Goulart appeased the military. But it also angered many of his Labor party followers who had come to believe that their minister was really one of the few men on whom they could depend. The president was prepared to ride out this storm. A subsequent one, however, he could not.

The episode that drove Vargas from the presidency and, indeed, brought about his death, centered around an assassination attempt on Carlos Lacerda, an invective newspaper publisher who had taken considerable dislike to *trabalhismo* in any form and had not failed to let his readers know about it. On one occasion when he attacked Vargas in print more viciously than usual, several of Vargas' closest associates, viewing their president's deteriorating position with considerable anguish, considered that if only Lacerda could be "removed" the situation might yet be salvaged. They suggested to the chief of the palace guard, Gregório Fortunato, a semi-illiterate who had served Vargas faithfully for more than 30 years, that he should "take care of Lacerda." While Vargas remained ignorant of the plot, his chief guard arranged for Lacerda's assassination. The problem was that Lacerda was only wounded. But his companion, an air force major, was killed.

Although the president had nothing to do with the assassination attempt, a storm of anti-Vargas indignation swept the country. The bluster was shrilly inflamed by the wounded Lacerda and sorely exacerbated by angry officers in the military. Aside from Lacerda's invectives and accusations, both the air force and navy drafted resolutions calling for their president's immediate resignation. Then the army came out with a manifesto suggesting that a presidential leave of absence would be the best solution. All this was too much for Vargas. On August 24, 1954, after writing an emotional note absolving himself of guilt and blaming all the country's problems on Brazil's entrenched traditional establishment, the president committed suicide.

All Brazil was horrified. As dramatically as sympathy had left Vargas in life, in death it returned. Most Brazilians seemed to absolve him of all guilt. Afterward it was the military and Lacerda's followers among the economic middle class who became concerned. The *trabalhista* movement targeted all its epithets in their direction. While Getúlio Vargas may have begun his presidential career as a traditional politician and later evolved into a quasi-fascist, there was little doubt that he ended it as a populist. Equally interesting, a great many people began to think of Jango Goulart, the deposed cabinet minister, as the dead president's political heir.

Stunned by their president's suicide, many Brazilians had dramatically shifted their political sympathies. But this certainly did not deprive the military, or Lacerda, or even their urban middle-class sympathizers, of political gains. Thus after Vargas' vice-president was quietly sworn in as Brazil's new leader, politics once again settled into something of a normal pattern. In the ensuing congressional elections, military conservatives as well as Lacerda's political following (mainly members of the UDN political party—União Democrática Nacional) no doubt were pleased to learn that ex-minister Goulart had been decisively defeated in his bid for a senate seat. As a candidate of Vargas' PTB party, Goulart's failure was all the more striking because it occurred in his home state of Rio Grande do Sul after a campaign based directly on the memory of his recently martyred mentor.

It was not that Goulart lacked continuing appeal among blue-collar workers in urban Brazil. His failure to gain a senate seat from Rio Grande do Sul was due partly to political infighting over the successorship to Getúlio's mantle. Yet Goulart's continuing popular appeal and the PTB's substantial strength in the cities was amply shown in the elections of 1955. In these Goulart emerged a victor, this time as the country's vice-president (running with Juscelino Kubitschek) on a coalition ticket—a marriage of convenience in the interest of winning elections—of Vargas' old PTB party, which was still strong in the cities, and the PSD party (Partido Social Democrático), a "machine type" organization commanding considerable strength in the traditional countryside.

As a former governor of Minas Gerais, Kubitschek held considerable influence among the traditional rural elite. Although these elite had been politically weakened in recent years because of the increasing importance of the cities, some of them nevertheless were still able to deliver large chunks of votes on a fairly predictable schedule. The Goulart-Kubitschek strategy, therefore, was to combine that strength with the PTB urban working masses and thereby achieve an overall voting majority. It was a marriage of political convenience over ideological purity. And it won elections.

One sector of the military was fairly unsettled over this turn of events—particularly with Goulart's victory. And Lacerda was furious. But what could they do? Very little, at least for the moment. Their problem seemed to be that the more moderate military officers had declared hands off political meddling. The people had spoken. And so the "Kubitschek era" (1955 to 1960) was allowed to unfold.

The new regime greatly accelerated the pace of modernization, heavily investing in the cities and directly and indirectly subsidizing Brazil's incessant march toward an industrialized economy. Moreover, the president conceived of and erected Brasília, the spectacular all-new national capital in the country's heartland. Kubitschek hoped that this one achievement would direct Brazilian energies toward developing the hinterland and toward a consideration of the greatness which Brazil had both a power and a right to become.

Yet Kubitschek's development model was doomed to eventual exhaustion. By 1960 the deficiency was clearly evident. The president had failed to carry out any economic or social reforms in the countryside. Little wonder. His own base of support lay with people who would suffer most if the agricultural sector were to be substantially modernized. Kubitschek, therefore, had made the political decision to leave rural Brazil alone and to concentrate nearly all his modernizing efforts in the cities. With population increasing and agriculture stagnating, however, the country's industrial complex began to suffer serious economic binds. Moreover, these and other problems contributed to a chastening rate of inflation. Lacerda was at the printing presses once again with cries of corruption (apparently considerable), malfeasance, and presidential incompetence. His readers grew in number, his admirers in faith.

In the presidential campaign of 1960 it seemed that nearly everyone was crying for reform. But it was also apparent that what some groups had in mind when they spoke of reform certainly would not be accepted by others without a struggle. The upshot was that Jânio Quadros, a quixotic "nonparty" man relatively unknown outside his home state of São Paulo where he had served as governor, won the presidency.

Quadros' equivocal campaign rhetoric had led all the major groups to believe that he was *their* man. As it turned out he had fooled everyone so well that even Lacerda, after some early hesitation, had eventually begged Quadros to accept his support and allow the UDN party to sponsor his candidacy. The military was well pleased also, for Quadros was not associated with Vargas' old political camp or the PTB party. Yet the new president eventually pulled away from groups that thought they owned him and energetically pushed the kinds of reforms they considered anathema. A political crisis of the first magnitude was in the making. It was also one that launched Goulart into the presidency. How did it all happen?

Actually Brazil's electoral laws of 1960 allowed voters to split tickets between presidential and vice-presidential candidates. While the enigmatic Quadros polled a substantial victory, his vice-presidential running mate, Milton Campos, did not. It was the old PTB-PSD electoral alliance (the one that had successfully placed Kubitschek in power six years earlier) which captured the runner-up spot, edging Campos out by a slight margin. Any guesses? None other than Jango Goulart!

Lacerda's "outs" had won the presidency, but the old PTB-PSD "ins" had retained the vice-presidency. Quadros was the only candidate in Brazilian history to win a plurality in every state. Yet Goulart's personal popularity was such that even this landslide could not inundate him. The electoral strength of Brazil's newly mobilized working masses was apparent. Indeed, the growth in voter turnout between 1945 and 1960 suggested as much. In the presidential elections of 1945 there had been only 5.9 million voters. In 1950, however, the number had increased to 7.9 million, and in 1955 to 8.6 million. By 1960, barely 17 years after Vargas had sensed the wave of the political future and had shifted the social base of his power to the lower half of Brazil's social pyramid, the country had an election turnout of 11.6 million. In no way could population increase alone account for such a dramatic growth.

The quixotic Quadros was not long in proving that he was no one's man. Dismay and reaction quickly mounted, much of it coming from his earlier erstwhile supporters: The urban middle classes defected because the president's economic stabilization policies, which he had designed to clear up the financial problems bequeathed by Kubitschek, were hurting their consumption habits as well as their pride. After all, Jânio had run for the presidency on *their* UDN ticket; now he paid them no attention. Then the traditional politicians and government bureaucrats were visibly upset because Quadros' anti-corruption drives and efficiency campaigns threatened their jobs and security. And for other groups the frustration was much the same. Businessmen feared that the stabilization program would produce economic stagnation. Labor leaders and the urban lower class were incensed because the continuing inflation seriously hurt their purchasing power. The military was alarmed because Quadros was redirecting Brazil's foreign policy—renewing, for example, trade and diplomatic relations with the Communist bloc and insisting on nonintervention in Cuba at a time when it was popular to plan paramilitary invasions. The president also supported the seating of Red China in the United Nations. Indeed, Quadros' trend to the left in foreign affairs was dramatized by his presenting to "Che" Guevara the "Cruzeiro do Sul," Brazil's highest award. Those who had voted Quadros into office were horrified. Carlos Lacerda, destroyer of presidents and now governor of Guanabara (greater Rio de Janeiro) led the attack.

This certainly is not a complete catalog of Quadros' problems, for in addition he faced a dwindling export market for coffee and serious difficulties in servicing his extensive foreign debt. Some argue that he also had some psychological disorders. Whatever may be the case, in August of 1961, barely seven months from taking office, he suddenly resigned and fled the country, charging that "sinister foreign influences" had prevented him from effectively serving as president. Although wags identified those "influences" as having been bottled in Scotland, humor could not deny the gravity of the situation. When Jânio Quadros resigned, his constitutional successor—João Goulart, vice-president and head of the Brazilian Labor party (PTB)—was on a goodwill tour of Red China! The anti-Communist military certainly did not fail to notice this.

JOÃO GOULART BECOMES PRESIDENT

If the officers had not been divided in their attitude toward Goulart, no doubt they would have denied him the presidency on the spot. The military ministers in Brasília desperately wanted to prevent the vice-president from taking the higher office. Indeed, they even attempted to obtain a veto. But they were not prepared to call for an internal military, or perhaps even civil war, to make their point. The rub was that the Third Army in Rio Grande do Sul, Goulart's home state, was prepared to fight anyone "on behalf of the constitution" to give the China-touring vice-president his just presidential dues. It was clear that the potential objects of threat included the military ministers and their respective commands. The fact that Goulart's brother-in-law, Leonel Brizola, also a populist politician with national ambitions, was governor of the state where the Third Army was headquartered lent credence to the seriousness of the confrontation.[6] If the crisis had not fallen on everyone so precipitously perhaps the military could have settled its differences and eventually reached an anti-Goulart accord. But the time required to hammer out such a consensus simply did not exist. Any action, whatever it turned out to be, had to be taken at once. Meanwhile, the civilian congress in Brasília, feeling a few heady oats, rejected the military ministers' veto demand.

The conservative officers, blocked by widespread dissension within the officer corps, a threatened pro-Goulart mutiny in the Third Army in Rio Grande do Sul, the congress' acceptance of Goulart as the new constitutional president, and prevailing civilian support for the legality of the succession capitulated— but not completely. They would not call the opposition's hand with military force if, and only if, pro-Goulart supporters would accept a compromise that would allow everyone to save face. Their proposition: a constitutional amendment that would make a figurehead and largely ceremonial role out of the presidency. The amendment would remove the executive power from the president and invest it in a newly created office of prime minister. Thus everyone could have their own thing. Brizola and the Third Army in Rio Grande do Sul would have their man in the presidency. And although the military would have to accept that, its rebuttal would be to leave the president little power except that of cabinet appointments. Goulart could nominate for the ministerial cabinet, but aside from that he would have to keep "hands off" the administrative fabric of the government.

It is true that both Goulart's supporters and the military ministers were cool to certain aspects of the proposal when it was first advanced. But it did seem to offer a way out of an otherwise very serious impasse. Thus to avoid what appeared to be imminent bloodshed, Brazil's politicians and its military officers created for themselves a figurehead presidency and a parliamentary regime. The compromise was eventful in its own right, but it also set the stage for near political and administrative chaos in Brazil's federal government.

It was a curious array of forces that made possible Goulart's becoming president. The conservatives, including Lacerda's UDN middle-class supporters and the right wing of the military, had always been against the vice-president. But they did permit him to take office. His major supporters, on the other hand, came from four separate groups: a growing nationalist and developmentalist wing in the military, a substantial number of "economic middle classers" (who were suffering as a result of the country's serious economic situation and could not agree with the conservatives or Lacerda on solutions), a majority of the elected congressional deputies, and a great many urban blue-collar civilians.

Yet it also seemed apparent that a majority of *non*-blue-collar civilians were much more "pro-constitution" than they were pro- or anti-Goulart. Their support, such as it was, was offered only conditionally and would last only insofar as Goulart maintained "good behavior." There was no disguising the fact that although a great many people, especially those in the urban economic middle class, certainly wanted the economic problems of the country resolved, they also genuinely feared that Goulart might attempt a dictatorial left-wing solution. Following the example of Juán Perón in Argentina, he might thrust the working masses into a favored position at the expense of the economic middle groups and the army. Thus, while these groups to some extent were willing to support the legality of the amended constitutional succession, their qualified support would last only as long as Jango served a truly "constructive presidency." But would Goulart behave himself?

It was a very cautious man who became the new president of parliamentary Brazil. Goulart certainly was not unaware of his political problems. Indeed, it was only by a very circuitous route that he had even dared return to Brazil from the People's Republic of China, refusing to face up to the last hop from Paris to Rio until after the parliamentary compromise had been reached. On returning to his homeland, Goulart wanted to be sure that he was entering the presidency—not a jail.

For the first six months of his regime (September 1961 to February 1962) Goulart played the figurehead role with consummate good taste. He included in his first cabinet a balanced representation of the major parties. Indeed, he gave his implacable foes in the UDN party an equivalent number of seats (two) to those that he granted his own PTB party. Moreover, he extended the very important portfolio of war minister to João de Segadas Vianna, a well-respected general who had acted as intermediary between the anti-Goulart military ministers and the "pro-constitutional" army officers.

In the succeeding eight months, however, Goulart carefully embarked on a strategy to regain full presidential powers. The new president disarmed the skeptical by consistently stressing his anti-Communist principles and unaltered devotion to the democratic process. He attempted to prove as much by visiting the United States, declaring his opposition to Castro's Cuba, and showing his enormous respect for the armed forces as the guardian of the nation. Yet propitious events played into Goulart's hands; he was not long in taking advantage of them.

One of these events, or perhaps we had better term it "realizations," was the horrible ineffectiveness of the parliamentary arrangements in meeting Brazil's social and economic problems. Economic conditions had deteriorated rapidly. To be sure, this may not have been the fault of the parliamentary system per se. But the inability of that system to rise to the challenge and effectuate solutions discredited it in the popular eye. Related to this was the enormous rate of inflation. Although inflation hurt nearly everyone, it seemed to fall most heavily on the urban working classes, provoking labor strikes which the regime was unprepared or unwilling to handle. The resulting food shortages were instrumental in inciting riots with attendant looting and some fatalities.

All these problems brought popular attention to bear not only on the new parliamentary experiment but also on the popularity of Goulart. A general clamor arose: "Do something, Goulart!"

If Goulart could produce solutions he might be a hero. If he could not there was little doubt that he would be finished politically. How should he move? The parliamentary system allowed him no power. Could he get that system changed? And if so, how? How strong were the various social forces allied for and against him? To what extent did his populist brother-in-law, Brizola, epitomize the new wave of Brazilian politics? If Brizola's was indeed the new wave, could it somehow be galvanized into a weapon capable of containing the conservative officers in the military?

THE LEFTWARD DRIFT

We do not know how Goulart analyzed the implications of these questions. But as the domestic situation under the parliamentary regime continued to deteriorate, the president did decide to cultivate the political left more forcefully. Indeed, some have suggested that he embarked on a purposeful plan to discredit the parliamentary system by sabotaging whatever workability it might have had. Would this strengthen Goulart's hand for a return to full presidential powers?

Regardless of the merits, the strategy had one grave weakness: the political left was very divided.

"As if to recognize this fact," Thomas Skidmore notes, "Brazilians often referred to 'the lefts' . . ., which included two principal groups. One was the moderate left (or 'positive left'), represented by San Tiago Dantas, a PTB politician-lawyer from Minas . . ., and by the young technocrats such as Celso Furtado, who shunned party labels but were important nonetheless. This group was respected by the center for the seriousness of its intentions. The radical left (or 'negative left'), on the other hand, represented by Leonel Brizola was more violent in its language and appeared ready to go beyond constitutional processes."[7]

As Goulart reentered the world of partisan politics his language was ambiguous, sometimes approximating the rhetoric of the positive left, yet at other times mirroring the negative left. Regardless of the rhetoric, however, what became apparent to many *conservatives* was that their president was losing his "good behavior." He had begun to talk of the kinds of economic and agricultural reforms that would occasion a redistribution of income, status, and privilege among Brazil's social and economic groups. Thus there was considerable concern in some circles about what the president's ultimate motives might be. To Goulart, however, it was all very clear. He wanted to be a real president of Brazil, a populist president, perhaps even one with charismatic qualities.

"Jango's" purposeful inefficiency under the parliamentary system, his shrewd manipulation of military promotions and transfers, the deteriorating domestic scene with its labor strikes, and the widespread impression that the parliamentary arrangement was largely responsible for the continuing crisis all provided the necessary background for a national plebiscite on the future of the system. In the midst of crisis Goulart was able to push through a plan that would allow Brazilians to decide whether they should continue with the parliamentary arrangement or return to a more powerful presidential system in which he, as their president, could more effectively deal with the problems confronting the nation. This proved to be very appealing to strife-torn Brazil. On January 6, 1963, Goulart's countrymen voted by a margin of five to one to return him to full presidential powers. The military, also alarmed at Brazil's deteriorating political and economic situation, made no threat of a veto, for the officers themselves were cowed with the chaos and uncertain about what to do.

Would a "powerful presidential system" produce the promised land? Hardly. The expectations of many Brazilians therefore, were soon to be frustrated. In 1963 the country's per capita GNP declined for the first time in years. Currency in circulation increased from 509 to 809 billion cruzeiros, and this fueled an already high annual rate of inflation up to an estimated 80 percent. A comparison with the short time Quadros was in the presidency is striking, since the cost of living in 1963 had reached 340 percent of its 1961 average and the federal payroll had grown fivefold. Foreign investors, wary of Goulart's leftist rhetoric and incensed over the efforts of his brother-in-law to nationalize the American Telephone and Telegraph Company in Rio Grande do Sul, began to reduce their investments. Moreover, the United States, critical of the regime for its shifting policies and implied anti-American stance, sharply cut assistance. Then to top it all off, "official" corruption, already high even by Brazilian standards, reached a level unprecedented in the country's history.

Later in the year, fresh from his success in the plebiscite and not willing to risk the unpopularity of an austerity-stabilization program to reduce inflation, yet convinced that something had to be done with the rising cost of living, Goulart sought renewed favor with the masses by bringing up the "basic reforms" questions again. If he could just implement these, he thought, his blue-collar supporters and intellectual sympathizers would not have to suffer the brunt of any stabilization efforts. The costs, as well as the benefits of stabilization would be more evenly shared by all Brazilian groups.

Goulart's strategy can be divided into two phases: one is when he was allied with the "positive left" and heavily influenced by Dantas and Furtado; the other is when he shifted over to his brother-in-law's camp (Brizola) and made a politically suicidal marriage with the "negative left." Thus, while the political left was divided into moderate and radical factions, Goulart preferred either one or both to the alternative—a support base that relied on a continuation of the social status quo. In Goulart's mind the political right (the conservative military, rural landlords, large segments of the middle class, and urban industrialists and their friends) espoused policies and values inimical to Brazil's long-range development. The country was at a crossroads, he thought. It was up to him to choose the right route before the onslaught of modernization caused utter social and political chaos.

Goulart at first thought the positive left, that is, the moderate social reformers, held the key. They wanted to stabilize the country's economy, but they also wanted to remove the structural blocks that were causing much of the problem. The young technocrats, particularly Celso Furtado, had already drafted a development plan. Moreover, San Tiago Dantas had some reasonable ideas on economic stabilization. Most important, none of these approaches appeared to include the political after problems inherent in most hard-nosed economic austerity programs. With a political vote of confidence, Goulart selected Dantas as his finance minister and Furtado as his planning minister.

The Dantas-Furtado approach to the solution of Brazil's economic problems was conceived in both long- and short-range objectives. These were to be accomplished with fairly heavy governmental intervention in the economy and, implicitly, in the reorganization of traditional social relations among the various strata of Brazilian society. Nevertheless, democratic processes and procedures were to be zealously guarded. The approach, although creating a furor among the traditional elite as well as the radical left (one group was up in arms because the proposed reforms were too many and the other because they were too few), nevertheless earned the respect of Brazil's moderates. Many of them were convinced that the plan was really the only viable solution open either to Goulart or to the Brazilian people.

The short-term objectives of the new economic formula were a creation of Dantas himself. He would achieve a reversal in inflationary trends and would gradually reduce the rate to manageable proportions, but without applying the kinds of austerity measures that had proved to be so politically unpopular in the past. The strategy included negotiations with Brazil's creditors for more favorable terms on a portion of the country's foreign debt, a request for more development aid from industrial countries in North America and Europe and, to show good faith, a squeeze on the federal budget at all possible points (especially the "unproductive" ones, which would include the discharging of excess federal employees and the canceling of programs not in the interest of national development). This latter item would please the IMF (International Monetary Fund), which then would be willing to negotiate some standby credits to launch the whole affair. For additional external help, as well as negotiations on debt service, Dantas intended to visit the United States, Europe, and even Russia. In fact, in those days Brazilians were speaking of "three separate great deals" which would help them buy enough short-term economic stability to be able to implement needed reforms in agriculture and basic infrastructure. The result, it was thought, would be long-range prosperity and stable growth.

Certainly, neither Dantas nor Furtado had any illusions that their programs could be implemented without some sacrifice to all Brazilians. For one thing, they knew that they would have to increase taxes. They would also have to close the many loopholes that socially and politically important Brazilians had been using for a long time. And they also realized that the results of their reforms vis-à-vis the lower classes would certainly not be felt overnight.

The long-range objectives were integrated into an impressive three-year plan, directed at the "structural bottlenecks" in Brazil's economy and society, which Furtado had been working on for several years. For some time a growing number of economists, following the early lead of the Argentinian Raúl Prebisch and his United Nations Economic Commission for Latin America, had pointed out the structural causes of Latin America's continual economic crises. Because much of the bottleneck in Brazil lay with a stagnant agricultural sector, one of the plan's most important sections dealt with agrarian reform. The contemplated reform was not to be carried out merely for its social and political consequences—although they certainly were important to Goulart—but primarily for the economic ones.

Aimed at enhancing the productivity of the agricultural worker and peasant, the reforms would create a whole new consumer class for the Brazilian economy. Industry would benefit as would all Brazil—more jobs and more growth. Accordingly, not only did the government plan to expropriate certain agricultural lands but it also planned to pass laws requiring state and private agencies or individuals to pay peasants a wage for labor on lands not subject to expropriation. (Many lords had long engaged in a form of "indentured servitude" that the laws effectively intended to abolish.) Moreover, the peasants who were to be granted lands under the program would receive credits and technical aid so that they could invest, produce, and later consume.

Aside from agrarian reform there was another bombshell in Furtado's plan. He had called for nationalization of all basic communications and energy-production facilities. Many of these were owned by United States corporations. In particular, the American and Foreign Power Company was singled out to be the first casualty.

Furtado's plan was impressive in its logic, well executed in detail, and probably could have accomplished, or at least could have facilitated, a move toward accomplishing the government's development objectives. But the reforms it called for would also have selectively destroyed or weakened the economic and social interests of several of Brazil's traditionally important groups—landlords in particular and, in general, the portion of the economic middle class that received benefits from foreign investors. Congress, heavily influenced by these interests, refused to pass favorably on the reform plan.

The exact nature of the denial was curious and somewhat more complex than that which can be explained by simple "reactionary conservatism," however. It came about as a kind of sabotage operation as much from the extreme left as from the radical right. The planned nationalization of the American and Foreign Power Company, for example, was attacked by both political extremes, each hoping, but for different reasons, that Goulart's experiment with the positive left would fail. Brizola led the attack from one end, charging that Dantas and Furtado were engaging in a "sellout," paying hard-earned Brazilian treasure to a foreign company that had for assets nothing more than a "pile of junk." Brizola's anti-Dantas invective was highly inflammatory. Then from the radical right came the indomitable and ever-present Carlos Lacerda. Already alerted to possible mileage that could be gained from these events, he led an impressive "pincers movement" on Goulart and his ministers. While Brizola wanted the American and Foreign Power Company expropriated without compensation, Lacerda shrilly condemned any expropriation at all.

If the furor over the proposed nationalization of the power company were not enough to seriously hurt the Dantas-Furtado plan, the agrarian-reform bill that Goulart had submitted to congress in March of 1963 (offering compensation in government bonds rather than in cash) provided whatever else was needed. Ultraconservatives from both Lacerda's UDN and Kubitschek's old PSD immediately attacked. Then in May a committee in the Chamber of Deputies voted by a margin of seven to four to reject the reform bill. Brizola, a congressional deputy from Rio Grande do Sul and also a member of the committee, responded to the defeat (he was very much in favor of *this* reform bill) by demanding that the army take up arms and rise to the need of social reform. The real rub for the government was that on a credit-touring visit to Washington, Dantas had already promised the Americans—as a condition of their aid—that Brazil could and would put through an agrarian-reform act.

Goulart, the political man he was, tended to view this struggle between the left and the right in purely political terms rather than on economic merits. Although he was concerned about the rabble-rousing from the radical right, it did not unnerve him nearly as much as did the continuous volleys from the extreme left. After all, it was his brother-in-law, Brizola, who was the leading supplier of left-wing invectives. Besides, Goulart's own political sympathies lay very much in a left-wing direction. Thus, as Skidmore has observed,

"Goulart seemed to become associated with Brizola's extreme views on stabilization (larger wage settlements), foreign capital (confiscation with minimal, if any, compensation), and reform (radical change with or without the Congress). During the April-May political crisis Brizola took center stage. He was everywhere, attacking the 'entreguistas' around the President, the 'reactionaries' in the Congress, the 'gorillas' in the Army, and the 'imperialists' in the American Embassy and the IMF [International Monetary Fund]."[8]

Although both Dantas and Furtado made impressive and sometimes valiant efforts to counter the Brizola-Lacerda volleys, it seemed that their president chose to do nothing. Goulart, it was said, had begun to lose his political nerve. In time he became much more interested in politicking than in defending his ministers' reform programs. The president was suddenly acting as if the *real* issue before the country was radical social reform, not the control of inflation and the gradual removal of structural blocks on the economy.

With a "so-what-does-it-matter" wave of his hand, Goulart scuttled Furtado's three-year plan as well as the short-term stabilization efforts proposed by Dantas. After this he dumped both ministers from his government and moved very quickly toward Brizola's open arms. And it was not long before Brazil's president began to argue that because of reactionaries in the country he could not promote needed reforms by peaceful and legal means. The combination of a predominantly conservative military, its middle-class supporters, and the external pressures from the United States made these changes impossible, he argued. A "popular revolution" was the only key. Accordingly, he increased his output of emotive slogans, presumably thinking that this would occasion "spontaneous" organization among the peasants and other lower-class peoples with whom he identified. And, of course, he continued to enjoy the militant support of the members of his PTB party. For them he was something of a charismatic leader. But had he read Brazil correctly?[9]

It was not surprising that Brazil's political moderates, her extreme rightists, and especially the conservatives in the military should have become fearful of Goulart's leadership. Their anxieties proved to be well founded. As cries of alarm from the right grew increasingly shrill in the wake of a continued presidential drift to the left, Goulart responded with a frontal attack. Beginning by closing down the Brazilian Institute of Democratic Action, a prominent right-wing group, he followed up with some hair-raising jabs at Lacerda and his most prominent associates. Goulart also implemented coercive measures against other civilian groups who opposed his plans for Brazil.

The more coercion he applied, however, the more Goulart alienated moderate Brazilians from his cause. Convinced as he was that the political wave of the future lay with the left, particularly the radical left, the president seemed little concerned about his relationship with the moderates. With utter abandonment he politically "wrote off" an important sector of Brazilian society. But as a result of his dramatic shifts, and particularly his closing down and outlawing of civilian anti-left groups, the burden of any political opposition by necessity fell on the military. It was among the officers that the conspiracy for Goulart's removal finally hatched.

THE MILITARY CONSPIRACIES

There was no *one* military conspiracy against Goulart but rather several, which in the initial phases transpired quite independently of one another. Some began early in Goulart's presidential career, others later. Jarbas Passarinho (then a colonel in the Amazon area and later, in successive order, governor, senator, minister of labor and, in 1970, minister of education) speaks of the conditions that augured for a conspiracy among his colleagues:

"Professional politicians and labor leaders linked up with the communists and initiated a truculent aggression against military commanders in the Amazon. . . . The agitation gained force in the labor movement, especially in the Petrobras Union [of government oil workers]. Strikes were encouraged, even by directors of the companies involved. The state of Pará had a Secretariat of Lands, linked to the Communist party, which sold the best vacant lands to great landowners from other regions. They fostered smuggling and extravagance."[10]

Alarmed at such militancy, particularly because much of it was directed against the military, the generals in the Amazon drew up plans for a preventive coup. Moreover, Colonel Passarinho himself began to organize groups of school children for counter-propaganda campaigns. Soon afterward anti-Communist articles began to appear in the northern newspapers. By association, of course, this also meant anti-Goulart propaganda, because by then the president had begun to drift over to his negative left stance, which included, as street-corner partners, Brizola and the Communist party.

General Morão, who reported an earlier conspiracy in Rio Grande do Sul, attended a meeting on January 8, 1962 which had been arranged by General Penha Brasil. Also in attendance was Dr. Saint-Pastoux, the leader of FARSUL, an agricultural producers' organization in the South. Says General Morão: "Until then I was asleep, but I awoke on seeing the exact extent of the reform that Brizola wanted to introduce."[11]

By 1963 another military group in Natal on the northeast coast had entered the anti-Goulart swing. Here the final spark had been Deputy Leonel Brizola's gratuitous insult upon General Antonio Carlos da Murici. Brizola had gone too far with his invective this time. Thirty-three generals, including Artur de Costa e Silva (later to become the second military president of Brazil after the 1964 coup), telegraphed their support to General Murici and expressed their particular dislike for Brizola. At the time Costa e Silva was reported to have said to his executive officer: "Resistance is now created in the armed forces. Our group is strong in the General Staff, but weak in the regional commands. We must be strong there too . . ."[12]

In Recife, center of the Fourth Army, General Castello Branco (the "swing man" who would become the first president of the "revolutionary" military government) turned his command over to General Justino Alves Bastos, the only commander from the four principal army regions who was to become a real conspirator. General Castello Branco was leaving the Fourth Army to become chief of the Army General Staff. Before departing, however, he created a new military office in Recife—"superior of the day"—to coordinate "defensive revolutionary plans" within the Fourth Army. The officers in Recife, at least those who were loyal to Castello Branco, were not yet prepared to initiate action against their presidential commander-in-chief. But they were certainly willing to resist such possible inroads on constitutional processes as Goulart's rumored intention to close congress. But Alves Bastos, the new commander of the Fourth Army, soon spurred on the conspiratorial efforts by enlisting civilian groups in Recife for the anti-Goulart cause, and by preparing them not only to initiate counter propaganda but also to undertake direct anti-government action if that should prove necessary. Yet Goulart never knew anything was brewing at all.[13]

So began the month of March, 1964. Still there was no central directorate for these and other conspiratorial groups. But the number of dissident officers certainly was growing. In all probability they would eventually attempt to link up. What was needed to finalize such an arrangement was some kind of catalyst. In due course it developed. Friday, March 13th, became bad-luck day for Jango.

JANGO FALLS

Faced with the growing clamor from the radical left, and misinformed about the extent of his support in the military, Goulart decided to preside over a series of mass rallies in the cities to mobilize support for his "basic reforms." Before mid-March 1964, his purpose was clear. This time he would strike at the very heart of a great many middle- and upper-class prerogatives. His basic reforms included rent controls, voting rights for illiterates and enlisted service men, tax reforms, the nationalization of foreign property, and a comprehensive program of land reform.

The first of the rallies to publicize his radical program was held on the night of Friday, March 13, in one of Rio's main plazas, Praça da Republica. The masses, approximately 150,000 persons, enthusiastically responded; it was indeed a sensational show. The president of the republic, his ministers (including those of the armed forces), his brother-in-law, Leonel Brizola, and the directors of several Communist-controlled labor unions were the most visible dignitaries. The government, disregarding the discomfort caused by a wholesale paralysis of the transportation system of a vast area, pressed buses and trains into service to bring workers' delegates to the plaza. Some had come long distances: textile workers from Juiz de Fora, steelworkers from Volta Redonda, oil workers from Duque de Caxias, and others from the industrial suburbs of Rio, all were gathered by their respective unions with assistance from Goulart's ministry of labor. Banners and signs were everywhere, all, in one or another fashion, demanding that the government carry out popular and nationalistic reforms. As might be expected, the demands corresponded closely to much of Goulart's rhetoric.

Seldom before had anyone seen such spectacular incitement to action. With consummate skill Goulart and his radical-left advisers had fabricated an event that they thought would galvanize the nation and create, with the support of the masses, the necessary climate for the reforms that they believed could only be carried out by popular and forceful demand. That night decrees were read and statements made that were nothing short of verbal fire bombs; they included immediate agricultural reform without cash compensation to expropriated owners, the amplification of the Petrobrás oil monopoly by expropriating specific private refineries, the nationalization of American Telephone and Telegraph (as well as the American and Foreign Power Company), and the imminent legalization of the heretofore proscribed Communist party.

Sitting in front of their television sets and noticing the presence of three military ministers on the stand (whom, as cabinet ministers, Goulart had ordered to attend), many Brazilians might have had the impression that the army, navy, and air force were all in complete support of the events transpiring before their eyes. Goulart had hoped for such a reaction when he ordered all other normal television programming preempted for the rally. But other officers in the three armed forces, viewing the same spectacle, reacted in a totally different and not too unexpected way. From their perspective the television programming only convinced them that if Jango Goulart were not stopped, he would lead the nation into a state of anarchy. Supported by workers' organizations and "left wingers" in the military, they feared that he could fashion a coup and put himself at the head of a Castrolike dictatorship. Observers close to the military reported that the telephones of numerous top officers had probably never rung as frequently as they did that Friday night following the rally. It would have been about 11:30 P.M. when the reportedly nervous and irritated dialogues among the officers began. The general tone seemed to go something like this:

"Did you see the demonstration? Did you pay attention to the speeches?"

"I did. He only needs one more chance against us. We must talk, before it's too late."

"That's how I feel—say when and where. . . ."

The meetings began very soon indeed, heavily attended by officers who feared that Goulart was beginning his own revolution and would lead the nation into a civil war. These officers considered it necessary to act before the country drifted further to the left, either domestically or in its foreign policy. Ten of the top-ranking commanders met and mutually covenanted to accompany a prestigious military officer, as soon as a willing one could be found, in an immediate preemptive action that would detour Goulart's hand.[14]

Meanwhile, despite the president's tight control over radical right-wing civilians, increasing numbers of moderates became more visibly alienated from his regime. Governor Magalhães Pinto of Minas Gerais vehemently criticized the government's agrarian reform plan. Governor Adhemar de Barros of São Paulo, Brazil's most economically important state, ordered his police to prevent federal officials from speaking at a student demonstration. Local authorities prevented Miguel Arrais and Leonel Brizola from appearing at a rally in Belo Horizonte. Moreover, in Rio de Janeiro, Carlos Lacerda, who had been mounting a verbal siege for years, increased his vitriolic attacks against Goulart. In mid-March, ex-president Dutra broke his habitual silence and declared that he could not support Goulart's government. Two days later, in São Paulo, 500,000 middle-class women and men united in a "March of the Family with God for Freedom"—an anti-Goulart demonstration, organized by the Feminine Civic Union, that had the blessing of the state's civil and military authorities.

These events helped the military conspirators find their "swing man," who turned out to be none other than Marechal Humberto de Alencar Castello Branco, chief of the Army General Staff and ex-commander of the Fourth Army in Recife. Castello Branco would become the new president of Brazil. But in the meantime he circulated to his conspiring colleagues, who had enlisted his prestigious services, his famous "lealdade ao Exercito" (Loyalty to the Army) document. Castello Branco's brief, articulate, and convincing statement soon became known to wavering moderate officers. It won many of these moderates over to the conspiratorial cause by its apparent clear-cut justification for forcefully opposing Goulart's rumored plan to use the government-controlled labor unions as a political base for overturning the constitutional structure of the country. Castello Branco also attacked the president's plan for a constitutional assembly, terming such an act merely a prelude to dictatorship. He also spoke of the historic role of the army in overseeing the Brazilian political process and in guarding the constitution. He then lashed out at those who would "reform" the organization of the army, charging them with wanting to make it into a "people's army" after the fashion of some Communist countries.[15]

Goulart had been warned. Incredibly, however, he paid no constructive attention. Within a week he had mounted a frontal attack on military discipline. This episode occurred as a result of the navy's arrest order of 40 sailors, including José Anselmo, an ex-university student who had joined the navy to help increase the mobilization of "popular forces" among the members of that service branch. These "radicals" had been actively organizing a "labor union" among enlisted men, many of whom had responded to the efforts with considerable enthusiasm. As soon as the arrest order was made public, more than 1000 fellow sailors mutinied, taking refuge in the headquarters of the sympathetic Metalurgical Worker's Union in Rio de Janeiro. When the president denied his naval minister's request to punish the mutineers, that admiral promptly resigned. And how did Goulart go about selecting a replacement? By consulting a list of "acceptable" officers that had been prepared by the General Confederation of Workers (CGT), a militant pro-Goulart labor congress. In effect, the president had given radical unions a veto right over appointment to one of the three highest military posts in the nation.[16]

The new naval minister appointed by Goulart promptly ordered all charges against the mutineers dropped. The sailors, in turn, celebrated that decision with a noisy parade through the center of Rio. Declared Brazil's president: "No one desires more than I the strengthening and cohesion of our armed forces. No one desires more than I the glory of our navy . . . but discipline is not founded on hate and inequities. Discipline is founded on mutual respect between those who command and those who are commanded."[17]

Much of Brazil's military establishment was not at all convinced by this kind of rhetoric. General Bastos blasted the press coverage of the parade and the demonstrations: "The repugnant photographs appearing in the Rio newspapers and magazines filled officers and sergeants in all parts of the nation with righteous indignation."[18] In retrospect, the general went on to express the opinion that this episode was the true trigger of the coup.

Other Brazilians, particularly opposition politicians in the federal government, were no less alarmed. Minority leader Pedro Aleixo, who happened to be in Recife speaking to a group of students at the time, declared: "The spectacle I witnessed and the information coming to me from different sectors of the country were convincing evidence that we were headed for civil war."[19]

With support among officers and higher enlisted ranks visibly crumbling, Goulart decided to increase his appeal to lower enlisted ranks and attempted to draw more support from forces already unleashed at the mutineer's rally. Thus three days after dropping all charges against the rebellious sailors, the president appeared at a banquet in the Sergeants' Club in Rio, smilingly conversing with José Anselmo, the recently released sailor whose arrest had sparked the mutiny. Goulart's minister of justice devoutly proclaimed this to be a true expression of democratic life—a table where cabinet members, sergeants, and the president of the republic sit in perfect equality with one another. Goulart's speech was televised nationwide.

It was Goulart's last public banquet. Already General Morão's troops were advancing from Minas Gerais and as were those of General Kruel from São Paulo. Troops placed in the field by Goulart to guard against such an event proved strangely inadequate to the task of finding the rebels. But when they did, many openly joined in the march on Rio.

On the morning of April 1, seeing that the situation was hopeless in Rio, Goulart flew to Brasília where he hoped to make a stand. But the situation there was equally bad. So he continued on to Rio Grande do Sul where the Third Army, which only a few months before had threatened civil war to insure his right to the presidency, was stationed. But this time that army had changed its mind, joining rather than fighting the rebels.

On April 4, 1964, João Goulart, President of Brazil, Labor party luminary, and heir to the Getúlio Vargas legacy, fled to asylum in Uruguay.

BIBLIOGRAPHICAL ESSAY

Rollie E. Poppino, in his seminal work, *Brazil: The Land and the People,* begins with the following paragraph:

"Nearly half a millenium has gone by since the first Portuguese explorer set foot on the continent of South America. In that time Brazil has evolved into a distinctive segment of the new world—*in* Latin America but not wholly *of* it. The surface similarities between Portuguese and Spanish-America imposed by geographical proximity, the common Latin origin of the dominant cultures, similar political and economic ties with Europe, and comparable experiences in conquering and displacing the native population, have sometimes over-shadowed real differences between the Brazilians and their Spanish-American neighbors. The most striking contrast, in fact and potential, is the vast size and political unity of Brazil. While the Spanish empire in America disintegrated into eighteen separate nation states, Portuguese America remained intact to become physically a giant among the independent nations of the world."

There is considerable truth to Poppino's statement. I have not talked with anyone knowledgeable about Brazil who has not found its history, its culture, and its contemporary affairs to be among the most fascinating of any developing country in the world. Brazil exhibits all the greatness, diversity, and complexity of any of the industrial nations of Europe. But it also demonstrates the kind of decay and instability in its political and social institutions that characterizes nearly all other developing countries of the world. Several famous Brazilian intellectuals and writers have attempted to come to grips with the meaning of these "internal inconsistencies." They have investigated the problem from cultural as well as social and political perspectives. Probably the most famous is Gilberto Freyre who, with his now classical work, *The Masters and the Slaves,* attempted to assess the contribution to Brazilian society made by African slaves, many of whom were more literate and culturally advanced than their Portuguese masters. In an important sequel, *New World in the Tropics: The Culture of Modern Brazil,* this eclectic "socio-historical anthro-pologist" has suggested that Brazil really is a "tropical China" and cannot be understood otherwise.

In the analytical-historical and contemporary research areas, Brazil's Hélio Jaguaribe (*Economic and Political Development: A Theoretical Approach and a Brazilian Case Study*) has attempted to demonstrate the reasons behind the special historical evolution of his country's social and political institutions. He lays great stress on economic variables as being determinative. Celso Furtado, another intellectual and also the minister of planning in the Dantas cabinet under Goulart, has had his economic history of Brazil translated (*Economic*

132

Growth of Brazil: A Survey from Colonial to Modern Times). He tells a similar, impressively argued story and includes much economic-historical data. The economic vicissitudes, the "busts and booms" about which Jaguaribe and Furtado speak and which they argue constituted conditioning influences on the foundations and evolutions of Brazilian society, are picturesquely and competently illustrated in Stanley J. Stein's regional study of *Vassouras: A Brazilian Coffee County, 1850–1900.* In this specific county Stein has impeccably documented the roles of planter and slave in the changing plantation economy.

For the modern day, no doubt the single most important and complete historical work dealing with the period 1930 to 1964 is Thomas E. Skidmore's *Politics in Brazil.* Names, dates, and events are recorded with impressive completeness. Moreover, in an intuitive way, Skidmore has effectively shown the relationship of social forces to political institutions. Following closely in importance, and time, are two recent volumes, "musts" for students of Brazilian society and politics: Ronald M. Schneider's *The Political System of Brazil: Emergence of a 'Modernizing' Authoritarian Regime, 1964–1970,* and Alfred Stepan, *The Military in Politics: Changing Patterns in Brazil.*

Other works of importance include Irving Louis Horowitz, ed., *Revolution in Brazil: Politics and Society in a Developing Nation*; Eric N. Baklanoff, *New Perspectives of Brazil,* and *The Shaping of Modern Brazil* (Baklanoff's contributions, both published by university presses, contain much historical and contemporary data relevant to modern-day Brazil). Also, for an introduction to the "structural block" argument in economics, see Albert O. Hirschman, *Latin American Issues: Essays and Comments.*

In addition to these volumes, I have found the following books and articles particularly useful in the preparation of this chapter: Frank Bonilla, "A National Ideology for Development: Brazil"; Glaucio A. D. Soares, "The Political Sociology of Uneven Development in Brazil"; Rollie E. Poppino, "Imbalance in Brazil"; Vladimir Reisky de Dubnic, *Political Trends in Brazil*; Roberto Muggiati and Jario Regis, "Quem Derrubou Jango"; C. H. Haring, *Empire in Brazil: A New World Experiment with Monarchy*; Bradford E. Burns, *Nationalism in Brazil: A Historical Survey*; Robert R. Daland, *Brazilian Planning: Development Politics and Administration*; Robert E. Evans, "The Brazilian Revolution of 1964: Political Surgery Without Anesthetics"; Hélio Jaguaribe, "Political Strategies of Economic Development in Brazil"; Nathaniel H. Leff, *Economic Policy Making and Development in Brazil, 1946–1964*; Bryant Wedge, "The Case Study of Student Politics: Brazil, 1964, and Dominican Republic, 1965"; and Albert O. Hirschman, *Journeys Toward Progress: Studies of Economic Policy Making in Latin America.* In addition, the United Nations' Economic Commission for Latin America (ECLA) publishes the *Economic Survey of Latin America* which contains a plethora of economic-related data.

CHAPTER 6

The Military Politicians; How to Foster Economic Growth and Avoid Political Development

The collapse of Goulart's "forces" was so sudden and final that even the military and civilian conspirators were surprised. The radical left proved to have neither strong leadership nor spontaneous followers. Brizola mouthed an exciting rhetoric but apparently had little ability to create and sustain a dynamic organization. Many of Goulart's urban workers, in spite of the inflammatory rallies, seemed to be resigned that their lives would go on in much the same way regardless of who held office in Brasília. Others on whom Goulart had based his bid for power were disenchanted with so much rhetoric and so little "pay off." Moreover, the considerable show of force from nearly all the military regions, and the widespread support this show had received from Brazil's "middle segments" and elite, no doubt cowed many additional "basic reformers" in the Goulart camp. Thus the workers certainly did not take to the streets to battle anti-Goulart forces as, indeed, Goulart had hoped and the military had feared.

Viewing their president's demise, the old civilian politicians—opportunists that they were—jumped into the traces posthaste. For a week they treated the military revolt as merely a replay of the crisis of 1954 when Vargas was ousted, or as a replay of the crisis of 1961 when Quadros resigned and Goulart first became president. In each of these two cases, as was the custom among Brazil's officers, the military had intervened to "set things right" but had eventually retired to let the civilian politicians go at it again. Many of the nation's political elite were convinced that the takeover would constitute nothing more than a political hiatus. There was no apparent reason to assume that the military would not turn the political system back to them again. The civilians, anticipating an end to military rule before it had scarcely begun, accordingly began to look for a new president within their own ranks. The power jockeying commenced nearly at once. Yet, not wishing to initiate a widespread purge of the "in's," the congress declined to formally recognize Goulart's ouster.

The military, however, was engaged in a new and aggressive internal struggle over what to do with Brazil's political system. Two groups of officers were highly visible—"hard-liners" and "soft-liners." A third, somewhat moderate, amorphous, and indecisive "middle group" also entered the arena. For their part, the hard-liners were convinced that the civilian politicians were not only totally corrupt but also decidedly beyond salvation. Too many times, they argued, had the military obligingly pulled them out of their stupid, corrupt, and selfish quagmires. The time had come for the military—the only group genuinely interested in the welfare of the whole nation—to take and maintain charge of the country until the officers could definitively clean up the political mess. Quite aside from getting rid of corruption, therefore, the hard-liners also called for drastic surgery on the political system itself. Artur de Costa e Silva, later to become Brazil's second military president, is said to have been very sympathetic to this view. So were other high-ranking officers. But they were neither sufficiently numerous nor powerful to assume control at will. Their "soft-line" and "moderate" brothers were holding back; they would either have to be convinced or neutralized.

The soft-liners, once the coup was an accomplished fact, wanted the military to proceed just as it had in 1954 and 1961—to act as a moderating force to correct critical inadequacies in the political system and then to return it to civilian control. In this regard, the desires of the soft-liners were not decidedly different from those of the politicians. They all wanted to uphold the constitution. But the officers also wanted to preserve civil liberties and rights. To be sure, many soft-liners were sympathetic to the need for domestic reforms—social as well as economic—but in recent months they had become concerned with Goulart's radical tendencies. There was nothing inherently wrong with the political system, they thought; Goulart had simply exceeded permissible boundaries.

Soft-line officers opposed their hard-line colleagues not only with persuasive arguments but with sizeable numbers. Between the two groups a stalemate existed. As neither side was sufficiently powerful to have its own way, and as neither wished to do anything to fragment the image of military solidarity, neither side moved beyond the realm of words. The resulting inaction, however, was as deceptive as it was disarming. It merely clouded the underlying tensions that were just beginning to surface.

If the balance of power or persuasion could be tipped in favor of one or another of the opposing military camps, the fragility of officer solidarity would become immediately apparent. Unknowingly, no doubt, the civilian politicians provided that service. Their unbridled pursuit of self-serving interests aided the coalition-building of the military hard-liners. For nearly a week following the coup—and with great confidence—the politicians machinated with impunity. Their "business-as-usual" attitude, however, contributed to an eventual destruction of their political livelihood.

The moderate "middle" officer group was not as influential for its convictions as for its strategic position. It held the balance of power between the hard- and soft-liners. It was a prestigious group, headed mainly by senior officials of the War College (the Escola Superior de Guerra) and other enlightened senior officers who were scattered throughout the various commands.[1] The middlers generally favored a pragmatic course between the extremes advanced by their colleagues. While they wanted to correct inadequacies in the political system they also wished to retain competent civilian advisers in government positions.

In addition, they held out for a continuation of most of the civil liberties that were not directly dangerous to the military. Above all, they wanted Brazil to get on its feet economically and begin to progress once again.

CONSOLIDATING MANEUVERS

Initially, the soft-liners and moderates prevailed. The hard-liners certainly were not dismayed, however, for they could readily see that as the civilian politicians continued their course, the result was to encourage many wavering officers to sympathize with hard-line thinking. The conversion process reached a threshold when the congress refused to formalize Goulart's ouster. Thereafter the persuasive advocates of a tough line progressively gained the upper hand. Within days they were in a position to demand—in the name of large segments of the military—that congress enact legislation that would permit the officers to purge the civil service of leftist elements and other undesirables notorious for graft and corruption. The hard-liners also demanded the right to revoke the mandates of elected federal and state officials.

Congress, still basking in the perceptual twilight of the 1950's, refused to acquiesce in these demands, responding instead with its own much milder— and from a practical perspective, essentially meaningless—emergency act. In the face of this civilian "insubordination," still more military moderates shifted to the hard-liner's camp. Soon the consolidation was sufficient. The alliance of hard and converted moderate-liners thereafter took political matters into its own hands.

On April 9, 1964, the three military ministers (who, when Goulart fled, had assumed executive power under the rhetoric of the "Supreme Revolutionary Command") simply ignored the congress' emergency legislation and issued their own decree. Designated as an *Institutional Act*, it became but one of more than a dozen that in due time the military would issue. The Act gave sweeping powers to the executive (the three military ministers). While it specifically preserved the constitution of 1946 it nevertheless stipulated that there would be certain modifications: the executive was to have power to submit constitutional amendments to congress. Congress, in turn, would have 30 days in which to consider the proposals and, by a simple majority vote (rather than a two-thirds vote) could approve them. Moreover, the executive would have power to propose budget expenditures and congress would have no power to increase them. Then the Act gave the nation's deliberating body a time limit in which to enact or reject bills and amendments submitted by the executive. Any bill escaping congressional attention or decision within that period would automatically become law.

Although all these constitutional and institutional modifications may not have been too upsetting, additional stipulations in the Institutional Act certainly were: the executive was given the power to proclaim (or to extend) for 30 days—and without congressional approval—a state of martial law. The Act also suspended for six months all rights of seniority and tenure in the civil service; and, it empowered the executive to revoke the citizenship rights of political undesirables for a period of 10 years. The military, in one fell swoop, created the strongest and most arbitrary central government that Brazil had known since Vargas' *Estado Nôvo*.

The officers further stipulated that a new president and vice-president must be elected within two days after promulgation of the Institutional Act. As if to ameliorate the dilemma that this posed for the nation's politicians, the document also canceled the constitutional provision that had made active military officers ineligible for election.[2]

On stage and in full color marched Castello Branco, former head of the Fourth Army in Recife, subsequently chief of the Army General Staff and, finally, the "swing man" among the military conspirators. A man well respected by both civilian and military plotters, his resources, stature, and prestige, had made the coup successful. He was, therefore, a natural—and willing—draft. An April 11, a cowed congress dutifully elected him president. As he received the oath of office he swore to uphold the constitution—as amended by military decree.

One of the most moderate of all the precoup conspirators was now Brazil's president. But could he please the hard-liners? Not, of course, unless he took a tough, no-nonsense approach to Brazil's political problems. After all, the military's right wing had demanded a political purge of nearly 5000 Brazilian citizens whom it considered to be "undesirable." Among those on the list were former presidents, numerous state governors, members of congress, labor leaders, intellectuals, diplomats, civil servants, *and* soft-line military officers. It was not surprising that scores of Brazil's most illustrious citizens chose voluntary exile. Celso Furtado accepted a visiting professorship at Yale and later went to the Sorbonne. Helio Jaguaribe lectured two years at Harvard and subsequently became a visiting professor at Stanford. Other illustrious Brazilians became faculty members at additional prestigious American institutions or took up residence at intellectual centers in Great Britain, Europe, and elsewhere in Latin America.

In spite of all the fears, how did Castello Branco *really* treat the situation? Only a small minority of the officers appeared to be totally reactionary. Indeed, even the hard-liners had a strong "young Turk" faction which had to be dealt with. Then there were the "Sorbonne moderates" who had their own ideas about things. Thus, after most of the logrolling was over, the only really solid and clear imperatives to emerge with Castello Branco's program were the ones of cleaning out corruption, moving Brazil ahead economically, and containing all Goulart-type politicians.

There was still dissent in the officer corps about particulars. But it was clear to all that such dissent had less to do with the nation's economy and society than it did with its polity. The officers' dilemma was how to deal with the conceptual dimensions of what we have earlier called "political modernization" and "political development." If for lack of political development and wise leadership Brazil's economy had stagnated and its society became disjointed, could the military compensate indefinitely by filling in the political abyss itself? Even if the officers had the technical competence to handle the economic questions (and this was not certain), what would the long-range social and political effects of indefinite military intervention be? How would people in a highly mobilized country like Brazil react when most of their institutions of meaningful voluntary political participation had been rendered impotent?

Huntington has shown that a military which intervenes politically in a mass-mobilized gap society (such as Brazil) has four general options open to it regarding its relationship to political modernization and political development.[3] One option is to indefinitely retain complete control of the political system (thereby perhaps inhibiting long-range political development). Another is to return the system to the civilians (either in a more modernized and developed state than when retrieved or simply with a hope that some development will occur once the tensions have been normalized). Then, the military can choose to acquiesce in the expansion of political participation or, finally, it can choose to resist that expansion.

A military that both retains political control and resists expansion of political participation (thereby electing not to absorb new social forces into the political system) has demonstrated a substantial lack of faith in the capacity of civilians ever to govern themselves appropriately. Whether or not such a lack of faith has objective roots, its expression in a policy of retention and resistance makes it difficult for the military to contribute substantially to political modernization or to political development. Such a military cannot develop politics because it avoids a recognition of their necessity. Apparently, in a mass-mobilized country like Brazil, it is only through a conscious leadership "will" that political development can occur at all. Even then it is a very difficult task. Yet, while the military may have the prerogative of creating such a will, it also may fail to see the need to do so. Castello Branco and his military colleagues had chosen both to retain the political system and to restrict political participation in it. However, would they make a conscious effort, while it was in their stewardship, to develop it?

Castello Branco's moderate inclinations and initial successful manipulation of his right-wing colleagues were amply shown in the three months following his elevation to the presidency. The military hard-liners had demanded an abrogation of the political rights of approximately 5000 persons. When Castello Branco had completed all the purging he felt was necessary, however, only 378 "enemies" of the regime had been affected. To be sure, the list included "three former Presidents—Kubitschek, Quadros, and Goulart—as well as six state governors, 55 members of the federal Congress, and assorted diplomats, labor leaders, military officers, intellectuals, and public officials."[4] Yet, though there was a great outcry of indignation among those immediately involved, most Brazilians acted as if they were tired of the same old unsuccessful faces. They seemed to offer no widespread objections to the purges.

The new regime, initially dominated by moderately inclined officers from the War College, pursued a fairly responsible course. While stabilizing political tensions (by the use of a moderate amount of coercion and the threat of more if necessary), the regime nevertheless employed the services of first-rate civilian economists and bureaucrats and began to stabilize the economic chaos that a previous succession of presidents had bequeathed. Roberto Campos, a long-time friend of the United States, was made Planning Minister.[5]

In due course the United States resumed its technical and financial aid. Indeed, the Johnson administration was so grateful to the generals for ousting Goulart and thereby taking the heat off American investments that his "warmest regards" telegram practically arrived before the coup was complete.

Yet in spite of the deflationary policies generated by Campos and his colleagues, the resumption of aid from the United States, and the beneficial loans from other decision-making centers, the economic results for Brazil were not immediately satisfactory. Soon the officers realized that Brazil's economic problems were so enormous that a bailing-out operation could not possibly be done within the span of Castello Branco's normal presidential term. There was a simple solution to that knotty problem, however. The military pushed through a constitutional amendment (by authority of its Institutional Act) which allowed their president to remain in office two extra years, until 1967. Perhaps by then the economic, social, and political problems would be resolved.

In the meantime the civilian politicians simply would not cooperate. From the government's perspective they did not even try to behave themselves. Constantly they attacked the regime for one or another alleged failure. Even some former prominent supporters of the anti-Goulart conspiracy became aggressively critical of the military's new economic stabilization policies. And Lacerda, the perpetual malcontent, was violently disrespectful.

In July of 1965, and in preparation for the upcoming state and federal elections (which were to be held at their normal time in spite of the extension of Castello Branco's presidential term) the officers moved to shape the political rules more to their own convenience. First they promulgated an "ineligibility law" which made it illegal for any former Goulart cabinet minister or other undesirable left-wing politician to run for office. Second, hoping to reduce Brazil's "splinter-party politics," the officers introduced incentives to encourage the development of a two-party political system (and therefore, they thought, a more stable one).

Civilian politicians among the opposition were not to be outdone by the new Statute of Political Parties, however. In their respective conventions, and especially in Guanabara (where Lacerda was governor again) and in Minas Gerais (where the Kubitschek machine was still quite intact), they kept nominating for office many of Brazil's political undesirables. These, in turn, were consistently ruled ineligible on the authority of the new laws. The nominations were clearly designed to inflame the hard-liners. And in that they certainly succeeded. Indeed, even the opposition candidates finally approved by the electoral board were distasteful to the military right wing.

When the election votes were counted, promilitary candidates had won in nine of the eleven state governorships. But the two that the officers lost were also the most important—Guanabara and Minas Gerais. The hard-liners were furious. They pressured Castello Branco to nullify the elections and to disqualify the winners in those two states. The president resisted this move but he did bow to a major compromise. It became known as the Second Institutional

Act, and the pressures that established it are now termed the "white coup," pulled off by hard-line officers.[6] This one established *indirect* elections for president and state governors (to be elected by the federal congress and state legislatures, respectively). It provided for an enlargement of the supreme court (with new judges to be appointed by Castello Branco). It authorized the president to suspend—at his discretion—the political rights of all Brazilians whom he considered to be a threat to the government. Moreover, it dissolved all existing parties and authorized the formation of two new ones. In one swoop Goulart's PTB, Lacerda's UDN, and Kubitschek's PSD, along with all other parties, were officially destroyed (although they did not fail to function "underground"). In their stead the regime created an official opposition party, MDB (Movimento Democrático Brasileiro), and an official government party, ARENA (Aliança Renovadora Nacional) or, as the Brazilians said, the party of "yes" and the party of "yes, sir!"

The Second Institutional Act was to remain in force only until the inauguration of Castello Branco's successor in March 1967. But, if the civilian politicians did not learn their lessons fairly soon, additional acts might have to be promulgated. And soon they were. As polarization continued, even the few remaining vestiges of constitutional formalities began to crumble. The widespread failure of civilian opposition politicians to understand the new rules of the game had allowed the military hard-liners to win the political jousting. The result was a parliamentary sham. Political development? The officers seemed to think that there were no politics worth developing. The military could get along quite well without them. Or so they thought.

When the civilians controlled Brazil's political system the economy suffered, gyrating nearly uncontrollably from exhilarating expansion to deep stagnation. In addition, and through it all, the effects of the ever-present inflationary spiral oscillated periodically from discomfort to nearly intolerable pain. Now the military, having foreclosed on all "nonproductive" political participation by civilians, was carrying a heavy self-appointed mandate in the political arena. Could it do better? Could it work the economic miracle that had so long eluded the civilian politicians?

Castello Branco's initial stabilization policies certainly left no doubt in the minds of many Brazilians. All sectors were hit simultaneously—and fairly adversely. Gone were the special privileges, the automatic wage increases, the considered favors, and even the compensating corruption. Lacerda and his group, for example, who earlier had conspired with the military for a coup, now seemed to think that the government had gone mad. Yet, somehow, Roberto Campos and his team seemed to be pushing at least some of the right economic buttons, because in time not only was inflation nipped (from an annual rate of approximately 144 percent in early 1964 to 55 percent in 1965), but eventually the economy began to expand once again as well. Indeed, the buoyancy was even seen in the traditional export sectors. A pattern of chronic trade deficits was arrested and, in 1965, a $300-million surplus reported. Thus as certain as the austerity of stabilization was felt, so also, eventually, were the benefits of further economic expansion enjoyed—at least by some. Contrary to many other stabilization schemes, those of Roberto Campos did not seem to sacrifice absolute growth for stability.

With such a felicitous turn of events, the economic anxieties for a great many people were reduced. Traditional exporters, while by no means exuberant, were at least doing relatively well. Businessmen and entrepreneurs were pleased because of the increased merchandise sales and factory orders. Economic middle groups sighed with relief as white-collar jobs expanded. While opportunities to participate in the political system were severely curtailed, the stabilization *with* growth—something of a wonder—seemed to be an adequate if not temporary compensation.

The experience of the blue-collar workers was somewhat different. In some ways we suspect one could argue that their economic lot also improved. For one thing, the *rate* of increase in the gap between wages and rising consumer prices was reduced. But, during this period at least, there did not seem to be much reduction, if any, in the absolute gaps. Later the gaps actually began to increase once again. Thus, unlike many middle and upper status groups in Brazilian society, the urban workers were not politically "diffused" by economic stabilization with growth. The government found it necessary to outlaw their strikes and to invoke severe sanctions on those who disobeyed. It imprisoned union leaders and placed "official stewards" in their stead.

Yet although some observers feared that Brazil was becoming a country where some people did not eat and others did not sleep for fear of those who went hungry, it was increasingly apparent that, for a great many people, Castello Branco was doing just fine. War veteran, fighter, humorless administrator, and (in spite of his denial of civilian politics) consummate military politician, the president was losing no ground.

THE MILITARY HANGS ON

As planned, Castello Branco ended his term in 1967. His military colleagues, however, showed no signs of releasing the country from their political control. Thus the federal congress dutifully replaced the "swing man" with Artur de Costa e Silva, one of the "moderately hard-line" military conspirators in the original anti-Goulart plots. Circumstances allowed the new president to be less concerned with deflationary stabilization than his predecessor—since a lot of it had already taken place—and he thus had more latitude in which to toy with economic expansion and development. As a consequence, Costa e Silva did indeed surprise many Brazilians, not so much for his hard, no-nonsense and sometimes paternalistic political line—which everyone expected anyway—but for his continuation and even expansion of the successful economic policies of the previous regime.

True, the new president was badgered from time to time. Students in Rio de Janeiro and elsewhere paraded periodically with protest banners announcing themselves as "students and workers against dictatorship." Prominent clergy decried the loss of civil liberties. And, from the other side, the hard-line officers continued to harp about the "imminent Communist danger" (in spite of the judgement of government observers that any Communist threat to political stability by then was virtually nil). Yet being of "harder" inclinations than Castello Branco, Costa e Silva pressed an increasingly dictatorial political course. But, in the first year, it was neither as severe as some had feared nor as complete as others had wished.

While some people seemed to receive ambiguous signals from Costa e Silva, his administrators and policy makers had little doubt at all where they were going. One leading official reported to James Nelson Goodsell of *The Christian Science Monitor:*

"It doesn't matter what the people think. They are often wrong and generally unable to know what is good for them. We intend to stay in office until we can clean up Brazil and prepare the way for a true democracy. We know what we are doing and silly protestations about lack of democracy will not deter us."[7]

Yet the students thought it did matter. Their disorders and protestations, until then relatively minor, began to grow.[8] So did the complaints of the Archbishop of Recife, Dom Helder Câmara, the most quoted left-leaning Latin American prelate. And workers became more restless.

Growing anxieties about the suppression of civil liberties were also expressed from the political right. Carlos Lacerda, never too concerned about preserving liberties for his leftist antagonists, was greatly angered that the military had begun to seriously circumscribe his own. Frozen from channels of political influence and contained by the government's increasing censorship of the press, the invective publisher complained that the military (whom he had helped to power) was "preparing a contraceptive pill to sterilize democracy in Brazil,"[9] was "marrying itself to the decadent oligarchy,"[10] and that "military corruption, or that protected by the military, is the worst of all, because it is armed."[11]

The military, knowing Lacerda's talents only too well, certainly did not take his remarks lightly. The hard-line officers' rabid counter denunciations exemplified the point. The Lacerda-military exchanges developed considerable acrimony when the publisher's competitors broadcast an account of his secret meetings with United States Ambassador John W. Tuthill. The ambassador, wishing to keep the channels of communication open to all "respectable" political groups (which excluded pro-Goulart ones), had met with Lacerda once at his residence and again in Petrópolis, a resort setting. One senator from the government's ARENA party called the meetings "inadmissible," adding that "the American Ambassador did not seek out a political opponent of the President but instead a man who preaches the overthrow of the regime and its institutions."[12] Costa e Silva was so furious that he refused to give the ambassador an audience. He also declined to publicly refute a series of anti-American rumors generated by students. These included charges that United States' aid to Brazil was being used to brainwash Brazilian youth and that United States interests planned to split Brazil into two nations and then to depopulate the Amazon region through birth control schemes to provide a haven for United States survivors of a nuclear war or, failing that, to have sufficient and suitable land for a concentration camp for militant Negro Americans.[13]

Because Lacerda enjoyed "high visibility" among important Brazilian groups, and because he previously had lent rabid support to the military, he had been one of the few old-line "traditional" politicians not silenced. (Subsequently, he did lose his political rights, however.) But the publisher's meetings with the ambassador—in light of his scathingly critical attacks on the government for its close ties with the United States—was nearly the last straw. Hard-line officers pressed for a termination of his political rights. Eventually they got their way.

Lacerda's social basis of political support was not nearly as secure as it once had been. The expanding economy had reduced the anxieties of many of his former middle-class followers. They were less inclined, therefore, to be influenced by his anti-government rhetoric. Accordingly, Lacerda's declining influence was related to the government's continuing economic successes. Following a pattern already set by Castello Branco, for example, Costa e Silva, in his first year in office, further reduced the annual rate of inflation to about 25 percent and increased the annual rate of real economic expansion to about 5 percent. Moreover, the president also maintained a rigid hand on wage increases, kept labor leaders in jail, and disallowed strikes. Employers and businessmen were pleased. For them, Lacerda's attacks on the government made no sense at all.

GROWING DISCONTENT ON THE LEFT

It was true that the progressively hard "democradura"—an amalgam of the Portuguese words for democracy and dictatorship—adversely affected all Brazilians in a political sense. And although the economic benefits deriving from the military's guiding hand were a sufficient offsetting compensation for many, still there were exceptions. Two of cardinal importance were the workers and the students.

Workers' complaints once again lay mostly with the increasing gap between the cost of life's necessities and the amount of one's paycheck. Much of the visible problem derived from the government's belief that, to fight inflation, it must place artificial controls on wages. Indeed, this was a central point in the regime's continuing deflationary program, having the effect of singling out workers and other lower income types for relatively higher sacrifices to put Brazil back in economically good stead. Castello Branco himself, in August of 1966, had frozen all wages for a year and had decreed penalties for employers who attempted to circumvent the regulation by paying bonuses or tips. The purchasing power of workers since 1964 had correspondingly declined by 40 percent. To top this off, the minimum legal wage hovered at $39 a month. A great many blue-collar working fathers were trying to support families on that amount. They said they couldn't. Yet, since the political outlets for dissent were stringently controlled, there was practically no public display of unrest. And threats were downright dangerous. After all, labor leaders dating from the Goulart days had received jail sentences of up to 30 years.

The ramifications of student discontent were different—as much in causes as in consequences. If the government's tight rein on television, movies, and the theater were not enough to uncouple an endemically alienated segment of the society, Costa e Silva's habitual "top-priority-for-education" speeches, after which nothing in practice was ever done, provided whatever else was needed. While the president never cut military funds to accommodate any general budget deficits, he always cut those for education. In fact, education's share of the national budget had dropped from 11 percent in 1965 to 7.7 percent by mid-1968. Among the consequences was the fact that a population of 85 million could boast fewer than 200,000 university students. Facilities were bad and were deteriorating. In addition the overcrowded universities in Rio were forced to turn away two out of every three qualified applicants. How does that affect an unlucky young man or woman's opportunity expectations and anxieties for personal progress? Visible protest was not long in coming. With it arose a new phenomenon among the normally compromising, agreeable, pragmatic, and placid Brazilians—violence.

NEW POLITICS: PROTEST AND TERRORISM

In March of 1968 Rio students expressed a vigorous challenge in the form of a protest march. Relatively peaceful in the beginning, it soon deteriorated into violent clashes. Police gunfire killed one student and fatally wounded a shipyard employee. Incensed by the police attack, the retreating students regrouped long enough to threaten more demonstrations in early April. The commander of Rio's military zone warned that his troops would treat any future disorderly demonstrators like "an enemy attacking the fatherland's territory and threatening the nation's basic institutions."[14]

The press had given the riot wide coverage. Costa e Silva was unbearably distressed about this. During a speech at an anniversary celebration of the Brazilian Press Association he reminded the reporters that there was a "strict connection between the right of freedom and the duty of responsibility."[15] The journalists did not appreciate the advice because, following a week of clashes among police, students, and some workers, more than a score of the newsmen and their photographer colleagues had been beaten or arrested. And one radio station had been closed.

Yet in the heat of the disagreement, the government reiterated its prohibition against publishing any political statements either from persons who had lost their political rights or from any of their associates. The officers, it seemed, had set on the "conspiracy theory" of disorders and, therefore, blamed most of the problems on professional agitators.

Costa e Silva's pressure on the students hardly deterred their energies, however. In fact, it seemed that his actions served more to radicalize than to enforce submission. In June the students marched on the Education Ministry to demand the resignation of its minister, Tarsol Dutra. Spokesmen for the minister announced in advance that he would not listen to grievances, offer sympathy, or resign. Two platoons of police made the point with tear gas and an anti-riot truck equipped with a water cannon.

Military hard-liners literally screamed for an immediate crackdown on this threat to national security—even if that meant abolishing the remnants of democratic processes still existing in the country. But it appeared that the president had a personal aversion to making decisions of this kind under pressure lest it force him to concede to subsequent pressures. Thus he temporarily brushed off the hard-liners, but not as completely as he did the students.

The president's intransigence only hardened the students' resolve. A week later they recruited ordinary citizens, writers, professors, workers, and Roman Catholic nuns and priests for a 25,000-member protest march along Rio de Janeiro's Avenida Rio Branco. It was the largest public demonstration in four years. Rio's Roman Catholic Vicar General, Bishop José de Castro Pinto, had given the clergy under his jurisdiction permission to participate in the anti-government demonstrations. Moreover, he issued a statement affirming that "we hold just the principal complaints of our youth."[16]

Visibly unnerved, Costa e Silva finally promised to name a "work group," including students, to draft plans for the renovation and improvement of the nation's schools. A report was to have been prepared within 30 days. But since the group would be only the latest among 54 to look into educational problems in recent years—with no subsequent action on the principal recommendations—there was widespread doubt that the new group would accomplish anything either.[17] "Abaixo a ditadura" (down with dictatorship) was the newest line of graffiti scrawled on buildings and walls. The growing clamor of politicians for open elections, of students for educational reforms, and of the Catholic Church for social justice and progress left the Costa e Silva regime tense and frustrated.

Why couldn't everyone just behave himself? How could the country progress with so much protest nonsense going on? Economic development must come first. Then many of the other problems would take care of themselves. At least this seemed to be the military's reasoning. Thus while the social disturbances were increasing, the government did not cease its efforts to find economic solutions to social and political problems. Yet in the local folklore the month of August seemed to pose special riddles of its own. Years earlier in August one national president (Vargas) had taken his own life, and another (Quadros) had resigned enigmatically. What would this August bring? All Brazilians waited.

Impatient students soon broke the calm. Throughout July and August of 1968 they had held their annual conventions (which even included participation by the outlawed National Union of Students, an anti-military, anti-United States, pro-Communist organization). Then in September they took to the streets once again. The military, believing that the outbursts had been planned in the July and August conventions, decided to put the student leaders in "preventive detention" and their respective organizations out of business. The assault was most severe at the University of Brasília:

"Some students were taking tests. Others were in their labs. Suddenly the campus and its buildings were enveloped in clouds of gas and dust. There were depredations, clashes, combats, aggressions, shots, prisons. Once again the University of Brasília had been invaded by the [military] police, this time invested with the mission of arresting five students. Only one, Honestino Guimarães, the leader, was detained. . . .

[Hearing the commotion, several congressmen came over to try to calm the disturbances. What happened to Deputy Santili was, the observer reported, a typical occurrence.] Santili Sobrinho, when he tried to protect his son, was surrounded by police who arrested him [and beat him with nightsticks], paying no attention to parliamentary immunity. The commotion soon quieted down, but the aggression against Deputy Santili had repercussions in the House of Deputies, whose president asked for an investigation. . . . ARENA and the moderate sectors of the government were perplexed. For them it was difficult to justify the invasion. Even the radical pro-government deputies, such as Sr. Clovis Stenyel, refused to defend such scenes as these."[18]

With treatment such as this, members of congress became increasingly hostile to the military rulers. That hostility was soon to be demonstrated.

Student riots continued in succeeding months.[19] Moreover, political assassinations, for example, that of Captain Chandler, a United States army officer studying Portuguese at the University of São Paulo in preparation for teaching at West Point, became more common. A veteran of Vietnam, he was found machine-gunned to death for "his war crimes against the Vietnamese people." The very same day the Brazilian authorities arrested the entire leadership of the National Union of Students (which, because it had been banned, happened to be holding a clandestine convention in the town of Ibiuna near São Paulo). But the remaining radical students were not cowed. In many parts of Brazil they continued their vigorous demonstrations. Then, in subsequent police-student clashes in Rio de Janeiro, four more students were killed. Finally, in October, workers in several parts of the country carried out strikes to protest police abuse, not only of students but of themselves.

The extreme political right, particularly air force officers, reacted very stiffly to all this. "There were reports that these officers, disgusted by student and leftist excesses, intended to seize a suitable opportunity to take the law into their own hands, or at least to force President Costa e Silva to get tough."[20] Shortly thereafter the first reports of police torture, virtually unheard of in Brazil before this time, began to be heard.[21] And the previously organized Communist Pursuit Commandos, or "death squads" (made up of off-duty police and military officers) began to strike at alleged leftists and criminals toward whom the courts, it was said, had been too lenient. Few Brazilians were immune to experiencing tension in these agitated times. The hard-line military coalition-building started once again.

The catalyst for a hard-line "internal coup" was once again provided by a congressional politician, this time a young radical opposition MDB deputy, Marcio Moreira Alves, author of two books and of numerous articles that hard-line officers had long considered subversive.[22] In a congressional speech he had called on the parents of all Brazilian children to boycott the military celebration of the nation's independence day, September 7, and also had suggested that freedom-loving Brazilian girls prove their devotion to their country by refusing to date military officers. Incensed at what it interpreted as a conspiratorial campaign to discredit it in public eyes, the military demanded that congress lift the deputy's immunity so as to allow his prosecution for "violating national security." A long congressional debate resulted. But Moreira Alves' colleagues adjourned for the legislative year before taking any action either for or against him. Unwilling to allow such a lack of action to go unchallenged, however, Costa e Silva called Congress back into session (at considerable expense) to act on the issue. This time the legislators voted 216 to 141 *against* ousting their fellow deputy, even though the committee set up to hear the initial arguments (packed with progovernment legislators) had recommended punitive action.

Clearly, even ARENA deputies were now unwilling to go along with an act that the executive considered essential. Thus the president was caught in a serious bind. On the one hand, at his inaugural, he had pledged to "humanize" the revolution. Yet, on the other, he had his hard-line colleagues to deal with. Pragmatically there was only one way he could act and still retain the presidency. In December of 1968, to prevent a "coup within a coup" by the air force, he announced the regime's Fifth Institutional Act which suspended all civilian guarantees and closed congress. While both actions were in direct violation of the existing constitution—a document that the officers themselves had imposed on the country after their 1964 coup—civilian uncooperativeness had made it all necessary. Other oppressive military decrees dramatically followed. These included total censorship of press, radio, television, and all international cables and phone messages. Many politicians and businessmen were arrested, including some of Brazil's most internationally respected journalists and scientists.[23] The nation was effectively returned to the situation that had prevailed immediately following Goulart's ouster in 1964. Political modernization? Political development? How well had the military used its four-year stewardship?

WHEN THE HARD-LINERS WIN

"We had a problem in stemming the tide within our own ranks," says a high military officer who, like almost all others, refused to allow his interviewer to identify him publicly. "We now have about 75 percent control of the situation, but many of the officers are still unhappy and the battle isn't over yet."[24]

In a social and political sense, of course, the larger battle never was—nor would be—over. But the coalition-building to which the officer referred was, indeed, moving in favor of the power-seeking military hard-liners. What is more, they even seemed to be improving their image among some civilian groups. "Brazil needs a cleansing and it will take the military to do it," said a leading banker. "If the military can stick to its efforts which came forward in December, we'll get the true revolution we expected when the military ousted Jango back in 1964."[25]

Yet in spite of the turning tide there was no denying the fact that the military remained deeply divided regarding its role in politics. Some of the "moderate" officers now wondered if they should ever have taken power in the first place. It seemed to them that, while the country as a whole had progressed economically,[26] not all Brazilians had participated in that progress as they should. The moderate officers argued that very little social progress could be registered at all in spite of nearly five years of military rule. If anything, the country had been backsliding. The needs of education, housing, and other social amenities—taking into consideration the increase in population during the previous five years—were more pressing than ever.

As the differing perspectives worked themselves up and down the various lines of command and influence, it was not surprising that the drama should produce apparent anomalies in public policy. For example, the Fifth Institutional Act, which had closed congress in December of 1968, also introduced economies in all governmental activities *except education*. Presumably the students had made a point. But to whom and for what? Certainly the hard-liners appeared to have little love for students—and the hard-liners were in power. In any event, when the military once again took over dictatorial powers, it also announced its intention to expand and improve schooling facilities at all levels.

What did the officers intend to do with the long-run political results of a new educational thrust? They already had more student problems than they cared for. A developing country needs a literate and skilled population, but its educational efforts cannot be made in total disregard of the product produced. In this respect one cannot ignore the ability—or the willingness—of a country to absorb its literate children into the mainstream of economic, political, and social life. If a nation's programs create the kinds of gaps that we have discussed, then the political results may overwhelm those in power. Reflecting on the political effects of one of the best elementary education programs in all Africa, and one held in great esteem by UNESCO and other world bodies, President Azikiwe of Nigeria nevertheless decided it was necessary to "undo progress." The social forces generated by his schools led him to conclude that education before industrialization and increased productivity was an unproductive social service. It was "unproductive" not so much from an ideal frame of reference as a practical one. There were serious political problems deriving from the high level of unemployment among his increasingly literate countrymen.[27]

The Fifth Institutional Act also increased the restructured Brazil's tax base. Evasion, widespread and relatively easy only several years before, became increasingly difficult as well as dangerous. The Act and its supporting laws decreed severe penalties for tax fraud. The punitive threats were made real by increased collection and auditing forces. Federal income tax revenues soon increased by 50 percent. But there was a new and rather unexpected element in this turn of events. Businessmen now came under the "illicit profit" surveillance of the military. Capitalists cheered when the officers broomed out the corrupt politicians. But now the finger was on them. What did it all mean?

In addition to increasing educational funds and moving in on corrupt businessmen, the government also introduced temporary price controls on food and many other products and services. In addition, it embarked on a modest agricultural reform program designed to assist small farmers to acquire land and to provide them with the necessary financial and technical means to cultivate it. All these reforms seemed to answer many complaints from urban workers and some peasants.

In the early months of 1969 the hard-liners continued to strengthen their control over the entire political fabric of the nation. They prevailed on Costa e Silva to decree an additional series of Institutional Acts. Embodying the psychology of the "carrot and stick," each was designed to attack one or more symptoms of political instability and social chaos. The Sixth Act reformed the courts (to undo the "leniency syndrome"), and the Seventh Act severely limited the number and autonomy of elected officials. As the series continued, the United States, which had granted the officers nearly 2 billion dollars in foreign aid since 1964, became visibly concerned about the growing "totalitarian" nature of the government. It called home its field representatives for consultations.

Relative civilian calm prevailed in spite of these new decrees. Little wonder, the coercive power of the state was everywhere. As an illustration, the press, with few exceptions, remained highly muzzled. Said one Colonel close to Marshal Costa e Silva: "The press was reporting all the news that goes on in Brazil and we could not permit that."[28] Another responded with, "you've got to realize that we do not tolerate criticism of the military, for we know what is best for Brazil and a critical press will only impede our efforts."[29]

The assertion that "the military knows best" was less obvious to the general population than the fact that the military was still very divided. The hard-liners had been chaffing for some time under the effective reporting of dissension within military ranks. In reading over editorials from 1968 and early 1969, a British resident in Rio judged that "one is struck with a feeling that the press got fed up with pious platitudes and the sense of drift evident here. And the press began to ask questions which the military leaders and their friends took as offensive."[30]

In March of 1969 Brazilians increasingly spoke of another "coup within a coup," meaning that they believed the hard-liners were accruing progressively more strength and control over Costa e Silva. In quick succession the government had arrested 470 more of its subjects and had processed 300 of them out of all of their political rights. This brought the total number of citizen-eunuchs to more than 800. What was alarming to many, however. was not that the arrests were coming with any greater frequency but that the rationale to support them was progressively more ambiguous. In any event, as the officers (in spite of five years of rule) considered the threat from the political left to be greater than ever before, they did not feel obliged to document the "counter-revolutionary" tendencies of many of those whom it arrested. In fact, one official of the Interior Ministry, commenting on the activities of the eleven anti-subversive agencies empowered to arrest and hold without charge anyone they chose, reportedly said: "Not one of them [those arrested] is a communist. They will be charged eventually, but with complaints of subversion of the regime."[31]

A hard-line consolidation was fairly clear by April when the government once again moved against the educational system. Having granted budget increases only months before, the rumors of impending student unrest apparently led the officers to suspect the "loyalty" of numerous members of the university faculty. Like many "intelligence gatherers," they placed great faith in the conspiracy theory of civilian unrest. The list of 68 professors purged from the federal university in Rio read like a "Who's Who" of higher education in the country.[32] Observers reported that "most of the retired professors could not in any way be regarded as political activists, and only a small portion, perhaps 20, could be considered mildly leftish. Some are known conservatives."[33] The ultimate rationale of the arrests, therefore, was logically ambiguous. Nor could it be determined. As the military held dictatorial powers, its actions, right or wrong, were not subject to judicial review. But to make their point—whatever it was—undeniably clear, the officers not only relieved the professors of their political rights for 10 years but of their professional ones as well. It forbade any other university to employ them and reportedly sent out an order to private business to refrain from hiring them.[34]

There is an old adage in Brazil: "The more Brazil is changed the more it remains the same." But would it? The officers purged their detractors; they cleaned up a considerable amount of private and public corruption; and they closed down virtually all civilian political participation. But by continuing the country's economic expansion they also set the stage for further social mobilization—and therefore for increasing demands for the very thing that the officers were unwilling to give—opportunities for political participation.

The United States State Department was worried about the political trends. But the Commerce Department was delighted with the continued economic expansion. Foreign-investment prospects were wonderful. Surely economic growth would solve the transient social and political problems.

In August of 1969 the urban guerrillas, having until then confined most of their operations to robbing banks, struck with a ferociousness seldom recorded in Brazilian history. The assassinations and counter-assassinations, and the kidnappings and ransoming of political prisoners were all the more spectacular because so many important people were involved. During the height of the tension, Costa e Silva collapsed with a cerebral hemorrhage and was permanently disabled. People speculated as to whether he was a victim of emotional frustration or of random biological aberrations. A military triumvirate, immediately preempting the succession of the the the vice-president, replaced the fallen leader and stepped up the arrests of dissidents; those still free responded by kidnapping the United States ambassador.

Incensed by this latest open and flagrant disrespect for authority, and blaming Costa e Silva's hemorrhage on student agitators, the military hard-liners responded to the American ambassador's abduction by promulgating their Fourteenth Institutional Act. It revived the death penalty (not used since 1891) for peacetime "subversion and terrorism." The United States government, how-ever, alarmed and fearful for the safety of its ambassador, placed great pres-sure on the Brazilian military to abandon this route and to open negotiations with the terrorists.

Within several days a dialogue was successfully opened, the ambassador was released, and numerous political prisoners were hurriedly enplaned for Mexico City. Mexico, in the spirit and tradition for which Latin America has long been known, had agreed to receive yet another batch of a sister republic's exiles. Like nearly all Brazilian political prisoners released in exchange for the lives of foreign diplomats these, too, spoke of electric-shock torture as a minimum; some reported severe beatings. The torture themes have been so consistent, and even acknowledged by Brazilian authorities, that few observers now seriously doubt that they have some reference in fact.

Before the military officers inaugurated their new president—a little-known general by the name of Emilio Garrastazú Médici—to replace Costa e Silva,[35] the hard-line faction assured its own position by establishing new military courts for alleged terrorists. An interesting sidelight of the new policy was that all those arrested had to be tried and their cases disposed of within 30 days of capture. While no *judicial* review was possible, even before this time, the new decree now seemed to assure that there would be no time for any possible *military* reviews either. Lower echelon officers could have a field day. And many of them did.

The new president had the aura of a gentleman. He seemed persuaded that what Brazilians needed most was a little fatherly reasoning. So confident was he that in one of his first pronouncements he promised a return to "normal democratic procedures" by the end of his term.[36] He also ordered the people—categorically—to cease using torture methods as a means of extracting informa-tion from their captives.[37]

The president's goodwill did not survive the first few months of 1970. His fatherly advice went unheeded. His subjects continued to be disrespectful and inconsiderate. In March, he therefore reneged on his promise of eventual democracy. What Brazil now needed, he said, was a *revolutionary state:* "The Revolutionary State will last as long as it takes to implant the political, admin-istrative, juridical, social and economic structures capable of raising all Brazil-ians to a minimum level of well-being."[38] What Garrastazú Médici really meant to say, of course, was that those who would not be convinced about the military's judgement of what was best for Brazil either would be coerced into silence and inaction or would be temporarily—or permanently—put out of business.

There is no question that many Brazilians were convinced of the rightness of the military's course of action. It is equally true that others were cowed into silence and inaction. But still others, and this was and is the continuing thorn in the side of the regime, have maintained their "revolutionary cause." The challenge and the coercion, the terrorism and the torture, the kidnappings and the ransoming, continued throughout 1970. If the ransoming should cease, there seems little doubt that the terrorists, desperate as they are, would feel obliged to call the government's hand. The radicals grew more violent and their kidnappings of international diplomats, in 1970, more frequent and daring. Nevertheless, the hard-liners have become more "hard" as well as more convinced of the rightness of their cause. The reports of torture have grown more commonplace and, in part, because the police assaulted and allegedly tortured several priests and nuns, several prelates of the Catholic church have become more disturbed and outspoken against their government.[39] But the government has relentlessly pursued the terrorists and has succeeded in crushing a number of their organizations. By 1972 terrorism had declined markedly.

The military's censorship of the press also has continued. From time to time the officers have permitted some "license." But,, periodically, they have it clear that the only acceptable publications on contemporary affairs are those that pay at least nominal deference to the established political arrangements. On occasion, several publishers tried slight "deviations" Some, for short periods of time, even seemed to get away with them. But in the end there has been little doubt about who retains residual, if not outright, determination of what the Brazilian people ought to know regarding their country's political and social affairs.

The basic issues of political conflict have never been resolved, just "treated." In December of 1971 the military government added an additional tool for treatment if not control when President Médici signed a new decree-law authorizing him to decree secret laws whose contents will remain secret, being noted in the official government paper, *Diario Oficial*, by title only. Brazilians are subject to what, no doubt, are essentially subversive-control laws that they can now neither read nor understand.[40]

Yet, economically, Brazil seems never to have had it so good, at least, not since the boom years of the Kubitschek era. The United States Department of Commerce, in its November 1970 summary of economic trends, confirmed the existence of a swift developmental pace during the first half of 1970: Gross national product rose at a real estimated rate of 7.1 percent; the value of goods exported rose by 27.7 percent, reaching $1240 million for those first six months; and gold and foreign currency reserves jumped by $330 million to reach a record of more than one billion dollars. Inflation was held to an annual rate of approximately 22 percent; industrial production rose by 8 percent, farm production rose by 6 percent, and income after taxes (in real terms—adjusted so as not to be inflated by inflation) rose by 13.7 percent.

If the breathtaking expansion of 1970 was surprising, that of 1971, in some sectors, was exhilarating. Figures on Brazilian production for the first four months of 1971, for example, show a continuing surge of growth, rising to a value of $157 million as against $125 million in the first four months of 1970. Exports (except for coffee and manganese which declined substantially in volume—29 and 41 percent, respectively) rose fairly consistently and, in some sectors, spectacularly. In spite of the coffee and manganese export decline, the total value of exports during January to April, 1971 was reckoned at $838 million against $751 million for the same period the previous year.

The role of the central government in the economy also increased substantially. One indicator was the nearly 39 percent jump in its revenues (from 5925 to 8226 million Cruzeiros for the four-month period, 1971 over 1970). Even when allowing for the depletion of the real value of the Cruzeiro due to inflation (7.7 percent for the period), the government's take was up at least 31 percent over that of 1970.[41] Such an increase is dramatic. Aside from the normal increased revenue that might be attributed to economic expansion, such added revenues also demonstrate that the military government had a better hand on tax collections and a surer control over corruption.

Brazil was not developing politically in 1971, but the same certainly could not be said of its economy. The military was pleased; how many Brazilians were equally as satisfied is a question of honest doubt. Insofar as rapid economic development further mobilizes Brazilians for new patterns of socialization and commitment, one can expect the officers' political problems to worsen, not fade away.

CHAPTER 7

Theory and Reality: Do They Match?

Does the Brazilian case coincide with any of the general patterns outlined in Parts I and II of this book (thereby advancing our general understanding of the topics herein discussed), or is there such a mismatch between the data and the theories that alternative middle-range generalizations must be sought? Indeed, are general explanations possible at all?

It is apparent to us, and we hope later in this chapter to demonstrate, that the exciting events in Brazil between 1930 and 1964 dramatically illustrate many (but, of course, not all) of the topics abstractly discussed (especially in Part II) relating to the rise of new social forces, to charismatic leaders, and to political parties, and how all these related to both old and new political institutions—and the military officer corps. From the case, one catches a glimpse of the processes of environmental change and the political and social dislocations associated with them. Brazil's economic system became progressively more complex, shifting away from predominant export-import enclaves to domestically produced substitutes for many consumer goods. Eventually, the country even launched some large-scale industrial production. Accompanying these changes were dramatic shifts in the way men organized themselves to carry out their new occupational roles and social functions. Differentiation and specialization occurred with rampant speed in society, business, and public administration. Population growth, urbanization, and the advance of literacy proceeded apace. From 1920 to 1964, for example, Brazil's population nearly tripled, from 27 million to 79 million,[1] while also the number of Brazilians living in cities of *50,000* inhabitants or more increased nearly *six and one-half times*, from 3 million to nearly 20 million.[2] The rate of urbanization was fully twice that of population growth. If we had comparable data for the smaller urban growth centers blossoming after 1946, the urbanization rate no doubt would appear considerably higher. In those cities and growth centers, traditions were undone and new values and expectations acquired; and new classes were mobilized for political participation. There Vargas was to found the PTB, and Goulart to take advantage of it.

Throughout the country per capita *primary* and *secondary* school enrollment also increased, in aggregative terms from 47 per thousand population in 1920, to 139 in 1964,[3] rising from 1.3 million pupils to almost 11 million. Also, *university* enrollment increased from 4000 to 142,000, advancing at a rate roughly eleven times that of population growth. And as industrialization in the

154

cities proceeded ahead, the per capita GNP originating in industrial activity increased from $26 in 1953 (the earliest date for which figures are available) to $50 in 1964, or approximately a 100 percent per-capita increase in little over a decade. These are dramatic shifts. They signify both a physical and an emotional dislocation. They are one index of the availability of people for new commitments and new patterns of socialization—social mobilization. The accompanying experiences frequently heighten expectations, hopes, ambitions, desires, and so forth, not to mention a capacity to act and an impatience with those who may wish to block action.

Pressures for changes in the structure of Brazilian society and its political system closely followed these dislocations and the social mobilization that accompained them. As pressures arose for a redistribution of wealth, status, and prestige, the society became strained. Reflecting this was a kind of "decay" in the old institutions and patterns of governance—the critical junctures being in 1930 when the old machine bosses lost much of their influence, and in 1964 when the military ceased its moderating role, cashiering the entire political system and following with an attempt to forge a new one more to their liking.

The problem with Brazil, as with many rapidly changing countries elsewhere in Latin America, Asia, Africa, and the Middle East, is that the decline in the legitimacy and governing capacity of their traditional institutions is rarely ever compensated for by a corresponding development of modernized political institutions and procedures. Other aspects of modernization just seem to "happen" once the process of change gets into motion. But adequate political development takes an enormous amount of compromising collective will. The new and old social forces in the society must come to terms with one another on new rules of the social and political game. The amoral way that these forces usually push their own interests, however, makes the fabrication of such a compromising national will extraordinarily difficult. This feat was certainly beyond the capacities of most Brazilians.

Into this gap generated by a decayed political past and a yet undeveloped political present arose charismatic leaders, collective protest movements, developmentalist ideologies, and military coups. At one or another time in their careers both Vargas and Goulart took on an aura of "situational charisma," at least for the Brazilian working class. They also generated an acceptable ideology for the new social forces whose interests they attempted to champion. *Trabalhismo*, they termed it, a mixture of social welfarism, working-class political activism, and economic nationalism. For some it was a new way of looking at the world. It laid down guidelines for them to judge what was right and what was wrong with their society, which social groups they should ally themselves with in their push for the "new Brazil," and who and what they should fight. Both Vargas and Goulart then attempted to give the new mood some institutional base by respectively forming and championing the Brazilian Labor party (PTB). As for the military, they choose to pull off their coups in 1930, 1945, 1954, and 1955 and, finally, in 1964, to take over the political system for themselves.

Since before 1930 much of Brazil had been in agony. On the one hand, the expectations of the newly mobilized groups—the working masses in the cities, and the new economic middle, business, and industrial classes—had far outstripped any possibility of their being realized. On the other hand, the traditional world of the landlords and the rural politicians was in jeopardy of suffering an imminent collapse. Some wanted; others would not give. The country had split into conflicting camps. The nation's political institutions were neither sufficiently modern nor sufficiently developed to manage the tension. An amoral society resulted.

When a country undergoes rapid environmental or value change, such as occurs during periods of rapid economic development and urbanization, a group's access to the opportunities it does not have but desires, or its retention of those it possesses but which it fears are under attack, is affected by the values of and relative power held by other groups in the society. When peasants want "modernizing" opportunities, for example, they must seek concessions from upper-status groups in the society—rural landlords, traditional politicians, and so forth. Likewise, when the privileges of established upper-status groups are under attack, it is the relative power and influence of those who wish to retain vis-à-vis those who wish to get—or give—that frequently decides the issue. Nearly always it is the political system and its institutions that are called on to find solutions to conflict with which the various mobilized groups can live in "pacific tension," or, failing that, can be forced to abide by through coercion or the threat of its application. Sometimes existing institutions can handle the tension. Sometimes they cannot.

Interestingly, nearly all newly mobilized groups thrusting upward from the lower end of the social pyramid have had to struggle for their gains. Not only do we have the case of the peasants, therefore, but of many other groups as well. The history of trade union movements throughout the world—even in the United States—attests to similar conclusions. The Brazilian labor movement (PTB) is particularly illustrative. Thus whatever success such a group may attain is attributable not only to its intensive search for opportunities but also to its capability for staging a convincing collective movement against the social and economic gatekeepers who have historically guarded the opportunity doors.

Upper-status groups, with a few exceptions, do not resist these movements out of ideological commitment so much as they resist them out of economic and social interest. As such, their resistance continues only as long as the social and economic costs of doing so do not exceed the benefits that may derive from attempting to preserve, by coercive force, the old opportunity order. Traditional upper strata are always *prone* to resist social and political change because such change does, in fact, entail at least a partial restructuring of the distribution of wealth, political power, and social prestige. Those wedded to the old order tend to believe, with some justification, in a more or less inverse relationship between their own opportunities and those of the newly aspiring groups. They frequently believe that any increase in opportunity for the lower classes must entail a reduction in their own. Accordingly, it is a loss or a fear of an imminent loss of opportunities long enjoyed that sets the stage for upper-class solidarity and "counter" collective action. A group or community—or nation, for that matter—never experiences more solidarity than when its cherished values are under physical attack and the apparent perpetrators are readily identifiable. Therefore, it is not surprising, in the face of a threat to traditionally held opportunities, that traditional rivals will resolve their traditional differences and join together for a struggle against the common enemy—the new social forces—that environmental and value change has mobilized and unleashed.

In the wake of rapid environmental change nearly all groups and classes suffer some structural and psychological binds or "gaps." But they do so for differing reasons. Among the lower classes the binds derive from expectations rising much faster than opportunities. But among the upper strata the binds primarily occur because traditional or newly won opportunities are decreasing or are under attack. In this case the "zero-sum game" mentality is not totally divorced from reality. If the peasants win land the traditional lords will have less. If the blue-collar workers win increased wage and fringe benefits, entrepreneurs may realize less profit. If too many aspiring members of the lower strata invade the economic middle class, the job security of those who have already "arrived" will be threatened. Regardless of the nature of the objective conditions, if one believes that his opportunities are falling or may imminently do so, and if he pinpoints the cause as deriving from a new social force, then he will frequently run to the bosom of his "natural friends." Accordingly, the stage is set for a possible counter collective action. Thus we are alerted as to why the feelings for Goulart among some groups underwent such drastic change over time. With these general observations in mind, we now proceed to an examination of the Brazilian data vis-à-vis some specific topical areas considered in Part II.

ON THE CAUSES OF CHARISMATIC AND MILITARY AUTHORITY IN BRAZIL

We have argued that the social preconditions for the rise of either charismatic or military authority are essentially the same, and that one of the key variables is a decline in the legitimacy of old traditional patterns of authority accompanied by a mobilization of people for new commitments, new values, and new expectations. The general observations in the preceding paragraphs illustrate the relationship of these factors to the failure of rational-legal authority to develop. The essential points are driven home more forcefully, however, by a specific consideration of three mobilized groups—the economic middle class, blue-collar workers, and the military—which played key roles in the processes of change that Brazil was experiencing. If we add to this a discussion of Goulart's leadership style, the picture that illustrates the rise of charismatic leaders and the occurrence of military coups should be fairly complete.

Economic Middle Class

From 1930 onward there had been an accelerated growth of Brazil's "middle segments" (a term used in the literature to account for the lack of class identification among Latin America's economic middle class). Brazil's cities had grown considerably, as had its manufacturing, professional, and white-collar service base. The acceleration was substantial because it was motivated by economic crisis. The enormous success of the country's semicolonial economy—exporting raw materials and importing manufactured goods—had precluded, up to 1930, the possibility of giving indigenous industry much consideration. It was not until the old economic formula entered bankruptcy during the Great Depression that Brazilians were forced to turn to other economic options. In the twentieth century there is only one alternative that most people consider acceptable—industrialization—and once Brazilians became convinced that there was no profit in the past they quickly lent their energies to the creation of a new economic order. Accordingly, it was within the context of "forced industrialization" that the new economic middle class really grew.

In many ways Brazil was remarkably successful in its new economic enterprise, sufficiently so, at least, to now be exporting heavy machine lathes and other manufactured items to none other than the United States of America. Obviously, one of the necessary and inevitable by-products of this adventure was the creation of new types of occupations for Brazilians of all strata. The economic middle class incorporated new kinds of professionals, excutives, managers, salesmen, and white-collar workers. Each of these categories rapidly grew in numbers; and those who entered them did so with increasing skills, competence, and education. More so than ever before, the middlers were equipped to relate to a world of technological change. We infer that their expectations for personal freedoms and material benefits rose. In addition, one gets the feeling that the economic middle class also believed it had every right

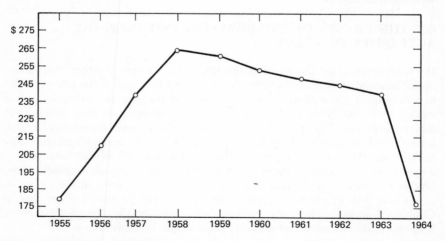

Figure 7. Change in Real Per-Capita GNP (in constant dollar equivalents), 1955 to 1964.
Arthur S. Banks, *Cross-Polity Time-Series Data,* p. 266; and International Monetary Fund, *International Financial Statistics,* January, 1965, p. 33, and April 1961, p. 29.

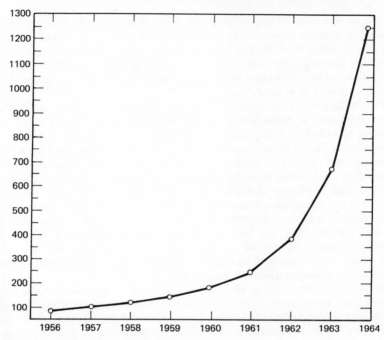

Figure 8. Cost of living price index, 1957 to 1963.
International Monetary Fund, *International Financial Statistics, Supplement to the 1971 Issues,* p. 25; and *Supplement to the 1967/68 Issues,* p. 42.

to demand, as do its counterparts in the more industrialized nations, that progress and development must continue indefinitely.

When we consider the area of compensating opportunities, however, we do *not* see a relatively constant and progressive rise but, instead, a rise *with a subsequent, and serious, deterioration.* The new economic middle class, we infer from the structural evidence, had reason to experience rising expectations, but its opportunities came in a curvilinear fashion. In the early years of post-depression industrialization and economic expansion, opportunity (particularly of the economic variety) rose because there was a heavy demand for all kinds of qualified administrative, managerial, professional, and white-collar service manpower. With slight ups and downs this continued for 25 years or more. But when the Kubitschek economic-development model gave out shortly after 1960, the cities began to join the countryside in a common dilemma—stagnation. Consumer demand tapered off, occasioned not only by inflation but by the fact that perhaps 50 percent of all Brazilians were still caught in the trap of a traditional rural social and economic setting. The entrenched politicians in the countryside had failed to realize that they could not have it both ways—traditional status and privileges on the one hand and a modernizing urban economy on the other. There came a time, therefore, when the rate of economic growth in the cities began to drop off rather sharply while inflation increased in like but opposite manner. The economic middle class, we are led to conclude, was among the first to feel the bind-producing effects. Figures 7 and 8 demonstrate the dramatic dilemma. The resulting anxieties were reflected in intense political behavior articulated by a search for political solutions. Janio Quadros, they felt, would save them.

The crisis came to a head when Janio Quadros "defected," instituting his tough economic austerity program in order, he hoped, to reduce the rate of inflation inherited from the Kubitschek era. Somehow inflation and poor money management had to be at the root of the country's economic problems. At least a review team from the International Monetary Fund implied as much. But, as usually occurs when classical economics are applied to unclassical situations, the resulting economic slowdown and unemployment—without, by the way, much control of inflation—brought cries of alarm from those whose material opportunities and benefits were clearly taking a tumble. Thus, during the period 1930 to 1961, we see relative opportunities (primarily referenced by economic indicators) of the "middle segments" increasing and then falling. The increase was gradual and fairly consistent until about 1960. Thereafter middle-class opportunities took a dramatic fall.

With expectations rising, and opportunities to realize them rising but then falling, the economic middle class was certainly entering "gap" conditions. What meaning would those involved attribute to these conditions? Would the "middlers" want to throw out the whole political system and start over with a charismatic leader or military rulers? Tensions were increasing. The political arrangements were not producing solutions, only aggravations.

Whatever meaning the present had in an objective sense, doubtless it was influenced by perceptions of future trends that the economic middle class could relate to their opportunity position. Perceptions of a good opportunity future would, no doubt, occasion a wait-and-see attitude, signifying a kind of continued faith in Brazil's political system. Perceptions of continued deterioration in their opportunity position would probably add a psychological bind to the already existing unfavorable objective conditions, occasioning a withdrawal of political faith, and thereby producing a readiness for a charismatic leader or, failing success there, a coup by sympathetic military officers who would "clean up the mess."

The structural evidence seems to justify an interpretation of an eventual deterioration in future opportunity perceptions, although the exact phasing of the shifts were not necessarily synchronized with any real objective conditions. But there are a number of indicators from which to infer an oscillating perception that probably exacerbated a sensitivity to the felt gaps and binds of the present. The probable nature of these perceptions, therefore, will help explain the middle segments' fluctuating warmth for the presence of Goulart, and eventually for the Brazilian political system. Let us look at some of the indicators that logically infer the perceptual trends.

In 1961 significant numbers (but certainly not all) of Brazil's economic middle class opted to encourage the military to abide by constitutional provisions for the presidential succession of Goulart. Why? The middlers had never held the constitution inviolate. After all, they had, from time to time, supported Vargas in his early quasi-fascist stages. They had also supported earlier military interventions. One is led to believe, therefore, that they supported the succession of Goulart out of the conviction that some kind of change was needed if they were ever to be relieved of their economic plight—and the dramatic Goulart, who had reform ideas and a personal flair, was more impressive than the indecisive military that seemed to have neither.

Goulart had let it be known that he did have ideas for change in mind. In addition, Dantas and Furtado, representatives of the new technocratic elite and potential Goulart collaborators, had argued all along that the standard economic austerity programs demanded by the International Monetary Fund and adopted by Quadros (and which had weighed so heavily on the economic middle class) were not the way to handle economic problems in a developing country like Brazil. These arguments could not help but please the "political center," some of which was composed of non-Lacerda affiliated economic middle groups.

The question of removing "structural blocks," also in the kit of things for the new economic technicians to do, may have provoked an ambiguous response. But if some members of the middle class were not behind a "block-removal" program, at least they were in favor of a much more mild austerity plan than the IMF had in mind. And Goulart was in agreement with that. Thus, in their own way, many middlers let the military know that they favored Goulart's taking office. It is logical to assume, therefore, that while they may have feared Goulart's "dictatorial tendencies," they also anticipated that their president-to-be would do some economic problem-solving—and fairly soon.

What was the nature of this perceptual plight? During the incredible economic expansion of the Kubitschek era, the middle class' perception of future opportunity availabilities undoubtedly rose. This class was prospering as, perhaps, never before. Kubitschek promised that there would be more of the same. The evidence suggests that the economic middle class, at least up until 1960, largely agreed with his economic predictions.

But with Quadros and his frustrating austerity programs, the disclosures of governmental corruption, the laying off of white-collar employees, the unceasing exposure of critical conditions in the economy, which Kubitschek had kept from public view until virtually the moment of collapse, and the official assertions that a lot of belt tightening would be necessary for the foreseeable future, one would expect that the perceptions of the fulfillment of future economic dreams would take a dramatic tumble. Whether or not they did, we can, of course, now only conjecture from logical and secondary empirical evidence. But if the laments and denunciations of the invective Lacerda meant anything—and Brazilians are inclined to say that in those days they did—we might even conclude that the effect of Quadros on Brazil's middle class bordered on shock.

The military probably aggravated the problem when it vetoed Goulart's claim to the presidency after Quadros' sudden resignation. The China-touring vice-president had made a number of statements that would have given the middle class some hope—structural reforms and rejection of the IMF austerity measures were only two of the more dramatic ones. In many ways Goulart did not seem to be all that much better than the quixotic Quadros whom he was attempting to succeed. But, at least, in the minds of many he was "less worse." It was this combination of events, along with the continuing expectations-opportunity structural binds, that led to a mild pro-Goulart position.

In any event, the military, very sympathetic to middle-class interests, perhaps because of its own alleged middle-class origins, eventually fabricated a way for Goulart to assume the presidency by virtue of the fact that it could not agree on a way to keep him out. Enter the parliamentary regime that made Goulart a figurehead.

Goulart had made, as we have noted, a number of "reform statements" that were pleasing to the economic middle class. There was some hope, with Jango as president and the constitutional crisis settled, that the economic situation would improve. Goulart had said he could and would improve it. He had revealed what he would do. And he was believed—at least with some guarded skepticism. The middle class mildly supported his constitutional claims if for no other reason than because they liked what he said about the IMF. Moreover, the military recanted and allowed him to assume a watered-down presidency. However, regardless of Goulart's potential or desire to fulfill these economic expectations—even under the most favorable circumstances—the military's decision to institute a ceremonial figurehead presidency in a new parliamentary system of government precluded his doing anything. Since the president was rendered powerless, how could he be held accountable?

Economic conditions continued to deteriorate. Many economic middlers were more prone to hold the military rather than Goulart accountable for them. Besides, within only six months of having taken office, "military accountability" was a theme that Goulart himself began to drag out for everyone to sample. The propaganda and the low public morale—fueled or exacerbated by the economic crisis that worsened daily—played well into the president's hands. As he wanted presidential powers restored, he was quite unwilling to do anything to take the military off the hook. The more heat the better. In the interim about the only gain for the middle class was the government's creation of thousands of positions in its federal bureaucracy. On balance, therefore, the actual economic opportunity position of the middle class seemed to worsen steadily. It appeared that the deterioration would continue as long as governmental changes were not forthcoming. Yet they could not take place because the military had placed the government in a state of parliamentary limbo. Thus we can infer that the economic middle class, suffering in the economic present and seeing that the military had tied Goulart's hands, took a continued downward spin in terms of how they perceived their future.

Obviously the actual expectations-opportunity structural bind was as serious, if not more so, as before. But the psychological impact had been greatly exacerbated by a doubtless continuing perception of a bleak future. Hence, the disrupting and anxiety-producing effects continued. We would expect the appearance of some intensifying problem-solving collective behavior—social forces mobilized for action. A greater need for leaders with charisma? Or authoritarian solutions? We shall see.

When Goulart made his move to cashier the parliamentary system and gain full presidential powers, the economic middle class overwhelmingly supported his efforts. Why? It seems the middlers were convinced that such a move would facilitate a resolution of their economic problems. After all, Goulart himself had promised as much. Thus as the results of Jango's overwhelming victory became known, many middle classers no doubt considered their future economic prospects to have brightened considerably. But what did Goulart do? He abandoned the very plan (the Dantas-Furtado formulas) that might well have solidified support from the political center. He then took an abrupt ride with his brother-in-law, Brizola, on an overnight express to the negative left. The economic middle class could see no justice in this. In spite of full presidential powers, Goulart was doing nothing about inflation, nothing about the stagnating economy and, therefore, nothing about middle-class employment security or deteriorating purchasing power. With such an unexpected turn of events, what could the future possibly hold? Again we see the middle segments in a discouraging position, one probably associated with another frustrating downswing in the perceptions of their future lot. Given the conditions with which the downward shift was associated, we would predict that the stage was once again set for probable middle-class collective action. But this time, because of the president's "betrayal," the action would of necessity be anti-Goulart in its thrust. Where else to turn but to the military, or to some alternative leader with lasting charisma?

Shortly, civilian groups began to link up with dissident officers and to conspire against their president. Finally, 500,000 middleclass men and women took to the streets in a "March of the Family with God for Freedom"—a kind of anti-Goulart manifesto written with one's feet. There was no hiding the fact that the march met with the overwhelming approval of conservative civilian groups as well as many officers in Brazil's alarmed military. Lacerda had won his day. An invective man all along, these events played into his hand and gave him a ready-made audience. He was not long in exploiting it.

The result. An important segment of Brazilian society was removed from Goulart's coalition of implicit support. Subsequently, it was available for coalition-building with other anti-Goulart forces.

Urban Working Classes

While the middle class took a vacillating position toward Goulart, the urban working classes, at least until near the military coup of 1964, considered him to be something of a constant liberator. The urban workers certainly were not devoid of frustrating structural and psychological binds or gaps. The evidence obviously is to the contrary. Their binds were serious. This is one reason why they were so influenced by Goulart's leadership style. The president was fighting, or at least he conveyed the convincing appearance of fighting, for their opportunities—wage increases to keep ahead of inflation, better working conditions to meet new aspirations; and freedom to strike; if necessary, to force their demands. Goulart was labor's man; labor thought it knew it.

The president's problem with labor was that he was only marginally successful in serving its interests. He promised; but he had trouble delivering. The working man's wage increases were always at least six months behind rising prices. Consequently, labor was nearly always in a state of agitation. Goulart did not necessarily dislike this state, since it offered him potential political gain. But, after all, he could only take advantage of the agitation as long as there was a belief that he could do something about the underlying conditions that caused it. While succeeding, by seemingly purposeful design, in alienating other groups in the society, Goulart could never really deliver even to his own.

Vargas had swung in the same direction back in the 1940's when he attempted to shift the social basis of his political support from urban middle classes and rural political machines to the new urban working masses. Thwarted once by a military coup, Brazil's Mr. Politician from Rio Grande do Sul had nevertheless moved toward a completion of his shift by the time he returned to the presidency in the elections of 1950. The urban masses were frustrated. They were mobilized, searching, unhappy, and yet expectant. They were available for organization by leaders with charisma. Vargas, and then Goulart, were happy to oblige.

In terms of social mobilization and the expectations-opportunity gaps that tend to accompany it, we see the following salient events taking place: the urban working masses were not only increasing in size as the industrial economy expanded but they were becoming more educated, more experienced, and more exposed to and involved in a world of modernizing change. Second generation migrants, born and reared in a world of dramatic urban change, were reaching the job market. Expectations, in relative terms, we argue were therefore probably increasing rapidly.

As for opportunities, the initial post-1930 years had witnessed many job opportunities going begging. Virtually any skilled worker could obtain employment. And while the salaries and wages were low, they were never as low as those in the countryside. Indeed, relatively speaking, even laborers were better off in the city. It was not too surprising, therefore, that the urban-based labor pool was not long in swelling as country cousins migrated to Brazil's cities to see for themselves if what they had heard from others was indeed true. However, industry, in spite of its rapid growth, could not absorb so much available manpower. Unemployment rose. Moreover, there were other opportunity problems. The main one appeared to be the incredible rate of inflation under Kubitschek and Goulart. Eventually the level of per-capita opportunity for workers really took a spin downward. The impact seems to have been somewhat more serious for them than it had been for the economic middle class, businessmen, and industrialists. The urban workers were the first to suffer; they also suffered the most.

The nature of hopes and perceptions about the future is difficult to infer for the urban workers. One sees a number of ambiguous gyrations occurring.

For one thing, Goulart had made a lot of promises, but he was only partially able to deliver on them. The nagging problem of inflation always made the present seem bleak and the future probably as bad if not even more dismal. If anything for many workers Goulart's unfulfilled promises and continuation of a dark personal financial situation accentuated the feeling of despair and frustration. Some workers were drawn into closer solidarity with their union-affiliated brethren and spent many long hours discussing their plight.

As could be expected, among the cohesive groups, collective action was not long in appearing. There were strikes of substantial proportions. Among these groups the rhetoric of both the communists and Brizola made substantial headway. Moreover, when Goulart called for the massive rallies, literally hundreds of thousands of urban workers responded. In the end, however, because of a lack of linkages with other, more powerful and well-placed groups in the society, and because Goulart's personal credibility was being rapidly spent, urban workers failed to respond to the defense of the radical reforms that their president had in mind. An additional critical factor was the coercive potential of the military. The workers simply were not prepared to test it. Had other circumstances prevailed, and had the workers been linked up with the middle class, mobilized peasants, or even modernizing officers in the military, they might have been able to pull off the "revolution" for which Goulart had prepared an ample stage. But the president's personal behavior, his opportunistic politics, and other complicating factors, conspired to make such an eventuality unlikely if not impossible. Goulart had fully alienated the other important groups in the society. They were unavailable for linkages with him. Having chosen to become the "legitimate" president of only one group of Brazilians, Goulart ended by being president of none.

Military Radicalization

Some militaries fight wars. Others occupy defense positions either at home or abroad. The military in Latin America, with rare exceptions, has done neither; it "guards constitutions." The Latin American officers, however, are frequently disunited about exactly what it is that they should guard. Witness the "hard-line" and "soft-line" factions in Brazil. Ordinarily, therefore, they cannot make and unmake guardianship decisions at the drop of a general's medal. As in the larger society, and particularly under conditions of rapid social and economic change, any given country has officers who are ideologically on the political left as well as on the political right. These extremes usually are not so great as in the larger society. But there is sufficient diversity to make political proselytizing among one's colleagues a necessary precoup enterprise.

There are probably some officers whose predisposition would always be to govern the country themselves—"scientifically"—regardless of the political winds. In Brazil these tended to be the "hardliners," fairly conservative in their political and social values. Such officers are probably among the first to begin any "restorationist" conspiratorial plots as, indeed, in Brazil they were. But, as we have seen, the early plotters must await the proper time to launch their conspiracy. It is necessary for them to swing powerful and influential colleagues over to their way of thinking; and it is very helpful if they have the support of strong social forces in the society at large—such as the middle class.

The probable success of a coup is increased when linkages are established throughout the various officer corps as well as with civilian groups who are already in a state of strong anti-government sentiment. One also desires to reduce to an acceptable level the risks of punishment in the event a coup attempt fails. Military solidarity and civilian linkages help to reduce those risks. Indeed, if there is anything that most officers abhor it is an internal war with their peers. One's military colleagues also possess the means of lethal force.

When the military intervenes in politics with a coup it nearly always does so when political instability is obvious, when corruption in governmental institutions is highly visible, and when an aggressive and, perhaps, violent "choosing of sides" is occurring among various civilian social forces. It it these conditions that sound the clarion of duty to the military. That duty becomes apparent very quickly if the processes of change and conflict in any way threaten military organization, discipline, or the relative status of the officers.

In Brazil individual officers participated in the social and political tensions of the period. And the military, as an organization, was threatened from time to time. Goulart rotated commands and pitted junior officers against their seniors. He resisted or refused pay hikes, dined with mutineers, and refused permission for officers to discipline their wayward men. Moreover, he spoke of a "people's army," an institution that, if created, would preempt the normal social and command functions of the regular military and, perhaps, totally replace it with a working-class militia. At least Kubitschek had provided the military with its needed equipment—aircraft carriers, submarines, super-jet aircraft, trucks; and plenty of practice ammunition. He had also watched after pay increases; and he had never talked about a people's militia. But Goulart was trying to run a tight military budget. Moreover, much of his rhetoric was implicitly anti-military. As a modern organization, the military ranked high in the area that we call value expectations. But consider what the events of the day were doing to its opportunities and perceptions of its future role.

The result produced structural and psychological binds among many of the officers and enlisted men. The situation, from their point of view, was catastrophic. To these frustrating conditions, to these binds, must be attributed the motivation of many of the officers to take an irreversible ani-Goulart stand. That similar gaps and binds existed in the society at large made the situation favorable for action. Thus the Brazilian military became ready for intervention because not only were substantial dislocations occurring in the larger society which the traditional political arrangements and their infant modern ones could not handle but also both these and the punitive politicians heavily and negatively impinged on it as an organization. Its independent survival was threatened. Thus, as we have argued, the search for answers to military coups in the modern day must first begin with societal variables, not military ones. The military reflected the problem of change. It even participated in it. But it did not create it.

While the military, along with other important groups and organizations, was suffering, the officers had advantages for recourse that other groups did not possess. They had linkages among themselves as well as with powerful civilian groups, and they had plenty of organizational, leadership, and material resources. Although other groups could be ultimately coerced into inaction, the military could not. Its resources were too powerful. It had ample materiel, communications, intelligence, and means to carry out physical violence. All it needed, therefore, were sufficient linkages among the plotters, both military and civilian, to make a coup possible and the risks of failure minimal. As we have seen, in due time the linkages were indeed created.

The only element lacking was a catalyst, or at least a series of accelerators. Goulart happily, although probably unknowingly, obliged (first by forcing the resignation of the naval minister who had called for disciplining the São Paulo mutineers, and second by staging his massive "people's rallies"). The final ingredient was also Goulart's final banquet as president. For all to see, Brazil's president smilingly embraced José Anselmo, the chief protagonist in the Rio naval mutiny. He then hurried, not voluntarily, into exile.

The critical threshold of coalition-building was reached when the military "swing man," Castello Branco, joined the conspiratorial cause. The swing man is usually "highly visible" and enjoys recognized prestige among his colleagues. Therefore, his joining provides all that is needed to bring numerous wavering or unsure officers into the conspiracy. This critical shift also establishes a margin of safety for the original plotters: the chances of a successful coup are enhanced; the possibility of an internal military war is reduced. Castello Branco played the swing-man role to consummate perfection. It was only natural, therefore, that he should become the new president. Convinced as he was that political decay and charismatic leadership in Brazil were both unredeemable and dangerous, his action allowed the military to attempt to control both.

Goulart's Leadership Style

Did Goulart *have* to behave the way he did? Were there no other, reasonably acceptable options open to him? To answer these questions affirmatively is to posit a reductionist absurdity. Goulart did not have infinite options, of course, but he did have some. To be sure, his universe was limited by his own world view—his political value system, if you please—which was highly sympathetic, rhetorically, at least, to the disfranchised and downtrodden. Hence, one limitation on the president was the political nature of groups from which he could derive ideologically agreeable political capital. Thus it is doubtful that Jango, under any realistic circumstances, could have become a servant of the traditional lords.

His options were limited in other ways. Decisions made earlier in his political career limited as well as expanded his facilities for manipulating the present. He had won friends but also had made many enemies. His strategy had to take this into consideration—including just who his friends and enemies were.

This, of course, was complicated by his family ties with Brizola, the prophet of the negative left.

Then there were exigencies that derived from the disastrous economic conditions inherited from Quadros. On the one hand, Goulart had promised economic recovery. Yet, on the other, the collapsed economy would require him to perform some politically unpopular surgery to revitalize it. Thus whereas the president received praise for his promises he was heavily excoriated for the eventual means he chose to realize them. Yet he picked the worst avenue of all —a suicidal drift to the negative left.

That was one thing Goulart did not have to do. At least so it would seem from the benefit of hindsight. He scuttled the one option that might have revitalized the economy without alienating the political center—the Dantas-Furtado plan for economic recovery and national self-determination. To be sure, Goulart would have incurred the contiuing enmity of the traditional elite—the lords and machine politicians in the rural areas—and also Brizola and the "negative left." But he probably would have retained the confidence of the political center and still would have been able to assuage the dismay among members of the PTB. Even more, by following the Dantas-Furtado plan, the president probably would not have established conditions favoring an anti-Goulart military conspiracy of such substantial proportions. The military was politically divided. Goulart united it—against him.

These difficulties illustrate many of the "traps," discussed in Part II, into which various leadership styles may fall, particularly under conditions of rapid social, economic, and political change when new social forces rise and political decay occurs. "Traditional" leadership generally fails in times of rapid modernizing change because it does not respond favorably, or adequately, to alterations in peoples' values, perceptions, desires, wants, or abilities. But we also know that rapid social and economic changes do not automatically bring with them a new "rational-legal" political order. Brazil is more typical than not on this dimension. For greater or lesser periods of time there is a kind of noninstitutionalized gap land in which great personalities rise and dramatic events occur. It is into this gap, into this climate of uncertainty and yet hope, that the charismatic leader steps. Vargas, then Goulart, played out such roles for the Brazilian laboring masses and the new social forces that they represented. When they chose to inflict "damage" on the military, however, they invited a coup.

A charismatic leader's power to command, as we have argued, lies as much in the eyes of his followers as in the programs that he pushes or in the personal attributes that he possesses. As such powerful personalities make many enemies, they must also be careful to maintain strong friends—particularly strong social forces—at their side. Yet time and events make this very difficult.

Of all the "dilemmas-for-charismatic-leaders" discussed in Part II, it was the "payoff" clause that finally uncoupled Goulart from the charisma that he had enjoyed among the one group whose interests he had chosen to champion. The PTB followers who once so ardently praised him failed to rally when he really needed them. Some may even have preferred military rule to Goulart's continued clumsy failure to put Brazil on its feet.

Charismatic leadership is important and sometimes decisive under conditions of rapid change. Some leaders have been successful in forging the kind of social, economic, and political order that in all likelihood would not have been made in their absence. Moreover, some leaders have successfully "routinized" their charisma and have institutionalized new leadership forms. Goulart, for many reasons—some related to personal inadequacies, some to ill-fated decisions, and still others to conditions beyond his control—failed to do either. In Brazil the military is still trying to compensate for that failure.

ON THE CONSEQUENCES OR EFFECTS OF MILITARY RULE IN BRAZIL

A curious thing is happening in Brazil. The rulers want economic development; they are getting it. And while the officers find that in the process they are obliged to abridge democracy—to muzzle some of their citizens—not too many Brazilians outside the intellectual, working, and peasant classes, and bosses in the old but now illegal political machines, seem to be overtly protesting. Indeed, some citizens even appear to be delighted with the relative calm and "progress with stability" the officers have brought to the country. If not pleased with military rule, others seem to have little present objection to the political arrangements. Why?

Part of the answer to Brazil's apparent stability lies in the military's power to coerce "stable behavior." Yet additional answers must also be sought in the way that the officers handled the chaos afflicting the nation. Propositions advanced in Part II suggest that those who support military rule would generally be those for whom the military—as it attacked the national chaos—effectively raised opportunity levels and, in the short run at least, reduced structural gaps and psychological binds. For them, the democracy of the past produced few economic satisfactions and many political frustrations, while the dictatorship of the present, on balance, provides more of what is wanted and afflicts with less that is not. The officers have answered these peoples' most immediate pressing need—economic security and social peace. In the short run those who are favorably affected are willing to exchange their political freedom for a secure, if not totally satisfying, economic and social pot. Life, for them, has been "stabilized."

Among those who are not so pleased—if not outright rebellious—our propositions would suggest that the opposite characteristics prevail. The military's development programs and political controls have increased their binds. There seem to be three general groups here: (1) those who deeply regret the loss of their political freedom and power—mainly students and intellectuals; (2) those who are upset with the loss of a combination of their economic status and political power—for instance, middle-class Brazilians swept out in the anti-corruption drives and old-style as well as new-style politicians whose losses include their political rights (when the ancient archenemies—Lacerda, Goulart, and Kubitschek—can meet together in a secluded retreat, as they did in 1969, to plot a political comeback, you know that things are fairly desperate); and (3) those who never really had much political power anyway but now are perpetually denied a satisfactory participation in their country's booming economy.

The latter group, being primarily peasants and laborers, has no particular reason to be pleased with—and many reasons to be resentful about—the commanding officers and their dictatorial rule. The military, by disbanding the unions, freezing wages, and outlawing peasant leagues, has denied both groups meaningful organizational status. The lower classes, therefore, have no effective means within the system to exercise organized pressure on the military's decision making in political and economic affairs. They have few if any advocates in high politico-military circles. They have suffered accordingly. In spite of their discontentment, however, most of them have been cowed and contained.

Because of the effective coercion only the truly revolutionary have become the urban guerrillas. Yet, in spite of their sensational behavior, as of late 1972 they seem to have had a fairly low level of effective power. The government continually rounds them up, killing a few in the process. Those who remain at large eventually retaliate with a political kidnapping, thereby acquiring leverage to bargain for the release of their imprisoned colleagues and other interested political detainees who prefer exile to prison. Then 50 to 100 Brazilians fly to exile in Mexico, Chile, or Algeria. Other acts of terrorism and counter-terrorism also prevail. The cycle, temporarily suppressed, grinds on. How long can it continue?

The indications now are that the military's surgical procedures will continue as long as substantial economic development in Brazil remains a reality and as long as there is no military "civil war" in which the soft-liners win out. How can this be? It is because, on the one hand, fortuitous economic circumstances encourage people favorably affected to maintain political and economic linkages with the government rather than with the revolutionaries or their friends. On the other hand, the dissident masses are successfully cowed because they have no powerful advocates among prestigeful groups or any effective collective power of their own.

These are nevertheless potentially precarious circumstances for the military because virtually any action that it takes runs the risk of negatively affecting the economic and social opportunities of the civilian groups that have supported it. In time, civilian support would, it would seem, tend to disappear as toes are stepped on. Moreover, the conflicting expectations of various groups in Brazilian society would seem to make it all the more likely that the military would run this risk fairly soon in its new political career.

For example, during the latter part of Goulart's rule the rate of inflation—a negative opportunity indicator for most groups or classes—was rising approximately 12 percent per *month*. Agricultural production had fallen, as had the country's industrial output. The Northeast was still an area deep in poverty.[4] Brazil's traditional foreign creditors were nervous and hedging. Foreign investors were reticent to commit funds. Bureaucratic corruption and graft were endemic. Money changed hands but there was little tangible product to show for it.

The military was expected to put a stop to all this decay and nonsense. But there were conflicting expectations: How should the officers do it? What should the eventual results be? While the landowners wanted Goulart out and his political rhetoric silenced, they nevertheless desired that the old economic system remain fairly intact. But the peasants, especially in the Northeast, wanted a program of land reform. The labor movement wanted to keep the gains it had made under previous presidents. But employers wanted labor's power curbed. The middle class wanted more social welfare programs for itself but fewer for labor. The military initially gave signs of wanting only to retain its traditional role as the "moderating influence" in Brazilian politics. The middle class agreed with this posture, wanting the resumption of constitutional forms of government as soon as possible, as likewise did the old traditional politicians who wanted the military to return to its barracks so that they could return to dominate the political and social system—but without having to deal with Goulart and his friends. But the military reneged, forsaking its moderating tradition and retaining the political system for itself. Then, for their part, the students and intellectuals wanted a totally new society. But the officers, now tired of both old politicians and students, would listen to neither. Finally, as if all this were not enough, there was the problem of migration from the Northeast to the prosperous South—and the unwillingness of the South to accept impoverished migrants. There was a desire to open up the frontier of the country—and a desire to live in Rio while somebody else did the "opening up."

The military leaders were therefore subjected to conflicting pressures when they decided to rectify their country's problems. A move in one direction would please some Brazilians but anger others. This is a dilemma of a serious kind for the military in Brazil, particularly if our propositions are correct, because the situation will tend to work against the military in the long run, not for it. Let us review the relevant propositions in direct reference to the Brazilian case.

1. As social mobilization has dipped down even to the level of the peasantry in Brazil, we have predicted that the social and political effect of military rule there will tend to be politically and socially "conservative." Social and political reforms, insofar as they entail a redistribution of income and power at the expense of the economic middle class or the military, will not be made, or if carried out, will be done only for "showcase" effect. Economic development, yes. Some structural reform, yes. But probably there will not be enough constructive change to reduce appreciably the gaps and opportunity binds among the mobilized lower classes. Also economic development will increase the rate of social mobilization and, therefore, the gaps and binds that those groups suffer.

2. In countries that Huntington has identified as "Praetorian" (which includes Brazil by virtue of the fact that the military and other groups there are always

raiding the political system for themselves) and in which social mobilization is high (again, characteristic of the Brazilian scene, as the evidence shows), we have predicted that the military will have little capability of fostering political development, although the officers may be highly successful in areas measured by aggregative economic indices. We say aggregative, because the distribution of the national economic pie will in no way be pushed toward equalitarian or "left-wing" ideals. Thus social mobilization will increase while political development does not, and expectations among the lower classes will consistently and increasingly outstrip opportunities for their satisfaction. The military has chosen sides in Brazil. But history, in the long run it would seem, does not favor them.

These propositions would seem also to be reinforced in Brazil by the apparent middle-class identification of much (but not all) of the officer corps, and the influence of the Escola Superior de Guerra on the development of a new military ideology that articulates security (anti-communism) and national development.[5]

We can "test" the validity of these propositions in the specific case of Brazil by cutting the analysis along lines of actual and perceived opportunities which the military has brought to various groups and classes in Brazilian society in the past seven years. If, in the wake of dramatic economic expansion, the relative opportunity position, particularly the economic and political opportunity position, of the lower classes has worsened or not improved, these predictions will be supported. If, on the other hand, the economic and political opportunity situation among lower classes is improving relatively, the propositions are negated and will have to be rethought. Let us analyze the events.

Economic Opportunities

Soon after the military took control of the government in 1964, and in its attempt to brake inflation, it applied a gradual austerity-stabilization program. Naturally unpopular among wage earners (because it tended to freeze wages perpetually behind price increases), the deflationary policies nevertheless succeeded in their attack on inflation. Moreover, they did so *without* causing widespread economic dislocations. From a projected annual rate of 144 percent (for the last year of Goulart's regime had he completed it), the officers trimmed the inflationary rate first to 80 percent and then, successively, to 45 and 30 percent, and even lower. In 1968 it was down to 23 percent.[6] By 1970 the rate dropped even lower, to approximately 19 percent. In comparison with United States standards this rate still appears to be very bad. By Brazilian experience it is phenomenally good.

In early 1967 the government instituted a program of currency reform. By lopping three zeros off the old currency issues, it made the 1000 Cruzeiro note worth one *Cruzeiro Novo*, or "new Cruzeiro."[7] Also it devalued the national currency by 23.2 percent to bring it more in line with its true relative value in the international money markets. Since 1967 the government has devalued the

Cruzeiro Novo several times, but on each occasion by several percentage points less than the time before.

The series of currency adjustments have had a curious effect. On the one hand, they have made Brazil's exports more competitive in international trade. On the other, they have discouraged foreign imports. Exports have boomed, and domestic industry, receiving the equivalent of a "tariff," has enhanced its position in internal markets.[8] Residually, temporarily at least, these changes have benefited employers and wage earners alike—creating more profits and, if not higher wages, at least less unemployment. Benefits have also extended to the nation's gold and foreign-currency reserves (sometimes considered an indicator of good financial health) which, as of late 1970, jumped to $1020 million.[9]

To secure needed investment funds for increased economic expansion, the officers reformed the country's tax base and beefed up its collection and anti-evasion forces. The increase in tax revenue has been phenomenal. Moreover, most of the monies received seem to be finding more productive outlets than the shoe boxes or private safes of corrupt politicians or the salaries of self-serving bureaucrats. The general increase in revenue and a careful control of expenditures have allowed the officers to trim the federal budgetary deficit from 54 percent in 1963, when Goulart was in power, to 11 percent in 1966.[10] There still is some deficit spending going on. But the amount for 1970 was reported to be less than the equivalent of 200 million dollars in United States currency, or about one percent of the gross national product.[11]

The whole economy seems to have picked up. By mid-1966 two new steel mills had been built. This allowed the country to satisfy much of its domestic requirements and still have 13 percent of production for export.[12] To take care of the increasing demand for petroleum products, two new refineries were placed in production and an additional one expanded. Aided by the discovery and exploitation of new oil deposits in the poverty-stricken Northeast, total petroleum production jumped by nearly 50 percent.[13] Hydroelectric power stations (in conjunction with dams for vast irrigation projects) have been built, especially in the São Francisco Valley (in the Northeastern state of Bahia) and along the Paraná River in the South. The Urubupunga project alone will be the third largest hydroelectric complex in the world. It appears that, finally, São Paulo will have an adequate source of energy for its factories.[14]

The officers have given incentives (through regional development projects and tax breaks) for plant construction in the underdeveloped Northeast. Investors have been attracted. With the construction of asphalt and cement plants, and soft drink and electric refrigerator factories, the area now has the beginnings of an industrial economy. As most of the installations are "labor intensive" they can use the unskilled or semiskilled labor that abounds in the Northeast. The area also has many new roads that link it to the rest of the country.[15]

Naval construction has become an important industry along the east coast. Automobiles and trucks are produced in the South. And in all these categories production has risen sharply since Jango's fall. The country's Army Corps of

Engineers has extended and expanded the road network throughout the nation. And the United States has reinstated its military and economic aid. The officers have produced benefits. Many Brazilian consumers now have more than ever before.[16]

Rural Brazil, a sector of endemic traditionalism, has also received some modernizing improvements. The Ministry of Agriculture, embarking on an ambitious pilot development program, has established guaranteed minimum prices and agricultural credit in some regions, has provided for crop insurance, has set up experimentation and testing stations, and has subsidized the use of fertilizers and mechanized equipment. Then, in the South, the ministry has aided in the diversification of the agricultural base, attempting to eliminate thereby the great market and climatic uncertainties associated with the one-crop economy of the region. Agricultural production has measurably improved.[17]

Potentially more striking, at least, in terms of the possible opportunity impact on large numbers of Brazil's peasants and tenant farmers, is a series of government programs aimed at changing the land-tenure system. One of them —primarily a colonization effort—is designed to settle the sparsely populated areas of the country, notably those around Rodonia and Acre.[18] If the relatively infant pilot programs are successful, the government has said it will then expand their scope.

A second program focuses on the Northeast. To improve the agricultural conditions of the small farmer, the government is beginning to undertake a more equitable distribution of landholdings,[19] is making provisions for irrigation projects, and is consolidating small farms (minifundias) into machine-workable sizes.

The Northeast, where life is so tragic that reality reads like a surrealistic novel, has a very uncooperative climate. Cyclical droughts have pushed peasants, in starving desperation, to stage mass raids on food storage depots. Conversely, the interior has received heavy flooding. Yet, although all these natural calamities are damaging to peasant opportunities, they may not be the politically critical variables at all. Frustrated rising opportunity expectations, generated by the government's announced programs, may pose serious problems unless the military puts a lot of rural-reform action where its mouth is. On balance, the officers' efforts thus far in the rural areas are too small to have had much actual opportunity impact, for peasants, but they certainly have been large enough to generate a lot of opportunity expectations.

On balance, the middle class, with some exceptions, is enjoying an economic upswing. Blue-collar workers, however, are still chafing behind wage controls which, since 1961, have reduced their effective purchasing power by up to 40 percent. Yet, because of the expanding economy, more jobs are continually opening up. Peasants have received some economic promises but not much to set their teeth into. Thus the benefits of Brazil's economic expansion have been largely confined to the middle-class minority, while the majority remains stagnated in varying degrees of poverty. Even President Médici concedes: "The economy is going well, the people not so well."[20] Médici feels that there is now a need to entertain a better distribution of the country's economic benefits. Yet the military tends to justify the idea on paternalistic humanitarian grounds. Thus although they now require employers to open savings accounts for all their employees and to deposit in them a portion of the company's profits, they only allow workers to make withdrawals to buy a house, to pay medical bills, or to pursue other economic goals that the government considers worthwhile.

Political Opportunities

The political system has been more closed since the ouster of Goulart. However, except for certain groups, the rigidity has not been uncomfortable because economic benefits have more than compensated for the loss in political freedom. For others, especially the peasants, there is little change. They enjoy as many freedoms under dictatorship as they did previously under "democracy." It is the old political elite, intellectuals, students and, to some extent, reform-minded priests who have been hardest hit. Blue-collar workers have also now lost even the illusion of political participation.

Whereas the traditional politicians wielded great power in pre-Goulart days and the radical students exerted great influence during Goulart days, now they are virtually ignored if not repressed. Yet, on the other hand, the economic middle class, even though it has lost its direct influence in political decisions, has nevertheless seen its desire fulfilled for honest, efficient government (at least, more nearly so than under Goulart and Kubitschek). But since most Army officers consider themselves—and act as if they were—"middle class," the interests of this group have not suffered.

The lower-class urban workers, in spite of Goulart's rhetoric when he was president, actually had little political say. They participated in national decision making only when the opportunistic president felt it was to his advantage for them to do so. Yet they thought that they were politically important—and certainly at election time they were. The objective political opportunities to influence government decisions, however, are probably not now reduced as much as the workers' current icebox status would seem to indicate. There appears to be a large reduction, of course, because of the formal denial of political participation and the collapse of labor-union autonomy.

The problem with all this is that psychological binds among the workers have probably been aggravated. Under Goulart the workers had a leader who conveyed the image of being a champion of their cause. They had their unions. And they had their labor leaders. They suffered economically but they had some compensation in the illusion of political power from which they had hoped economic improvements would derive. Now they have neither the compensation nor the hope.

In some respects labor is therefore worse off, in some respects about the same, and in others perhaps a little better. The workers may be frustrated, full of anxieties, and wreathing with discontent. But such was life under Goulart also.

For the economic middle class, the capitalists, and the "new rich," the conditions that would give rise to structural and psychological binds have been reduced. As far as these groups are concerned, therefore, the linkage patterns consistently gravitate in favor of the military. The consequences of military rule have not, of course, favored the status-quo politicians, self-serving bureaucrats, leftist humanitarian priests and intellectuals, or radical students whose binds, on balance, have become worse. But, unless effective anti-government linkages are established, the officers will remain virtually invulnerable.

The coalition-building problem for the dissidents is acute. The old politicians have little love for leftist priests and students, so there is little possibility of an anti-government coalition's being made with them. Students, intellectuals, and priests have established linkages among themselves, but the absolute numbers of these groups alone are much too few to combat the overwhelming physical superiority of the military. The only revolutionary avenue open to left-leaning dissidents, therefore, is to establish linkages with a soft-line faction in the armed forces and then to make an alliance with urban workers and mobilized peasants. But although the military is still very fragmented in its political philosophy there is no indication that any linkages are possible there—yet. On the other side, the ambiguous position of the workers—aided by the government's effective control over all worker organizations—has pretty much removed labor from linkage consideration, at least, for the moment. The same is equally true for the peasantry.

The linkage or coalition-building dilemma is aptly seen in an anecdotal illustration (below) of one of the elements of political opportunity—absorption. Keep in mind that, in economic terms, the officers have been very "absorptive" for a great many Brazilians. Thus the contented have not demonstrated much collective worry about being governed by a military dictatorship. For other people, however (who for ideological or other reasons have refused to accept economic palliatives for the loss of their political freedom, or who have not participated in the economic benefits that the officers have showered on others), it is another story indeed.

Military Response: Coercion, Absorption and Political Development

During the first few years of military rule there was much citizen satisfaction with the way that the officers "cleaned up" Brazil's political mess. Stories, like the following, were told approvingly: just after the revolution, an influential army officer went to visit one of the national congressmen well noted for his ability to accumulate money and property. The congressman, anxious to make a good impression with the new rulers, showed the officer around his house pointing out the "picture I got from so-and-so for doing this" and the "suits I got from so-and-so for this" and the "forty pairs of shoes I got from someone else for doing this." As he went from room to room the officer watched in reserved silence. Finally, when it came time for the man to leave, the congressman showed his visitor to the door and said: "If there is anything you want, let me know and I'll do it for you! After all, it's easy for me—I'm a congressman." The officer quickly replied, "You mean you were."

Military rule implied an honest and efficient rule; this delighted many Brazilians who had not shared in the fruits of corruption. For virtually the same reason many supported the institutional reforms that the officers introduced into the political system. In an interview in mid-1967, Congressman Rafael de Almeida Magalhães, an ARENA representative from Guanabara, expressed the following views about the old and new political structures.

"Civilian authorities refused to experiment with a two-party system. Look, it's obvious that this [two party] system, even though imposed by decree, allows for better representative functions. . . . Two strong, well-organized parties will have much greater influence than pulverized currents split into diverse groups. . . . And even if the two present parties are artificial, so were the previous ones, which were controlled by dominant personalities who manipulated them merely to satisfy their personal ambitions. There is no domination of military power over civil power. What exists is an attitude of flight in the face of new realities. . . . The politicians can lead the process [toward a new Brazil] *if* they destroy their old preconceptions and adopt a new frame of mind. This is a time for greatness, imagination, and public spirit. The responsibilities are already defined. It is necessary that all of us have a vision of what must be done. The new Brazil needs a new kind of political behavior."[21]

Such talk was welcome for a while. But as the economic situation improved and the threat of communist takeover grew faint, some sectors of the population, in spite of their early approval, began to grumble about the officers' authoritarian rule. Some of the more extreme leftists, their programs ignored by the government, their access to political decision making denied, and their participation in the expanding economic benefits only marginal, began to set off bombs in public buildings. When the next set of street demonstrators came along, the police—unable or unwilling to distinguish among moderate, radical, and extremist activists—responded with indiscriminate repression. In subsequent encounters the demonstrators returned the complement. The cycle of action and reaction proceeded along its counter-productive way. By December 1968 (when the hard-liners pulled off their "coup") torture was beginning to play a role in police interrogations. Thus when the stroke suffered by Costa e Silva and the kidnapping of the American Ambassador occurred within a few days of each other, restraints on interrogations of "subversives" were lifted with abandon.

Since 1968, interrogation with torture is believed to have become widespread and to have been indiscriminately applied. Yet it is these methods—whether true in fact or simply believed—and the images they convoke—that have produced the most difficult problems for the officers, not the isolated acts of terrorism. Indiscriminate repression has created a backlash from a growing but still small number of previously moderate civilians. It has encouraged the enmity of a growing number of Catholic prelates. And it has sparked international protests from countries of all political persuasions.

The most serious consequence of governmental repression of moderates is that it radicalizes them. An illustrative example was voiced by a minor member of Brazil's opposition MDB party after the police had interrogated him regarding his relations—erroneously alleged, as it turned out—with political extremists. Leaving the custody of the officers with a disfigured hand (from having his fingernails pulled out and the palm burned with cigarettes) he announced: "If I had known where to find a terrorist group I would have joined immediately."[22]

The mounting campaign against liberal and moderate priests has also dragged the Catholic Church as an institution in the political arena.[23] Most of Brazil's 245 bishops signed a petition demanding that the government "investigate the problem of torture of political prisoners in depth." And Pope Paul found the evidence impressive enough to make what he described a "duty-bound intervention" in behalf of political prisoners.[24] Some elements in the Catholic Church, therefore, have begun to challenge the government. If present events continue, the stage could be set for an open confrontation of two very powerful influences in Brazilian life: the church and the army. The church, goaded by the army, may provide the linkages that thus far have eluded the radical political left wing.

It would seem that here the officers have made a tactical error. Until 1968 they had managed the structural and psychological binds (which the civilian population had inherited from Goulart's days) quite well. True, some Brazilians suffered. Some suffered greatly. Yet in spite of the cyclical ups and downs and the increasingly harsh acts perpetrated against some of Brazil's best-educated and most prominent citizens, control was easily maintained. Among the dissidents there never were sufficient anti-government linkages to pose any serious threat to the prevailing political order. But much has changed in Brazil since the "happy" stable days of 1966 and 1967. The officers are as much at fault as any. Their aggressive and counter-productive social-control measures have fostered a wave of antagonism that they may not be able to ride out.

At first, the officers applied coercion selectivity, mainly to those whom everyone felt was guilty of doing at least *something* wrong anyway. Later, as the government turned to more repressive measures to suppress nominal dissent, the men in the field went totally overboard with their "interrogations," especially of students and left-wing clergy. Students have parents—mostly middle-class parents. They suffer the pains of their children. They are capable of focusing on the source of that pain. Moreover, the use of torture against moderates, Catholic clergy, or even students radicals, for that matter, may produce the initial solid elite linkages that are needed to direct large-scale resistance. If any kind of economic recession occurs that severely damages the opportunity position of workers and the middle class, or if the officers' linkages with the United States are ever cut, then it would seem that the present regime will be in very serious trouble.

WHO SHALL OWN THE NEW BRAZIL?

The survival of the military dictatorship in Brazil depends on its ability to manage structural and psychological binds among large, important segments of the society and to successfully coerce into political inactivity anything left over. In a modernizing and rapidly changing country, however, "military fascism" suffers many of the dilemmas of contemporary modernizing monarchs. Huntington calls one of these a "success vs. survival" dilemma.[25] Several analogies are worth drawing because they are so illustrative of the inherent long-range contradictions in these kinds of regimes. As with the monarchs, the economic success of military fascists is matched by the inability—unwillingness —of the officers to absorb the newly mobilized masses into full-fledged economic and political citizenship. Absorption means sharing. It means an expansion and an eventual distribution of political power and economic benefits.

In the final analysis, absorption also means the modernization and development of a complex political system capable of arbitrating demands among competing groups. It means that it must provide some way for all groups—at least nearly all of them—to have a responsible stake in their country's present affairs and reason for hope about their future position in it. All military dictators have had trouble with absorption. Frequently they just give up and turn the political system back to the civilians. But military fascists have had particular problems because the whole process of political development, from their perspective, is little more than an unwarranted encroachment on what they feel is "right" for the economic development of their country. Yet, insofar as the implementation of their rightness does produce successful and rapid economic development, it also contributes to the rise of new social forces that, if they remain "unabsorbed" for long, will try to push the officers out of a job.

As with modernizing monarchs, the economic success of military fascists, in the long run, does not augur for the stability or nonrevolution for which they had hoped. Nor does it augur for their own longevity. Time is not on their side. The great problem for the officers—given the pressures—is that their intransigence does place time on the side of counter-ideologies (for example, Communism), particularly if the officers bungle the economic development process and, after a period of increasing benefits, find that their country suddenly suffers a "J-curve" economic decline. Communism, as other socialist ideologies, thrive (as a counter-ideology) on the existence of political and economic "gaps" between expectations and opportunity. We have seen that, in the long run, political opportunity seems to be as sought after as economic opportunity. Military fascism may provide one kind, but it cannot provide the other unless, of course, it decides not to be what it obviously is—a single right-wing clique running the entire societal show.

For the moment, Brazil's officers seem to be safe enough even if the same cannot be said for some of their civilian subjects. In November 1970, for the first time in four years, popular nationwide balloting was allowed for congressional deputies. One should not be led to believe that the military would have permitted itself to be voted out of power under any circumstances. But the election results—insofar as they were honestly reported—are illuminating.

The ARENA party (the official government party) increased its former two-to-one majority (over the loyal MDB opposition party in the federal congress) to, at least, three-to-one. Moreover, of the 30 million ballots cast to choose 46 senators, 310 deputies, and 702 seats in state assemblies and municipal councils, only about a million were blank protests. Most of these turned up in the urban areas of Guanabara and Rio where civilian unrest has been endemic. But in Minas Gerais, out of 3.8 million registered voters, 900,000 stayed away from the polls despite a warning from the governor that those so doing would be fined 5 percent of their monthly salary.

Now we are brought back to some aspects of the "consequence" discussion in Part II. It seems apparent that Brazil currently approaches, in Samuel P. Huntington's terms, a "mass-praetorian" condition. The gap between social mobilization and political development is huge. All sectors of the society, from the old lords to the new peasants, have become mobilized and, at one time or another, have launched collective movements to push their interests. Huntington's theory holds that under these conditions the role that an intervening military takes is likely to be one that is politically conservative.

In Brazil this prediction tends to be born out. To be sure, the officers certainly have been economic activists, calling for—and implementing—much state intervention in the economy. But this has not obviated the fact that the political system which they head remains rigidly closed except to those who generally agree with the current order of things. Political development? In the final analysis the really tough politics are determined at the point of a United States made rifle, not through legitimate and powerful political institutions.

Eric Nordlinger's predictions (that officers simply act out their middle-class interests) also tends to strike home in the Brazilian case. If a military is politically revolutionary during early stages of modernization, it is because the oligarchs have kept it and its middle-class reference group out of the political arena at a time when they have become socially mobilized and desperately want in. But when social mobilization has dipped down into the social pyramid, the officers and their middle-class reference group (who now are "in") take on a politically conservative posture and, in essence, attempt to fabricate a new kind of "oligarchy of the middle class."

The Brazilian case tends to bear out both Huntington's and Nordlinger's generalizations. In the days of Vargas it was the military *tenentes* who were the radical revolutionaries. Thirty-five years later, when the Brazilian masses had become mobilized, the same officers took on a new stance. Now they hope to contain the new revolutionary breed.

A country already experiencing a substantial gap between the rise of new social forces and the development of integrating political institutions—one that has dipped deep into its social system—will probably find, therefore, that its military will not be highly disposed to wielding much pressure for modernizing political and social change. Economic development, perhaps, yes. But even this will be done primarily within the framework of the existing, or perhaps slightly modified, social order. Economic development is thought of more as legitimatizing what exists rather than as facilitating a change toward the "new world."

"When New York has become only a palid memory in the history of mankind," reads a caption beneath a photo of the new Brazilian federal capital, truly one of the great wonder-cities of the modern world, "Brasília will be the headquarters of the modern world." Only prophets are competent to predict the future. Even they have enough trouble. But politics tell us that for a country like Brazil it will take more than the dictatorial guidance of the military to make such a prophecy come true.

For those who wait, or can wait, the future never ceases to become the present in Brazil. But what if the structurally- and psychologically-bound dissidents—now mostly students, intellectuals, priests and workers—link up with an extracontinental socialist power? What happens if an economic depression shatters the aura of economic expectancy? What happens if the military ever turns the political system back to the politicians? Will Brazil be more politically developed than before? Will it be more secure and less amoral? And if not, will the amoral cycle simply repeat itself? The answers—or nonanswers— seem to hinge, in large part, on whether Brazil politically develops and politically modernizes. It will be interesting, and no doubt eventful, to see how the stewardship of the military continues to unfold.

PART IV

The Monarchy and the Officer Corps in Libya or How to Create a Nation but Lose a Throne

CHAPTER 8

The Making and Unmaking of Monarchs

"Some day," King Farouk of Egypt ominously predicted before he fell to the now legendary Colonel Nasser and his associates in 1952, "there will be only five Kings in the world—the King of England and the four in the deck of cards." The world is now one king closer to Farouk's forecast. In September 1969, 79-year-old King Idris of Libya fell, a victim, as Farouk, of forces that modernization unceremoniously unleashed.

If King Idris were appreciated for what he once was rather than condemned for what he had failed to become, no doubt he would continue to enjoy residency in his kingdom. "After all," declared one of the young military officers who had helped overthrow the Monarch, "you have to remember that Idris is the father of our country." He also was—on the presumably valid word of the King's grandfather—a direct descendant of the Prophet Mohammed. Legend notwithstanding, Idris, as his grandfather before him, certainly had been a widely recognized spiritual leader in Islam and an important tribal dignitary. In earlier years many of the King's followers had blessed him with a near-fanatical devotion. Now, in the twilight of his life, they raised little more than a shout of protest at his dethronement.

For many observers it was all so strange. Not only had Idris enjoyed a devotion reserved especially for leaders of the faithful, he had also accumulated impeccable credentials as a nationalist. In the 1930's, partly from exile in Egypt, he had spearheaded and helped sustain an impressive and lengthy resistance against his homeland's brutal Italian overlords. Subsequently, after World War II, he had done his best to patch up the mess laid down by Rommel and Montgomery as they seesawed across his native country with their tanks and cannons, land mines and firing squads.

So impressive were Idris' efforts, that, when independence finally came in 1951, he was the only logical choice for the nation's standard-bearer. His Middle East countrymen, under the watchful eye of Adrian Pelt of the United Nations, decided to make him a monarch and to call his domain the United Kingdom of Libya.

"In the name of God the beneficent, the merciful," they began in their constitutional preamble, "we, the representatives of the people from Cyrenaica, Tripolitania and the Fezzan, meeting by the will of God in the cities of Tripoli

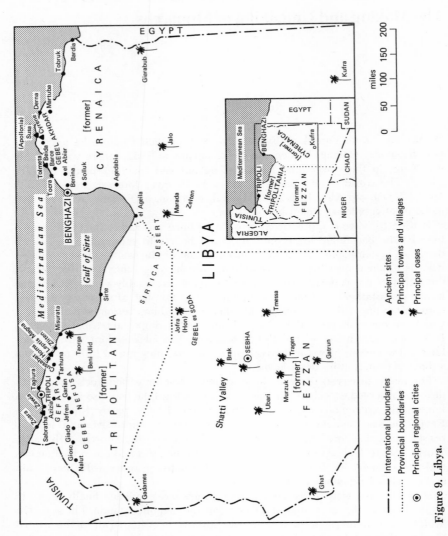

Figure 9. Libya.

and Benghazi in a National Constituent Assembly, have agreed and determined to form a union between us under the Crown of King Mohammed Idris al Mahdi al Sanusi to whom the nation has offered the Crown and who was declared constitutional King of Libya by this the National Constituent Assembly." Idris, Emir of Cyrenaica, head of the powerful Sanusi Moslem brotherhood founded by his grandfather,* descendent of Mohammed, and dedicated nationalist, accepted.

The new king had slightly more than a million subjects. Most of them were nomads or oasis dwellers—and illiterate. But he did count about 60,000, mostly in Tripoli and Benghazi, who could do more than sign their name; and there were three university graduates among them. His real estate was about two and one-half times the size of Texas. But 94 percent of it was desert; and the per capita income was barely $35.

At a ceremony at the Manar Palace, residence of a former Italian overlord, Idris nevertheless proudly declared: "We joyfully proclaim to the noble Libyan people that . . . our beloved country has, with the help of God, attained independence."[1]

PRE-INDEPENDENCE NATIONALISM

The birth of Libya as a nation, and the making of Idris into a monarch, derived less from any strong sense of nationhood before the 1951 Declaration of Independence was read than from external pressures imposed by foreigners. Indeed, "nationhood" required such pressures. Libyans had long cherished an almost fanatical regional and tribal identification. They did not give it up easily. Thus even though for decades the outside world had been calling Idris' subjects "Libyans," they nevertheless had always referred to themselves—and continued to do so—as Tripolitanians, Cyrenaicans, or Fezzanese, names deriving from the country's three prime regions.

Before the Italian invasions and eventual occupation of those regions (beginning in 1911 when Rome landed an invasionary force to drive out the Turks), the term "Libya" had never been applied to a well defined territory. It was not that the word had never been used. However, for Herodotus and the ancient Greeks it meant the entire North African area. For early Roman and Arab geographers, it referred to two entirely different regions. For others who had either settled in or run over Libya, including the Phoenicians, Greeks, Numi-

---

* The Sanusi brotherhood preached a return to the rituals and beliefs of early Islam as set forth in the Koran. The Order, stopping short of asceticism, was nevertheless noted for its "puritanical" way of life. From the original headquarters at Jaghbub (1855), it spread its gospel of Islamic reform by teaching and missionary work until its influence was felt from Morocco to Constantinople. As usual in the Arab world of those days, with spiritual authority went temporal power. Thus in the 1880's the Sanusi order, under the leadership of al Mahdi, the father of Idris and son of the original founder, held political influence over the nomadic tribes of the Libyan desert. Moreover, it counted among its followers Arabs from practically every prominent tribal or religious family in Cyrenaica and Tripolitania. Wherever Sanusi influence spread, security, justice, education, and trade tended to follow. For an authoritative treatment on this movement, see E. E. Evans-Pritchard, *The Sanusi of Cyrenaica* (Oxford: Oxford University Press, 1949).

dians, Romans, Christians, Barbarians, Vandals, Byzantines, Arabs, and Turks, the name referred to an ambiguously defined territory. And all this long before the Italian Fascists came around in the 1930's attempting to revitalize the old Roman grain bins and fabricating, as a consequence, a "fourth shore" for Italy out of Tripolitania and Cyrenaica.

It was no accident, therefore, that in preparation for independence in 1951 the writers of Libya's new national constitution felt obliged to mention specifically the three regions that had united to form the "federal kingdom." In fact, so strong were the regional identifications that the constitutional framers had to set up two capitals of equal importance—Tripoli in Tripolitania, and Benghazi in Cyrenaica. Between them, the government and the bureaucracy would alternately reside and function. The relatively underpopulated and austere region of the Fezzan, to its chagrin, did not merit such equalitarian attention, although it would have liked it.

It has been argued that in spite of regional differences, Libyans have long enjoyed a "sense" of nationhood, sharing, as they have, a common language and cultural background. Thus even though the ancient "national" North African Roman metropolises died (as the Empire itself waned in the fifth century) and the skillful irrigation systems—including dams and aqueducts, wells, cisterns, and terraces—fell into disuse following the invasions of the nomadic Arabs in the seventh and eleventh centuries, the spirit of national identity has lived on. It is true that the Arab ethnic element and language in the Libyan population today, the Islamic religion, and many social customs which trace from the Arab invasions have indeed given a certain pre-independence common ethnic and cultural flavor to Libya. But flavor is hardly sufficient to establish a strong Libyan national identity, particularly when those involved are less aware of it than are foreigners who think they see it. Thus the average Arab in the region nearly always called himself a Tripolitanian, a Cyrenaican, or a Fezzanese, not a Libyan. So we have concluded that the "roots of Libyan national identity," which some observers thought they saw within Libya itself, were, in fact, a product of foreign intervention in the domestic life of the respective regions. How did it all happen?

For one thing, in varying degrees, a great many Tripolitanians, Cyrenaicans, and Fezzanese shared a common revulsion toward the Italian invasions and occupation of their homeland (1911–1943). This was especially true in the 1930's when Mussolini and his Fascists sent Italian colonists to confiscate and resettle the best Arab lands and an Italian army to make sure that the conquest was permanent. In the process, the settlers and their military protectors deprived many of the tribes not only of their traditional leadership but sacred customs, religious practices, and opportunities for modernizing development as well. Although Arab resistance to the Italian occupation was most intense in Cyrenaica because of the greater strength of the well-organized Sanusi brotherhood there, residents in all the regions nevertheless made some cooperative efforts to rid their homeland of the Italian oppressors. Here was a case of "negative nationalism." Thus the common denominator for the three-region Arab cooperation in this instance was the Italians, not the concept of a new nation.

The heat and passion generated against the Italians were striking. Decreed to serve the interests of Italian settlers, stripped of their mosques and religious practices and deprived of their lands, the Arabs, especially in Cyrenaica, hotly resisted. The Italians retaliated brutally until they had snuffed out or rounded up the last resister. The conquest was eventually complete, and maps which showed all Libya to be Italian no longer lied. Yet, if the ownership of real estate changed hands, so did the mood of the Arabs. They emerged more united than ever before.

A mild antipathy toward foreigners, perhaps even an incipient negative nationalism, developed during the earlier 360-year Turkish occupation of Libya (1551–1911). But the Turks had generally left the Arabs alone, only stepping in from time to time to exact tribute. Besides, the Turkish occupiers and the Arabs both prayed to Allah and they both paid deference to the sacred Caliph who resided on Turkish soil. Thus the Italians were surprised to find that when they landed their invasionary force in 1911, the native Arab population, rather than join the Christian "liberators," sided with the Turks, fighting and resisting valiantly, but futilely, for nearly 20 years.

One important side effect of the long ordeal with the Italians was the emergence of new kinds of Libyan leaders. As their struggles transcended regional boundaries, so did their personalities and news of their exploits. They became the first "national" leaders the indigenous population had ever respected, if one excludes, of course, the Turkish Caliph and Sultan. And Idris, the king-to-be, the Cyrenaican nationalist and standard bearer of the powerful Sanusi brotherhood, became known to and appreciated by Libyans everywhere.

In addition to stimulating "negative" nationalism, the occupation of the homeland by a foreign power also precipitated—as has been the case in much of the contemporary Third World—a positive thrust toward national identity or consciousness. Thus, while the Italian occupation generated conditions conducive to an emergence of Arab leaders with a supraregional identification, it also enhanced communications and social and economic intercourse throughout the society and, in a sense, domesticated a lot of it. The Italians built roads, towns, and ports; and they set up small scale industries in Tripoli and Benghazi. The occupiers also extended cultivation in the better-watered northern regions and established numerous agricultural communities. All these improvements were, to be sure, primarily for the benefit of the Italian colonist. But the Arabs nevertheless shared in some of the residual benefits. They acquired new skills from employment in the growing small-scale industrial and service centers. Some Arabs obtained an Italian education, and still others learned how to deal directly with one another across tribal boundaries without having to defer to traditional tribal authority for guidance.

While many Arabs resisted changes which struck at their traditional privileges—even with fanatical zeal in some places—the evidence nevertheless shows that the Italians did induce permanent alterations in many Arab life styles. No doubt some Arab norms and values also changed. Thus there was much voluntary migration from oasis dwellings to towns as well as to Tripoli and Benghazi—not to seek oppression, but to participate in the modernizing benefits which the Italians had brought. Some of the nomadic Bedouins, particularly the younger ones, even took up urban residence and sought their fortune in a new and, for them, radically changed world. The whole process was terribly ambiguous for the Arabs. The Italians were brutal toward those who resisted the destruction of Arab traditional life. The Arabs loathed—and frequently resisted—that, especially in Cyrenaica, the homeland of Idris and his Sanusi brotherhood. But Arabs were also intrigued with what the Italians were doing.

In terms of modernizing abilities, the Italians helped to develop the very people who later, in alliance with traditional tribal leaders and the British and the French, would rise up against them. To be sure, there were Arabs, especially in Tripoli, who temporarily opted for "integration" with the Italians to avoid their brutality. Yet on balance, the occupation helped to break down the walls of traditional Arab regionalism. Communications, contacts, resistance movements, migrations with new experiences in towns and cities, education—all these tended, albeit in a weak way, to help establish the basis for a national identity larger than Tripolitania, Cyrenaica, and the Fezzan.

There was at least one additional way in which foreigners fostered nationhood. This time the entire collective world community holding membership in the newly formed United Nations was involved. Following World War II the allies had engaged in much discussion regarding what should be done with the colonies of the vanquished powers. Obviously the colonies would not be turned back to their former occupiers—although they might be occupied by new ones. Libya, however, was a special case. Toward the close of the war the Italians had undone Mussolini, hung his body in a street, and switched from a virtually defeated Axis power to an Allied servant. Thus, when the war ended, the "victorious" Italians argued that they had a right to reclaim their old colonies. Diplomats from other Allied countries were not at all impressed with this line of argument, however. They quickly agreed that Libya should not revert to colonial status, at least under an Italian brand. But what status should it acquire? Independence? There was a lot of discussion on that, too. Eventually a determination for independence was made, however, and the United Nations began to set up the machinery to make it all possible.

The Libyans, while desperately wanting independence, nevertheless seemed incapable of cooperating or agreeing on the form it should take. Each of the three regions wanted to go its own independent way. The bickering between the Fezzanese, Cyrenaicans, and Tripolitanians regarding the exact form an independent Libyan state should take was so bitter that finally, the United Nations told all of them to patch their regional differences or have no independence at all. Faced with such an unhappy alternative, the quarreling sides compromised their regional demands, authorized a kind of federal kingdom which allowed considerable autonomy to the three regions, set up the two capitals in Tripoli and Benghazi, and declared Idris to be their King.

IDRIS THE KING

Libyans conversant with events beyond their borders realized that in material things their country held strong candidacy for membership in the club of the world's five poorest. Not only were most Arab Libyans illiterate and pitiably poor, but all of them lacked training in organization, management, and industrial and agricultural enterprise. Yet, regardless of material and human limitations, there really was a striking mood of optimism in the country at the time of independence. Visions of progress and development seemed to permeate nearly every household. The sun had risen over a new Libya; and now it rested upon a "democratic, representative, constitutional monarchy." Most Libyans seemed to be happy for it.

In his maiden speech at the moment of national birth, the first Prime Minister captured much of the flavor of the new Libyan vision. The representatives of the people, he affirmed, intended to revamp the entire legal code and bring it more into harmony with model Egyptian laws. (Idris' 20-odd year exile in Farouk-land had acquainted him with Egypt's modernizing experience, and he liked it.) The central government also intended to vigorously push educational reforms, and, within a few years, bring a majority of Libyans to the world of books and newspapers. The authorities also promised that they would develop communications, industry, and services—all this despite the painful realization that there was very little developmental money around. In fact, in reflecting on the level of national wealth, the United Nations had affirmed that Libya had insufficient resources even to support a 1000 man standing army.

Literacy was a cardinal concern. Deliberations regarding it occupied much of the time of both national and provincial authorities. If Libyans were educated, these authorities said, the tendency for cohesion and solidarity among the three provinces would be enhanced. This in turn would serve to strengthen the national consciousness and prepare a foundation for the realization of Libya's destiny.

The euphoria vaporized more quickly than even the pessimists had expected. The United Kingdom of Libya was hardly two months old when an internal crisis demonstrated to everyone the union's actual fragility. In preparation for the February 1952 national elections, the Tripolitanian National Congress Party, a coalition of endemically discontented urban Arabs in Tripoli, established a slate of candidates to oppose the government. Earlier, the Party had challenged Idris and the Sanusi order on the idea of a federal constitution. For regional advantage, given that Tripolitania was the most populous and developed part of Libya, the Party had preferred a unitary arrangement by which it would have had more relative national power. Cyrenaica and the Fezzan were not ignorant on this issue, of course, and they resisted. The resulting debates were aggressive indeed and, in Tripoli, the tensions flamed into a riot. It was then that the United Nations had tendered its ultimatum. Yet Idris won on this issue, due in part to Tripoli's warring political factions on the one hand and the well-disciplined order among the Sanusi on the other.

The incumbents in the upcoming election had not forgotten this struggle. Being provisional office holders (their pre-independence appointment or election to office was to be either validated or negated in the first round of national elections), they were defensive, perhaps overly so. Some of them were also afraid of the National Congress Party.

Voting in the cities was by secret ballot. There, the Party logged heavy gains over incumbent office holders. But in the rural areas the exercise, as the law provided, was handled by the "Registering Officer." The officers did not observe voting secrecy and, according to National Congress Party officials, placed considerable pressure on the tribes to "vote right." Whether for this or other reasons, the Party's efforts in the countryside proved to be a total disaster. Thus when the announced election returns gave the government 44 out of the 55 national seats in the House—at a time when the Party faithful fully expected to capture 35 (and therefore a majority)—the National Congress leadership literally came unglued. Organizing protest demonstrations in Tripoli, they aimed to call world attention to the "fraudulent" election and the existing government's abuse of power.

Armed men, allegedly recruited by the Party, infiltrated Tripoli by night and turned the protest demonstrations of the following day into riots. Property was damaged, a dozen Libyans killed, and a hundred others injured. An alarmed government ordered its police to quash the rebellion and arrest its leaders. Later, the authorities totally dissolved the National Congress organization and deported Sadawi, its captain. In one fell swoop the government effectively eliminated all important opposition, at least in the form of political parties, both inside and outside Parliament.

The crisis with the National Congress Party was only one of numerous challenges to attempts to make a nation out of Libya in fact as well as in name. The internal disunity was continuous, characterized by severe clashes between federal and provincial politicians and the King's official representatives. Thus while all Libya suffered from cleavages between oasis and city, and while it also witnessed numerous conflicts between tribe and political party, the clashes among its elite were singular indeed. An interesting point is that a peculiar constitutional arrangement facilitated it all: While the national electorate sent the central government its politicians, it was the King, through his constitutional powers of appointment, who provided an analogous service for the provincial governments by appointing all their governors. Constituencies and lines of authority were therefore not only divided but frequently in conflict. Several Prime Ministers and their respective governments were brought down by this division.

If the conflicts among the elite were severe, no less so were those between the city and countryside, between the traditional past and the modernizing present. Because there were no national political parties—indeed, no parties at all—nearly all political activity tended to revolve around the personal and tribal interests of traditional leaders in the country and a new, but weak, group of modernizing national bureaucrats and politicians in the cities. There was no national structure—except the King and his entourage—designed to integrate the disparate parts. Political organizations which might have done so had been proscribed. Nor could Parliament pull in the slack. There, cliques revolved around personalities and local family and business groups as well as the Royal Family. Moreover, little or no machinery existed for amelioration of conflicts except the ultimate power of arbitration afforded the King—a power which Idris used wisely and effectively for some time.

If all these threats to national survival were not enough, quarrels among the oligarchs and their children over the successorship to Idris' throne provided an additional divisive sideshow. In October 1954, 38 princes, unable or unwilling to contain their ambitions to the royal chambers, staged a series of internecine scandals which culminated in a political crisis of major proportions. The princes, all members of the Sanusi order and descendants themselves of the King's grandfather, figured they could, or should, either sit on Idris' throne when the old man was no longer around or, barring that, at least decide among them who would. But the King had a different opinion. He liked to distinguish between his office as monarch and his office as head of the Sanusi order. Reasoning that while any of his grandfather's blood male relatives could legitimately become the next head of the brotherhood, it was nevertheless his prerogative alone to designate the heir to his throne. He wanted that heir to be his own son—if he could only father one who would live beyond infancy. Failing that, he would make his own suitable choice. But it would be his own, not that of the princes.

As the princely quarrels grew more intense, and their objection to Idris' opinion more aggressive, several of the young upstarts devised a stratagem to resolve the problem. They would assassinate Ibrahim al-Shalhi, one of the King's most devoted and trusted advisors, and one who also seemed to be at the headwaters of the King's restrictive view on successorship.

The assassin, Prince Sharif, was successful. But his mistake was to kill Shalhi openly on a street in Benghazi—an act which resulted in his immediate arrest. This set into motion consequences which were far from what the plotters had imagined. For one thing, as soon as the King realized that numerous members of the Sanusi family were implicated, he had them all put under house arrest. (Some observers noted that Idris' action may have been partially motivated by a concern for the princes' physical safety. The rumor-mongers were reporting that members of the powerful Barasa tribe of Cyrenaica, to which the dead advisor was related, were preparing to avenge his murder in accordance with an old Middle East custom: "An eye for an eye," and so forth.)

Within two weeks Idris also announced that he was exiling seven younger members of the Sanusi order to the oasis of Hon. Subsequently, he opened the reactive floodgates, proclaiming that all other family members, except those in direct line of succession (which he determined to mean his own or his brother's families) were to lose their royal titles as well as their right to hold government posts. Prince Sharif (grandson of one of the King's cousins) was tried for murder, found guilty, and subsequently executed (February 1955). To make the point indelibly clear, it is said that Sharif's body was exposed to public view for 20 minutes at the exact spot where Shalhi had been shot.

The crisis, of sufficient proportions to bring into serious question the survival of the monarchy, permeated the whole realm. But the King resolved it all by acting forthrightly and dramatically. As he honestly desired to be a wise moderator of the "oligarchical politics" of his new country, in no way could he allow the Royal Family to undermine the principles on which such a moderating power had to be based. Thus, faithful to the notions of justice and law to which Libya's monarch and her first national politicians had dedicated themselves, Idris, in heated anger, turned upon his own royal family.

In the first years of the realm it was a wise and skillful Idris who compensated for the fragility of the nation, moderating the petty quarrels of its oligarchs and attenuating the divisive national political influence of the Sanusi order of Cyrenaica. And while oligarchical infighting and maneuvering continued to cause numerous cabinet reshuffles, the King's abilities were sufficient to soothe the tensions. Indeed, by the time Libyans celebrated the tenth anniversary of their independence, their brittle, fragile, and somewhat artificial kingdom was indeed showing considerable resiliency. Yet it was not "political development" but rather King Idris' wise interpretation of his powers which seemed to make it all possible. While the rather frail, scholarly King was probably divided in loyalties between Cyrenaica—his homeland—and the whole of Libya—his kingdom, his wise leadership was certainly eventful if not crucial for the entire realm.

In spite of constitutional designs to the contrary, it was not the federal government (which existed until 1963) or the unitary one replacing it (abolishing the three regions and creating in their stead ten administrative districts) that provided the real unifying link between Cyrenaica, Tripolitania, and the Fezzan. It was the King. Indeed, three prime ministers (Muntasser, Sakisli, and Bin Halim) resigned their portfolios because the King, putting national stability and unity ahead of petty oligarchical and regional interests, had overruled them by royal decree.

Removing himself to Tobruk to a kind of self-imposed isolation, Idris placed himself above factional rivalries and allowed competing leaders to air their differences and grievances in his presence. But he refused to take sides on the basis of personalities. As a result, while the country continued to be torn by tribal feuds and rival houses vying for leadership, the King, as a remote and wise guardian of his country, became a figure of great prestige who wielded ultimate power.

There was a long-range price to be paid for this momentarily fortunate arrangement. As long as the King could successfully perform the integrating functions which developing political institutions should but did not do, there was little likelihood that any would develop. Thus in their day-to-day proceedings parliamentary portfolios, as well as politics, continued to be decided mostly on the basis of personalities and cliques who seemed to relish the mild sense of crisis generated each time they swapped appointments. No one seemed to feel the need to encourage the emergence of a modernizing political party. In reviewing those days, John Wright concludes that "government was a remote affair over which the urban voter had little control and the country folk, represented in the national and provincial assemblies by their traditional leaders, neither expected to control, nor hardly felt the need to do so."[2]

As with dreams of people, those of nations frequently fall short of aspirations and expectations. Such was Libya's fate in the initial seven or so years of the kingdom, not only in terms of national unity but in aspirations for economic development as well. Yet in spite of the fact that the country suffered divisive conflicts and, by any standards, was a realm of utter poverty and squalor, there were national gains that should be noted. When the Italian occupation ended in 1943, for example, there were virtually no Libyans in any government bureaucracy. Moreover, by a combination of purposeful Italian design and the disruptive effect of the war on the schools, no Libyans were attending secondary schools. Yet by independence day (in part because of the British military occupation "progress policy" which removed artificial shackles on Arab mobility) 80 percent of the civil servants in Cyrenaica and 71 percent of those in Tripolitania were Libyan. In the early years of the kingdom the federal government, with Idris' prodding, raised those figures somewhat higher. In the space of a few years Libyans had emerged from the status of servant to that of master technician in the realm.

Idris and the new Libyan nationalists also set up new elementary and secondary schools for Libyan children. And 1000 students were enrolled in the new national university (with classes held in both Tripoli and Benghazi). The regime also made some progress in roads and communications. But, in view of the need, progress was negligible until 1961. Illiterate men from the country continued to drift to the towns, sometimes taking their families with them, sometimes leaving them behind. Nevertheless, they remained illiterate. Seeking to earn more money and to buy more goods, they frequently found that they ate no better and lived worse, especially in the exploding shanty towns of Tripoli and Benghazi.

OIL!

No traveler could possibly escape the boulevard scenery. The long line of Mercedes-Benzes, Fiat 600s, half-ton pickups and diesel trucks moved too slowly. Traffic jams and exhaust fumes, and American supermarkets, coin-operated laundries, and bowling alleys had come to Tripoli. Indeed, one could even see the Chicken on the Wheels and the Red Cat—two recent additions to Tripoli's night life. Big men in big hats drank there, uncorking 40-dollar-a-bottle champagne almost as if it were Seven-Up.

There were freeways under construction and already caravans of dusty cars, trucks, and horsedrawn *gharris* had descended upon them. The harbor was choked with ships waiting to unload cargoes of equipment, building supplies and consumer goods. The surrounding landscape was peppered with hundreds of construction projects in various stages of completion. Thousands more were in some stage of planning. Plain evidence existed that a dramatic change had come to Libya—oil. There were vast amounts of it. The atmosphere was frantic.

"Until the 1950's," John Wright affirms, "the presence of oil in North Africa was barely suspected; the oil and gas fields of the Sahara do not betray their presence by such obvious clues as the 'Eternal Fires' of Azerbaijan or the asphalt ponds of Iraq."[3] Yet the Italians, when they found traces of petroleum and methane gas in their water wells, certainly had a deep suspicion that something lay under the inhospitable sands. One of them, Professor Ardito Desio, followed the tracings while making a geological map of North Africa in the 1930's. Later he submitted to the Italian Government a confidential report based on his observations. He pointed to Libya's Sirtica, that totally barren expanse of sand lying between Tripolitania and Cyrenaica, as one of the most promising oil producing areas.

Wishing to test the matter, the Italians moved in. But they had neither the equipment nor the techniques to handle the tough desert drilling conditions or sink the wells to the required depth. Twenty years later, however, American technology did tap the Sirtica. Desio would hardly have been surprised—not about the Americans, of course—but of the massive deposits of oils they found. By 1961 it was flowing to Mediterranean ports.

Aside from proximity to European markets, Libyan crude oil has another great advantage: it is remarkably free from sulfur. Most Middle Eastern oils, especially those from Kuwait, are highly contaminated. When this kind of oil is burned, pollution-sensing instruments come alive. People complain, more so now than before. Thus the Libyan crude oil has been in continuing demand. Indeed, Western Europe has clamored for it. Of the world's major oil producers, only Nigeria enjoys deposits with a lower sulfur content; but, because of the distance factor, Libya nevertheless has been in a favored position.

The uncertainties of Libya's political future held up oil exploration until independence was granted and, even then, it was some time before interest reached a point of clamor. In 1953 the government passed its Minerals Law under which prospecting permits were issued to nine major international companies. But if it had not been for a 1955 strike at Edjeleh in the Algerian Sahara near Libya, perhaps the Libyan fields themselves would still remain unknown. They were hard enough to find as it was. With the Algerian strikes, however, there was real evidence that North Africa did indeed contain oil-bearing sands.

The Libyan government went to work immediately and drafted its first, fairly far-sighted, Petroleum Law. Declaring all subsurface mineral resources to be the property of the State, it mapped out exploration zones and laid down rules of the exploring game so that potential fields could be found and exploited as soon as possible. The government further decreed that the state's share of the oil revenue would be 50 percent of the oil companies' net income. The companies were happy. So was the government. And the task of letting concessions commenced almost immediately. Within three years, concessions covering 55 percent of Libya's land area had been allocated to 14 international oil companies.

After 18 months of discouraging "dry holes"—and an accompanying expenditure of over $100 million—Desio was vindicated. In 1959, Libya Esso Standard finally moved into the Sirtica near a lonely landmark known as Bir Zelten. The well came in at 17,500 barrels per day, a rate that was nearly as good as anything in Kuwait or Saudi Arabia. A mammoth "pay zone" lay beneath the sands, at less than 6000 feet.

In the early 1960's, as oil began to flow and revenues deriving from it piled up in the government treasury, King Idris found it wise to caution his people of approaching dangers—"a thirst for wealth and an indulgence in luxuries, pompous display, idleness, and waste."[4] The King also warned that "the struggle ahead will not be less strenuous than during the past 10 years. Prosperity has its own problems. . . ."[5] Nevertheless, he felt moved upon to acknowledge God's hand in the discovery of the new national wealth.

Prosperity? Indeed! In the short space of 10 years (1957-1967) Libya raised her per capita gross national product from approximately $50 to $1,018. The trend was geometric, witnessed by the fact that increase for 1967 over 1966 was a startling 42 percent. By 1970 Libya had risen to the fourth largest and fastest growing oil producing country in the world. Dollars pouring into its national treasury increased 25 fold in eight years, from 40 million in 1962 to nearly 1 billion in 1969, and to nearly 2 billion in 1971!

The changes such activity wrought upon the Libyan people were substantial. Many dated even from the period of early exploration. As the oil crews moved onto the hot sands, they found it necessary to hire laborers to clear land mines (left over from World War II), and to assist in seismographic explorations, water well drilling, and the moving and supplying of oil rigs. Most of the Libyans so engaged were "casual" laborers hired from the small communities near the scene of operations. Wages soon rose to $1.20 a day, making the income for many rural Libyans better than that of any other Middle East country. By 1968 wages had doubled.

There were other benefits. One of them was full employment for any Libyan who could drive a nail, operate a tractor, or manage people. The demand for skilled workers was high. Wages and salaries were substantial, even two to three times higher than those in Egypt. The government erected hospitals and offered free medical care to Libya's urban citizens. It began to plan for decent housing for Libya's new workers and, in other ways, facilitated an improvement in the quality of life for many people.

Educational improvements were no less dramatic. Children served by the nation's schools rose from 33,000 in 1951 to 170,000 in 1965. In five short years enrollment nearly doubled again. Moreover, the more than 300,000 children attending school in 1970 included at least 85 percent of Libya's school-age population. One Libyan in six became a student. Yet Libya was so short of teachers that it became necessary to import foreigners to take up the slack. Fully 25 percent of all teachers in the schools during the initial expansive years were Arab nationals from other lands, primarily Egypt.

Nor did the government confine its educational efforts to the elementary and secondary levels alone. It erected a national university with campuses in Tripoli and Benghazi. Moreover, it demanded that the educators who staffed those campuses prepare their students to enter the main stream of Libyan economic life—as managers, entrepreneurs, bureaucrats, and perhaps even as technicians. Qualified students who could not be accommodated in the national university were encouraged to study in Cairo.

A new generation of Libyans was rising—one that could scarcely remember the rumble of Rommel's tanks, the atrocities of the Italians, or, for that matter, the traditional regional fanaticism of the old Tripolitanians, Cyrenaicans, and Fezzanese. What they did know was more immediate. Some of that came from Egyptian Arab nationalist teachers whom Idris had hired to staff his new schools, and there were also substantial inputs from Cairo's "Voice of the Arabs."

In due time, young men, perhaps even to their own astonishment, became aware that their training and experience gave them the capability to get things done in what always had been a sluggish, traditional society. In addition, there were employment opportunities everywhere. The government as well as private enterprise was investing in and profiting not only from oil, but new commerce, business enterprises, and service industries. Moreover, the government's investment in infrastructure alone, resulting in the creation of 3000 miles of new roads, a tripling of electric power capacity, and the providing of drinking water for 20 urban centers, was an additional boon. In the lives of many people the hopelessness of poverty gave way to a sense of purpose that even survived the heat of the Libyan summers. Per capita national income continued to skyrocket.

By 1969 it was apparent that all these facts were dramatic both for what they did and did not say. No one doubted the existence of a feverish economy —including inflation. Few objected to the government's transfer of its oil wealth to the building of a modernization-supporting infrastructure in agriculture as well as small-scale industry. But much of the prosperity was a big lie—at least for the majority of Libyans. Rather than create happiness and contentment, the discovery of oil beneath the Sahara sands had done exactly the reverse.

For one thing, it created unbearable disparities between those who participated in the new wealth and those who only saw it, like an evil mirage, always beyond their grasp. While some Libyans became millionaires, others remained on the outskirts of time. The per-capita income for most peasants remained at $45, roughly where it had always been. But their purchasing power had actually declined. Inflation. "The gross beneficiaries of the oil boom—financiers, industrialists, contractors, palace courtiers, speculators and adventurers—were certainly not numerous," said Eric Rouleau. "But they were ostentatiously visible. They lived in sumptuous homes, drove about in Cadillacs or Mercedes; frequented the night clubs . . . and vacationed in Florida or the French Riviera where they were noted for their lavish spending."[6]

Ten percent of Libya's population received more than half its billion dollar annual oil income. Of course, there were substantial service industries rising to fill the earning-power needs of some of the other half. But the feelings of relative deprivation remained, accentuated by the ostentatious living of Libyan millionaires and their American oil friends, many of whom, it is said, delighted in sporting their Texan "ten-gallon" hats in the Red Cat and the Chicken on the Wheels.

Relative deprivation and consequent frustration were encouraged by a government that, in spite of its developmental plans and public investments, was inactive and corrupt. The younger generation in Libya had long been restless over this problem, particularly as they watched their elders enriching themselves from the petroleum bonanza while the nation's aspiring youth were frequently left, as beggar children, on the outside.

A kind of proper political docility, in addition to family connections, was needed for entrance to the public trough. The graduates of the Libyan university in Benghazi were particularly incensed over this. It was said that their alma mater was the only institution in the country where academic success was achieved through merit rather than family connections, positions, or money. Yet the graduates were consistently denied access to key command posts in the economy unless, of course, they showed proper, and to many of them an increasingly distasteful, deference to Idris.

It was a vicious cycle for the new generation. They were more urbanized, literate, and sophisticated than their parents. More nationalistic, too. And those in the volatile urban centers were more numerous. While, in 1957, 80 percent of all Libyans lived in rural areas, farming and tending their flocks, ten years later more than two thirds of the population had migrated to the cities, according to information available to the *African Recorder* (April 8, 1967, p. 1602). There, they became educated, informed, and were introduced to new ideas and ways of thinking. And this occurred at the same time that the Libyan political system was being run by men whose lives dipped into the traditional past, whose behavior was nepotistic and personal-advantage seeking, and whose leader first uttered his childhood cries only 25 years after the final shot of the American Civil War was fired.

Governmental corruption highlighted other developmental ills. Ministers seldom held their jobs for more than a year or two, but in that period many of them found it possible to become millionaires—even if they started from fairly humble, but politically important beginnings. Foreign oil companies seeking concessions reported that they sometimes had to pay as high as a million dollars in bribes just to get their applications in the hands of the proper government officials. Then, to get them out of those same hands with a concession award cost another million or two. One foreign oil man is quoted as saying that "Libya was the most corrupt country I've ever seen."[7] More importantly, an angry Libyan nationalist, representative of thousands, was led to declare: "We felt that our country had become a Western whore. We were humiliated by the aimless drift. . . ."[8]

One of the factors encouraging corruption in Libya was that money was being poured into the country considerably faster than it could be productively used. It was like dumping gold into the laps of students majoring in the humanities and asking them to build roads, dams, and canals with it. Money, therefore, found its way into the pockets and hands of government bureaucrats and the nation's royal family—and some of its foreign visitors. Similarly, it was not uncommon for government officials to appropriate state drilling equipment, tractors, and water trucks for use on their private farms. So institutionalized was the corruption that, if asked to return illegally appropriated items to the state, the officials often became indignant.

Idris was King of the Libyans and father of his country, and he enjoyed much prestige among many of his countrymen. But his immunity to criticism decreased as fast as oil revenues rose. Students—as usual—were among the first to become seriously disaffected. They even expressed their discontent from time to time in mild urban skirmishes with the police. Impatient with government ministers whom they believed had concerned themselves only with personal gain—and fired by a Nasserite brand of Arab nationalism—they began to demand an elimination of the Anglo-American military bases. They also argued for a genuine independence that would liberate them from foreign domination. The newly emerging federation of Libyan workers (20,000 strong in 1963) identified with these themes and, along with the students, became exceptionally combative. Intellectuals and some small property owners joined in. A little muscle flexing in Tripoli in early 1964 set off a serious, and destructive, riot.

Idris and his government reacted very strongly to all this nonsense. The repression they ordered was not only bloody but done with a certain amount of uninhibited glee by the police who participated. Indeed, so complete and so unfettered was the application of coercion that only the increasingly nationalistic Libyan army remained physically untouched. But even it was psychologically deterred from any anti-government action: the King's loyal Cyrenaican Defense Force was just as well equipped and had twice as many men!

In the days and months which followed the riots of 1964, the King and his government forbade any organized political activity, proscribed the holding of public meetings or the carrying out of worker's strikes, muzzled the press, and paralyzed Parliament. While in the face of all this, the country remained calm; but it was only by the grace of the local police, the Cyrenaican Defense Force, and foreign intelligence that national stability could be pulled off. The throne was guarded—and so were the people. The discontented lost their voice. Few channels existed through which urban interests could be aggregated and expressed. Students were contained, workers manipulated, and the jails increasingly filled with political prisoners. Only the army could make some demands. Yet, as we have seen, even that was counterbalanced by tribal militias and the Cyrenaican Defense Force.

A new nationalism had come upon Libya. It was not a nationalism of the oligarchs—largely anti-Italian, anti-colonial, and pro-independence in nature. It was a nationalism of the young, the new students, new workers, new property owners, new emerging middle class, and new junior officers in the military. It was a nationalism born in Cairo, swaddled in Tripoli and Benghazi, and, finally, cast upon the whole of urban Libya like the infamous *ghibli*, the hot unbearable south wind from the Sahara. Few post-war Libyans remained ideologically unaffected.

The old generation of oligarchs was content with its gains. It had won its freedom and independence and had become rich and powerful. But it was also corrupt and decadent, at least so in the minds of the young who aspired but found the doors to opportunity open only ajar. The national image for them was a scandal. The country was being occupied by American-serving Arab sycophants who would sell their motherland for the legendary pot of porridge.

THE ARAB-ISRAELI WAR

It was into this background of rising frustration, discontent, and coercion that news burst of the 1967 humiliating defeat of Egypt, Syria, and Jordan at the hands of the Israeli Jews. Even if Idris, who not only disliked but feared Nasser, had wanted to, he was too weak to lend any military effort to Libya's Arab brothers. But many of Idris' subjects nevertheless emotionally shared Nasser's shame. They were furious at their impotence and angry with their King for not having prepared them to avoid such a tragedy. Waves of spleen-rupturing, antiforeign and anti-Jewish sentiment swept the land. Libyans from many walks of life were caught up in the excitement, indiscriminately demanding the evacuation of the large Anglo-American military bases, expulsion of the Jews, and a Holy War with Israel.

Frustration negated the fear of coercion. Students, workers, junior military officers and intellectuals flooded the streets in Tripoli and Benghazi to register their discontent. The disorders, riots, and killings which resulted shook the Idris government as would an angry dog his tormenting feline.

Idris, the wise man that he had once been, finally began to pay some attention to the new mood. While his police did play a bloody repeat performance a la 1964 on striking trade unions who wanted to prevent the exporting of oil to the "accomplices of Israel," the King nevertheless also began to announce some new nationalist-appeasing policies. First, he would strengthen Libya militarily, increasing the size of the country's armed forces to 10,000 men. Correspondingly, he also gave tacit approval for negotiations with Britain to supply a Rapier low-level missile system to handle any attacking aircraft flying below radar cover. This was how the Israelis had gotten to Egypt's airfields, it was said. Libya's 250-member American-trained air force with its jet trainers and piston-engined transports wanted none of that. The missile system would also include the famous Thunderbird apparatus for interception of high and medium level aircraft. (Critics suggested the King was protecting himself from Egypt, not Israel.)

Second, the King would foster a new nationalistic program geared to a general "Libyanization" of the realm. Toward this end, he appointed as his new Prime Minister Abd al-Hamid Bakkush, a brilliant young lawyer educated in Cairo. Only 32 years of age, Bakkush was acclaimed to be the youngest premier in office.

Seeking men of confidence, Bakkush's first act as Prime Minister was to drastically lower the average ministerial age, bringing into the new cabinet several of his contemporaries who had proven their ability as undersecretaries or as heads of government departments. Here were men young enough to participate in the ideals of Libya's newly mobilized youth, yet sufficiently mature to understand and sympathize with the problems of the preindependence generation.

Bakkush was progressive and ambitious, and also very aggressive. Among other innovations, he set up ministerial committees on which student representatives could serve, and he invited everyone to participate in the government process. Moreover, he took upon himself the task of encouraging national consciousness and political participation, not only through broadcasts, which were frequent, but by personal appearances in the various administrative districts of the land. The new ministers were as self-confident as Bakkush. They seemed to give the country a new sense of purpose and a stronger personality of its own.

The powerful Shalhi family of Cyrenaica, along with other rich and powerful families in the realm to which the King had long been intertwined, was horrified over the appointment of Bakkush as Prime Minister. Less perceptive and less wise than their Monarch, and certainly more avaricious than perhaps the King himself even realized, they could see little good and much to fear in Bakkush and his colleagues. Their status, their privileges, their way of life— all were at stake. Bakkush intended to eliminate corruption from government. He demanded that people be allowed to pursue opportunities commensurate with their capabilities. And he definitely was turning the government into the hands of young Libyan nationalists, if not Cairo sympathizing revolutionaries. Nearly as soon as Idris had made the appointment, therefore, the families began to bombard him with pleas that he undo it.

The pressure on Idris was so intense that within 10 months he buckled, fired his Prime Minister, and replaced him with a civil servant who promptly ended the reforms and reinstituted the old ways. The urban nationalists considered this to be a blow to Libya's national destiny, and many of them became convinced that peaceful reforms would never be possible within the existing political system. They were humiliated and angry over the Libyan establishment's visible lack of enthusiasm either for Libyan nationalism or the Arab cause. Once again they went to the streets. The reaction was once again the same. The King's police made the point rather clear with their truncheons.

THE DISAFFECTION OF THE MILITARY

Some Libyans had been in uniform since World War II. They had fought side-by-side with the British in the desert campaigns against the Axis. They were British-trained and had been British-led. Now they were the senior officers in Libya's fledgling army. But the King, if not fearing them, had at least slighted them. Most of the money, most of the equipment, and most of the perquisites of office had gone to the Cyrenaican Defense Force, another legacy of the desert war that remained a semiautonomous police force linked by clan and history to King Idris. All this had been a source of irritation to the regular military for some time. The discontent was only partially attenuated with the abolition of the federal system of government in April 1963 and the subsequent placement of all provincial police under the control of the national government. This greatly strengthened the hand of the national professional army. The senior officers were happy. But this said nothing about their juniors.

For years a progressively growing number of young officers had been receiving training outside Libya. Their political ideas, for this or other reasons, had been developing along lines compatible with those held by students, workers, and intellectuals. They wanted a new Libya, a modern Libya, and a nationalistic Libya. If they were disloyal to the King, they nevertheless felt powerless to confront him. Those who openly sympathized with them were still too few; the senior commanders were still too powerful. Indeed, senior officers and the Cyrenaican Defense Force had helped put down the anti-Western and anti-Jewish demonstrations in Tripoli and Benghazi in 1967. And in 1968 the army had rounded up 110 Palestinians and other members of the underground Arab nationalist movement. It was said that the detentions were ordered because of rumored plots to overthrow the monarchy and invade the Americans' vast Wheelus Field. Subsequent prison sentences ranged from 15 years to life. Yet it was by an increasingly tenuous thread that such commands could be given and executed. The young officers were plotting.

Years earlier, as King Idris calmly listened to his Prime Minister's recitation of national goals at his country's independence ceremonies, he very positively reacted to one which called for the creation of a Libyan army as soon as possible. "This is the dearest wish of our hearts," he told his visitor, Henry Villard.[9] By 1969 Idris may very well have wished to reconsider his feelings. Within one year after the fall of the Bakkush government—and the disappointments which the firing represented—the young officers had made their move.

Perhaps it all was inevitable. As Idris built up his modern army, navy, and air force with American and British help, he found that he had to recruit his officers from among the newly mobilized masses. The sons of the rich were too busy making money from oil to put on a uniform. It was many of these young officers that the Cyrenaican Defense Force—recruited from Libya's small traditional middle class—had put down after they, along with students and workers, had erupted in violent demonstrations following the 1967 Arab-Israeli war. Many of the young officers had been jailed.

Coming from relatively humble families, the junior officers had first been frustrated by a society which offered them few opportunities. Enlisting in the army to gain stable and remunerative employment and enjoy the prestige of a uniform, they once again saw their channels of mobility blocked. They also perceived that their seniors really did not care about Libya, its strength, or its destiny in the Arab world. So they coveted Idris' power. They detested his handling of the economy and they were sickened with the national corruption.

"How could they," said the King when the coup eventually came. Had he not provided them with schooling and education, a uniform and training, life and purpose? But then there is an old Libyan proverb which advises: "If a man hands you a rope, tie him up with it."

CHAPTER 9

Soldiers in Islam

The armed children of modernization had risen. Young, brash, inexperienced, "laughing stock" of the Tunisians, stepchildren of Egypt's Nasser and an enigma for the United States Ambassador in Tripoli, they rapidly charted a new course for Libya's future. Foreigners were aghast. What kind of political religion was this? They could wonder. Few countries had so suddenly experienced a marriage of contemporary socialist thinking and ancient traditional absolutes. "You can find in the Koran the answer to all your questions," declared 27-year-old Muammar al-Qaddafi, one of the prime conspirators of the revolution and eventual first officer in the ruling Revolutionary Command Council. "Arab unity, socialism, rights of inheritance, the place of women in society, the destiny of our planet after the invention of the atom bomb—all is there for the man who can read the Sacred Book."[1]

Armed with such assurance and righteousness, Islamic purity quickly jumped to a priority position on the officers' list of concerns. Once the country was "purified," they thought, then their attention could turn to the revolutionary socialism they had all been talking about since the early days of listening to Radio Cairo. Accordingly, in spite of their socialist rhetoric, the initial casualties of the revolution were not the oil companies, foreign businessmen, or private property. The scimitar of Arab nationalism would fall upon some of these later. First to fall were the gambling casinos in Tripoli. With their tables hooded, no longer would some lucky oil engineer's happy cry of "hot dawg!" rise above the background of the clicking roulettes and the excited chatter at the dice tables.

Moslem fundamentalists do not gamble, at least in casinos. And they do not drink alcohol. So why should foreigners? Thus the country's visible stock of liquor soon suffered the fate of its gambling tables. And customs officials were tough on replacements. Hundreds of bottles of confiscated dark brown bourbon and light tan scotch, fine white and red wines and brandies piled up in the ports of entry. Even the desert was declared "dry." Said one disgusted oil man: "Who ever heard of drilling for oil in the desert without a can of beer." They would learn. And other things, too. Orthodox Moslems do not eat pork. No more of it passed customs either.

Libyan Arabs speak Arabic and write in Arabic script. Why were there so many signs in English and Italian around the country? "Signs aren't written in

Arabic for our benefit in New York City," said one of the officers. "So why should we accommodate you with English signs here in Libya?" The names of banks, the Pepsi-Cola signs, the hotel marquees, the bilingual road signs, even the lettering on ash trays in hotel lobbies were all painted over, taken down, or scratched out. Americans and Britons frequently had to stop at intersections to ask directions. Oilmen worried that their English-speaking personnel in the field would suffer a rash of accidents if deprived of safety signs they could read. And travelers at the Tripoli airport sometimes made rapid retreats when they confused the Arabic equivalents of "Ladies" and "Gents."

For many people, such rashness and zealotry made Qaddafi as enigmatic as the Sword of Damocles. Marvine Howe of the *New York Times,* for example, found Qaddafi's meticulously correct English, sober manner, and personal reserve to be in marked contrast with some of his actions.[2] Yet, there he was. And there would be more of him, too. Tripoli's Catholic Cathedral, dedicated to the Sacred Heart of Jesus, was destined to become the Gamel Abdel Nasser Mosque, complete with a picture of Muammar al-Qaddafi plastered on the crucifix.

While the country was being spiritually purified, returning to the bosom of Mohammed, preparations were also under way to make radical changes in the functioning of the political system. Once the conspirators had secured the near-bloodless neutralization of the Cyrenaican Defense Force and satisfied themselves regarding the loyalty of the provincial military commands, they began to make their move. One of the first was to auction off the fleet of 600 Mercedes Benzes inherited from King Idris and his coterie of government officials.

The officers then struck out at the British and the Americans. Not the civilian oilmen—for whom protection assurances of life and property were given—but their uniformed countrymen who occupied strategic portions of the Libyan homeland. The officers affirmed immediately their unwillingness to renew leases (expiring in 1971) on the huge military bases. Moreover, they reiterated to the Americans in particular, that since Libyans did not desire a foreign military presence on their soil, the only sporting thing would be to abandon the vast Wheelus air base immediately. The American ambassador, under some duress, finally agreed to begin dismantling equipment and removing personnel.

As long as foreign "occupation" forces remained on national soil, the young officers' freedom for maneuver could be threatened. After all, when King Idris, vacationing at a Turkish health spa, first received incontrovertible word that he had been deposed, he sent Omar Shalhi to Britain to plead with British Foreign Secretary Michael Stewart to use his Libyan-based troops to restore the throne. Although Stewart refused, the British troops he might have used were nevertheless still a problem. They were closely tied to Idris' Cyrenaican Defense Force.

The young officers also knew a little about United States relations and activities in the Middle East. For example, they were well aware that in the 1950's Eisenhower had lent the services of the CIA to the Iranian Shah. The Shah, having fled his angry subjects for reasons of personal safety, nevertheless

returned "victorious." It was said that CIA bribes and payoffs were considerable. America's oil interests, endangered by the Shah's nationalistic opponents,
had been preserved.[3]

"From now on, Libya is deemed a free, sovereign republic under the name
of the Libyan Arab Republic," stated the officers in their Proclamation on
September 1, 1969, "ascending with God's help to exalted heights, proceeding
in the path of freedom, unity, and social justice, guaranteeing the right of
equality to its citizens, and opening before them the doors of honorable work—
with none terrorized, none cheated, none oppressed, no master and no servant,
but free brothers in the shadow of a society over which flutters, God willing,
the banner of prosperity and equality." The captains would have the Proclamation voluntarily if they could, enforced if they must. But one thing they did not
want was foreigners hampering them while they ruled the country. And so, in
addition to negotiating a withdrawal of American and British military personnel
from Libyan soil, the officers also terminated the residency of the economically
powerful Italian community.

The process had all the logic of a Bedouin's dream. Confiscating bank
accounts and personal property held by Italians (with the exception of minor
personal effects), and denying them any rights to gainful employment, the new
regime nevertheless guaranteed their personal safety for as long as they wished
to remain on Libyan soil. No one was surprised that flights to Rome and Milan
were solidly booked. The "tyrannical Italians" had usurped the property of
Libyans long enough, Qaddafi said. Eventually, all of them (variously estimated from 18,000 to 40,000) some of whom had never set foot on Italian soil,
went "home." Confiscation of Jewish property derived from the lingering
effects of the 1967 Arab-Israeli war. But the Jews, at least, were compensated
with 15-year Libyan bonds. The Italians received nothing. Rome was infuriated
and even refused to buy any of Libya's liquefied natural gas.

"If foreign experts are real experts, and they are helping us, and we need
them, they are welcome to stay. But if they are not. . . ."[4] American oilmen
were temporarily needed. Italians and Jews were not. Libyans had been prevented from getting good jobs by those people, the officers said. The new
republic would stand for no more of it.

What the officers really wanted was a nation filled with the principles of
"freedom, socialism, and unity" for their Arab countrymen. They affirmed their
tireless dedication toward the building of such a society of equality and justice.
"Our socialism is the socialism of Islam," said Qaddafi in an address in Benghazi
on September 16. "It is the socialism of the true faith. It is the socialism which
springs from the heritage and beliefs of this people."[5] It was not, he hastened
to assure, a socialism of Lenin or Marx, but rather one which would suit the
circumstances of the republic as it removed itself from the "exploiting classes,"
yet at the same time remained anchored to Islamic social justice. Except for
the property of foreigners, it would therefore respect individual private
ownership—which Islam blesses.

How would the new political ideals be implemented in day to day administration and governance? No one seemed to know. Initially, the officers were

unclear and presented every evidence of not having previously thought about the matter. Even their first moves were political, not administrative. For instance, they declared that they would not remain glued to their office chairs—as they alleged the case had been with King Idris' bureaucrats—but would go to the people to investigate their problems and deal with them in a "scientific" way. "The age of dealing with the problems which disturb the classes of the toiling masses by means of counterfeit promises from air-conditioned offices has now irrevocably ended."[6] But what was the scientific way? Answers were not forthcoming. Thus the one clarity amidst the post-coup confusion was not so much *where* the new regime was going but that the direction, whatever it was, would not be given from an air-conditioned office.

The meticulous planning which had gone into the coup itself did not appear to have been accompanied by any concrete ideas about what was to be done in the event it was successful. The functions of government became paralyzed as senior military officers and civil servants were jailed and minor functionaries told to "watch it." The resulting day-to-day administrative decisions seemed to emanate alternately from the radio stations in Tripoli and Benghazi. No one appeared to know who would carry out the numerous decrees, orders, and commands. Those who might have done so were either in jail, or afraid they might soon be.

SOME POLITICAL THINKING

If the victorious captains had no administrative clout, the same certainly could not be said of their aspirations to acquire some clout of a political variety. It was only natural, therefore, even though the various ministries were still quaking from post-coup aftershocks, that the reforming officers should turn their attention toward considering the kind of political structure they would substitute for the monarchy. Yet at first they were much more clear on what they would *not* have than what they would. For example, civilian politicians were out; they had done enough corrupting. Moreover, no longer would the oligarchs run Libya as if the country were their private domain. Indeed, no longer would they run anything. Nor would the officers allow any political partisanship. Libyans were to be united, not divided into feuding parties. No action was to be taken against leaders of underground parties who had been working for the overthrow of the monarchy, but after September 1 no one was in doubt that any continuation of those activities would be considered an act of treason.

How could political unity and political participation be achieved so that the ideological goals of the revolution might work themselves out? Qaddafi, who had quickly surfaced as the spokesman for the Revolutionary Command Council, gave some insights as early as November into the probable thrust the new regime would take. The officers, he said, would set up a "popular organization" embracing all the republic's working forces. While it was true that this would afford the new leaders great opportunities for manipulation and political control, it would also provide the people an opportunity to develop a sense of political participation in the affairs of their country. Within a single political organization would be represented all the various "laboring" groups: teachers, workers, farmers, doctors, lawyers, students, and others. No immediate rush was made to bring the organization into existence. But a considerable amount of intellectual energy was invested toward thinking out the problem. "Incorporating the masses" into the revolution was a must. The young leaders saw that they could not institute lasting reforms without the support of dedicated followers.

What the officers had in mind, of course, was a "mass party." Organized from the top down, such a party would give Libyans a subjective sense of participation but without having to allow them power to determine government decisions. No doubt Qaddafi and his colleagues had Nasser's Arab Socialist Union in mind as an acceptable prototype. If parliamentary life returned to Libya, therefore, it would be through the officers' selecting the people's "true representatives." "Directed democracy" was to be the watchword.

ISLAM'S SOLDIERS

When most young men their age were still tending flocks, paying for their first new bicycle, or perhaps beginning a career, Libya's young officers had captured a country and made it their own. To be sure, some were "faceless" men and they preferred to remain such—anonymous, secretive, yet influential. Others, such as Qaddafi, were not only intelligent, articulate, and energetic, but unabashedly flamboyant as well. Declared the great Gamel Abdel Nasser during a break in meetings at an Arab summit conference held shortly before he died of a coronary: "I rather like Qaddafi. He reminds me of myself when I was that age."[7]

Qaddafi was born in a nomad's tent a few days before "Pearl Harbor." Thus he was still in his 27th year when he became ruler of an oil-rich desert. A product of Benghazi University—where merit and qualifications meant something—he had graduated from that institution in 1963 with a history degree. From there he moved on to the Libyan Military Academy. Idris had established and generously funded that school in order to enhance the professionalism of his national army. Little did the King suspect that the end product of his careful educational planning would not be loyal commanders, but rather a fresh batch of revolutionary conspirators. The Academy's 1965 and 1966 graduating classes contributed almost the entire membership of the Revolutionary Command Council. A "placement" success to rival that of any school, it nevertheless was not exactly the kind of mobility that Idris had in mind.

Qaddafi must have demonstrated considerable acumen and loyalty during his years in the University and the Academy, because in 1966 he was selected to spend a year at Britain's Royal Military College at Sandhurst. Yet, from Idris' point of view, it all went for naught.

Of all the members of the new Revolutionary Command Council, Qaddafi stood out not only for his zeal and energy, but for his unpredictability as well.

He would appear "spontaneously" in the various districts of the land to make speeches about the revolution. Later, at the most unpredictable hours, he was known to "drop in" on his Arab friends in other Middle East countries, leaving a million or so dollars to help finance the campaign against Israel. At the very least, the Captain-suddenly-made-Colonel frustrated all the protocol officials. Pomp, ceremony, fancy clothes, arrival at the appointed hour; all these he disdained.

So faithful was Qaddafi to his Pan-Arab colleagues—in spite of his other unpredictable features—that when Premier Gaafar al-Nimeiry, his counterpart in neighboring Sudan, was temporarily deposed by Communists, Qaddafi had his Air Force order down a British Airways Boeing 707 flying over Libyan air space so that he could extract two of the alleged prime conspirators. He then turned them over to Nimeiry for interrogation—and eventual execution. The British government was furious. But it had long since lost its influence in Libya.

Handsome, an Arab's Arab, and the kind of man many said they would like to be, Qaddafi quickly emerged as the standard-bearer of nationalists not only of his own Middle East land but of others as well.

Like Qaddafi, Prime Minister al-Maghreby (who quickly surfaced as the regime's number two man) was also well trained. In fact, he received much of it in the West. While no one seemed surprised that he held a law degree from Damascus University, the news that he also had earned a Ph.D. in Petroleum Law from George Washington University in the United States national capital was sufficient to raise many eyebrows. Returning to Libya—with all his degrees —he had been hired by Libya Esso Standard. The company promptly fired him, however, when he vigorously advocated the cessation of oil shipments to the West after the Arab-Israeli Six-Day War. Maghreby was less prone to rhetoric and more dedicated to the actual chores of "rationalizing" Libya's relations with the oil companies than was Qaddafi. Thus nearly immediately, while Qaddafi was making his speeches, Maghreby was drafting documents for extracting higher revenues from the companies. When the inevitable face-to-face discussions began, American oilmen quickly realized they were confronting a very knowledgeable, if somewhat biased, adversary.

Ahmed Shetwey became Libya's new Minister of Petroleum Affairs. Curiously enough, he probably received much of his requisite education while serving as Prime Minister al-Maghreby's cell-mate following the Six-Day War. He also had come up against Idris' oil-shipment policies—which included a hard clampdown on anyone threatening to disrupt Libya's favorable relations with the West. Shetwey and al-Maghreby (both were under 30 years of age) were intensely nationalistic, and it was obvious they were willing to take risks.

Colonel Saaduddin Abu Shweirib eventually surfaced as the army's new Chief of Staff. Although slightly older than his colleagues—he was in his thirties—he nevertheless came with many of the same youthful credentials. Foreign experience: he had studied at the United States Army Command and General Staff College at Fort Leavenworth. Nationalistic sentiments: he had been sacked from the army in 1967 because Idris' Generals suspected him of having pro-Republican sympathies. Occupational humiliation: since his firing from the army he had worked as a notary public.

Colonel Adm al-Hawaz, the Defense Minister in the newly formed regime, was considered by many observers to be the real theoretician of the revolution. While keeping himself somewhat removed from public view, he nevertheless demonstrated considerable personal courage and valor while arranging for the disarming of Idris' Cyrenaican Defense Force. Once that operation was taken care of, the potential threat of a counter coup greatly diminished.

The "faceless ones" also sat in the higher councils, and, along with those members of the Revolutionary Command Council noted above, also thrust themselves into activities which, they hoped, would remove Libya from its prostration before the West, purify the nation, relieve it from oligarchical corruption, and introduce equality, justice, and economic development for the Libyan masses.

ECONOMIC DELAY AND POLITICAL RESOLVE

While the ritual of national purification unfolded, and the terror of administrative chaos ran its course, Libya decayed economically. Expulsion of the Italian colony—which constituted the bulk of Libya's skilled labor force—helped bring construction to a halt. Whatever other working forces remained were also idled when the officers began to investigate rich landlords who had been investing in quick-profit luxury apartments and office buildings. Indeed, it was not long before construction around Tripoli ceased altogether.

There were other problems. Foreign currency reserves dropped because the officers called for a temporary reduction in oil exports. They were fearful that Esso Standard and others were wrecking the long-term productivity of the fields by withdrawing Libya's wealth too rapidly from its oil-bearing sands. Then, the muddle at Libya's ports became so bad that shippers had to levy a 25 percent surcharge on all freight movement.

As could be expected, in light of all these events, urban unemployment rose, first to 12 percent, then to 20. And inflation kept right on climbing. As a result, while the country's oil revenues continued to be deposited in the various banks to which they habitually had gone, no one could quite figure out what the officers were doing with the accounts.

It seemed to some observers that before too long the social consequences of such economic chaos would bring Libya's new leaders straight out of their dreamland. If unemployment and discontent increased, particularly among workers and merchants in the cities, the regime's principal support would be alienated. How then would it function?

The foreign press was scathingly critical of all this. Increasingly they pointed to the youth, "incompetence," and arrogant brashness of Qaddafi and his friends. "Hillbillies of the Middle East," they said. Even Tunisians poked fun at what they called Libya's temporary "Nasserite spree." Others downgraded the capabilities of the officers, calling them all "children of Radio

Cairo" and alleging that Nasser's powerful radio transmitter was the only cultural influence they had ever had in their Cyrenaican desert garrison.

Yet the observers disregarded—or ignored—the fact that nearly all members of the Revolutionary Command Council originated from homes in or near metropolitan Tripolitania, that some of them were well traveled, and that not a few were well educated. Thus, in some ignorance, no doubt, even Algeria's President Boumedienne was reported to have referred to Qaddafi as a child who knew too little to speak.[8]

The young officers were many things, but hardly all those they were accused of being. Yet one thing was certain. Even if the nation did suffer catastrophic economic decline, Qaddafi and his colleagues would not be deterred from their task. There were some moments of indecision, and even a minor "second coup" attempt by some officers. But they were contained, and those who remained faithful hardened their resolve to march forthrightly ahead.

NEW OIL AGREEMENTS

How long could such nonsense last? That was an international question. Yet as the days and months came and went—with little evidence of a collapse—speculation became academic. In its place came hard realities. Particularly was this true for the Americans who found they had to start paying attention to what the officers were doing. Aside from the airbase question, Qaddafi and his ministers had also begun an incessant campaign to extract higher tax revenues from the oil companies. In due time the companies caved in, agreeing to *double* King Idris' requested increase of 10¢ per barrel in the posted price.

The first major agreement was with Occidental Petroleum Company. Not only did it raise its posted price from $2.33 to $2.53, but it also agreed to increase periodically that price by two cents for each of five ensuing years. Moreover, it allowed the officers to augment their tax take by several percentage points (by increasing the 50 percent tax negotiated under the Idris regime a decade earlier to 58 percent, but dropping the requirement that 5 percent of pretax profits be paid for agricultural development purposes). Since it was on the basis of the posted price of oil—not the market price—that taxes were levied, state revenue did indeed jump. Some oilmen were aghast. How could such unreasonable demands be met? Did not the officers know that their very livelihood depended on Western oil technology and the companies who knew how to use it?

The renegotiated contracts with the various oil companies literally doubled Libya's annual take from its oil treasure, climbing from $1 billion in 1969 under King Idris to an annual rate of nearly $2 billion in 1971. What would the officers do with their incredible bonanza? The whole world waited to see.

THE PENULTIMATE ACT

No one should have been greatly surprised—although not necessarily undismayed—as the officers played their hand. Indeed, on numerous occasions

Qaddafi had announced the intentions of the Revolutionary Command Council. It would concentrate its efforts, and therefore its money, on three fronts: national purification, preparation for war, and economic development; probably in that order of priority. Thus the deteriorating economic conditions following the coup excited foreign observers more than most Libyans, and, in particular, much more than the officers running the national show. That is one reason why the officers were so slow to implement any corrective measures.

National purification itself—the elimination of the oligarchs and their corruption; foreigners and their language, culture, decadence, and many of their skilled workers—required some surgery which, in the short run at least, was recognized to have deleterious economic effects. In any event, before the economic problem could be countered, attention had to be directed toward strengthening the military. This was necessary so that national authoritative moves could be made with some assurance that they would be respected by any foreign power or domestic group intent upon restoring Idris to his throne. Thus Libya's chaotic administrative and economic conditions during the first few post-coup months—which led some to conclude not only that the officers had absolutely no idea of what to do but had no competence to do it—were misleading. Qaddafi and crew knew exactly what they were about—or at least what they wanted to be about. The immediate correction of economic chaos was not one of them. That problem lay in the eyes of foreign beholders who had not registered the proper priority sequence.

Consolidating and institutionalizing the first of the three priorities—national purification—would require a near total reconstruction of governmental bureaucracy, including all ministries and agencies. The officers seemed to have no illusions that they could accomplish this overnight. They probably also knew that government paralysis would be one of the short-term consequences. However, when the cancer is deep the cure is more complicated and requires more patience. From where the officers stood there was little doubt that the thoroughly disease-ridden bureaucracies would require massive surgery. Money would have to be spent to train workers, to remove corruption, to modernize facilities, and so on.

The second priority, military preparation, was where most of the attention turned after the excitement of national purification began to ebb. In addition to ensuring protection for the nation, the officers also saw a need to expand militarily in order to participate in causes of common concern to all Arab lands. While the "common concern" may have, and indeed was, interpreted variously among the several Arab states, to the Libyan officers it was a code word for the reconquest of Palestine.

In this area, as in none other, Libya has excelled. Army pay doubled; contracts were signed with France for the purchase of 100 Mirage jets; Russia and her bloc agreed to supply tanks and armored personnel carriers; and other arms-manufacturing countries placed themselves on tap to supply smaller weaponry. Where have Libya's fortunes gone? A sizable amount, obviously, has been invested to prepare for war.

"We pledge all our material and moral capabilities to the Palestine cause," declared one member of the Revolutionary Command Council. "Our relation with other states will be on the basis of the position of these states on the Palestine cause."[9] So it has been. Along with investment in armaments, therefore, Qaddafi and his colleagues have showered an annual subsidy of $55 million on Egypt, have made sizeable donations to Syria, and have contributed to al-Fatah, the group of Palestinian Commandos who, until mid 1971, harassed Israel from Jordanian and Lebanese soil with considerable strength. Correspondingly, because of a "vacillating" attitude toward the reconquest, Qaddafi has extended negative, and sometimes abusive, treatment to Kings Hussein of Jordan, Faisal of Saudi Arabia, and Hassan of Morocco, the three remaining Middle East Arab monarchs.

Profiting from a happy marriage of personal ambition, religious zealotry, and a Pan-Arab leadership vacuum in the Middle East, Qaddafi has retrieved Nasser's mantle, donned his cloak, and become the foremost contemporary spokesman for Arab unity. It is not unity for unity's sake alone he seeks, but rather one which will lend strength and power for the task ahead—the crushing of Israel if the Jews do not relinquish the Arab lands they have occupied since the Six-Day War. Accordingly, as a result primarily of Qaddafi's prodding, the governments of Libya, Egypt, and Syria in August of 1971 finally agreed to a new, loosely structured federation which would allow them to unite their forces for the common struggle. The Sudan, scheduled to have joined an earlier abortive federal attempt in 1970, has said it will join at a later date.

There may be many nonmilitary related residual benefits deriving from an Arab federation (if, indeed, a federation can remain together, since other attempts have failed), such as a complementing productive utilization of the vast agricultural potential of the Sudan, the capital generating capability of Libya, and the skilled manpower resources of Egypt. However, there is little doubt in the minds of most observers that the immediate impetus for a federation is not so much for economic development as for a resolution of the Palestine question. If, in an earlier day, Qaddafi reminded Nasser of himself when he was young, there is now little question that Qaddafi believes as much. With a near-fanatical zeal he has set himself the task of finishing what Nasser began.

With so much energy and so many resources invested in national purification, military preparedness, and the advancement of the Arab cause in Palestine, what could be left over for economic development, the third priority in Libya's scheme of goals to accomplish? There have been solutions, as well as energy and money, but not enough to put Libya back on its economic feet. Qaddafi has doubled his oil revenues, and that has helped. He has imported 50,000 Egyptian technicians to fill skilled labor tasks, many of which were left vacant by the departing Italians. He has attempted some economic diversification, making investments in agriculture. Nevertheless, all planning to the contrary, economic progress has been slow and bottlenecks appear everywhere: money lies unspent in development budgets; construction has not recovered; and half-finished projects lie idle. How long the "Palestinian question" will take the minds of Libyan workers off their own domestic economic difficulties is anybody's guess.

Middle East skeptics have already relegated the new Arab Federation, if not Libya itself, to the garbage heap of history, prophesying that when the oil fields are depleted the country will revert to the world of the nomads, to be forgotten as were the ancient Roman aqueducts. Yet it is too early to make such rash judgments. Although the odds do not appear appreciably in the officers' favor, it is an unnecessarily premature judgment that says Libya's young, abrasive, and energetic leaders cannot also be nation builders.

It is too early, also, to suggest that no long-range developmental benefits will derive from the country's oil treasure. Indeed, it is too early to suggest that Libya has no other resources which might be tapped. Only in 1970, for example, the president of Boyle Engineering Company announced that engineers from his firm are certain the country has a treasure potentially more valuable than even its oil. *Water*. Analyzing the evidence from wells drilled for oil, they estimate their find could easily supply water in quantities equal to the flow of the Nile River for 1000 years. The vast underground basin, located between 25 and 175 feet below the desert sands, is thought to cover approximately one thousand square miles.[10]

Placing such a vast resource to productive use may facilitate Libya's Arabs making as many roses bloom in the desert as do their Israeli enemies. If the two historical gladiators can somehow resolve their differences short of mutual annihilation, there may yet be metropolises along the shores of North Africa which can rival those ancient ones built, and forgotten, by Rome.

BIBLIOGRAPHICAL ESSAY

The presumed relative unimportance of Libya before it was found to be sitting atop a black sea coincided uncomfortably well with the relatively few good books and journal articles written about it. This makes a striking contrast to the amount of newsprint generated since 1969, when the West's access to the treasure sea was potentially threatened. Libya has suddenly been "discovered."

Among the few good foundation books on the country is one that also is truly outstanding: John Wright's *Libya,* published in 1969. (Complete entries for all works are to be found in the bibliography.) While doing in-country research in the mid-1960's, Wright attempted, without success, he says, to locate a good general history of the country. Although he came across several competently written, specialized books on Libya ("Haynes on the antiquities of Tripolitania, Evans-Pritchard on the Sanussis, Khadduri on modern political development, Kubar on the oil industry"), he remained unsatisfied. Since the book he wanted apparently did not exist, at least in any European language, he decided to write it himself. It is superb, both in detail and style.

In addition to the specialized authors which Wright notes, there are others who are worthy of attention of any student of Libya. One such author is Adrian Pelt. His magnum opus, *Libyan Independence and the United Nations,* deals with the emergence of Libya from colony to independent state. Pelt concentrates primarily, but not exclusively, on the years 1950–1952. The book falls into the category of "best," partly because Pelt is brilliant, but also because he was the actual representative of the United Nations on the scene and had firsthand access to personalities and documents.

Closely following Pelt in importance, although somewhat dated now, are works by Khadduri, and Halpern, and one commissioned by the International Bank for Reconstruction and Development. Khadduri's work, *Modern Libya: A Study in Political Development,* although almost totally without analytical content, is nevertheless richly endowed with data which the author has arrayed to create an important descriptive political history of the land. Halpern, with his *The Politics of Social Change in the Middle East and North Africa,* bores into the meaning of some kinds of political and social change. The International Bank has placed in *The Economic Development of Libya* a wealth of pre-1960 economic and natural resource information and also some important notes on history and manpower.

If one enjoys a highly readable, largely anecdotal treatise of kings and their followers, he ought to leaf through the pages of Villard's *Libya: The New Arab Kingdom of North Africa.* The author, a United States Foreign Service Officer stationed in Libya during the time that Idris, Adrian Pelt, and the United Nations were putting the new country together, gives a firsthand

215

account of some of the drama. In addition, Agnes Keith, wife of one of Villard's contemporaries in the Foreign Service, gives (*Children of Allah*) a highly readable, anecdotal followup of the newly created nation, its people, and its desert territory.

Useful journal articles on Libya have surfaced relatively recently, all of them within the past ten years, and most in the past five. Those found highly useful in the preparation of the case study are: Ragaei El Mallakh, "The Economics of Rapid Growth: Libya"; Frank Ralph Golino, "Patterns of Libyan National Identity"; Eric Rouleau, "Oil and Monarchies Don't Mix"; James D. Farrell, "Libya Strikes it Rich"; Charles E. Brown, "The Libyan Revolution Sorts Itself Out"; Robert Wylie Brown, "Libya's Rural Sector"; Frederick C. Thomas, Jr., "The Libyan Oil Worker"; Hisham Sharabi, "Libya's Pattern of Growth"; Charles O. Cecil, "The Determinants of Libyan Foreign Policy"; and Ali R. Bengur, "Financial Aspects of Libya's Oil Economy." A Documentary entry in the *Middle East Journal*, "The Libyan Revolution in the Words of its Leaders," (Spring, 1970) helped in capturing some of the rhetoric and ideology of Libya's new leaders.

More casual, but nevertheless useful, articles on Libya include a well-written if not unnecessarily biased one by Francis Hope, "The Tripoli Hillbillies." More objective, in tone if not substance, is Trefor Evans, "The New Libya."

For other relevant entries published prior to 1959, one should consult R. W. Hill, *A Bibliography of Libya*.

Some of the best newspaper and newsmagazine entries on Libya may be found in the bibliographical entries for John K. Cooley, George W. Herald, and Bertram B. Johansson.

CHAPTER 10

Modernizing The Maghrib

The introduction of Arab Libya into a world of modern technology and organization was an exciting, if not frustrating, adventure for that part of the North African Maghrib. Emerging so recently, and yet so quickly, into the twentieth century, the country scarcely had time to adjust to the inundating effects of Italian colonization before it was flooded once again, this time by revenues from its incredible underground treasures. While oil and the bounties deriving therefrom were considered to be Allah's blessings, in due time some Arabs nevertheless began to wish that He would have hurled them out a little more slowly.

Yet the drama, and the intensity of its unfolding, are not without redeeming qualities, particularly if the Libyan society and polity ever catch up with their racehorse environment. In the meantime, the events afford dramatic illustration of several modernization themes raised in this book.

MODERNIZATION AND MODERNITY

Modernity, we have argued, is both a state of mind and a state of being, dealing as much with people's attitudes and values as with their physical world. Within the attitude and value side of that definition reside several important variables. One of the most suggestive is psychic mobility—a frame of mind which allows one to role play and to be adaptable to changing occupational and life-style requirements. This variable, in addition to others—such as a belief in the efficacy of science; a desire, indeed, an ambition, to progress and to develop oneself; a general rejection of traditional "ascriptive" norms and an adoption of those of an "achievement" variety—set some of the important psychological hallmarks of the modern man.

Aside from the "mind variables," modernization, as we have seen, also involves "structural variables," those which relate to the physical world and to how people organize their living in it. Primarily but not universally, modernization of "structures" is seen to entail an increase in the use of scientific technology, the appearance of dynamic urban centers, and the development of complex and differentiated social organizations capable of facilitating increased productivity and maintaining the necessary ecological and life-style arrangements to make it all work.

217

In Libya, environmental modernization (primarily technology and organization) was introduced in the twentieth century by the Italians. Into a world largely inhabited by nomadic Arabs and governed by traditional Ottoman Turks were thrust radical environmental changes and a complex and differentiated set of social organizations to make them stick. At first, even when the Italians consciously encouraged it, the Arabs were reluctant to participate fully in those changes. Indeed, some fought to reject them.

Yet, as Rome constructed new cities or added to old ones, blocked out and settled its farms and ranches, and generally thrust itself toward revitalizing the old Roman grain fields and thereby reincorporating the "fourth shore" into a homeland lost since the fall of the Empire, some Arabs began to drift in. By law they were relegated to a "second-class" participation. But this did not necessarily reduce the volume of experiences which resulted. However, before most Arabs could be a party in their own right to those "structural" changes, they had to clear two substantially high hurdles. One of them we might call the *"mind hurdle."* It required a leap out of much of the psychology and values of the nomadic and tribal past to the mind reference of an urbanizing, increasingly literate, mobile present. The break, no less so among the Arabs than among many other peoples, was never total, of course, but it was substantial.

The other hurdle was colonialism. The Italian overlords were not in Libya for the benefit of Arab Libyans. Regardless of an Arab's desire or motivation to modernize, it was the Italians who held the keys to all the doors of opportunity. With independence in 1951, the Arabs hurdled some of the obstruction; with the "revolution" in 1969, they hurled the rest of it out to sea.

It might be argued that the generation which won independence—Idris' generation—was motivated to fight more from its desire to *resist* Western values than to incorporate them into Arab life. Fair enough. Certainly there was plenty of anti-Western sentiment in the early years of the Italian occupation. Nevertheless, when the Italians implanted structural change on the North African shore, they introduced some Arabs to dissonance-creating experiences. The pattern was accelerated with World War II and the subsequent discovery of oil. For an increasing number of Arabs, traditional village life and tribal values were called into question. Dissonance was reduced by adopting the new life-styles and adjusting one's value preferences to accommodate the change. Thus, while the old men still lived, a whole generation of their literate, urbanized, symbolic sons could be extraordinarily keen on incorporating technology —particularly war technology—into their lives. Young Arabs might make an effort to preserve—or even to enforce—certain traditional Islamic values (dietary absolutes, for example), but such activity in no way precluded their participation in, and creation of, modernizing structures or adjusting their value matrix accordingly. Nor did it prevent their obliterating much of the rest of the traditional Arab past. By 1970 the country was being run by ambitiously modernizing men consisting of college graduates, military officers, and a Ph.D. The *Ulemas* and *Sheikhs* had long since been cast aside. Scientific technology and modern social organization? The new generation was ingesting it as rapidly as it could learn how.

The great psychological struggle for the Libyan masses now is the continuing need to adapt to an environment which shows absolutely no sign of becoming static, driven on as it is, by the oil and the symbolic holy war with Israel. Structurally, the conflict will revolve around the need to create—and the resistance against—modern and developed organizations which can facilitate a political incorporation of the masses into the new North African republic. It is a matter of national survival.

DEVELOPMENT AND DECAY—PROTEST, REACTION, AND REVOLUTION

A spectacular development of new social forces was a central theme in Libyan life, consisting of new soldiers, students, rising middle class, and second-generation urban immigrants. Another central theme, and a critical one for the political evolution of the nation, was the accompanying rigidity and semiclosed nature of the country's institutions, first when they were under the command of the Italians, and later when they had largely been taken over by Idris and his followers. The resulting "gaps" were, therefore, not only a theoretical problem, but an intensely real one in the lives of thousands of Libyans. Few of Idris' subjects remained outside these tensions.

The early Italian denial of traditional Arab rights (opportunities) created the kinds of structural and psychological binds that force-fed the anti-Italian resistance movement. The collective action itself, facilitated by the ready availability of competent traditional leaders (Idris and Mukhtar are prime examples) and a well-disciplined traditional organization (the Sanusi order), could capitalize upon the rich Arab traditions of tribe and clan and make a good showing against the Italians. The fact that the traditional forces became mobilized at all and could even consider "linking up" across clan and tribe, however, derived from the undercurrents of opportunity deprivation and the application of substantial amounts of coercion Italian style. Nevertheless, one whole generation was left under the branding iron until midway through World War II.

Given the manner in which Libyan history unfolded thereafter, it is not at all curious that the post-Idris generation of urban Libyans should encounter a new iron, although one of a different heat. The sons of World War II were also truly the children of modernization, suffering, as all such children do, from "expectation-opportunityitis." Environmental and subsequent value changes produced an eventual social mobilization which crystalized into collective action. Idris, who had once led the fight for the freedom of his own generation, became the new oppressive overlord, denying the new aspirants access both to political power and the public trough.

More urbanized and literate than ever before, the disenfranchised were also ignored by the nation's headstrong oligarchs and the middleclass sycophants who catered to them. Having resolved their own bind (or having had it done for them), the lords were not of a mind to extend that same opportunity to their nations' newest mobilized children who were forced to resolve much of the dilemma in the same way some of the oligarchs had earlier attempted to resolve theirs—by force.

The failure of the old order to adapt and respond, and its technique of sending out the Cyrenaican Defense Force to put down everyone who yelled in protest, was more indicative of weakness than strength and of decay than development. Idris, through the image of his person, and in spite of the many disagreeing tribal factions and city groups with which he had to work, had given his homeland a sense of identity and nationhood. He had gotten Libya off to a good start. He failed, however, to arrive at second base, refusing to sponsor the development of absorptive institutions and proscribing the institutions that attempted an analogous function on their own (political parties, for example). The regime's nepotism, the requirement of political docility, the necessity to extend favors, and the need to ignore bureaucratic corruption in order to acquire mobility in the absence of family connections were not only insufficient means of absorption but clearly unacceptable ones as well. Idris had allowed Libyan politics to deteriorate because of the machinations of cliques, self-serving exchanges among traditional lords, and "profit-taking" among corrupt, incompetent bureaucrats.

The moral, we suspect, is that it is only under unusual circumstances (as, for example, when there is a colonial presence) that new social forces and traditional institutions, especially political ones, can get along. In the absence of such a "negative unifying force," the legitimacy, or utility, of the old order and its leadership decays; and it becomes increasingly necessary to maintain order by coercion—police power, jails, harassment, deportations, and executions. In Libya, values and attitudes of the new socially mobilized groups had changed. The old monarchy and the religious and clerical foundation upon which much of it rested—including the Sanusi order and traditional tribal organization—were seen as standing in the way of progress.

IDEOLOGY AND LEADERSHIP

In previous chapters we have argued that under conditions in which social forces remain unassimilated into the political and social fabric of a country (and particularly if those forces are being severely "persecuted" by upper status groups, colonial overlords, or occupation forces), "revolutionary" ideas will tend to emerge among them. When articulated by a "charismatic leader," sometimes those ideas take on an "ideological" tone. As such leaders tend to surface only among people suffering from severe structural and psychological binds, however, they, as well as the ideology they preach, frequently command the allegiance and faith of something less than the whole nation. More frequently, a charismatic leader heads only a faction in the population, albeit, a frustrated, discontented, and unabsorbed faction. If such a leader ever becomes the national captain, it is because he and his group, pulling off a win in the interplay for national power, have simply installed themselves in the palace. They have expelled foreign troops, forced the withdrawal of colonial masters, or cowed all domestic dissidents. Indeed, sometimes they may have to do all three.

Especially during the Italian occupation Idris seemed to participate in an aura of charisma (among his Arab brothers, of course, not the Italians), even though his orientation was more traditionalistic than it was modernizing. Yet it was he who made nationhood possible and who held the country together during its early turbulent years. When new unassimilated social forces arose, however, they cast Idris aside. In popular jargon, the King had "lost" his charisma. In reality, of course, he had not lost anything personal at all. The newly mobilized Libyans had simply come to perceive the Monarch as being unable or unwilling to lead them into the symbolic promised land. A new leadership need had arisen because a new Libyan had come into existence. His leader needed to be able to shed light on paths simultaneously leading to modernization, nationalism, Arabism, and hatred of foreigners—and to show how to fight Israel besides. Nasser had filled that need for Egypt. After the discovery of oil and the Arab-Israeli war, Idris could not possibly do it for Libya.

It is within this context that one must understand the present role of Muammar al-Qaddafi, and of his taking on the mantle of Arab nationalism at home and abroad. Qaddafi presently enjoys the "Nasser syndrome," aided, in part, because his style—rhetoric, flamboyancy, and unpredictability—embodies that of the deceased Egyptian president. Not unexpectedly, therefore, Qaddafi has emerged on the back of an accelerating acceptance of "socialist" ideology. Like many other Libyans, he is in fact a child of Radio Cairo, not so much from the consequences of radio transmissions as from the rhythmic compatibility of their meaning with new Libyan expectations.[1]

Qaddafi and his group have articulated an ideological synthesis, a kind of "pragmatic Arabism," if you please, which combines the Koran with the exigencies of the modern day. Those exigencies are related to the existence of Israel on the one hand, and to a need to develop Libya economically on the other. As yet, the ideological tone, while employing a lot of socialist and anti-Israeli rhetoric, has nevertheless been compatible with the continuing presence of foreign oilmen on Libyan soil. Nevertheless, the next military round with Israel, if there is one, will probably be accompanied by a nationalization of Libya's entire oil industry.

While "gap people" sometimes are attracted to the revolutionary ideology of communism, large numbers of contemporary Libyans do not seem to be among them. Any exceptions to this general observation have no doubt by now gone "underground." In earlier years, of course, Idris rounded up and imprisoned or deported Palestinians because he said they were communists working for the overthrow of his monarchy. Today, Qaddafi does the same thing, not because he is unsympathetic toward the Palestinian cause but because his Palestinians might also be communists. The apparent paradox (rabidly supporting the Palestinian cause while imprisoning Palestinians who also support that cause) is logical from Qaddafi's point of view. He wants his Arab nationalism and ideology to be uncontaminated by any foreign influences that might ideologically or materially subordinate the interests of Libya to some undesirable, international cause. The message is "Arabism." Any other socialism is clearly suspect.

Charismatic leaders, as ideologists, suffer from a frequently fatal disease—

time. Success and failure work against them. Success, particularly in economic development—at least in the short run—reduces, binds, and attenuates conditions which fertilize charisma. Failure, on the other hand, is proof that the leader is no good. In the event of leadership success (by meeting many of the expectations of followers and therefore "paying off") longevity of one's tenure in office is enhanced if he can somehow "routinize" his charisma and then have sense enough to step down in good time and pass the mantle of office on to someone else. The survival of charismatic features in Qaddafi's relationship with the Libyan masses, therefore (in an atmosphere in which he is too young to step down if he succeeds but, in any event, probably has cause to be more concerned with the possibilities of failure, both in economic development and in the development of modernizing political institutions) probably depends on the maintenance of hostilities with Israel.

MILITARY REGIMES

In Chapter 4 we formulated two dependent variables relating to political activities of military officers in the Third World. We wanted to know (1) what motivates the officers to attempt a coup d'etat, and (2) when they do, and are successful, what the expected social and political consequences of their reign would be.

Regarding the causes of military coups, we argued that the search for answers must begin first with societal variables (particularly the "gap" creating ones), not military variables. This does not mean to imply that military variables (for example, social origins of the officers and the national or extranational colleagues with whom they identify) are not important. But such variables seem to be crucial only if larger system-wide social preconditions are met. Those conditions are a constellation of factors setting off system-wide disturbances which neither traditional political institutions nor, if there happen to be any, underdeveloped modern ones seem capable of handling. In the contemporary world, the military intervenes in that twilight period when social mobilization and institutional rigidity have combined to produce a new, intense, and recalcitrant social force. Indeed, the whole society may be amoral and corrupt. Its modern institutions are relatively undeveloped if they exist at all. Its traditional institutions, on the other hand, have suffered from rigor mortis and decay. The old guard has resisted developmental change for too long, thereby "aging" beyond repair.

Certainly this constellation of factors was fully evident when Qaddafi made his move in 1969. However, the officers themselves had been discontented since at least 1959, evidenced by the fact that a subversive Movement of Free Officers was formed in that year. But the group was too weak to act in the face of Idris' then fairly strong position. The only thing the dissident officers could do was plot. But when fairly substantial system-wide social disturbances arose in 1964 and 1967, they made their move.[2] On both occasions, however, they bungled the whole affair, partly because the disturbances had not yet made an impact upon the royal guard which surrounded Idris. Many officers as well as civilians were imprisoned as a result. The only alternative to detention was territorial escape—to Cairo or Rome—an option that many people took.

By 1969, however, there were manifest system-wide breakdowns throughout the whole society. Students were rioting; "intellectuals" were hatching plots and junior military officers were joining them; religious, government, and tribal leaders were exercising all the coercive powers at their command; and the oligarchs were making off with most of the country's money. When coupled with a rising frustration in the Army itself (in part because the King had noticeably favored the Cyrenaican Defense Force), it was all sufficient to give the young officers the freedom and the opportunity they needed in order to act.

It was a "text-book" coup, foreign observers said. The precision was nearly absolute. Other Arab regimes quickly sent observers to find out which foreign power had masterminded the whole affair, but they all drew blanks. While the image of Nasser may have inspired the officers, everything else was totally initiated in Libya—including the social disturbances, the breakdown of political legitimacy, the development of new unabsorbed social forces, the amorality, the riots, the strikes, and the plots. Some say Idris picked a wrong time to have an extended Turkish bath on the other side of the Mediterranean. However, it was only a matter of time.

Because of Idris' inability, or lack of desire, to develop his regime politically, he eventually had to pay political, social, and economic deference to his junior military officers. In the long run, therefore, the King's destruction of political party activity and his failure to create alternative means of productively channeling the energies of the socially mobilized (such as Nasser had done with his Arab Socialist Union), greatly served to produce a legitimacy vacuum. As the old traditional patterns of social control broke down, few new ones, except the point of a gun, ever emerged.

In the failure of positive action, Qaddafi and his friends will be no more immune to legitimacy dilemmas than was Idris. Additional coup attempts can be anticipated (one was reported in December of 1969) if the young men fail to develop institutions that can satisfactorily absorb the newly mobilized into the social and political system. The key is not so much "ideological happiness," we suspect, as it is the reduction of unbearable abrasiveness in daily living. Some countries, in spite of presumably good intentions of some of its officers, never make the grade. Bolivia, for example, has had over 180 coups (and an unknown, if not uncountable, number of attempts) in its 150-year history as an independent state. If Qaddafi does not accompany his anti-Israeli kick with some institution building at home, he will be left mounted on his own version of the blind, enraged, camel.

As for the second dependent variable, the anticipated social and political consequences of military coups, we might also interpret this to include the social and political programmatic thrust the officers can be expected to take whether they are able to successfully implement it or not.

As argued in Chapter 4, the answer, or at least clues to it, are to be found in a particular combination of societal *and* military variables. The societal variables includes (1) variables that produce structural and psychological binds and that eventually led to system-wide disturbances, and (2) the degree of inclusion of various social strata in those disturbances. The strongest military variable, on the other hand, seems to be the social origins of the officers, or in the absence of any clear-cut uniformity there, the "reference group" to which the officers are emotionally or ideologically attached.

Various combinations of these variables tend to produce differential effects as regards postcoup programs. If, for example, social mobilization with accompanying evidences of severe structural and psychological binds has reached only part way into the social system (touching an aspiring middle class but not involving the peasantry), the tendency will be for the officers to engage in a little radical "reform-mongering." Particularly will this be so if their social origins dip into the more disadvantaged classes who are attempting some "middle class" status but find an intransigent oligarchy preventing them from getting it. Access to status requires the moving of the oligarchs and their coterie out of power. These conditions approach the "radical praetorian" societal type established by Huntington and demonstrate why a society so characterized is both amoral and corrupt.

On the other hand, if the two constellations of social variables are patterned in such a way that system-wide disturbances have reached down even to socially mobilized lower classes, particularly if the officers themselves have by this time developed a "middle class identification" if not exactly a middle class origin, the tendency will be for postcoup programs to take a more conservative stance. The social conditions established by this type approximate Huntington's "mass praetorianism." Brazil is a case in point.

Even when tendencies for mass praetorianism exist it is still possible, however, for the officers to take on a modernizing if not paternalistic social and political reform role if their "middle class" interests have been contaminated by experiences which have broadened their perspectives. Such seems to be the case in Peru, our next case coming up.

The predictions emerging from these hypotheses in many ways coincide with the events in Libya. A society with "radical praetorian" tendencies and system-wide disturbances was overthrown by a group of middle class aspiring officers who, along with a lot of recently urbanized civilians, had been frozen out of the social and political fabric of the country. Radical reform ensued, not the least of which was a dismissal of the oligarchical class. Obviously, Qaddafi did not have *them* in mind when he said "the interests which we represent are the true interests of the Libyan people."[3]

Curiously enough, some observers of the Libyan scene have called the 1969 military coup a "conservative" one. This is an unfortunate allusion to the intense religious fundamentalism of the regime. "Conservative" within the normal usage of the word at least, is applied badly in this case. For one thing, aside from the oil wells, there was precious little in the country that the officers seemed desirous of conserving. Religious fundamentalism, absent from Libyan cities for decades, might be revitalized but certainly not "conserved." Moreover, if the regime were truly a "conservative" one, it would have been out to legitimize the monarchy, not destroy it; invite Western exploitation of the land, not retch at the thoughts of it; and so on. Much of what might have been conserved was soon being put to the torch. This is fairly radical political conduct regardless of whether one wishes to refer to Islamic dietary and social values as somehow being "traditional."

The expulsion of the foreign business community (particularly the Italians), the wholesale remaking of the bureaucracies, the incipient development of new organizational bases and patterns of social behavior (including the kinds of political participation that will be allowed) are certainly radical in every sense of the word. On balance, therefore, the Libyan case, as far as the predictions regarding the political and social effects of military rule are concerned, substantially supports the generalizations advanced earlier in the book.

In the excited first hours following the coup the officers read their now heralded Proclamation of the Republic. Ending on what may be a continuous note of beginnings, the young men laid out the challenge: "Extend your hands, open your hearts, forget your rancors, and stand together against the enemy of the Arab nation, the enemy of Islam, the enemy of humanity, who burned our holy places and shattered our honor. Thus will we build glory, revive our heritage, and revenge an honor wounded and a right usurped. Oh you who witnessed the holy war of Omar al-Mukhtar for Libya, Arabism, and Islam. Oh you who fought the good fight with Ahmad al-Sharif. Oh sons of the steppe. Oh sons of the desert. Oh sons of the ancient cities. Oh sons of the upright countryside. Oh sons of the villages—our beloved and beautiful villages—the hour of work has come. Forward!"

PART V

Disquietude in Central Peru or How Peasants May Overcome a Rigid Environment and Introduce Themselves into the National Economic, Political, and Social Fabric of Their Country.

In the Brazilian and Libyan cases we have scanned some of the processes of environmental and value change and their political and social consequences as if we were looking through the large end of a telescope. We have attempted a synthesis of both attitudinal and structural change processes through time, including therein many economic, social, cultural, and political factors. We have, therefore, covered a wide area, touching, as it were, relevant attributes of mind as much as the nature of structures and institutions in Third World countries. To penetrate the reality of modernization further, it is necessary to turn the telescope around, to magnify one small part of national reality and thereby hold it up for closer inspection.

Accordingly, in this section we shift our identification from macro-society to a micro-group so as better to see not only internal modernizing dynamics but also more clearly to perceive the relationship of newly mobilized groups to the larger institutional fabric of a country. Peru is our country and some of her peasants our people.

Then, in the final two chapters of this section, we shall attempt an abstract synthesis in terms of a "model" of political and social change, focusing explicitly on dynamic mobilizing forces among the peasantry, and thereafter using it to interpret the Peruvian data.

CHAPTER 11

The Man and the Movement

Peru's sierra begets several breeds of man. Some are lords; most are peasants. Some become leaders; others live to be led. A few remain unflinching traditional zealots. Many become actively involved in a world of modernizing change. Only the names of a scant few ever surface on the pages of an academic publication; of these still fewer enter from the mainstream of peasant life. Certainly this does not happen because the peasants do not have a story worth telling. The problem is that only infrequently do they have a chronicler. Thus still untold in any detail is the story surrounding one peasant—a leader and a reformer—whose peasant forces came to represent one of the most important organizational happenings in Peru's central sierra. Both he and his followers merit much more attention than they have yet received.[1] Aside from the data, therefore, one purpose of this chapter is to record important events in the public lives of this leader and his followers.

The events take place in two separate geographical areas of central Peru. Both are in the department (state) of Junín. One covers the central highlands from Chongos Alto to Tarma; the other consists of a reduced area in the central eastern region loosely converging on Satipo (see Figure 10).

THE NATION AND ITS PEASANTS

The presidential years of Fernando Belaúnde Terry (1963 to 1968) are noted (depending on one's perspective) for Communist infiltration into government, for monetary inflation and near national bankruptcy, for improvement in middle-class social and occupational mobility, or for unprecedented opportunities for politically marginal citizens to become involved in the politics of a modernizing nation. For the peasant (*campesino*)[2] it was a time in which pent-up organizational drives and ambitions could be realized. Accordingly, when Belaúnde came to power in 1963 some villagers literally "exploded" with relief and promptly invaded ranch lands long considered a source of festering relations between themselves and their lords.[3] Other highly motivated peasants took a slower posture directed nevertheless toward similar ends. They wanted a chance for progress and they wanted it now. After building an organizational base and linking up with modernizing national bureau-

229

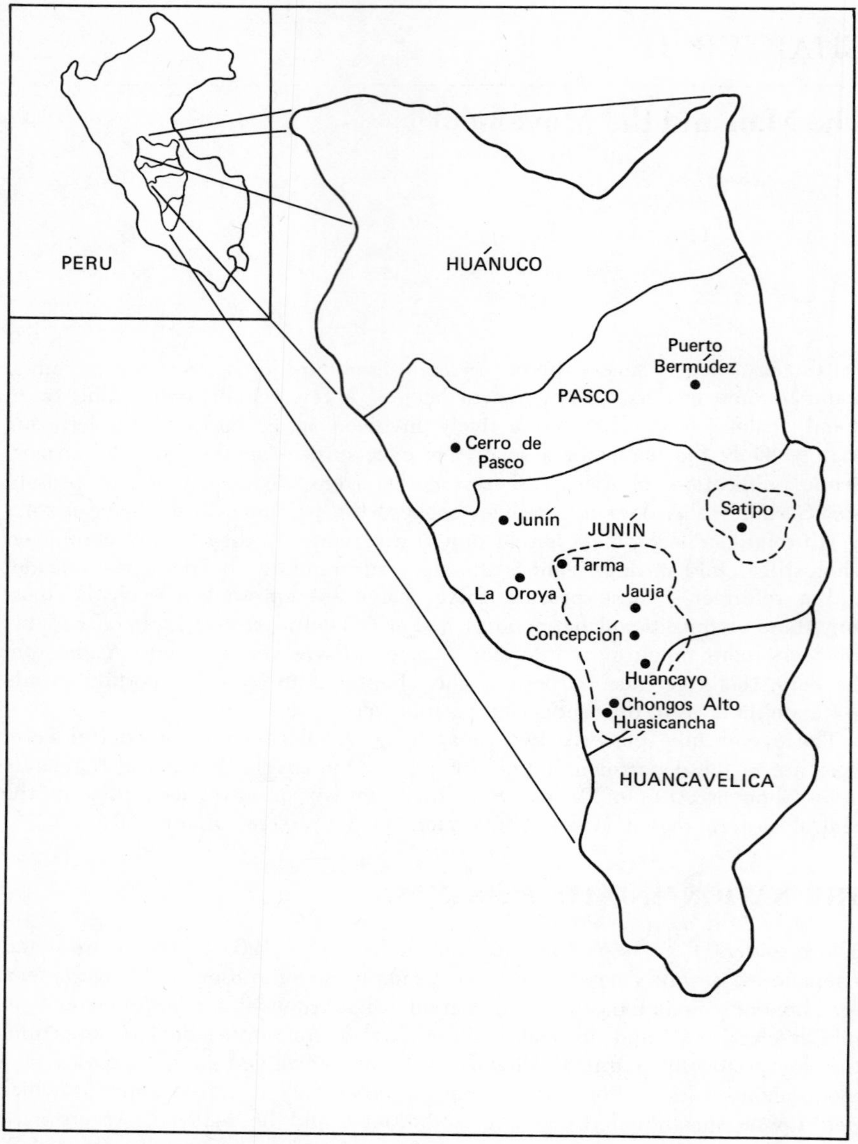

Figure 10. Central Peru.

crats, they began the political task not only of making demands on their
government but of expecting that government to hear them in all seriousness.
Indeed, as the Belaúnde presidency wore on, it seemed that with increasing

frequency peasant organizations, along with their demands, were cropping up virtually everywhere. The following representative announcement of a regional sierra group (which had linked up with urban nonrevolutionary reformers) illustrates the spirit of the times, complaints of the past, and hopes for the future.

Huancayo, April 7, 1967

FRENTE DE DEFENSA Y DESARROLLO DE LAS COMUNIDADES DEL CENTRO DEL PERU

FREDEC invites all Presidents, Solicitors [*personeros*], and Peasants in general of the *Comunidades* [a kind of reservation village] of the Departments of Pasco, Junín, Ayacucho, Huánuco, Huancavelica and Lima to the official inauguration of our central offices . . . in the city of Tarma, Saturday, April 8, 1967 at 10:00 A.M. The inauguration will be attended by the Minister of Agriculture, Dr. Javier Silva Ruete.

President, Solicitor of your Comunidad, fulfill your village obligations. Attend the inauguration of your organization's headquarters.

This act marks a historic step in our struggle against all the exploiters who have abused us with deceit and force. We seek to unite all of us in the successful struggle for an authentic Agrarian Reform; we demand the prompt and immediate expropriation of the ranching estates [*latifundios*] of Cerro de Pasco and all others of the region.

Fellow peasant [*hermano comunero*], you have an obligation of honor Saturday, the eighth of April, in Tarma.

FREDEC is Unity, Hope, and Revindication.

LET THE WELFARE OF THE PEASANTS IMPROVE: LONG LIVE PERU.[4]

Organized activities of this and related kinds brought into sharp relief a struggle among Peru's elites—between those who pushed for social and political modernization and those who considered its impending arrival (especially when that presumed a mobilized peasantry) to be a sign of uttermost decadence. Accordingly, strong and determined national forces impinged on the villages both in an attempt to set them free as well as to shut down their boiling energy.

In decades and centuries past in the Peruvian highlands, many peasant resistance movements broke out in the name of freedom or restoration of a traditional life that was lost. But they did not have much success. The peasants were consistently exploited, cowed, and suppressed. Wherever peasant organization began, leaders were jailed, deported, or exterminated. If complaints were registered, nearly always the complainers rather than the objects of protest were dealt with—usually harshly. Sanctions were heavy, administered to child and adult alike. Such "retribution" was possible because the land barons historically were amply bolstered not only by parliament but also by other important national institutions—the army, the civil guard and, in many instances, the church.

In the 1950's the peasants in many parts of the sierra and eastern uplands of the Amazon's basin again initiated waves of protest. Before opposition forces could move in to shut them *all* down in the traditional manner,[5] however, political and social modernizers "infiltrated" the national government and began to throw up protective walls around the peasants. Indeed, by 1963 these modernizers had captured major portions of the national government, including the presidency. Hence, in comparison to earlier times, peasant political activism was mirrored by numerous important and powerful people strategically placed in the national culture. Fernando Belaúnde was one of these apostles of change.

For years many Peruvians had called for an end to and, from time to time, even protested in their own way against what they deemed the criminal neglect of their peasants. Largely through the efforts of intellectuals associated with the Apra reform party[6] there had developed a national consciousness of the "Indian problem." Indeed, even during the repressive dictatorship of Manuel Odría (1948 to 1956) the government had begun to set up and finance some agencies to tackle the problem of integrating the peasant into national life. However, the efforts were largely paternalistic and produced no important reforms. But as the shanty towns grew and the *barriadas* (the slum districts) of Lima increased, the need for action became imperative not only in human terms but also from a conservative's political point of view. Something simply had to be done to save Lima: hundreds of thousands of destitute peasants were leaving their ancestral homelands and inundating the capital.

It was really Belaúnde, however, who articulated a meaningful reform philosophy—a kind of ideology—reincarnating the ancestral habits of popular cooperation long heralded as a hallmark of the old Incan Empire. The president-to-be mirrored, awakened, and rekindled among the peasants many dormant hopes and aspirations that in earlier years the Apra party had wished to but had failed to champion. During his many visits to the backwater villages of the nation, he continually declared that the old regime must fall, that new blood and new changes must be introduced, that Peru's peasants must cease to be the forgotten people of the Americas. With these words and these thoughts, Belaúnde captured the imagination of hundreds of thousands of his countrymen. Indeed, as early as 1956 he ran a campaign for the presidency. But he was defeated. Afterward, the opposition responded to his audacious statements on social reform by incarcerating him for a short time in El Frontón, the Alcatraz of the southern Pacific. While there, not only did Belaúnde refuse to recant, he also undertook a dramatic protest fast. All this did not go unnoticed by the peasants of Peru.

With all these and subsequent acts Belaúnde thought he was gearing up for an experiment in "modernizing-elite gradualism"—reform from above. The national government could aid in carrying out nonviolent change, he argued. If it did not act, if it did not begin reforms, radicalism and revolution would inevitably result. As far as the countryside was concerned, he believed that the keys lay in cooperative efforts in agrarian reform and community development.

Immediately on assuming the presidency in 1963 (an act permitted only because the military had so willed it), Belaúnde set about trying to bring the resources of the central government to bear on those difficult tasks.

Peru's president was soon to feel personally the debilitating effects that his country's rigid social system had always imposed on attempts at reform. Agrarian reform on paper was one thing; getting it implemented was quite another. Community development materials for the willing hands and strong backs of thousands of anxiously awaiting villagers was a fine idea; but parliament, controlled by the Apra-dominated opposition, would supply few funds. While accomplishing some reform and considerable village development (aided with United States loans), Belaúnde nevertheless did so neither in the magnitude that he had hoped nor at the level that he had promised the peasants. This, along with the pent-up energy of long-suppressed villagers, established an unhappy prelude to a period (1964 to 1966) of intense agitation, additional land invasions, and guerrilla warfare. Yet these skirmishes presented Belaúnde with an impossible situation. To save his administration from Peru's omnipresent and increasingly vociferous elite guardians, he was forced to succumb to many of their coercion-and-no-reform ultimata.

In 1956, and certainly in 1963, the peasants felt that Belaúnde was, if not one of them, at least with them; as time wore on many became unsure. If the plague of a corrupt, inefficient bureaucracy and a majority do-nothing parliamentary opposition were not sufficient to occasion the eventual fading of his reforming star, inflation, devaluation, and the near total loss of hard currency reserves in late 1967 provided whatever else was needed. Finally, in the latter part of 1968, the military ousted the president and sent him into exile.[7] Peru's experiment in democratic gradualism had ended.

Nevertheless, it was unlikely that peasant forces unleashed during Belaúnde's administration would ever return to the old position of subordination vis-à-vis Peru's rural elite and absentee landlords; and they have not. As before, they have continued to organize—especially into cooperatives—and they have continued to demand reforms from the present military dictatorship. An index of their success is shown by the shock among conservatives who had originally heralded the coup. Among other things, the old elite expected the military to put an end to "extremism." Primarily, that referred to peasant demands for lands. Instead of shutting down the peasants however, the new government actually accelerated the pace of reform, awarding to "insistent" villagers and plantation workers at least part of what they had been struggling to obtain. Thus, shockingly for some, the officers have expropriated lands belonging not only to United States business corporations in the Peruvian highlands but those belonging to many absentee Peruvian lords as well. The government has even "invaded" some of the rich coastal sugar-producing plantations.[8]

Enthusiasm has been running high. In promulgating the new agrarian reform law of June 23, 1969, President Juán Velasco Alvarado announced:

"From now on Peru's peasantry will not be anymore the Pariahs nor the disinherited people who lived in poverty from the cradle to the grave and who looked helplessly to a somber future for their children. From this happy 24th of June on, the Peruvian peasant will be a truly free citizen whom the father-land has finally granted the right to enjoy the proceeds of the soil he labors on and a place of justice in a society where he no longer will play the role of a second-class citizen, a man to be exploited by other men."⁹

For the present moment, at least, the military government *has* made a difference for the peasants in Peru. That difference lies not so much in the official rhetoric—which is little altered from that of the Belaúnde years—as it does in the potential consequences of it. The officers apparently have power to carry out virtually whatever reforms they desire, a power denied Belaúnde in his greatest hour of need. Nevertheless, the reforms thus far continue to be primarily defensive, carried out in specific areas where peasant activism has been the most demanding and their protest the most insistent.

MUTATING PEASANT GOALS
AND ORGANIZATION STRATEGIES

The student of Peru would be considerably misled if he assumed that the thrust for modernization and change has been an elusive or even a pre-dominant domain of the country's modernizing elite. On the contrary. Forces for change were arising in the countryside quite as soon as elite rumblings of any notable intensity were being heard in the cities. There is a prevailing myth that peasants are virtually inert and so tied to their traditional way of life that only outside pressure for change can activate them. If it were ever true as far as Peru is concerned, it is a myth that now ought to die. This case study, as an illustration, will show that by the late 1950's, when elite modernizers began to have some influence in Peru's national politics, the peasants out in the countryside had already shifted a number of gears.

In particular, these changes in the countryside were as follows: increasing numbers of peasants developed an awareness of a world larger than their village region; new kinds of peasant leaders surfaced; growing numbers of peasants and leaders alike resolutely and articulately pushed for goals related to modernizing change and increasingly rejected those related to traditional stability; more peasants became associated with stronger, better established organizations and frequently launched movements to protest abuses, to partici-pate in the political system, and to improve progress; and the peasants, through their own initiative, established more linkages with national modern-izers. The great importance of shifting leadership style, institutionalized organ-izing, and national linkages will soon become apparent. In the meantime, a brief look at some of the early and then some of the more recent goals that the peasants sought will give one a feeling for the rather impressive changes occurring in the peasants' world view.

The goals of older peasant movements, with the possible exception of the infrequent "Messianic" variety, derived from what one might call immediate "low-horizon" concerns. To be sure, then as now the energies were protest oriented and generally directed against upper-status groups. But the old thrust was to eliminate particular abuses, not, as now, to restructure a major portion of the peasant world. The concern was with excessive work or personal service obligations, land-tenure disagreements, evictions, corporal punishment, and imprisonment. Usually, when a lord's specific excesses were eliminated, the peasants returned to life-as-usual unless, of course, some new particular abuse arose and became intolerable. Thus, as Ánibal Quijano affirms, older peasant agitation breaking out from time to time in the sierra was always characterized by its sporadic, ephemeral, and isolated nature, encompassing only a specific and usually small region.[10] Indeed, most frequently the action was relegated to one simple village.

In the 1960's, however, the peasants demanded broad-spectrum reforms that dealt not only with an "authentic agrarian reform" (which held first place on every modernizer's list of things to do) but also with community development, with modification of the water code, with agrarian justice, with communal cooperative banks, and with the availability of such modernizing inputs as education, communication, and transportation. Thus, in addition to moves directed at reforming the land-tenure system, the peasants have been anxiously engaged in the formation of cooperatives—both purchasing and marketing—in the creation of communal enterprises, in the building of schools, medical posts, and municipal buildings, and in the installation of culinary water and sanitary disposal systems. They have not been content to live a life of subsistence, much less to return to a life-as-usual vis-à-vis their lords. Accordingly, the movements —the rise of social forces—of the decade of 1960 have involved a major part of the Peruvian sierra, eastern region, and the coast. Moreover, they have frequently been affiliated with federations encompassing one or more departments (states). In recent years, literally hundreds of villages and scores of thousands of peasants have been brought into the communications network of these organizations.

Four general patterns of activity are noted: (1) increased peasant-initiated legal prosecutions against large landowners; (2) unionization or syndicalization of peasant tenant farmers or wage earners and creation of cooperatives among landholding peasants; (3) land invasions; and (4) guerrilla warfare. This is the general intensity spectrum of movements of the last decade. In nearly all cases, even with the new union movements and the acceleration of legal prosecutions in the courts, the peasants are no longer willing to settle simply for a readjustment of their relationship with upper-status groups within the rubric of traditional patterns of exchange. They are calling for a total reorientation of these relations and for their repositioning within the structure of Peruvian society.

Let us look at two examples:

COMMUNAL MOVEMENT OF THE CENTER

In the central sierra the critical year for the new peasant activism was 1958. That bench mark derives from a cheerless juncture in the life of a one-time peasant, Elías Tácunan. It signaled his irrevocable break with the Apra political party. Unfortunately, for the party, one of its most able labor organizers took leave and never returned.

Born in 1909 in the isolated village of Huasicancha in the high central sierra near Chongos Alto, Tácunan experienced in his early youth the anxieties and pains of a peasant's life. Eventually he emigrated to the sierra mining centers in search of opportunities that village life did not offer. While there, the man from Huasicancha joined the Apra reform movement. It is even said that he cultivated a close and harmonious relationship with the founder, Víctor Raúl Haya de la Torre.[11] The reforming ideas articulated by Apra ideology impressed Tácunan, and he dedicated years of his life to the growth of the party. Such dedication was costly, however, primarily because Apra was not at all appreciated by Peru's elite. The party's labor-organizing activities posed a threat to established order. Thus in 1936 the national government forced Tácunan and many other party members into a temporary Chilean exile. Later, in 1948, a massive purge sent thousands to jail. Tácunan himself was sentenced to two years in El Frontón.

Between the political purges Tácunan gained considerable experience in organizing Apra affiliated labor syndicates. No sooner had he obtained employment with the American-owned Cerro de Pasco mining corporation in 1945, for example, than he set out to found, at its smelting plant in La Oroya, the Federación Regional de Trabajadores Mineros del Centro. In those days there were many brilliant Apra organizers in the mining and smelting industries. Tácunan was one of the best.

For Tácunan, Apra had other attractions. The party was interested in peasants—at least, some kinds of peasants. Thus, when the purges were relaxed, the party decided to extend its organizing activities into the coastal agricultural plantations. Accordingly, and for this purpose, it created a subsidiary organization, Fencap (Federación Nacional de Campesinos del Perú). Tácunan was very pleased. Haya de la Torre had said all along that it was necessary to incorporate the peasants into national life if the country were to progress. Organization on the coast was a start; then it would take place in the sierra— perhaps even in his mountain village of Huasicancha where his relatives and friends lived.

Years passed. Yet Fencap, while pursuing a vigorous strategy of labor organization on large coastal plantations where it could make political mileage, steadfastly refused to engage Tácunan's own sierra homeland[12] where the cries of his nonvoting people increasingly reached him.[13] For Tácunan this was betrayal. In 1958 he left Apra, quit his job in La Oroya and went home, back to the village of his birth.

An experienced man had returned to his people. He was a leader; they were ready to be led. The villagers had begun to long for a new life, for freedom, for opportunity, and for progress. I am unaware of any prior time when such massive numbers of peasants would have been willing to receive a "high-horizon" Elías; for he truly came not only with a message of "let my people go!" but "let my people progress!"

In 1958 Tácunan could see that, although much remained the same in the villages, there had been perceptible change in the last decade or so. To be sure, the primitive roads and trails were still there (although some motorized transport was available from time to time out of the district's capital of Chongos Alto).[14] Moreover, because of the villager's strategic location, adjacent to extensive grazing lands prized by some of Lima's well-to-do and politically important families, neither the lords nor their administrators were much changed. While the lords no longer—or at least not as randomly and unabashedly—expropriated village land and livestock (or sometimes even village labor forces), Tácunan could see that the villages nevertheless still remained highly contained.

Yet other circumstances that Tácunan had known in the 1920's had been greatly altered by 1958. The transformation was not so much in physical surroundings or in relations with the land barons as in the peasants themselves. As such, a casual observer might have detected little change at all. True, there were a few more thatched-roof huts—and considerably more people living in them; and, because of the increase in population, the landholdings were smaller than those of the 1920's. But the market system had expanded. Moreover, the villagers no longer relied primarily on barter in their dealings with the *llameros* who, with their llama pack trains, visited the region to trade simple manufactured goods for sheep's wool, potatoes, and grains. Accordingly, Tácunan could see that many of his people not only knew the value of money but were using it with considerable confidence. Besides, instead of making wage payments in kind, some ranchers had begun to pay cash to their peasant laborers who "commuted" each day from nearby villages to render services.

What Tácunan noticed, above all, was that his people were thinking differently. Moreover, they were engaged in forms of behavior scarcely known decades before. For one thing the formal organization of village leaders (*junta comunal*) was involved in activities that reached far beyond the traditional ones of settling disputes, seeing to the care of the village saint, supporting the church, and maintaining the cemetery grounds. In 1958 the symbols of council activity related more to this life than to death or the life hereafter. Among other things the village elders had been discussing what might be done, if anything, about the ranchers who periodically invaded their lands. Moreover, they had engaged in agitated discussions about how best to protect themselves from moneylenders and shopkeepers in the district and provincial capitals which they visited with increasing frequency. In addition, they were concerned with getting the attention of government bureaucrats who, according to government propaganda, were supposed to be rendering services to them. Village leaders were particularly piqued at the enormous delays of the Ministry of Indian Affairs in the departmental capital of Huancayo. It seemed that the office's employees always had an excuse for not paying attention to village representatives and their needs. The peasant leaders were convinced that those who earned money from the state ought to "get off" their lord syndrome and perform the proper functions of their office. A good place to start, they argued, would be to allow village leaders to enter the office's front door rather than to require them, as habitually they did, to enter through the rear. In addition, the leaders stressed that the bureaucrats ought to know that peasant leaders are busy men; they do not have time to spend three or four days in Huancayo waiting for officials to tire of "flirting with their secretaries," stopping only occasionally to give out their great "mañana" speeches. "We are not aborigines who can be treated like that!"[15]

Aside from organizational activities, another era of dramatic change that Tácunan noted related to literacy. In the early 1950's many village councils had created school committees and instructed them to set up educational programs—at least one or two years at the elementary level—for all village children.[16] Interested adults were also allowed to attend. As the peasants entered the money economy in the postwar years they could see that power, influence, and, above all, protection from deceit lay with those who could read and write and sign their name. It seems that this simple observation, more than anything else, caused the villagers to want education for themselves and their children. In any event, the committees went to work and founded many schools in the region. As a rule the committees remained active and continued to work for the development of their school programs. They sponsored fund-raising projects and participated in the formation of local school policy. Moreover, they concerned themselves with the moral and professional behavior of the teachers who came to their communities, becoming progressively more concerned over time in light of their experiences with a profession that had long exhibited a contemptuous treatment of the highland peasant.

Once the desire to have schools was manifested, two mutually reinforcing events seemed to make their founding possible. First, Peru's entrance into a post-World War II money economy had left the peasants with a small surplus which could be invested (and they chose education as the target). Second, Peru had a surplus of teachers in those days. Many who could not obtain more satisfactory employment were willing to begin their services in a small village even if the schools were not officially recognized by the Ministry of Education. Besides, some villages even paid higher wages for beginning teachers than did the ministry, although in neither case were teachers' salaries anything but meager.

There were educational changes occurring elsewhere in the region as well. Some of the *hacienda* villages had taken an interest in founding schools, sometimes even over the heated objections of their owners. (The hacienda village was different from the *comunidad*—Indian reservation village—in the sense that it was part of the ranching operations of a great land baron and existed primarily for the purpose of securing a dependable labor pool. The reservation villagers had land titles; the hacienda villagers did not.) Many of the hacienda lords were then absentee types who came only to collect the annual increases in the herds and flocks. They had little immediate concern for village schools, or any other "human resource" improvements for that matter. They therefore paid little attention to the villagers' educational efforts until it became apparent what the schools were doing to the children. On one ranch in the Yanamarca valley to the north (between Tarma and Concepción) an angry landlord confronted the peasants' schoolteacher one day and screamed. "What have you done to all these Indians? They used to kneel down before me and kiss my hand; now they're all insolent!"

In some villages the schools became extraordinarily popular. At times even the parents attended if for no other reason than to learn to sign their names and thereby carry the pretense of literacy. It was the children who benefited the most, however. Yet they, in turn, gave advantage to the village. The practical utility of having even semiliterate children around was apparent to nearly everyone. When the first groups of youngsters finished the initial primary grades, the villagers frequently raised more taxes, initiated the second grade, and scouted an additional teacher, or teacher's helper, to staff it. In time, some villages were able to establish a full five-year elementary program and, on occasion, even to convince the Ministry of Education to "nationalize" their schools to pick up the salary costs of the teachers. Such happy events usually occurred only after innumerable petitions and visits to the Ministry's headquarters in Huancayo. The social impact was substantial, however, for in the process of discussing new problems and attempting to establish a primitive system of education, numerous villagers traveled considerably more than they otherwise would have done, met many more people, were introduced to extraordinarily different and challenging situations, and became much more aware of a complex and changing world outside their village.

Still a third area of organized activity had increasingly become apparent in Tácunan's absence. Some of the villagers had established athletic or sports clubs. Interest had grown as travel increased to the larger cities in the region where the national sport of *fútbol* (soccer) was firmly established. Once a village had a club it frequently began to participate in athletic conferences comprising as many as five or ten villages. For a special game in another settlement the entire village population might make the trek along with its team. The clubs thus functioned not only as a locus of enthusiasm, unity, and solidarity for the entire village but, more important, as a mechanism to broaden the peasants' experience and to introduce them to new issues and events. In addition, the games created situations in which large numbers of people gathered to talk informally about their world.

A fourth area of change, one that had been of considerable interest to Tácunan over the year, related to youth who had emigrated to the cities and mining centers. Rather than become totally alienated from their village of origin, many of them had maintained organized contact with it. Tácunan had been one of these, but he certainly was not the only boy to have left Huasicancha. Many of these sons—and at times daughters—organized themselves into social groups in the various places where they settled. The groups literally became urban colonies of the home village, frequently setting up a form of club government that paralled the structure of the village council. Sometimes these clubs even formed a kind of "shadow cabinet" contributing to village development and aiding it in its problems with the outside world. Thus, in addition to serving as city couriers for community interests, these clubs frequently participated in the planning of the village schools and in securing teachers for them. Not infrequently it was the clubs who donated the writing desks and other equipment—which, incidentally, always included a soccer ball.

Another variant of this phenomenon showed the clubs functioning to facilitate the urban integration and placement of successive new crops of emigrating youth. Moreover, as the clubs were a gathering point for social activity and communication, the migrating sons were able to keep in touch with their village and learn of hometown happenings. More important, however, when these seasonal workers returned home they brought with them considerable new information derived from other club members as well as their own experiences. The "gossip chains" were kept chattering well into the nights.

These were some of the more important changes that occurred during the years of Tácunan's absence. They contributed to his finding many peasants of the region not only frustrated with their world but also rallying around him whenever he said: "Now is the time to throw off the abuses which are heaped upon us daily." To be sure, others for some time and with increasing frequency had been saying the same thing. But here was Tácunan, one of their very own, one who knew all about the outside world, about organizations, labor unions, political parties, politicians, and how to defend oneself when the going is rough. Tácunan had been through it all with the Apra labor union movement in the decades of the 1930's, the 1940's, and early 1950's. Now the peasants were ready. They also wanted to become a recognized part of the Peruvian national state.

How do we account for these dramatic social and cultural changes in an area relatively isolated from the regional centers of communication and commerce of Huancayo and Jauja in the Mantaro valley,* an area long touted as being atypical, because of its dynamic progress, to the rest of the Peruvian sierra? Causes usually are multiple, and here as elsewhere different observers have their respective lists.[16a] In the case of the altiplano region around Huasicancha, however, two causal factors of importance stand out: One is the pressure of increasing population on a fixed land base; the other is the sierra mines, especially those exploited by the famed—and foreign owned—Cerro de Pasco Mining Corporation.

With the man-land question, the Spaniards, and then their descendants and cultural heirs had taken over much of the best grazing lands of the contiguous altiplano and, eventually, had begun to commercialize a sheep and llama industry there. On the land retained under peasant control, an increasing campesino population was left to fester. Exempted from this frustration, perhaps, were those campesinos who could market themselves as wage laborers to the cattle barons. But commercialization ruptured many traditional peón-patrón benevolent relations and only heightened disparities between those successful in obtaining nearby employment and the majority who did not.[16b]

A progressive release (beginning around 1925) from these frustrating circum-

---

* Isolation is, of course, a relative term. When Tácunan returned, Huasicancha was still 2 hours' walking distance from Chongos Alto, and five hours from there to Huancayo by motor transport, infrequently available.

stances was caused by the increasing emigration of village sons who found it necessary, if not desirable, to leave the area in search of seasonal or full-time employment. "Where else but the mines," they said? In fact, the mines, especially the huge complex of the Cerro de Pasco Corporation eventually became for many a stepping-stone for residence on the coast, sometimes even in the city of Lima, itself. Thus while man-land pressures were becoming increasingly unbearable, outside opportunities for alternative vocations became increasingly visible. The mines had been in a heavily expanding phase (facilitated by the construction of a railroad to the coast) for less than 25 years when sons of the altiplano ventured in with a show of general interest.

How long the land pressure was felt before emigration in substantial proportions began we do not know. Numerous village sons of the generation of Tácunan followed him. Subsequent generations proceeded apace. Tácunan was just one of the more illustrious from the region; one of his village brothers gained great prominence in the central sierra operation of Fencap, the peasant league of the Apra political party.

In the mines and smelters these men came into contact with new ways, new thinking, schools, and political organizers. Above all, they acquired new technical capabilities and seemed to develop a greater sense of self-worth. Their frequent, and sometimes prolonged returns to the villages in the high sierra had their eventual effect. If land pressure compounded by the commercialization of the sheep- and llama-raising industry had made continuation of a traditional village life impossible, the village sons readily taught an alternative that was increasingly perceived to be worthy of attention.

If it had not been for the land pressure, however, incentives for migration, and incentives for the elders to listen to whomever migrated, would not have been nearly as high. Thus a combination of declining assets (land) and rising expectations (through the mines and the sons who worked there) opened up the area culturally and, in a sense, politically. Hence, when Tácunan returned to his people, they were "ready." And so was he.

Tácunan first surveyed the regional situation and made himself well-known in numerous villages. Then in March of 1958 he called for a five-district convention of village council leaders, members of school committees, and officers of other village organizations. The districts, each with numerous villages, included not only the main one of Chongos Alto, but also Huasicancha, San Juán de Jarpa, Colca, and Carhuacallanga. In the first general assembly 80 village council leaders and more than 200 representatives of other organizations voted to form a federation of villages. They selected Tácunan as their first secretary-general. An organization representing approximately 30,000 people was born.

Thus it was in Tácunan's homeland that the infant beginnings of the Communal Movement of the Center began, the first politically independent league of peasant villages anywhere in the department of Junín. The initial opposition to the federation was substantial. The land barons' reasons derived from the nature of the federation's goals. The peasants had organized not only to handle better the development and progress already begun in the villages and to defend themselves in their relations with city and town bureaucrats; they also had organized to exercise their rights against the powerful cattle and sheep barons—the *gamonales*.

Yet this was only the beginning. Tácunan organized convention after convention in the isolated districts. Membership grew so rapidly that in time it became necessary to change the organization's name—from Communal Movement of the Center to "The Provincial Federation of Comunidades of the Province of Huancayo." Tácunan's organizing activities had spilled over from the high zones of the Mantaro right down to the valley itself where more than a hundred villages were located. A majority of them became affiliated with his movement. Shortly, in September of 1961, the new and larger provincial federation hosted in the strategic Mantaro village of Sicaya the "First Regional Congress of Comunidades, Municipal Councils and *Colonos* of Central Peru."[17] Here it was evident that Tácunan's interest had expanded into the international sphere. Aside from the perpetual agenda item of "authentic agrarian reform," one of the purposes of the convention was to see how the federation could "zero in" on John F. Kennedy's Alliance for Progress.

Tácunan's grass-roots organizing went right on into the national elections of 1962. In an attempt to maximize peasant participation in them, the man from Huasicancha launched his campaign as a senatorial candidate for Junín— sponsored by his "communal" peasant movement. "We must gain access to parliament," he argued, "or we may not be heard for a long time." The country seemed to be opening up to all its citizens. (Indeed, the peasants could see that Belaúnde was running again after his defeat in 1956 and appeared to have a winning chance.) Why not try to beat the system at its own game? As a result, Tácunan managed to pull in nearly 40,000 votes. However, because of literacy laws that presumably kept many of his peasant supporters away from the polls, this placed him only fifth in line after candidates sponsored by Belaúnde's Popular Action Party (206,000), the Apra (159,000), the National Odriísta Union (156,000), and the Liberation Front (53,000). (All figures are rounded off and are for the state of Junín only.)

The loss mattered little, however, since the military cried "fraud" (some say because Apra, a party it detested, had done so well), invalidated the national elections, and took over the country.[18] With this act, peasants virtually everywhere could see a bleak future of "more of the same" as far as their own position in society was concerned.

But this time the peasants refused to become resigned to a fate that they thought they had escaped.

Up and down the entire sierra they began to chip away at the social floodgates that for so long had held them back. During the seven months following the coup, peasants in the Convención valley east of Cuzco (Cuzco is a departmental capital in southern Peru and ancient center of the Incan Empire) carried out continual strikes, land invasions, and guerrilla war. Those in Cuzco participated in bloody riots, and those around Cerro de Pasco in the central sierra erupted into intense agitation. The Cerro de Pasco episode alone, less severe than that of the Convención valley, required the dispatching of 500 government troops to control it. There the fatalities were numerous (the government reported 7; the peasants stated there were 43).

It was after these outbursts, along with worker unrest in the mining centers, that the military government announced the discovery of a widespread "Communist plot" and declared a state of modified martial law. The government then struck with lightning speed, rounding up agitators, Communists, and suspected Communists from cities all along the coast to hamlets in the high sierra. One of those incarcerated was Elías Tácunan. After several weeks in jail he was set free, however, because the military could establish no real foundation for the charges made against him. Nevertheless, he was warned to avoid any further organizational activity among his people.

After lying low until the military considered the crisis over, Tácunan resumed his work with greater energy than ever. Before long it was necessary to change his movement's name once again to reflect more accurately its enlarged scope of operations. It became the "Departmental Federation of Comunidades of Junín" (Fedecoj). In the beginning barely comprising five districts in Huancayo province, and later only the province itself, Tácunan's movement finally emerged as an influential federation encompassing the entire department (state) of Junín.

In January of 1963 the military, reacting to the initial period of peasant agitation throughout the sierra, announced a land-reform program in the areas hardest hit by violence. The first to benefit to a minor degree were the villages in the Convención valley, seat of the most prolonged agitation. Token reforms were made elsewhere. But it was only with martial law that a peace of sorts was achieved throughout Peru. Thus town dwellers continued to fear that a spark of any kind would ignite the passions and hatred of the approximately 3 million sierra Indians and produce an inferno from which traditional Peru might not recover.

In spite of the tension, by February 1963 there was sufficient superficial order throughout the country to encourage the military junta's moving ahead with plans for a new round of mid-year national elections. Tácunan turned his major efforts this time toward registering voters. At his prodding, the Catholic bishop of Huancayo announced that there would be no cost for birth or baptismal certificates (documents required for obtaining an electoral voting permit) for the 45 days preceding the closing of voting registration. Tácunan pushed hard in this area. His experience in the annulled 1962 elections convinced him that in national politics an organization with few registered voters counted little. Literacy was not the problem it once had been because many of his people could now pass the tests. The question was getting through all the red tape required for a voting permit (*tarjeta electoral*).

Tácunan did not enter again as a candidate. Instead, he threw his weight behind Belaúnde and the senatorial candidates sponsored by the Popular Action party. That strategic move, he considered, would net the greatest mileage to the peasants in the long run. The elections were held on schedule and were reported to be among the most honest Peru has ever experienced. Belaúnde won.

Although on the surface the country was calm, it really was into a volatile atmosphere that Fernando Belaúnde Terry stepped as president of Peru on July 28, 1963. Within days the fragility of the peace that the military had established in the central sierra became painfully apparent as scores of villages mounted a siege on the traditional social order. It all started with the communidad of San Pedro de Cajas near Tarma in the department of Junín. On July 30 more than 1000 villagers launched a massive invasion of 20,000 acres of ranchland that they claimed by ancestral rights, a fact attested by ancient documents in their possession. For 30 years the village had been suing the rancher for the return of the lands; but the costly litigation had gone unresolved in the courts. Now the peasants had invaded the disputed lands and had declared that they would not be moved by anyone. As proof, overnight they erected hundreds of dwellings and moved their entire families and belongings to the invaded zone. It is said they even ran up the Peruvian flag and joyously sang the national anthem. Diverse persons, organizations, labor syndicates, and other villages from the central region sent congratulatory telegrams and interested observers. Tácunan's Departmental Federation of Comunidades of Junín quickly conveyed its approval and offered strong support. The invasion pattern was thus set as well as approved. Within days numerous other villages with similar litigations, buoyed up to the apparent success of San Pedro de Cajas, also began to invade disputed lands.

Belaúnde's government moved into high gear with consummate speed, responding to the invasions in a pattern already established by the military—minus the dispatching of government troops. That is, by decree it carried out on-the-spot land reforms in the areas of violence. No sooner had one spot cooled, however, than a dozen more broke out. Thus in the early weeks of Belaúnde's regime his government frantically moved from spot to spot in the central sierra carrying out local reforms. On August 10, 1963, for example, only 13 days after his inauguration, he declared the necessity and public utility of expropriating approximately 200,000 acres from 13 ranches in the central-sierra departments of Junín and Pasco. Fifty thousand of those acres belonged to the United States owned Cerro de Pasco mining corporation; 20,000 to the ranch invaded by San Pedro de Cajas. At the same time Belaúnde continued to push parliament hard for meaningful land-reform legislation.

These acts in no way resolved the problem. As the month of August wore on, the land invasions not only increased but moved progressively from the north toward the city of Huancayo. Members of the Regional Association of Agriculturists and Ranchers of Junín, centered in that city, were absolutely rabid. Shrilly they demanded that the government use the army to put an end to the invasions.

Belaúnde responded by issuing a communique warning the peasants that further land invasions would not be tolerated. Moreover, he advised them that a continuation of the radicalism would only delay a true (*auténtica*) agrarian reform. Nevertheless, he continued to respond to the rural-estate invasions, since they did not cease, not with troops but with expropriation of specific lands that he made available to the villages.

Belaúnde did make an important tactical concession to the ranchers, however. He agreed to expropriate lands only where invasions had occurred or were considered imminent, and only then after having consulted with the respective owners about compensation. The landowners' organization reciprocated by agreeing to the general principle of expropriation at a fair price (payment in cash) of roughly 10 percent of the ranchers' property for village use. Alternatively, the ranchers would enter into direct agreements with the villages to sell them land. This flurry of activity occasioned more land reform in the central sierra than any previous happening within living memory. Even so, considering the demand, it was pitiably inadequate.

Unfortunately, Belaúnde simply could not satiate the peasants in this piecemeal manner. Rural agitation and invasions continued into September, most occurring in the central highlands where population density was high. Daily news dispatches from various parts of the country gave them banner headlines. As the situation worsened, Belaúnde continued to sign decrees authorizing the expropriation of hundreds of thousands of acres in cases where the invasions stemmed from long-standing court litigations with the ranchers. In situations not fitting this category, Belaúnde's technicians were sometimes able to persuade the peasants to withdraw in exchange for promises of land under an agrarian reform plan that the president had submitted to parliament shortly after his inauguration.

Although Belaúnde could continue to expropriate some lands by decree, it was necessary for him to pay for them in cash at a fair market value. But his funds were limited. Obviously, if he were to carry out his reform program and were to anticipate the peasants rather than simply respond to their violent action, he would need broad authority to expropriate and make payment in bonds. At least that was the rationale behind his agrarian reform bill. Roughly, it called for a cash payment for all improvements plus 10 percent of the land's value. The balance would be covered with 20-year bonds. The ranchers' reaction to the bill was immediate and intense. The National Agrarian Society declared it unconstitutional, confiscatory, and a cause for suspending any new private investments in lands then under production. In the meantime, Belaúnde continued as best he could on a cash basis, concentrating most of his efforts in the highlands of Junín and Pasco.

Early in September, as the land invasion excitement increased, Belaúnde made a trip to the central sierra, visited Tácunan and other peasant leaders, and pleaded with them not to invade any more ranches until such time as he had done all he could toward a true agrarian reform. Tácunan pressed Belaúnde hard on this point, and the president answered him this way: "I ask of you a space of two months in order to initiate agrarian reform. All of us desire that the aspiration of justice will become a reality in our country. In two months we will initiate that reality." Belaúnde warned the peasants that further agitation might provoke a new round of military intervention, thereby risking the nullification of all reforms. He further reminded them that there were "dark forces" in the nation who, for their own personal gain, wished to create a struggle between the government and its people. As such, a return of lands to their rightful owners could only be done through legal channels and not by violence. "Violence is the energy of worthless men," was Belaúnde's parting admonition.

As the president met with Tácunan and representatives from scores of villages associated with the departmental federation, he convinced them of his sincerity. Thus, a few days afterward, Tácunan called a department-wide convention of all villages and relayed Belaúnde's story to hundreds of peasant delegates. The message: "Belaúnde has assured us that our hour of justice has finally arrived. He will implement that justice through a broadly based agrarian reform program. The program will include not only the redistribution of land but also education, technical aid, and credit facilities." Tácunan convinced the village representatives that what Belaúnde needed most was collaboration, not violence and obstructionism. In light of these convincing events the convention passed a resolution which, frankly, amounted to a vote of massive confidence for the president: "If President Belaúnde has asked for two months to resolve the agricultural problem for our villages, we will reciprocate by giving him twelve."

The pact held reasonably well in Junín even though Belaúnde was never able to pay off with his hoped for and frequently promised agrarian reform.[19] Opposition in parliament was too strong. However, he did send into the sierra regions of Pasco, Junín, and selected spots of Huánuco and Huancavelica, virtually every rural-action and village-development program he had. Indeed, of the 10 national development agencies under his influence or direction which worked in the areas of social and political change, seven had exclusively rural functions and two of the remaining three had rural-action programs.[20] He used these generously in Junín and Pasco.

The combination of Belaúnde and Tácunan was dramatic. With the exception of a peasant organization in Satipo, affiliated with Tácunan, and several villages in isolated regions of the Junín area, no more violence occurred for more than a year. It seems that the enthusiasm deriving from all the government concern and activity remained sufficiently high to temporarily blunt the immediacy of the land-tenure question. Thus the villages energetically entered a phase of road building, school construction, adult education, and technical-aid programs. They created medical-aid facilities, developed marketing and purchasing cooperatives, and set up transportation companies.

Though blunted, the land-reform question was always present, and Tácunan certainly did his best not only to keep the president aware of that fact but also to keep his peasants convinced that the federation did not consider the issue dead. For the most part, however, Tácunan's group was supportive of Belaúnde whereas Fencap, the Apra-sponsored peasant league that finally developed a sierra interest in 1961, was not. Thus it was to the president's interest and advantage to see to it that Tácunan's group could report some "successes." Even though Belaúnde could not meaningfully respond to the rhetoric of land reform, he could insure Tácunan's marginal success as a nonviolent reformer by patronizing his group with much of the state development aid destined for the villages. The president helped furnish materials and tools; Tácunan helped organize labor forces to utilize them.

Tácunan's astute handling of the issues, and his linkages with the president, allowed him to continue to enlarge his organization's scope while also maintaining considerable grass-roots support. Only the most radical of the peasant groups pulled away and left him. Thus by February 1967 he had meticulously carried out plans for a *national* convention of *comunidades,* hacienda peasants, and *colonos* to be held in Huancayo City. Land reform was still high on the agenda; the president was still making hopeful promises. Peasant delegates from all over Peru had accepted an invitation to attend.

Sudden death from a heart attack deprived Tácunan of realizing this dream (which heirs to his organization carried out in a partially successful manner in May 1967). But, "Elías Tácunan, strong man of 500 villages," is the epitaph engrained in the minds of his followers. He long will be remembered in the sierra.[21] The man's importance was recognized by Ciro Alegría, one of Peru's most internationally famous and frequently exiled protest writers. Dedicating to Tácunan a volume of his classic work, *Broad and Alien is the World,*[22] above his autograph he carefully penned: "To the New Rosendo Maqui of Peru." Maqui was the hero of his novel and the indefatigable and trusting peasant fighter for the rights of his people.

There was a double tragedy in Tácunan's death: one for the peasants, another for Belaúnde. After February 1967, with Tácunan gone, the peasants began to realize that the land reform they had hoped for would not be forthcoming. As 1967 drew to a close many began once more to speak of land invasions. By 1968, when the military again closed the halls of parliament and took the country for its own, the invasion rhetoric was highly pitched. Very quickly the military began to carry out the kinds of land reforms that it hoped would forestall revolution.

FEDERATION OF PEASANTS AND COLONOS OF SATIPO

While the events of 1961 to 1968 were transpiring in the central sierra, considerable violence, agitation, and guerrilla warfare occurred from time to time in other areas of Peru where Belaúnde's promises were heard but neither his reforms nor his pleas for restraint made any headway. One of these places centered around the frontier town of Satipo. A brief social and political backdrop to the area will set the stage for a description of the radical events that took place from 1961 onward.

The entire region had been a near-virgin wilderness on the eastern side of the Andes, recently made accessible by a tortuous and serpentine roadway leaving the Mantaro valley through the district capital of Concepción. The plan of several governments (Odría, Prado, the Military) had been to resolve most of the land-tenure problems in the sierra through resettlement programs in this and related regions. There were other advantages as well. Such a move would avoid the hot political question of the expropriation of sierra land. Accordingly, for several years prior to Belaúnde's inauguration in 1963 emigration from the central sierra to the area of Satipo had been encouraged. Many peasants had gone. Some had returned to the sierra, of course, but the net balance was in favor of Satipo. Even Tácunan's group tried to facilitate such a move by organizing a colonizing company in 1961 and sending out 50 families. The announced goals of the various governments had been to deed Satipo lands to "homesteaders" (*colonos*) and thus to encourage immigration. However, on-the-scene administering bureaucrats served more effectively to sabotage the land settlement program than to insure its success. They made the obtaining of a deed so difficult that only with extreme persistence over several years, and frequently not even then unless inducements were offered, could a peasant hope to see a document in his hand. For "important people," however, the task was easy. A former mayor of Satipo, later a regional assistant director of Belaúnde's Popular Cooperation program, affirmed that for people of his status the task was simple and required only a few days. As his vigorous championing of the peasants' cause had put him on the local police list, however, he found it necessary to leave the area. Thus the well-placed and their friends gradually began to take over most of the land opened up by the new roads. Moreover, they also began to establish in the area a tropical version of the sierra hacienda—with tenant farmers and the rest. Recipients of most of the good and accessible lands, therefore, were not peasants; they were lords. They intended to preserve their lordship.

The peasants who migrated from the sierra to the east were exceptionally brave. Fears of tropical disease and isolation were rampant, yet they migrated anyway. Not only were they highly motivated, but undoubtedly they expected their life to improve. Whereas many of their acquaintances had migrated westward to the coast or to the sierra mining centers, these chaps chose the exciting frontier of the Amazon uplands. The irony, as it turned out, was that while Satipo indeed was a frontier, many migrating peasants found themselves living and working in only slightly improved conditions from those to which they had earlier been accustomed. Moreover, the local police were extremely oppressive where sierra migrants were concerned—whether they held land deeds or not—and the national government seemed unwilling to do anything about it.

It was in 1961 that these *colonos* and peasants (the former being the peasants who had been successful in acquiring a little land, the latter being unsuccessful and, therefore, mainly tenant farmers) began vigorous organizational activities. The Apra party's national peasant league (Fencap) was then interested in Satipo (as, indeed, it was in the central sierra where it had been looking for a toehold in Tácunan's domain). Fencap moved in with assistance, sending (with considerable financial backing) professional organizers from Huancayo. The initial pleasure of the Satipo peasants and *colonos* with this service soon soured. Fencap seemed to be interested in them more as political resources than as men with problems to be resolved. The peasants promptly severed relations, cashiered the organizers from Huancayo, and sent them on their way. The Apra party was incredibly incensed over this act, particularly when shortly thereafter the Satipo group sent an aid request to Tácunan. He happily obliged. In the latter part of 1961, with Tácunan's guiding hand, the peasants and colonos of Satipo held their first regional convention. The police, and later the Peruvian Special Investigation Bureau (PIP), watched closely.

The first leaders of the Satipo organization were extremely vigorous in their denunciation of the government, alleging that it had protected the new wave of oppressive landowners and had ignored the peasants' rightful claims for deeds. With every meeting the tension seemed to increase substantially. Indeed, the rhetoric was such that by mid-1962 extremists and Communist ideologues had been attracted and were observed joining the organization. The intensity of the rhetoric continued to increase. Eventually it began to take on revolutionary symbolism. As leadership extremism increased, however, several from among the rank and file got "cold feet" and pulled out, thus fragmenting the organization's solidarity and strength. The radicals responded to this turn of events by enlisting the Campas Indians (a tribe natural to the region) to fill the void. Hundreds of the natives readily responded. They, too, were in a state of agitation.

In 1962 Tácunan again made a trip to Satipo—this time to participate in the second regional convention of his peasant affiliate. While there, he attempted to dissuade the extremists from their obvious course. But they would have none of his advice. The sessions were loud and aggressive. In the final meeting one man who stood up and vigorously denounced the organization's extremist tack was thrown into the street and nearly stomped to death. Only Tácunan's dramatic intervention (in which he bodily threw himself over the man) saved him.

There was a not-too-curious result of all the rhetoric and agitation. Satipo's public authorities announced their intention to expedite paperwork for land titles. They also agreed to be more receptive to demands for the state services that they controlled (including those relating to agricultural development). Moreover, it was said that the police would be more civil. However, the peasants very soon realized that, promises notwithstanding, the interest of the public authorities was more in removing Communists and extremists from their organization than in reforming anything.

Thus the situation, largely still in the realm of words even as late as March 1963 (four months before Belaúnde became president), was becoming sufficiently tense to encourage the PIP's Huancayo office to send in 16 "students and sociologists" for a study of peasant and colono "needs." The information derived from this outrageous deceit resulted in the arrest of two Cubans, several peasant leaders, and a former leader of the Peruvian Communist party who, earlier, had renounced his membership. (All were whisked off to Lima for intensive interrogation.)

The peasants and colonos were not only greatly alarmed about this turn of events but they honestly felt that their government had betrayed them. The immediate upshot was aggressive verbal confrontations with Satipo public authorities. However, now that the PIP had broken the ice and demonstrated the national government's intention to insure law and order, the local police responded to the "insolence" by jailing scores of the protestors and, by intimidation and threats, successfully cowing the remainder. The less hardy remained cowed; others later rallied around new leaders who shortly entered into a formal alliance with urban revolutionaries working out of Huancayo.

Tácunan denounced this alliance as loudly as he had the oppressive treatment heaped daily on his Satipo brothers. But, considering the tense times, he believed that the Satipo group had gone too far. Fearing that his whole movement would be crushed if he allowed an affiliate group to become subversive, he expelled it from the federation. It must be remembered that just two months previously the army had rounded up and interned Tácunan along with extremists from all over Peru. He saw no solution, therefore, but to rid himself of the Satipo organization.

Into this vacuum once again entered the Fencap league of the Apra political party, attempting to organize under its wing all the "cold footed" peasants and colonos. It called a convention for August, 1963—the same month that Belaúnde, who had assumed the presidency in July, was moving his government about the central sierra, attempting to keep the highlands from erupting. His attention never turned to Satipo because at the time the area seemed reasonably quiet. That quiet did not derive from "functional equilibrium," however, but from harassment, intimidation, and police deterrence, points Fencap realized in the wake of its failure to rally even the "moderate" ones to a new organization. The peasants and colonos were too fearful; the police too oppressive; the future too ambiguous and unsure. But the atmosphere was volatile.

If Belaúnde had been aware of the gravity of the situation in Satipo, no doubt he would have intervened, especially if he had known that all during 1963 and 1964 the remaining militant directors of the crippled federation were holding clandestine planning meetings. As a result of those sessions, "barbudos" (bearded ones) were seen among the peasants in the latter part of 1964. Then in 1965 Guillermo Lobatón and his professional revolutionaries from the Peruvian MIR (Movement of the Revolutionary Left)[23] went into action, organizing guerrilla bands that nearly brought Satipo and the surrounding region to its knees. *At the same time other professional revolutionaries bent on similar action entered the central sierra, but the peasants there rudely refused to cooperate.*

Guerrilla war placed Belaúnde on the horns of a dilemma. The flammable Satipo situation presented an effective rallying point for disparate groups in the "coercion-and-no-reform" opposition who, for more than two years, had been trying to shut down his program anyway. Their hysterical cries of "Communist takeover" seemed justified. After resisting for several weeks, Belaúnde was forced to send in troops or suffer the consequences—a loss of the presidency via a military coup.

In the meantime the land-reform program Belaúnde had hoped for, which had emerged practically stillborn from parliament in 1964, was being bled to death as it lay about the offices of the Christian Democratic-controlled ministry of agriculture. This was a price the president had to pay to that political party for its formal support on other matters. (The Christian Democratic party had agreed to a parliamentary alliance with Belaúnde's Popular Action party only if the president was willing to give it control of the ministry of agriculture.)

In Satipo large numbers of peasants, colonos, and Campas Indians were attracted to the guerrillas because they preached "land and liberty" and said they knew a way to get them both. However, following a protracted period of bloodletting and violence in the region, the army gained the upper hand and definitively put the peasant and colono organization out of business. It killed its president and numerous directors as well as the professional guerrillas. However, it was sufficiently "touch and go" for a time that, had it not been for the effectiveness of the hundreds of United States trained elite rangers rushed to the area (and the defection of some Campas Indians who betrayed the staging areas of the guerrillas after the Peruvian Air Force bombed several of their villages), the history of Peru since 1965 might well have been written with a different color of ink.

Since the guerrilla activities, public authorities in Satipo have been replaced; land titles are more easily obtained; technical assistance is now available; and the government is building a new road and an airport. What will the future bring?

BIBLIOGRAPHICAL ESSAY

Much of the data for the case study were gathered in 1967 during field research made possible by a grant from the Foreign Area Fellowship Program of the Social Science Research Council and the American Council of Learned Societies. Both qualitative and quantitative village-level data were reported in my *Lord and Peasant in Peru: A Paradigm of Political and Social Change.*

In recent years social scientists have taken an increasing interest in Peru, in part, I suspect, because of the vast social, political, and economic changes wrought there during the past 15 years. Not only have American scholars been involved but also a rapidly growing number of competent Peruvian nationals have been as well. Julio Cotler and José Matos Mar, both affiliated with the Institute of Peruvian Studies (Instituto de Estudios Peruanos) as well as Lima's San Marcos University, are cases in point.

I shall make no attempt in this essay to cite all the important historical, anthropological, sociological, economic, and political works that deal with Peru: there are too many—and I do not presume to be acquainted with all of them. I shall merely refer to a representative sample of works that I have found helpful in the preparation of this chapter. Aside from the footnote citations already made, I must say that William Foote Whyte, who has been conducting an extensive research project in Peru for several years, has stimulated much of my interest. His "Rural Peru—Peasants as Activists" touches several themes relevant to this chapter. Cotler, one of Whyte's colleagues, has added an important work that deals with change-preventing devices in the structure of Peruvian society. See his "The Mechanics of Internal Domination and Social Change in Peru."

Of course, some of the peasant "activists" of the present day about whom much is being written not only have broken the bonds of traditional social control and have considerably improved their position in life, but many have also joined the "amoral society" and turned on their former kind rather than retain a sense of community and solidarity with the village. The psychological and social implications of this have been portrayed, in a very interesting and brilliant way, by Carlos Delgado in his "An Analysis of 'Arribismo' in Peru."

The general political climate, specialized bibliographical references, and notes on the instability of national politics may be found in James L. Payne, *Labor and Politics in Peru: The System of Political Bargaining;* Arnold Payne, "Peru: Latin America's Silent Revolution"; and David Chaplin, "Peru's Postponed Revolution." A class-structure emphasis is added by Anibal Quijano, "Tendencies in Peruvian Development and Class Structure." In a somewhat controversial work, the Frenchman, François Bourricaud, *Power and Society in Contemporary Peru,* explores similar themes.

252

Specific works dealing with the villages and regions portrayed in the chapter's case study are by Richard N. Adams, *A Community in the Andes: Problems and Progress in Muquiyauyo;* Henry F. Dobyns, *The Social Matrix of Peruvian Indigenous Communities;* Eileen Maynard, *Patterns of Community Service Development in Selected Communities of the Mantaro Valley, Peru;* and José Matos Mar, *El Valle de Yanamarca.*

Reports of the successes and failures of Belaúnde's Popular Cooperation program may be found in Jack H. Hopkins, *The Cooperación Popular Movement in Peru.*

Selected information relating to recent national political trends vis-à-vis the peasantry is found in Marcel Niedergang, "Revolutionary Nationalism in Peru," and Richard Lee Clinton, "The Modernizing Military: The Case of Peru."

CHAPTER 12

New Social Forces: A Model for The Peasantry

Social mobilization and the rise of new social forces are two of the more important characteristics of modernization because, unlike many other kinds of related changes, the consequences of these directly impinge upon the functioning of the economy, the distribution of status and reward in the society, and the tensions that the political system will be obliged to handle. As we have shifted from a macrosociety view (Brazil and Libya) to a higher degree of magnification of a small group (peasants in Peru) with our data in order to gain a better understanding of selected aspects of modernization, so is it required that we do the same with our theory.

What I would like to do now, therefore, is explore the "new social force" idea in some detail, attempting to sort out specific variables that may help us to understand not only why socially mobilized people are sometimes capable of collective action, but what the consequences of various kinds of actions are. Thus, while we continue to look at a special set, albeit an important set, of modernization-related phenomena, at the same time we shall enhance our understanding of the relation of social mobilization to politics and to many of the other modernization phenomena already taken up.

Aside from an exploration of the substance of this chapter, I have an additional purpose in presenting the discussion. It is to give the beginning student further experience in dealing with theory, variables, and hypotheses, to sensitize him to the way they are used, and to demonstrate how answers to complex questions might be sought from them. In this regard, the model presented is only one of many (although the substance dealt with would not necessarily be the same) that might fruitfully be employed. I personally like this one because it has helped me to understand the rise of new social forces, emphasizing, as it does, the relation of social mobilization to the broader institutional fabric of a modernizing country. Moreover, it brings into sharp focus the role of structural differentiation and specialization, of changing attitudes and values, and of the functions of ideology, charismatic leadership, and political development.

Many of the variables employed in the model have been operationalized in the real world. Thus, the model has some scientific as well as pedagogical value. Making an effort to understand it will help prepare one to understand some of the more complex theories advanced in the social sciences.

This "middle-range" theoretical exercise is directed toward an explanation of two very specific dependent variables: (1) why new social forces rise, and (2) when they do, why some become more intense or revolutionary than others. While we have already gained some insight into these in previous chapters, we need to do so in a much more rigorous manner. At the same time we continually need to check back into the world of reality to see if what we say theoretically makes any sense in reality. Thus, following the model, we shall move to integrate the Peruvian data with it.

The vocabulary of the model is specifically oriented toward peasants so that data from the Peruvian case can easily be associated with it. Nevertheless, the model is suitable for a general investigation of the rise of social forces and their relation to political institutons.

Some years ago, Oran Young argued forcefully aganst the "collection of empirical materials *as an end in itself* and without sufficient theoretical analysis to determine appropriate criteria of selection."[1] Reflecting on Young's statement, Albert O. Hirschman offered a complementary critique of an opposite but equal folly—"the tendency toward *compulsive and mindless* theorizing— a disease at least as prevalent and debilitating . . . as the one described by Oran Young."[2] Hirschman proceeded to launch a devastating attack on the "quick theoretical fix" and the "extravagant use of language" that intimates "that theorizing can rival sensuous delights."

Hirschman might well be misunderstood if one were unaware of the man's own important theoretical contributions—that do include, by the way, models and paradigms.[3] What Hirschman is against, or so it seems to us, is not theory *or* data but the mindless excesses of both. Neither compulsive data gathering nor mindless theorizing necessarily serves social science; the latter may even do it considerable damage.

Without abstractions we cannot, of course, even begin to think. A particular choice of certain abstractions may aid our thinking, another may confuse it. Some models (ordered or structured forms of abstractions) may therefore be termed good—if, of course, one values a clarity of thought that penetrates to some of the world's reality. Yet other models may in fact be bad. The test, it seems to us, lies in a model's ability to explain as parsimoniously as possible the social phenomena under examination (dependent variables), doing so with a "cognitive style," to use Hirschman again, that neither straitjackets the future, disallows the unexpected, nor "thinks" wishfully and therefore claims too much for itself. Within these parameters, are there theoretical tools, in addition to the ones we have already looked at, that could serve to sharpen our analysis of social forces and their relation to political institutions?

In responding to the general challenge of sharpening analysis, Hubert M. Blalock, Jr. not only thinks there are many theoretical tools to be explored but that the ones we now have need to be made better. In one of his books (a volume, incidentally, which eventually must become one of the more important methodological works of recent years), he opens by asserting that "most social scientists seem agreed on the need for more adequate theories. . . ."[4] He proceeds to argue for a largely deductive, testable theory, one sufficiently complex to give really new insights, yet couched in order to permit its testable hypotheses to be moved from verbal to mathematical formulations. As such, the causal relations among the verbalized variables must be so specified that ambiguities are minimized in every way possible. Although Blalock writes a tall order it does seem to us to be one to which social sciences will increasingly dedicate more attention. It is an order that has occasioned the structure of some of the content of this chapter. Thus we have focused on dependent and independent variables in a manner that gives them explicit causal, rather than primarily correlational, formulations. For the most part the resulting hypotheses are probably amenable to mathematical reformulation and, insofar as empirical scales are possible, they are "testable."

For the moment, we want to explain two dependent variables: (1) the origin of new peasant social forces and (2) their intensity. The range and interrelation of the seven independent variables which we believe help to explain the above two will become apparent within the context of the model.

TWO INDEPENDENT VARIABLES

Models generally use abstractions cast in the form of variables. These variables either may be "dichotomous" (meaning they are somehow "broken in two," showing high-low or presence-absence characteristics only) or "continuous" (reflecting numerous possible gradations between the variables' extreme positions or ends). Thus, *temperature,* a variable, may be "high" or "low," or it may also reflect a hundred or more positions in between. The preference is for theory that facilitates the employment of either dichotomous or continuous variables. The choice is not arbitrary, of course, but rather dictated by the nature of the data at hand. Such flexibility allows both case- and large-sample comparative studies using statistical methods to be employed to test the theory's hypotheses. The model in this chapter may be used with either type of variable. Case studies generally require the use of dichotomous variables; large-sample comparative studies frequently use continuous variables.

The object of using variables is not only to refine abstractions but to hypothesize and test their interrelationship as well. Thus if we want to know "why new social forces among peasants rise" (a dependent variable), we begin the search for a combination of general explanatory abstractions (independent variables) which will explain that phenomenon. Accordingly, the model here uses dependent variables (the origin of new peasant social forces; the intensity of the collective action taken) and independent variables (the first one being "capacity").

Before moving to a theoretical discussion of the capacity variable itself, however, a preliminary note must be made regarding the relation of abstract independent variables to the real world. Although the note deals explicitly with the capacity variable, it serves to clarify as well the other independent variables. The crux of the problem is that, in order to use a variable for purposes of empirical measurement, one must move down the abstraction ladder and make contact with the factual world and touch base with some concrete indicators. In the operational stage of research, therefore, measurement and description depend on factors (indicators) which lie outside the rubric of the main theory. This "bridging problem" of theory with the real world arises because a deductive theory cannot be tested directly without the aid of an auxiliary set of assumptions linking its theoretical variables to the required operational indicators.[5] However, the relation of those indicators to independent variables, such as capacity, is of a different quality than the relation of the independent variables themselves to the dependent variables of the theory. The factors or indicators that serve to link the theory with the real world are more concrete than either independent or dependent variables. They require a certain *a priori*, and perhaps untestable, assumptions to be made concerning the causal linkages involved. Thus, there are recognized problems in establishing "epistemic correlations" between theoretical abstractions and operational indicators.[6] I assume, in light of justifications later in the text, that the operational factors and indicators selected for this study adequately relate to the underlying abstract variables. However, they are not the only indicators possible; they may not even be the best. This point must be considered in addition to possible errors in the hypotheses themselves. With these observations in mind, let us move to a discussion of the first independent variable.

Capacity

Capacity is a variable suitable for describing the relative degree to which individuals or groups are capable of understanding complex modernization-related information. Frank W. Young, in a more specialized "information-processing" frame of reference, created the variable (which he called *differentiation*) for purposes of establishing a general structural description of modernization (when used as a dependent variable in his theoretical scheme) and also to help him explain "solidarity" and "relative centrality" among social groups (when used as an independent variable).[7] The capacity variable is highly abstract and links up well with the psychological and structural variables of modernization discussed in Chapter 2.[8] Briefly, the theoretical assumptions are that people, no matter who or where they are, always process information of some kind about the sound, behavior, and artifacts they hear, see, or feel. Among any group (such as a peasant village) the aggregate (average) level of such information processed may be high or low, depending on the extensiveness of knowledge about the symbol (antibiotics, for example, or any of the thousands of other symbols associated with modernity—internal combustion engine, corporate organization, political equality, and so forth), and the diversity of symbols that are processed. With appropriate indicators, individuals or groups can be compared and ranked according to their capacity. Thus, if the information a group processes is diverse and complex, and if, on the average, the group can process that information with high perception and knowledge, then the group is said to have high capacity. On the other hand, a group that handles only a few modern information symbols, or perhaps many but about which it has a very low level of knowledge or perception, is said to have low capacity. The greater the diversity of symbols and the more complex

the information related to them, the higher the capacity. Thus, while traditional Eskimos have something like 52 words in their vocabulary to describe
icebergs of various kinds, and while they no doubt have a higher capacity to
process information about icebergs than almost anyone reading this book, in
the aggregate they rank lower than groups which are capable of processing
complex information about symbols not tied strictly to the local environment.[9]

The theory assumes that, on the average, the more one is exposed to modern
symbols and increasingly learns about them, the higher will be his capacity
to process information regarding them. The same is true for groups. Thus, the
more urbanized—reflecting on the structural and institutional arguments in
Chapter 2—literate, differentiated, and specialized a society is, the higher
the probability that more of its citizens will have high capacity. This general
pattern says nothing, of course, about motivation or other features differentiating those individuals who search out new symbols from those who do not;
nor does it say anything about what the acquisitive ones choose to do with
their newly-found capacity once they acquire it.

The second of the above two points—what happens when capacity is raised
—is treated later in the model. The first, motivation, obviously suggests that
not everyone exposed to a new symbol will take hold of it in the same way.
Some peasants exposed to the use of insecticides will not adopt the practice
on their own farms; others will adopt it but fail to understand the function by
which the chemicals work. Yet others not only will adopt the practice, but
also will acquire a working knowledge about the causes and effects of its use.
Obviously, therefore, the simple "diffusion model" of Chapter 2 is not sufficient
at this point either to explain modernization or to account for the rise of new
peasant social forces. What we will argue later is that the factors serving to
produce the new forces—capacity being a critical one when taken in conjunction with other variables—in turn *sometimes* feed back to motivate the acquisition of an understanding of more symbols and information.[10] Blalock speaks
of a "block-recursive" feedback system for situations of this kind.[11]

In any event, there is a whole body of theoretical and empirical literature
which supports the assumption that, on the average, the more one is exposed
to and acquires knowledge about modern symbols, the greater will be his
capacity. We refer in particular to the effect of the content of new communications media,[12] of the awareness of consumption patterns of others,[13] of contact
with missionaries,[14] of traveling or being associated with people who travel,[15]
of getting a formal education in the Western sense of that term,[16] and even of
being associated with "listening schools" operated over the radio waves.[17]

Capacity is a general index of what we had earlier called "social mobilization." On the whole, people with high capacity are also highly socially
mobilized. Thus, we can see that, as capacity is raised, values are changed,
attitudes are reformed, and people's relationship to the political institutions
under which they live—or are obliged to live—comes up for review. A general
rise in a group's capacity, one index of an increase in the level of its social
mobilization, prepares its members and, under circumstances that we will later
specify, makes them available for new forms of collective action.

The most obvious concrete factors affecting an increase in the level of capacity among peasants are experiences with a money economy; formal education; work outside the village (especially in mines and industry where labor unions exist); membership in formal organizations (federations, councils, syndicates, school committees, cooperatives); travel (especially when this is facilitated by the existence of urban peasant colonies); and contact with modernizing politicians. Other factors of lesser importance may play a role also; and in the lives of particular individuals, there may be important events falling totally outside the scope of the above indicators. In general, however, the factors listed do seem to be the most determinative in occasioning a rise in the information-processing capacity of peasants. Some, but not all, of these indicators would also apply to other groups in the society. Yet linking up any particular group with the variable may require an on-site inspection of the experiences which, for the group, seem to attach it most logically to the capacity variable. This is the "bridging" problem we spoke of at the beginning of the chapter.

The concrete factors themselves have "real-world" symbols, of course, and for structural measurement and case-study analysis one must get hold of the symbols. Some measurable village-level symbols serving to link the reality of the peasant world with the abstract variable of capacity are: functioning schools, travel linkages or work migration patterns for seasonal labor, village-urban political and social linkages, and the existence of various kinds of organizations. Other kinds of symbols may also be suitable. By using such symbols, the relative level, or changes in any given level, of capacity of groups may be structurally measured or roughly inferred from case-study data. Various groups may then be rank-ordered and compared on the capacity variable,[18] or the process of change of any single group may be followed through time. If we let "C" represent capacity, and a plus or a minus sign the relative level of capacity (thinking of it in dichotomous terms), then a group may be represented by $C+$ or $C-$, depending on its status on the variable vis-à-vis other groups against which it is compared. A group may change its capacity over time, of course, and the direction of change may also be noted: $C\uparrow$, capacity increasing: and $C\downarrow$, capacity decreasing. Or, capacity may be high or low but simply go unchanged through time: C_o^+, or C_o^-.

Opportunity

The model's second independent variable is *opportunity*. The most practical idea it brings to mind is "access channels" through which capacity may be exercised or operationalized. In functional theory, perhaps one would look for "equivalents" between the two variables. We are not sure the search would be operationally fruitful, but the notion nevertheless helps conceptualize the relation of opportunity to capacity. Suppose a peasant has learned to read. An appropriate opportunity channel would be access to books or other written media. Of course, he would, by continuing to read, probably enhance his reading ability. So we see that the exercise of some opportunities also produces, for a later time period, a rise on the capacity variable. Sometimes opportunity indicators in an initial period, because of "feedback" effects, can subsequently be considered capacity indicators. Another example may help: For a peasant having the capacity to handle modern agricultural technology, an appropriate initial opportunity would be access to the technical inputs. Similarly, one can think of the opportunity variable as relating to an entire peasant group, such as a village.

Conditions of "disequilibrium" likewise serve to illustrate the relationship of the capacity and opportunity variables. Thus, for a village having the capacity to increase its agricultural output by 1000 percent, subject only to an alteration in the land-tenure system, the question of land ownership undoubtedly will be raised. And a village that sees its population doubling every 25 years will raise the same question, perhaps with even more intensity. In aggregate uses, opportunity, as is the case with national income, must be understood in per capita as well as distributional terms. For example, if land is an opportunity indicator, increasing its availability for peasants still will not occasion a per capita increase unless the amount exceeds the rise in village population, and the distribution is widely shared.

Generally, the most dramatic opportunity indicators in the contemporary world of Asia, Africa, Latin America, and the Middle East deal with the peasants' participation in certain economic, political, and social events, usually in combination with one another. With rising frequency, peasants are on the search for better opportunities in these areas. From their point of view, the factors serving most adequately to link their world with the abstractness of the opportunity variable are:

Economic Factors

a. *Land reform,* because of the incredibly unequal distribution of land in most countries with significant peasant populations while at the same time population density increases.

b. *Production costs,* especially those related to fertilizers and insecticides, because the peasants now frequently consider their use to be necessary.

c. *Markets,* because the middlemen historically have been "gougers." Peasants are now beginning to know that alternatives to this dependency pattern do exist.

d. *Jobs,* because economic stagnation hits the peasant first. He is the last hired and the first fired on any outside job he may obtain.

e. *Medical facilities,* because the villagers are increasingly turning away from traditional cures and toward Western medicine.

f. *Transportation,* because the peasants no longer wish to be tied exclusively to their village. They relish the idea of circulating about in search of one or more of the factors noted above.

Political and Social Factors

a. *Organization,* because peasants are learning that most of their gains in economic symbols derive from corporate action.

b. *Social mobility,* because increasing numbers of peasants no longer wish to be considered vassals, owned by the lord of the manor or highly subordinated by the rural aristocracy.

c. *Political participation,* because they are beginning to feel that they now have a voice that ought to be heard in national politics.

d. *Social respect,* particularly for the highly mobilized, because they consider they ought to be nearly as equal as government bureaucrats.

e. *Social justice,* because peasants, with greater insistency, are now seeking, and expect to receive, equal treatment before the law, from the police, and by the politicians.

Again, when we consider the feedback effect, it is important to note that participation in new opportunities in one time period probably serves to enhance the rise of capacity for a later period.

In terms of their effect on other variables in the model, the economic, political, and social factors sometimes reinforce each other and sometimes substitute for each other. No matter the variety, however, they suggest a relationship of the village to the outside world that cannot be ignored. It is primarily by concessions from superior status groups that peasants are able to obtain access to the economic, political, and social opportunities they desire. *Thus, whereas the capacity variable relates internally to the village unit, the opportunity variable deals with the relation of the village to the larger society and environment.* Analogously, if we were focusing upon industrial workers as our "unit of analysis," the capacity variable would refer to them specifically, and the opportunity variable to the way they related to—and were treated by— the larger society.

We can now see how the opportunity variable relates to the discussion on political development and political decay discussed in Chapter 3. If the political institutions of the country are developed, or developing, they will do what they can to open up new opportunities for newly mobilized people and thereby retain a "broad interest coverage" and a "wide scope of support." Decaying traditional political institutions frequently are unable or unwilling to do that. This is one reason why the newly mobilized—those rising on the capacity variable—reject them.

From the peasants' perspective there are two general ways in which they are most likely to change their aggregative position on the opportunity variable. They may make their own opportunities by reaching out and acquiring the symbols they desire from upper status groups through force or persuasion. Or they may be beneficiaries of state-action reform programs designed to promote the availability of such opportunities.

As with capacity, we can take the opportunity variable and express a group's static or dynamic position on it in terms of symbols. Thus, $O\uparrow$ means opportunity is rising; $O+$, opportunity is high; $O\downarrow$, opportunity falling, and so forth.

Obviously, there is a commonsensical relationship between capacity and opportunity. In general, people with low capacity are incapable of handling a massive number of opportunities, regardless of their availability. Moreover, one would suppose that, the higher the capacity, the higher would be the motivation to acquire commensurate opportunities to utilize that capacity—a point we will turn to in some detail later. Also, there is a feedback relation between the variables. Participation in information-processing opportunities sets into motion events which tend to enhance further development of capacity —and a new cycle may begin. For the moment, however, let us continue to handle the model in its more simple variations.

SOLIDARITY: A PRECONDITION FOR COLLECTIVE ACTION

We have made reference to some commonsensical relationships between the variables of capacity and opportunity. Another approach is to subject some aspect of their relationship to theoretical analysis. One way of doing this is to relate the abstractions to one or more additional variables that logically derive from the underlying theory. Let us take one variable, solidarity, as a starter and put it into a dependency status vis-à-vis capacity and opportunity and see what theoretical conclusions are possible. First, however, it is necessary to see how the variable itself logically fits into the theory.

If we assume that information structures and the meanings attributed to them are an integral part of any society, then capacity to process the related symbols, and opportunity to apply that capacity, are but two aspects of a larger whole. A third deals with the values people give the information and its associated symbols. Aside from the scope and complexity of the information processed, therefore, it is necessary to look at the degree to which the processing itself evokes similar or diverse symbolic meanings. Take the symbol of money. What is its meaning for peasants? Is it a medium of exchange facilitating the buying and selling of goods; or is it a device employed by town merchants to deceive the Indians? What do the police, the courts, antibiotics, and the church cathedral mean? These, respectively, are symbols of state authority, Western medicine, and religion. They, as all others, carry some meaning for anyone who processes them.

Clearly, each symbol may evoke highly diverse or very similar perceptions among people who process information about them. If peasants attribute a similar meaning to each of a broad array of symbols, then it can be said that they are processing the associated information according to a highly unified value format. If any group processes an extremely wide variety of complex information in this way, they will be united in global understanding and harmonious in their thinking about the "really important things." Their perceptions of issues, problems, and solutions will be remarkably similar. Moreover, internal frictions within the group will be progressively minimized as an increasingly larger variety of symbols come to carry essentially the same meaning for everyone. There will be a coordination of minds in such a way that a sharp and definitive view is created among the peasants on any one or more of a number of issues—and the more unified the interpretation of information on those issues, the more unified the village will tend to be. In practice, this unification of symbolic meanings creates, maintains, and subsequently projects that united view to the rest of the world with resulting attitudes of "weness" and "theyness." Sometimes an articulated ideology surfaces among such people, particularly if they have a charismatic leader around pushing one. Frank W. Young, who formulated this variable for the context in which it is used here, calls it *solidarity*.[19] A group of peasants may exhibit high or low solidarity depending on how it globally interprets the information it processes. As with capacity and opportunity, through the use of appropriate indicators, it is possible to rank villages of a selected region on this variable and compare them.[20] It is also possible, through longitudinal analysis, to trace out the development, or the decay, of a village on this variable through time.

A relatively high state of solidarity has a curious effect on peasants. (The conditions giving rise to solidarity are noted below.) *It creates among them a potential for collective action which does not exist when they are in a state of nonsolidarity.* For one thing, they are in agreement about the really important things and therefore find it easier to organize for the attainment of many goals of common interest. This is a point of some significance, because it is the existence of some degree of solidarity which explains the basic disposition of peasants toward collective forms of what John T. Dorsey once called "energy conversions."[21] *It is the precondition for the rise of a new social force.*[22] People may become individually mobilized, but only when a number of them enter a state of solidarity has a new social force been born. The questions to be answered now are "How does the solidarity phenomenon arise and what is its relationship to the capacity and opportunity variables?"

The basic hypothesis is that solidarity derives from a *discrepancy* between the aggregate (average) *capacity* of a natural group (ethnic, religious, cultural, class) and the group's relative *opportunity* to apply that capacity. The discrepancy of interest here is of only one kind—capacity higher than opportunity. This particular variable combination produces *structural binds* and psychological anxiety or frustration among those involved. It is these binds and anxieties that set the stage for the appearance of solidarity.

To be sure, solidarity is only one of several possible social phenomena that binds may foster. Under certain conditions they also may occasion migration or perhaps even some kind of psychological resignation—two possibilities we will want to sort out from the chain of events which frequently lead to solidarity. A careful look at some of the intervening variables and conditions below will help to clarify the differing processes.

For one thing, the formal stage (a structural-bind situation) upon which group solidarity, individual migration, or psychological resignation all may be enacted with equal vigor presents only the "props" of the play and their supporting stage crews—the environmental givens—not the specific actors themselves. How the actors actually relate to the props is affected by two important variables. One is called *expected availability of local future opportunities* and the other is simply designated as *opportunities for migration*. Thus, people acting out their life roles under structural-bind conditions in which they perceive that future opportunities in the local environment will exceed those which might accrue through migration will tend to develop a state of solidarity.

In the absence of opportunities at home, but in the presence of opportunities for migration (with the anticipated expectation of rewards at the end of the journey), people tend to become disgusted with their homeland and leave it.[23] This, of course, reduces the probability of collective action because the activist cream is continually skimmed off through migration. In a different but related context Albert O. Hirschman has argued the consequences. When people can "exit" with ease, the probability that any protest will be exercised, collective or individual, is sharply reduced. Thus, he argues, "Voice," or what we would call collective action with its solidarity base, "is likely to play an important role in organizations only on condition that exit is virtually ruled out."[24] On the other hand, if neither opportunities at home nor opportunities for migration exist (in the presence of structural-bind conditions), people tend simply to become resigned to their "fate." High rates of vagrancy, absenteeism, alcoholism, suicide, or other indicators of frustration and despair, depending on the local culture, may abound.[25]

In summary, a structural discrepancy between capacity (high) and opportunity (low) has a tendency to produce a psychological state of group solidarity, an individual disenchantment with one's environment (with accompanying tendencies for migration), or a "defeatist" and frustrating resignation to the life one feels he is forced to live where he now is. The solidarity, migration, or resignation effects are primarily explained by present expectations of local future opportunities and opportunities for migration. Figure 11 illustrates.

The specific combination of variables producing one or another effect, that is, group solidarity, individual migration, or resignation, is best explained with the aid of a typology. The three general types and their variations presented below certainly do not exhaust the possible list, of course, but they will be sufficient for the moment.

Type I: Rising Capacity—Static Opportunity

The structural features of this bind-producing combination are simple enough and are shown by the capacity and opportunity lines in Figure 12. In this type

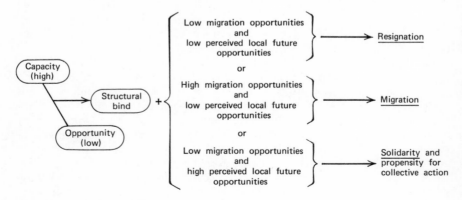

Figure 11. Causes and differential effects of structural binds.

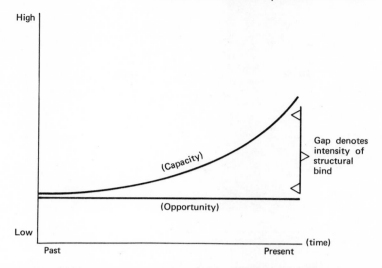

Figure 12. Structural binds under conditions of rising capacity and static opportunity.

it is the development of aggregative capacity that has created the structural bind, the relative extent of which is noted by the gap between the two variables. With the passage of time the gap becomes progressively greater.

The "meaning" of the gap for the participants and how they will react to it, however, is determined by their expectations of future opportunities either at home or somewhere else to which they may have a chance to migrate. Structurally bound individuals may therefore develop a sense of *solidarity*; they may *migrate* or they may become *resigned*. But the exact pattern depends on their judgment of what future opportunities the environment—at home or at the end of one's migration—either will render or extract from it. Thus the rise of a new social force, quite aside from its individual members being socially mobilized, also is influenced—and immediately—by the processes of economic development and political change transpiring in the society at large. These processes have a direct impact—for satisfaction or frustration—upon the opportunity, the perceived future opportunity, and the opportunity for migration variables.

If the peasants expect no change whatsoever in the prospects of future opportunities where they live (as illustrated in Figure 13) because of factors outside their control (lack of governmental concern with rural development; containment policies of the rural aristocracy; unresolvable man-land pressures; and so forth), as individuals they are likely to suffer a kind of "emotive alienation" from their environment. Such peasants are likely to emigrate to urban areas, new land frontiers, or mining centers in search of the opportunities their own environment will not or cannot deliver and may not be expected to produce in the future. Indeed, one entire generation, individually or in small groups, may simply move out—a phenomenon certainly not peculiar to any

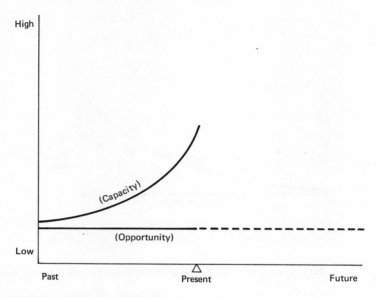

Figure 13. Structural binds with perceived static future opportunities.

given class of countries. We know several "old timers" who felt challenged and fulfilled on a 180 acre homestead in the arid American West. The homestead remains. But who among their grandchildren will return to its "good life?"

If "escape" from the environment from which one has become alienated is blocked for one reason or another (as, for example, by government policy prohibiting migration, landlord control over "indentured servants," discrimination that makes assimilation into a new environment virtually impossible, or simply a lack of opportunities elsewhere), then environmental alienation is likely to result in a form of resignation—resignation to a life that Hobbes once called "solitary, poor, nasty, brutish, and short." In such a state there tends to develop something analogous to the "amoral familism" Banfield found in his southern Italian village.[26] Those who are able—or are permitted—leave the village. Those with little or no "hope" remain. It is also under these conditions that the structural binds themselves can endure in a village almost indefinitely. People are incapable of resolving their problems because they lack the will to engage in aggressive corporate political, social, or economic action. They see only their own individual or family problems, not those of others. They are born and reared, and die in a sea of complaint with no expectation of improvement. Thus Gurr has found that among people of this kind, one generation is likely to do no more than "pass legends on to the next about the good life that was lost, and teach the new generation that they should demand the restoration of what was taken from their fathers or grandfathers."[27] There was no "good life" that was ever actually lost, of course. People's perceptions about what constitutes the good life, or ought to constitute it, have changed, while their environment has not, and they feel incapable of doing anything about their tragic circumstances.

All these variable relationships are, of course, theoretical suppositions. But they have alerted us to some of the essential things to look for as we examine social mobilization and the rise of new social forces. Some of the respective propositions have been examined vis-à-vis the real world and have proven to be useful predictors. Yet, as with all theories, it is necessary to continue to hone and refine them.

As discussed in Chapter 1, by creating variables and then postulating the likely effects deriving from some of their many possible combinations, we are creating *hypotheses*. These predict consequences or effects from a structured relationship of independent variables. The predicted relationship can then be tested in the real world to see if its premises and predictions bear out. If they do, and consistently so in a wide variety of cases, then our understanding of human behavior is enhanced. We may formalize these relationships (hypotheses) and give them identifying numbers.

HYPOTHESIS 12:1

Peasants experiencing marked structural binds (capacity high, opportunity low) who perceive that the local environment will offer clearly unacceptable future opportunities will, if migration opportunities exist, tend to emigrate.

HYPOTHESIS 12:2

Peasants experiencing marked structural binds who perceive that the local environment will offer clearly unacceptable future opportunities, yet at the same time find that migration opportunities do not exist, in time, tend to become "resigned."

Some students in the social sciences find it easier to keep the essential variable relationships of hypotheses in mind if those relationships appear "symbolically" rather than in verbal form. Thus, following a trend set by the economists several years ago, a growing number of scholars are attempting to refine their thinking in this way (the stimulus deriving primarily from the stringent demands of clarity for computer application). Thus, the hypotheses shown above may also be presented symbolically.*

---

* Hypothesis 1:

$$(C\uparrow) + (O_{\bar{\sigma}}) + (FO_{\bar{\sigma}}) + (M+) \longrightarrow B_e\uparrow$$

Hypothesis 2:

$$(C\uparrow) + (O_{\bar{\sigma}}) + (FO_{\bar{\sigma}}) + (M-) \longrightarrow B_r\uparrow$$

Where: $(C\uparrow)$ = Capacity rising over time
$(O_{\bar{\sigma}})$ = Opportunity low and static over time
$(FO_{\bar{\sigma}})$ = Future opportunity availabilities (perceived) in the local environment are low and static

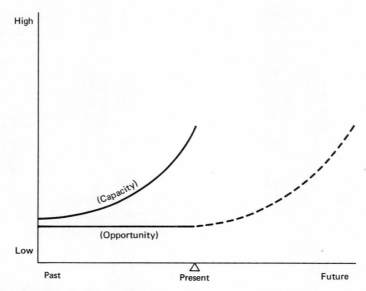

Figure 14. Structural binds in a relatively static environment but with expectations of increasing future opportunities.

Aside from alienation and resignation, structural binds may occasion at least a third response. This one is the most important for the focus here because it constitutes one avenue through which solidarity may arise (Figure 14). If aggregative capacity is raised in a static opportunity environment, yet broadly shared expectations for future improvements on the opportunity variable nevertheless exist (along with declining opportunities for emigration), then peasants tend to look inward to their village or group and begin to develop a sense of community and "oneness"—in short, *solidarity*. This may occur, for example, when a national government convincingly promises a massive development program for the peasantry, or the peasants for other reasons feel that through their own actions they can enhance their opportunities. If some outmigration occurs, the emigrating peasants still maintain close contact and identification with their village of origin. There are mutual hopes to talk about, mutual strengths to be found in togetherness, and dramatic promises or potential opportunities to consider. Agrarian reform, village development, political protection, and social jus-

(M±)	=	Opportunities away from the local environment (possibility of emigration) high or low
$\longrightarrow$	=	Have a high probability of leading to
$B_e\uparrow$	=	Emigration-producing structural and psychological binds increasing over time
$B_r\uparrow$	=	Resignation-producing structural and psychological binds increasing over time

tice are just a few of many possible topics. Under these conditions massive emigration and full-scale resignation tend to be shunted aside in favor of increasing solidarity. The peasants' perceptions of issues, problems, and solutions tend toward a unity in direct relation to increases in their binds. Moreover, internal group frictions are progressively minimized as an increasingly larger variety of symbols come to carry essentially the same meaning for all the peasants. The causes of the binds are talked about and agreed upon. Perhaps the landlord is blocking land tenure changes when capacity is high. If so, it is nearly certain that he will become the focus of attention. The villagers will begin to interpret many of their problems as deriving from his intransigence. Or, suppose the binds are thought to be caused by national bureaucrats, policemen, the church, other peasant villages, or dominating towns. The effect is the same. The villagers tend to perceive, in a unified way, the symbols displayed by those people or institutions. Thus solidarity at this state is not necessarily motivated by rational or utilitarian ends; it just happens. With these thoughts in mind, we are able to formulate another hypothesis.

HYPOTHESIS 12:3

*Peasants experiencing structural binds (particularly when capacity is rising, but opportunity is low and unchanging) who perceive that at least marginally acceptable opportunities can be extracted from the local environment will, if declining opportunities for emigration exist, tend to develop a sense of solidarity.**

Type II: Rising Capacity—Rising Then Declining Opportunity

There is, of course, a variety of capacity-opportunity combinations which lead to a structural bind.[28] In addition, we have seen that the bind itself, when mediated in certain ways by expectations of future opportunities and opportunities for migration, may produce solidarity, emigration, or resignation. For the sake of theoretical brevity only a few of these combinations can be noted in this chapter. One additional grouping in particular is worth mentioning, however, because it tends to produce some rather dramatic solidarity effects. In this case the structural bind arises in the manner shown in Figure 15; but its solidarity-

---

* The symbolic formulation for this set of circumstances is:

$$(C\uparrow) + (O_{\bar{o}}) + (FO\uparrow) + (M\downarrow) \longrightarrow B_s\uparrow$$

Where:	$(C\uparrow)$	= Capacity rising over time
	$(O_{\bar{o}})$	= Opportunity low and static over time
	$(FO\uparrow)$	= Future opportunity availabilities in the local environment are perceived to be increasing
	$(M\downarrow)$	= Opportunities for emigration declining
	$\longrightarrow$	= Have a high probability of leading to
	$(B_s\uparrow)$	= Solidarity-producing structural and psychological binds increasing

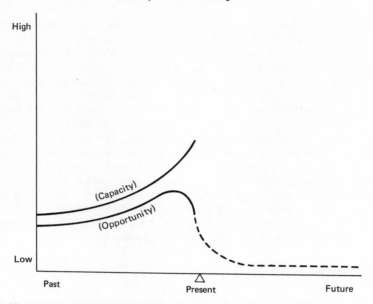

Figure 15. A pattern of structural binds and opportunity expectations producing intense solidarity.

producing effect is compounded by an anticipation that future trends on the opportunity variable will simply be a continuation of the present relative decline. The peasants feel threatened.[29] Their world is coming apart. Their hopes and expectations are being shattered.

Peasants experiencing these conditions are drawn together not only because of the solidarity-inducing binds themselves but because they believe they know exactly where the threats to their continued progress are coming from: the government—perhaps its reform program has collapsed or its police forces have gotten out of hand or its bureaucrats have suddenly become unresponsive; the landlord—perhaps he has just returned from a long period of absence and has decided to reestablish old labor obligations. The result is a "double action" solidarity, so to speak, first from the binds and second from the object perceived to be their cause. Solidarity is further enhanced if compensating opportunities for emigration are clearly unacceptable or nonexistent.

While the above circumstances set a fairly volatile stage, there are more potentially explosive ones as well. These tend to arise among the environmentally alienated who, having migrated in order to resolve their problems, arrive only to find themselves on the short end of a rather long but still hopeful rope. Their trauma frequently is more intense, and their state of emotional agitation more pronounced.

The phenomenon of "rising capacity—rising then declining opportunities," establishes conditions very similar to those noted by James C. Davies' "J-curve" hypothesis: "Revolutions are most likely to occur when a prolonged period of objective economic and social development is followed by a short period of sharp reversal."[30] Revolutions become possible, of course, only when aggrieved people are capable of corporate action. A state of solidarity makes that capability highly possible if not probable. It is under these conditions, compounded by anticipation of further opportunity decline, that the more dramatic movements among peasant social forces can be expected to occur.[31]

Summarizing key aspects of this argument, we have another hypothesis.

HYPOTHESIS 12:4

Peasants experiencing serious structural binds (particularly with the binds deriving from rising capacity and rising then falling opportunity) who perceive that under existing conditions their declining opportunities will continue to decline, yet who see no acceptable solution to their problem through migration, will tend to develop a fairly intense state of solidarity. *

Type III: Differential Increase in Capacity and Opportunity in the New Home of the Immigrant

There is still another type of solidarity-producing structural and psychological bind worth noting. Indeed, with four independent variables (capacity, opportunity, expectations of future opportunities, and migration possibilities), a fairly large number of possible combinations could be isolated. But let us stay with the more dramatic ones.

Type III is a fairly common bind in modernizing "permissive" societies where socially mobilized people may migrate from area to area as their desires and means permit. The binds resulting from a differential increase in capacity and opportunity (capacity and opportunity both increasing, but the former faster than the latter) may take several generations to reach a solidarity-producing stage, however. But the net effect forces one to discuss "peasants in cities" as well as peasants in the villages.[32] Thus, in the initial stages of the bind, the first individuals to feel its effects are likely to experience the "emotive alienation" syndrome, pack their bags, and hustle off to the city or some other area where the "promised land" presumably exists. The phenomenon of emigration may go on for generations, selectively tapping those with the highest

---

* Symbolically, the formulation is:

$$(C\uparrow) + (O\wedge) + (FO\wedge) + (M-) \longrightarrow B_s\uparrow$$

Where:

$(C\uparrow)$	=	Capacity rising over time
$(O\wedge)$	=	Opportunity increasing then declining
$(FO\wedge)$	=	Rise and subsequent perceived deterioration in availability of future opportunities in the local environment
$(M-)$	=	Opportunities for emigration are low
$B_s\uparrow$	=	Solidarity-producing structural and psychological binds increasing over time

binds, those most highly motivated, and so forth. (It is a point worth noting that via this process nineteenth century America did in fact receive the "best" of Europe—the best in the sense that those who came were highly motivated to take advantage of the opportunities opened up by a new frontier.)[33] Back home, however, nothing is done in the village or region to create opportunities and resolve the binds. There is no need to. Sufficient pressure for needed reforms is not there. The frustrated solve the problem by leaving it. This is a process that theoretically could go on until the "homeland" becomes a ghost town or depopulated wasteland. At the very least, the process takes care of much of the natural population increase. Massive population shifts occur for as long as emigration is possible and the emigrees still have hope.

Yet there is a long-run dilemma. What happens if for one or another reason the actual benefits of emigration become less and less attractive, or perhaps cease all together? Eventually this happens. The general pattern is for the modernizing country's larger urban society and economy to eventually become "saturated" with emigrees from the backlands. In time the "ghetto" of the city can offer no more opportunities at least not those of the expected kind—than does the village of the countryside. Yet "hope" impels the migration to continue and the urban slums correspondingly to swell.

While the migrant may be better off than before, or think he is, or even resign himself to a fractured hope, his children do not. They share the binds of their parents but not their resignation. They have no "memory" of the old rural life—of a life perhaps more terrible than the one they currently experience. What they do have is high capacity and a hope instilled by their parents and nurtured by experiences from city life. Their binds tend to be more acute, their patience much less pronounced. The caldron eventually takes in a new product, and that product is frequently intense solidarity among the cities' ethnic groups or lower classes (although resignation may appear in time if an oppressive and powerful government convincingly demonstrates that nothing can be done about declining opportunities).

What does one do if he already is in the "promised land" but that land fails to meet the promise? Both inside and outside the ghetto, in the heartland as well as the environs, those involved tend to develop a sense of solidarity. Their solidarity increases rather dramatically if they become convinced that under the present conditions the opportunities for which they had held such high expectations will not be forthcoming to the degree and quantity they had expected. However, it must be remembered that this particular solidarity phenomenon tends to be highest among second- and third-generation immigrants. Figure 16 offers a graphic illustration. Capacity has been increasing faster than opportunity, but a critical stage for solidarity is set when those involved see the "opportunity future" in a dimension similar to that depicted by the dotted line. It is under these conditions that people begin to make corporate demands on upper-status groups. Moreover, the long-range tendency of this structural situation and the individual psychology associated with it definitely tend toward violence.

This is a particularly difficult situation for upper-status groups to under-

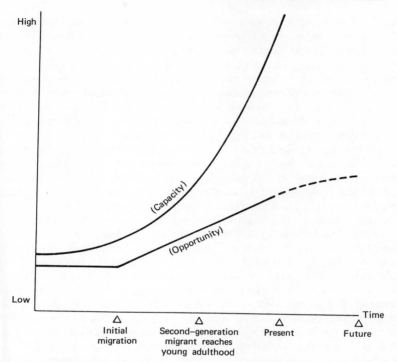

Figure 16. Differential increase in capacity and opportunity showing the effect of migration under conditions of eventual saturation.

stand. They see that the ethnic or other lower-class groups are much better off, in objective terms, than they ever have been. Indeed, much of their progress may have derived from reform efforts carried out by the nation's elite. But, as the pressure mounts, these elite may retort in disgust. "The more they get the more they want," "Give them an inch and they'll take a mile."

Summarizing key aspects of the argument, we arrive at another hypothesis.

HYPOTHESIS 12:5

Immigrants experiencing marked structural binds (with the binds deriving from rising capacity and rising but increasingly lagging opportunity) who perceive the opportunity future to be bleak, particularly if those involved are second-generation immigrants, will tend to develop a fairly intense form of "anti-establishment" solidarity.

SOLIDARITY MOVEMENTS: THE BIRTH OF COLLECTIVE ACTION

In Chapters 3 and 4 we argued that new social forces rise in modernizing countries because the socially mobilized participants are convinced that some

form of collective action is necessary to advance new collective interests. Col
lective action grows out of a prior state of solidarity. We have looked at severa
hypotheses that theoretically account for its appearance.

We have also now seen that not all socially mobilized people experience
solidarity producing structural and psychological binds. Social mobilization
is not, therefore, a sufficient explanation of the rise of social forces. Sometimes
the socially mobilized emigrate, or they may simply fall into a state of frustrating apathy and resignation. But all new social forces in the modernizing world
are composed of socially mobilized people. Modernization has enhanced their
capacity but has not done nearly so well in satisfying their opportunity expectations. The social forces rise to correct this discrepancy, placing as much
pressure as they can on the political system to do so. They want reforms—
redistribution of land, wealth, and income. Depending on how the political
system can—or is willing to—respond, opportunities, and therefore the extent
of the structural and psychological binds, may be decreased or increased.

Solidarity is a kind of "potential energy force." When that potential is converted from "kinetic" to "dynamic" status, a new social force is born—hence
the term *solidarity movement*. Yet, while the capacity, opportunity, future
opportunity, and migration variables explain the rise of solidarity, other variables must be employed to explain the appearance and intensity of the solidarity
movement. It is to that shift—from solidarity to solidarity movement—that we
now direct our attention. To be sure, the variables outlined here may affect a
variety of dependent variables. Their most dramatic impact, however, appears
to be in facilitating, impeding or mediating the intensity of the shift of the
potential energy associated with solidarity to the expressive energy of a solidarity movement. Before beginning a discussion of these variables, however,
it will be useful to describe some characteristics and functions of the resulting
collective action.

One thing a peasant solidarity movement frequently attempts to do is
enhance the availability of peasant opportunities. Thus, even though Ted Gurr
argues that *rebellions* or *revolutions* are characterized by the participants'
" 'nonrational' motivation to act violently out of anger,"[34] solidarity movements
of less intensity certainly are shot through with utilitarian motives. The peasants
have a problem—they are relatively overcapacitated vis-à-vis the opportunities
open to them. They probably do not talk about the problem precisely in these

---

* Symbolically, the variable relationship is:

$$(C\uparrow) + (O\uparrow) + (FO_o) \longrightarrow B_s\uparrow$$

Where: $(C\uparrow)$ = Capacity rising over time

$(O\uparrow)$ = Opportunity rising over time but at a slower pace

(FO_o) = Future opportunity availabilities in the local environment
are perceived as being static (or perhaps declining)

$B_s\uparrow$ = Solidarity-producing structural and psychological binds
increasing over time

terms, of course. But if they are in a state of solidarity (rather than emigration or resignation) they are likely to attempt a corporate resolution of their dilemma. Under uncomplicated conditions one would expect them to try to bring their opportunities more into line with their capacity. One would expect not only to hear rhetoric and observe strategies but witness actual programs and policies take shape as well. The peasants may decide on any number of things to do: build access roads, hospitals, and irrigation networks; reclaim lands; erect municipal buildings; and, perhaps, even introduce electricity. Or, in extreme cases, motivated by a combination of intense anger and utilitarian visions, they may invade lands, organize revolts, or perhaps engage in guerrilla warfare. Even in these more intense movements the utilitarian motives for organization consistently and strongly appear. Specifically, the peasants want more land, more water, more roads, more "infrastructure"—or they may just want the rural aristocracy and police to leave them alone. Generally, they want to remove themselves from their low opportunity position in a very rigid social structure.

One can see that most peasant social forces are likely to occasion opposition from the larger society. With the exception of millenarian and Messianic varieties (that still may occasion opposition but for different reasons),[35] the movements make as their prime objective a rise in the peasants' economic, political, or cultural status under conditions in which they must seek concessions from superior status groups in order to realize their goals.[36]

If the larger society did not place great blocks on the collective action of its peasantry, the policies, programs, and rhetoric that arise at the village or regional level would tend to develop gradually, more or less synchronized with the development of peasant solidarity. There would be no need for the peasantry to become radicalized. The larger society would be amenable to, and might even encourage, such opportunity indicators as agrarian reform, village development, occupational mobility, legal and social justice, and so on. As capacity increased, and to the extent that it were accompanied by solidarity, corporate attention would be turned to infrastructure—schools, roads, buildings, services—and the acquiring of land and the introduction of modern agricultural technology.

Whether such ideal conditions prevail or not, there is always considerable reinforcing feedback between the solidarity movement and the capacity and opportunity variables. For example, a successful movement hatches at least two major offspring: (a) an increase in the peasantry's capacity to handle or process more information and symbols, thus allowing the incorporation of more "meaning structures" into peasant life; and (2) an increase in the peasantry's relative access to whatever opportunities are available to the nation (or social subsystem) of which it is a part. The successful movement, therefore, enhances both psychological and structural aspects of modernization. In one aspect the peasants acquire more opportunities. In the other their corporate endeavors and personal energies expended toward that end enhance their information-processing capacity. Frequently the movement becomes infectious, involving progressively more people.

Radicalization or Moderation: The Influence of the Larger Society

In the face of actual or potential peasant social forces, the larger society rarely stands by unconcerned. Frequently it is not cooperative at all. Peasants do not live in a political vacuum. In order to attain opportunities they frequently find it necessary to direct their demands at privileged-status groups accustomed to exclusively running the national show. Yet sometimes there is a sprinkling of modernizing national politicians in that larger society who mirror the goals the peasants seek and make a vigorous effort to assure that reactionary elements in their society are, if not contained, at least motivated to make some concessions.

Suppose, for the sake of argument, that the big question for the peasants is land, and, moreover, that their cry for tenure reform is strongly echoed in the halls of the nation's parliament or among the elite of its ruling dictatorial party. The government's response to peasant activism, under these conditions, may still include some forceful deterrence, but probably it will not be of the traditional visceral variety that status quo regimes have favored. On the contrary, the nation's great thrust will be toward reforming itself. The governing elite will attempt to "absorb" or "integrate" the peasants into the mainstream of national life. They hear the knock at the door; they permit, indeed, encourage an entrance into the national fabric of society and economy. This absorptive response is one of several alternatives open to the larger society and is symbolized by "SR_a," *Societal Response—absorption*. The larger society is amenable to helping peasants obtain the opportunities they seek.

The effect of high absorption (SR_a+) on peasant solidarity and collective action may be derived from the basic solidarity hypothesis itself. If the government is actually successful in containing the reaction of landlords and traditional elite and therefore accomplishes some effective opportunity-extending reforms, one can see that the intensity of the solidarity-producing binds very well may decrease. If opportunity increases sufficiently and the peasants' structural and psychological binds are relieved accordingly, then the underlying conditions supporting intense forms of collective action are eliminated. Under these circumstances, one would look for a continued moderate amount of organized activity among the peasants. Habitually, they continue to form marketing and purchasing cooperatives; to expand their schools or found new ones; and to progressively become concerned about Western medicine, communication, transportation, and modern agricultural technology. Moreover, they begin to make some effort themselves to become integrated into the national state. In so doing the peasants tend to retain their "own" leadership, reaching out for outside advice only as needed. They do not voluntarily subject themselves to outside revolutionaries or other types of political extremists. Should any of these appear on the scene, the peasants are very apt to alert the authorities. The peasants are "loyal." Why shouldn't they be? The state has not blocked their goals but rather facilitated their attainment. These circumstances directly relate to Hypothesis 12:3 and demonstrate why the peasants could expect future opportunity increases in spite of present stagnated conditions.

The absorption variable directly relates to Huntington's important work on political institutionalization discussed in Chapter 3.[37] If, as in his framework, the modernizing institutions of the state are sufficiently adaptable, complex, autonomous, and coherent to respond vigorously to peasant social forces in the manner outlined above, then a considerable amount of stability can be expected. The existence of such institutionalized political organizations and procedures serves, in Ted Gurr's words, to increase men's value opportunities, i.e., their repertory of alternative ways to attain value satisfaction."[38] Basically, all it does is increase opportunities and afford people hope in the future.

On the other hand, suppose national modernizers do not have an influential hand in the nation's capital. Or, as sometimes may be the case, suppose they simply do not exist. Under these conditions if villagers demand cash wages from a rancher unaccustomed to paying for services, he will take quick notice of the insolent peasant behavior. Similarly, should the peasants form a labor syndicate, when absolute dependence on the lord has previously been a way of life, the lord will register grave concern and can be expected to exercise some harassment. Should the peasants invade and take over the lands, the lords' screams will be frightful indeed. If the lords are in a position to influence or direct the activities of the national army and the police, these institutions will take appropriate action against peasant threats to law and order. The state will attempt to shut down the movements and "put the peasants back where they belong." Under these circumstances, the larger society responds by attempting to block peasant collective action. It therefore frequently denies the peasants a realization of their opportunity goals. This is a *coercive* alternative to peasant social forces which the larger society may elect to employ. It is symbolized by "SR_c," *Societal Response—coercion.*

When a state opts for high coercion (SR_c+) as a general response to peasant movements, effectively shutting them down and discouraging their reemergence, it is clear that the state has denied the peasants a realization of the goals they sought—a move upward on the opportunity variable. As such, the structural and psychological binds among them remain even though the state maintains law and order.

In the long run, if a sufficiently high level of coercion is maintained, the peasants may drift into a state of resignation (if they otherwise cannot "escape"). In the short run, however, it is only the visible forms of their pent-up energy that are shut down or prevented from emerging. Thus moderate movements arising under the circumstances suggested by Type II ("rising capacity— rising then falling opportunity—deteriorating availability of future opportunities") may retreat. But they also may simmer and subsequently explode.

The same phenomena may occur with peasants who are deterred from action in the first place because they consider the costs too great and their own position too weak to risk collective action. They may have programs, policies, and rhetoric in mind to change their status and bring their opportunity more in line with their capacity, but they may choose to await a more propitious time.

In all cases when high peasant solidarity and high state coercion exist side by side, the peasants' aggregative capacity may go right on increasing until an intolerable threshold of binds is reached. An explosion then "suddenly" occurs.

The deciding factors usually are the presence of some kind of facilitating agents (resources, linkages, accelerators, or catalysts—points to which we will turn shortly), and the capability and willingness of upper status groups to continue to increase the level of coercion in the system. In any event, in the face of high levels of coercion one does not expect to see moderate kinds of peasant movements. Instead, one looks for all peasant social forces either to collapse or to intensify.[39] Figure 17 notes this phenomenon along with other probable rela-

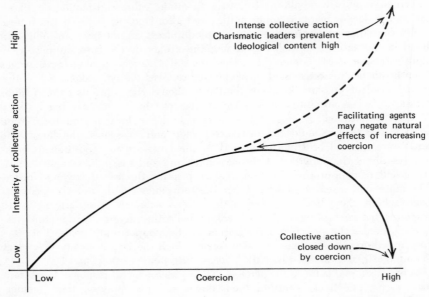

Figure 17. Hypothesized intensity of collective action under increasing structural-bind conditions at varying levels of coercion.

tions of the collective action and coercion variables.[40] The combination directly relates to Hypothesis 12:4 and demonstrates why the peasants could have such dismal expectations of future opportunities. They know the larger society is out to deny them realization of their goals. This perception may produce migration or resignation, but it may also increase a resolve to strike out against those manning the blockade.[41]

In summary, the conversion of solidarity into a solidarity movement and the intensity of the movement once it has taken off are affected by the way the larger society relates to the people involved. If the society opts for reforms and successfully absorbs or integrates the peasants, moderate movements can be expected. If, however, the society responds strictly with coercion and attempts to wrest from the peasants gains already acquired, then it should be prepared for a possible struggle. The application of coercion under these circumstances, in the short run at least, will serve to radicalize the peasantry and increase their solidarity and resolve. Thus Gurr can conclude that "the use of coercion to control discontent and maintain stable patterns of social action has complex and potentially self-defeating consequences."[42]

"Absorption" permits opportunity expectations to function along the lines outlined by Hypothesis 12:3 (capacity rising in static opportunity environment but with expectations of future improvement). The likely result is moderate solidarity movements. "Coercion" sets into play the opportunity expectations outlined in Hypothesis 12:4 (rising capacity—rising then falling opportunity with expectations of future opportunity deterioration). High coercion may contain the movements; but under the specified conditions it also sets the stage for possible radical movements that may indeed occur if the intervening energy-facilitation variables to be considered shortly come into play.

By combining the above arguments with those of Hypotheses 12:3 and 12:4 (in Hypotheses 12:3a and 12:4a that follow), we are able to detect some of the "feedback loops" relating to the respective roles of peasant social forces and the larger society vis-à-vis the intensity of the collective behavior.

HYPOTHESIS 12:3A

Peasants experiencing marked structural binds (with capacity rising, opportunity low and unchanging) who perceive that at least marginally acceptable opportunities can be extracted from the local environment because of the larger society's favorable reaction to peasant needs will, if the marginal attractiveness of emigration continues to decline, tend to develop moderate (non-revolutionary) solidarity movements.

Under these conditions such solidarity movements do, of course, eventually bring increased opportunities for the peasants. In subsequent time periods they also facilitate incremental increases on the capacity variable, and probably enhance the expectations of future opportunities. These are some of the positive feedback effects that may result when the larger society reacts favorably to peasant social forces. Thus, the larger society can never "slightly reform" itself and conclude that pressures for change will have been permanently taken care of. A more exact understanding of this relationship may be grasped from the symbolic formulas.*

* Hypothesis 12.3a showing time-sequence feedback effect on the opportunity, capacity, and future opportunity expectations variables.

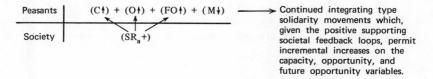

Preliminary time phase:

Peasants	$(C\!\uparrow) + (O_0^-) + FO\!\uparrow) + (M\!\downarrow)$	Moderate solidarity movements which, in a subsequent time phase, result in an increased level of opportunities for the peasants.
Society	$(SR_a\!+)$	

Subsequent time phase:

Peasants	$(C\!\uparrow) + (O\!\uparrow) + (FO\!\uparrow) + (M\!\downarrow)$	Continued integrating type solidarity movements which, given the positive supporting societal feedback loops, permit incremental increases on the capacity, opportunity, and future opportunity variables.
Society	$(SR_a\!+)$	

If a favorable societal response enhances the evolution of moderate solidarity movements, a coercive response does something else indeed.

HYPOTHESIS 12:4A

Peasants experiencing marked structural binds (particularly when the binds derive from rising capacity and rising then falling opportunity) who perceive that, because of the coercive response of the larger society to their efforts and also because no acceptable solution to their problem lies in migration, will, even if temporarily contained, tend to "gear up" for very intense (revolutionary) kinds of solidarity movements. *

*Preliminary time phase:

$(C\uparrow) + (O\uparrow) + (FO\uparrow) + (M\uparrow)$ ⟶ Increasing solidarity, with perhaps some manifestation of a solidarity movement, which evoke a coercive societal response.

Subsequent time phase:

Peasants	$(C\uparrow) + (O\frown) + (FO\frown) + (M\downarrow)$ ⟶ A possible containment of the
Society	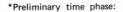 (SR_c+)

solidarity movement, but also to a setting conducive to very radical kinds of collective behavior.

Where:
$(C\uparrow)$	=	Capacity increasing over time
$(O\uparrow)$	=	Opportunity rising, but not so much as capacity
$(FO\uparrow)$	=	Future opportunity availabilities in the local environment are perceived to be increasing
$(O\frown)$	=	Opportunity rising then falling because of coercive response of the larger society to the movement
$(FO\frown)$	=	Rise and subsequent perceived deterioration in availability of future opportunities in the local environment
$(M\downarrow)$	=	Chances for emigration declining
(SR_c+)	=	High coercive response from the larger society

Where:
$(C\uparrow)$	=	Capacity rising over time
$(O_{\ddot{o}})$	=	Opportunity low and static over time
$(FO\uparrow)$	=	Future opportunity availabilities in the local environment are preceived to be increasing
$(M\downarrow)$	=	Opportunities for emigration declining
$(O\uparrow)$	=	Opportunity increasing over time
(SR_a+)	=	High absorptive response from the larger society

Accelerators

An additional set of factors that has some bearing on the intensity of collective action, once the structural and psychological binds are set, is collectively known as "accelerators."[43] Accelerators serve to shift the energy of moderate movements into a greater intensity. No doubt many real-life factors potentially could serve an accelerator function. An important one relates to promises. There is an old saying that "unkept promises make enemies of friends." In a general way, the adage captures a dimension relevant to peasant social forces and may be refined in the following way. While unkept promises may make enemies of friends, unkept promises to peasants in a state of high solidarity encourage vigorous action. In the face of rural agitation, a government may attempt to placate the villagers by promising reforms and benefits commensurate with good peasant behavior. This may indeed have a psychological impact affecting the peasants' expectations of future opportunities and create, in the short run, the kind of quietude the government is after. If the government does not fulfill its promises within a reasonable time, however, the tendency is for the failure itself to aggravate the underlying binds, convincing the peasants that opportunity is falling or will fall. The probability of intense collective action therefore becomes higher than ever. Thus a government finding itself under peasant fire and wishing to respond with reform rather than coercion had better do much more acting than talking. Moreover, the acting had better be something more than simple piecemeal response.

The accelerator effect is represented by hypothesis 12:6.

HYPOTHESIS 12:6

Peasant social forces which are led to believe that the larger society, because of its promises, will enhance their opportunity position but then find that the promises remain largely unfulfilled will become more disposed to intensify their collective action.

The relationship of the variables from which this hypothesis derives is better shown symbolically.

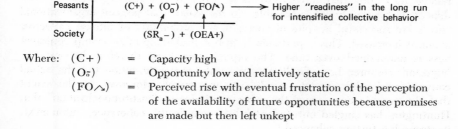

Peasants	$(C+) + (O_0^-) + (FO\frown)$	$\longrightarrow$ Higher "readiness" in the long run for intensified collective behavior
Society	$(SR_a-) + (OEA+)$	

Where: $(C+)$ = Capacity high
  (O_0^-) = Opportunity low and relatively static
  $(FO\frown)$ = Perceived rise with eventual frustration of the perception of the availability of future opportunities because promises are made but then left unkept

(SR$_a$−) = Low actual absorptive response from the larger society
in spite of promises to the contrary

(OEA+) = Opportunity expectation accelerator (which may take on a
number of actual forms in the real world. In this particular
formulation, "unkept promises" are seen as a critical factor)

Energy Facilitators

The variables in this section have their most dramatic impact when the
"subsequent time phase" conditioners of Hypothesis 12:4a are met (increasing
opportunities—high level of coercion—declining chances for migration). They
serve to facilitate the conversion of high solidarity into intense solidarity movements. They do so by negating or neutralizing the restraining effects of coercion. Neutralization may reflect objective reality. If so, the peasants will win
in the power struggle with the establishment. The facilitating effect may simply
derive from false perceptions of reality. In this case, the peasant solidarity
movement will probably be crushed. In either case, the effect on the solidarity conditions established by Hypothesis 12:4a (and others of a similar nature
where a status quo society, employing high levels of coercion, has allowed
rebellious energy to be stored up) is to facilitate an intense collective action.
(Refer to the dotted line in Figure 17 for a graphic illustration of this relationship.)

If moderate peasant movements arise and are not blocked by the larger
society, it is a sign that the upper strata are either purposefully flexible or
unintentionally weak; that high levels of coercion cannot or will not be applied;
and that the peasants have properly perceived the situation. If an intense
movement arises, however, it suggests that the upper strata not only have been
inflexible but also that their coercive powers have been liberally and successfully applied for a time. Energy potential has been building up, awaiting an
agent which could facilitate its explosive eruption. That agent may relate to
one or perhaps both of the following variables: *group resources* and *group
linkages*, symbolized respectively by EF$_r$ (energy facilitation—resources) and
EF$_l$ (energy facilitation—linkages).

Resources

As solidarity rises, the peasants attempt to build an organizational base to
relieve the binds that have fostered it. Coercion makes organization more
difficult but certainly not impossible. To the extent that peasant organizational
efforts are successful in spite of coercion, the probability of intense collective
action is increased. This is particularly true if leadership-followership cohesive-
ness is maintained over time. The organization itself therefore becomes an
important resource base, facilitating not only corporate action but the actual
conversion of solidarity into a solidarity movement. Moreover, to the extent
that the organization enjoys the other attributes of "institutionalization" that
Huntington has singled out (adaptability, complexity, coherence, autonomy),
its strength is further enhanced.[44]

Other observers have noted that competent leadership and complex organization enhance dissident institutional support.[45] Such support is increased if large numbers of peasants find themselves in solidarity-producing structural and psychological binds. And it is under these conditions that competent leadership is most powerful and influential because it is the "charismatic" type, discussed in Chapter 4, that frequently surfaces. Accordingly, under few if any other conditions is it possible for political leadership to function as such a powerful "independent variable" affecting the course of human events. Competent leaders may steer the energies of the movement in a variety of channels and, in fact, may even have a substantial moderating influence. Particularly is this true if the leaders are committed primarily to the enhancement of their own or members' opportunity positions rather than simply to expressive violence. Thus "they will adjust their tactics to the exigencies of the situations they face. If tactical considerations suggest that gains are best achieved with minimal violence, they are likely to control their followers to minimize rather than increase violence."[46]

From the preceding arguments several implications are clear. While the leaders have an enormous energy pack under their command, the application of coercion by the larger society increases the probability that the command, to be exercised at all, must be done under conditions of intense collective action. Thus as coercion increases, the charismatic leaders, in order to remain in a position of command, frequently sound the horn for counterattack. If they are competent, the resource base facilitating intense and perhaps sustained collective action is greatly enhanced.

As discussed in Chapter 4, still another important resource for peasant social forces, when the conditions of Hypothesis 12:4a are met, is ideology, particularly if it is of the emotive variety. *Fidelism* (Fidel Castro), *Maoism* (Mao Tse-tung) and *Hoism* (Ho Chi Minh) are contemporary examples. Only a few peasants need to understand much about the philosophical underpinning of the ideology. The catchword slogans are sufficient for the rank and file. The result is not only the creation of Apter's "framework of consciousness,"[47] which functions to guide political and social action, but a formation of a kind of secular religion as well. It is a belief system, a codebook for the future, in which the peasants place enormous faith.[48] Structurally and psychologically bound peasants feel a need for ideological sloganizing. When high coercion is also an ingredient in the solidarity formula they become very receptive to "missionaries" who purvey an acceptable brand. The more intense the structural and psychological binds, the more likely the ideology will be revolutionary. To the extent that these conditions are met and are associated with complex and strong organization and competent leadership, the probability of radical peasant activism increases dramatically.

Finally, material resources enter the picture and became particularly important if they enhance the peasants' power (weapons) or their ability to resist the effects of imposed isolation or pursuit in which normal sources of supply are destroyed or confiscated.

Organization, leadership, ideology, and matériel are important resources for peasants under conditions of solidarity, affecting not only the intensity of their movements but their potential success as well. When the "subsequent time phase" conditions of Hypothesis 12:4a fall into place (increasing capacity— rising then falling opportunity—expectations of deteriorating future oppor- tunities—high level of coercion—declining opportunities for "escape" through migration), these factors enhance the probability of intense collective action. On the other hand, when conditions of Hypothesis 12:3a are met (rising capacity—static opportunity but with expectations of future opportunities because of absorptive response from the state), complex organization and competent leadership nevertheless facilitate the orderly expression of moderate solidarity movements. Here revolutionary ideologies and volatile charismatic leaders do not have a high "take."

Linkages

There is another class of facilitating factors that take on dramatic effects when solidarity arises under conditions of Hypothesis 12:4a. These are *linkages* of peasants either with powerful and well-placed elite in the national culture who serve to protect them, or with a counter-elite who effectively convince them that an alliance will produce the same result. The linkages enhance the prob- ability of intense energy expressions because they directly inhibit, or the peasants think they inhibit, the rural establishment's coercive capability. Or, the linkages may also provide effective channels for building up the resources noted above that the peasants may later utilize to protect and assert them- selves. Thus in the face of high coercion one of the most obvious protective pursuits for a peasant organization is to create, or at least to attempt to create, linkages with powerful people or organizations in or out of the national culture who are capable and willing to take up their cause. The outgrowth is an open- ing of the floodgates, so to speak; and to the extent that the linkages are powerful, and effectively maintained, the intense energy expressions do not cease until opportunity rises and binds are relieved. In the absence of absorption, the state will be obliged to increase substantially its coercive response.

Catalysts

Frequently there is a final "spark" associated with intense movements. These are usually one-time happenings that (1) dramatically focus the peasants' attention on the presumed causes of their binds and provide them with a feeling that violent response is called for, or (2) expose the inability of the elite to maintain its monopoly of force. As Chalmers Johnson argues, "these are not sets of conditions but single events—events that rupture a system's pseudo-integration based on deterrence."[49] The spark may be a jailing, a murder, or even the appearance of a charismatic leader, particularly if he is in a position to convince the peasants that the power of the traditional rural elite has evaporated or somehow can be negated by forceful action. A catalyst does not *cause* an intense movement in the strictest sense so much as it inflames the underlying conditions and pushes the peasants to the boiling point.[50] Thus, once a catalyst has triggered the conversion of potential energy into the real thing, one had better not look for moderation. An intense movement will have been born.

The final set of hypotheses, which follows, utilizes these additional variables as a way of explaining the appearance of revolutionary forms of peasant solidarity movements and the probable effect of national policy on them. Hypotheses 12:7 and 12:8 have too many interrelated variables to lend themselves to easy verbalization. By now it probably is not necessary anyway.

HYPOTHESIS 12:7

Where state policy has been based on what Johnson calls a "pseudo-integration based on deterrence," that is, coercion.

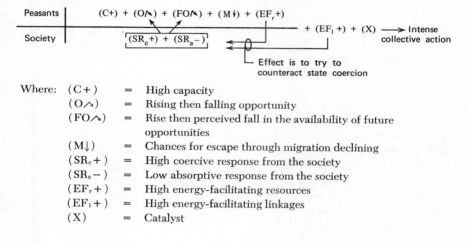

Where: $(C+)$ = High capacity
$(O\wedge)$ = Rising then falling opportunity
$(FO\wedge)$ = Rise then perceived fall in the availability of future opportunities
$(M\downarrow)$ = Chances for escape through migration declining
(SR_c+) = High coercive response from the society
(SR_a-) = Low absorptive response from the society
(EF_r+) = High energy-facilitating resources
(EF_l+) = High energy-facilitating linkages
(X) = Catalyst

HYPOTHESIS 12:8

Where state policy, in the face of a failure to integrate by deterrence, is based on attempts to integrate by unfulfilled promises of reform:

Peasants | $(C+) + (O_o^-) + (FO\wedge) + (M\downarrow) + (EF_r+)$
Society | $(SR_a-) + \overline{(OEA+)}$ $+ (EF_l+) \longrightarrow$ An eventual intensification of the solidarity movement, or perhaps to a second round of intense collective action
$+$
$\underline{(SR_c-)}$

Where: $(C+)$ = High capacity
(O_o^-) = Low, static opportunity

(FO↗↘)	=	Perceived rise and subsequent fall in the probable level of future opportunities
(M↓)	=	Chances for escape through migration declining
(OEA+)	=	Opportunity-expectations accelerator
(SR$_a$−)	=	Low absorptive response of the larger society, promises notwithstanding
(SR$_c$−)	=	Low coercive response of the larger society
(EF$_r$+)	=	High energy facilitating resources
(EF$_l$+)	=	High energy facilitating linkages

Aside from the usual policy insights (identification of critical points for manipulation) that models give, there is one curious insight that derives from the above hypotheses. It is that piecemeal absorption (reform) as a means to quiet social unrest is dangerous because it is both illusory and counterproductive. In the short run, some "stability" may derive, but eventually such activity will simply accelerate more demands for change and reform. Piecemeal reforms are hardly ever sufficient to relieve structural binds and therefore reduce antiestablishment solidarity. However, they usually do increase hope and capacity and thereby exacerbate the intensity of binds already felt. A clever government is soon found out. A smart one puts forth more action than public rhetoric to reform efforts.

Another policy observation relates to the role of "conspirators" in radical political behavior. Controlling them treats symptoms rather than causes. While such control may be in the interest of the larger society, failure for it to act on the causes of unrest (usually opportunity deprivation) only provides fertile ground for a new round of "outsiders" to be attracted to the cause. Arresting leaders, conspiratorial or otherwise, may dampen social protest energy, but it does not solve problems. New leaders nearly always surface to remind a "resigned" population of its plight.

CHAPTER 13

The Model and Peru

Case studies, like theoretical models, are frequently interesting for their own intrinsic value. Nevertheless, sometimes it is useful to move beyond intrinsic interest to evaluate data and "test" the insights of a given set of theoretical hypotheses. This is one form of analysis. At this point, therefore, we conveniently bring the Peruvian data to focus on the two main dependent variables advanced in the "peasant model," that is, why peasant social forces—or solidarity movements—rise, and when they do, why some become more violent than others. Of course, we are also interested in why some become more successful than others in attaining their goals, and perhaps in a host of other possible dependent variables. For the moment, however, we shall confine ourselves to the two prime dependent variables. Keep in mind, however, that much qualitative data can be fruitfully used in the social sciences if a systematic way of analytically exploiting these data are established. In modernization studies this is, perhaps, the only way we can profit from the "lessons of history" as recorded by those who had no idea of the kinds of questions that we would be asking.

Tácunan's movement in the central sierra hovered very closely to the "moderate solidarity movements" about which the model speaks. The peasants' thrust was toward the building of village infrastructure and the extraction of economic and social benefits from the larger Peruvian society. Tácunan did not call for a destruction of the society, only an elimination of its most abusive parts. Although in August of 1963 he was sympathetic with individual villages that carried out land invasions, at no time did his own movement sponsor any such action. Certainly, Tácunan was working for a demise of the feudal hacienda system. But the point is that he scaled his movement's energy along moderate, essentially nonviolent lines. Illustrative of this route was his expulsion of the Satipo organization from his federation and the October 1963 successful forging of a truce in the central sierra against further invasions. On balance, therefore, Tácunan's federation served more as a moderating force than as a propagator of widespread aggressive agitation.

This does not presume to suggest that the peasant-become-leader, at one of several critical periods, could not have set the appropriate spark and incited his movement to intense activity. During some periods the conditions were appropriate and his position within them sufficiently propitious to place such an eventuality probably within his power. A limiting factor, of course, might have been the clutches of the PIP, the police, and the army. The point is that, for reasons sufficient to him, Tácunan chose moderation. This man's role was therefore critical in the central sierra. Nevertheless, the fact that he could play it at all at the level of his own choosing derived from several factors at work within the national political system, a point that we shall consider shortly.

In Satipo it was another story indeed. Among the peasants there the voice of Tácunan had little effect. The federation leader certainly did not fail to try; but his influence was at best negligible and, perhaps, even counter productive. National political factors aiding Tácunan's role in the central sierra had no influence in the eastern uplands. This "charismatic" man—inherently the same individual in the sierra as elsewhere—was therefore left in Satipo sounding like the "Uncle Tom" of the Peruvian peasantry. The Satipo movement increased in intensity and finally burst into guerrilla warfare. The affiliated members made efforts to destroy the system under which they lived. No longer did they seek reforms from within it. Even some of the "cold footed" ones eventually were attracted to the guerrillas, if not as direct participants then as sympathizers, couriers, scouts, or specialists in logistics.

This is the summary panorama of peasant protest and goal-seeking activism in two regions of central Peru, 1958 to 1968. The empirical questions to be answered are: (1) Why did the movements arise in the first place, and (2), after they arose, why did the peasants in the central sierra eventually pursue moderation while those in Satipo either sympathized with or joined a guerrilla war?

WHY THE MOVEMENTS AROSE

One set of hypotheses from the model (numbers 12:3 and 12:4) posits that the preconditions for the rise of a new social force, whether moderate or intense in its collective behavior, derive from a discrepancy between the aggregative capacity of a group to process information (high) and its relative opportunity (low) to utilize that capacity. Depending on the state of expectations for future opportunities and the status of migration in relation to the discrepancy-producing conditions, one possible result is a state of solidarity—the immediate foundations of any collectively pursued action.

Given that the movements in central Peru occurred, were they preceded by the structural and psychological conditions established by the model, or by alternative conditions which might be specified, or by factors about which we yet know very little? If the structural factors outlined by the hypotheses are consistently present, and if the psychological conditions of which they speak can be reasonably inferred from secondary indicators, then the hypotheses are supported. However, if the evidence is not consistent with the hypotheses, then there may be cause to reject them and, perhaps, even the theory itself.[1] Let us examine, therefore, the general dynamics of the areas under study.

Capacity, Opportunity, Future Expectations, and Migration

When we consider Tácunan alone for a moment, it seems obvious that at various times practically every capacity indicator that we could imagine entered his life. He had traveled, had received a formal education, had associated with labor activists as well as with an activist political party, had spent time among political prisoners, and had been exiled to a foreign country. While all this was occurring in his personal life, Peru continued to be governed as one huge hacienda. Opportunity for men such as Tácunan, although no doubt increasing, still remained relatively low. Labor leaders frequently found it necessary to hold meetings clandestinely to prevent arrest. Organized pressures for wage increases were dealt with harshly. Political participation in the existing system was restrained—held to limits acceptable to the aristocracy. Moreover, the traditional elite considered peasants to be chattel property. And if all this were not enough, the Apra political party, the one with all the reform ideas, consistently failed to move in the direction in which Tácunan felt it should. It thus denied him the very vehicle that he had hoped would rectify many of the opportunity limitations imposed on his people. One sees an enormous discrepancy between capacity and opportunity developing in the life of this man. If the binds had occurred with him but with no one else in his homeland, the model would argue that regardless of his commitment, competence, or enthusiasm he would not have been able to arouse the villagers as he did. Thus whereas a case of "personal bind" may alienate one man and dispose him to action (emigration), if group solidarity is to arise, the binds must be broadly shared. We have argued that peasant solidarity did indeed rise. Was it preceded, therefore, by the binds about which the model speaks?

With respect to the capacity variable we notice that by 1958 many villagers had been to school; some had traveled to the large cities, even taking up residence in them for a time; others had worked in the mining complexes of the sierra or as seasonal laborers on the coast and had later returned home. Nearly all had been introduced into a money economy. In addition, a great many peasants had been touched by Belaúnde's 1956 political campaign. Some were even infected with his reform ideology which awakened their nascent popular spirit of cooperation and mutual self-help and excited their hopes for a future of progress and development. Moreover, many of the villages had established schools and also had put together some impressive development and protection organizations.

During the same period of time, however, the evidence points to only a slight increase, if any, in the level of per-capita opportunity for sierra villagers. Within the realm of political participation and social relations there was virtually no change. Peasants could not vote; they could only work, frequently without pay. They were not to be pitied so much as they were to be put up with—and then just as little as possible. Some economic betterment had occurred in the central sierra (a money economy and cash wages for some), but initial improvement here was eventually offset by a growing population on fixed land resources. Thus, little or no actual opportunity increases were observed. Expectations, however, were whetted. And nationalist reformers, such as Belaúnde, came along to make their promises.

Many of the first peasants to suffer serious binds attempted to resolve their initial frustrations, as had Tácunan, simply by emigrating to where the promise of opportunity was thought to be higher. One sees the effect of the conditions set by hypothesis 12:1 (The tendency for collective action, in the very short run, at least, is reduced when mobility opportunities are perceived to exist). However, in due time, as increasing numbers of peasants began to feel the frustrating experiences of structural and psychological binds in their villages, it became apparent that emigration no longer was an acceptable solution—at least, not for everyone. The entire village could not pack up and move off. There were no formal or legal restraints on such a move, of course—except for some hacienda villagers and other peasants who owed labor debts to their landlords—but opportunities elsewhere for everyone simply did not exist. Besides, the costs of moving (social as well as economic) were considerable, not to mention many of the obvious uncertainties about what the opportunity results might be. With this conjuncture many of the villagers, some of whom had already been out to the cities, mines, and eastern uplands, had found opportunities there wanting, and thus had returned to their villages, began to experience the solidarity-producing conditions of hypothesis 12:4 (capacity increasing—opportunities increasing slightly but then falling off with expectations of further decline—declining attractiveness of emigration) although, no doubt, in a less dramatic way than suggested by Figure 10. The general pattern, although weak, still fits. From the peasants' perspective their situation was becoming very uncomfortable. Something simply had to be done. Thus they began to organize to assert themselves vis-à-vis the larger society. Obviously, the underlying conditions conducive to Tácunan's success had been in preparation for some time.

A look at the Satipo area in the late 1950's and early 1960's occasions similar observations. The great exception is that the peasants who migrated there were already in a state of psychological tension. It is reasonable to infer that in their personal lives they suffered fairly high discrepancies between capacity and opportunity because it was only with great uncertainty, difficulty, and hardship that they could have moved from the sierra to the region of Satipo in the first place. It was common knowledge that sometimes these efforts were rewarded with death from illnesses to which the immigrants were unaccustomed. Thus, in general, one would think that the peasants who did emigrate would be among the most highly alienated individuals in the sierra. They, therefore, were probably among those placing highest on the capacity variable as well.

The reason that the uprooted peasants did not find the opportunities they sought did not lie at the feet of a combination of increasing population, a largely static environment, and social rigidity as was the case in the sierra. Rather, it lay with government bureaucrats in Satipo who were suffering from what some Peruvians call the "coastal complex." For them the peasants were an object to be exploited rather than helped, development legislation not withstanding. It is not curious, therefore, that as soon as the peasants ran into these opportunity blocks, they began to organize to remove them. The conditions of hypothesis 12:4, therefore, are also met in Satipo, but with a much greater severity than in the central sierra. Thus the evidence supports the theoretical contention that structural binds and a psychological state of solidarity are preconditions for the rise of peasant social forces whether those forces engage in moderate or intense collective action.

THE INTENSITY OF THE MOVEMENTS

Central Sierra

Two main phases stand out in the central sierra movement. One began about six months before Belaúnde became president and ended two months after his inauguration. The other was initiated by the president's pact with Tácunan and continued into late 1968.

At the beginning of the first phase the evidence points to the kind of high-energy potential outlined in the "subsequent time phase" section of hypothesis 12:4a: solidarity-producing structural and psychological binds were present; the radicalizing effect of declining opportunity per capita was also apparent; and "escape" through emigration was becoming less attractive, if possible at all. Moreover, the level of coercive control over peasant activism was still high (the military was in control) and liberally applied from time to time. In fact, in the months preceding Belaúnde's election, the popular feeling was that the military's stabilization of the sierra derived precisely from a "pseudo-integration based on deterrence." Moreover, the military had compounded the solidarity movement formula with an accelerator. The officers had actually promised land reform but had never really delivered the goods. And yet "potential" was all that existed, for during the six months preceding Belaúnde's election there were few if any anti-establishment peasant solidarity movements.

Belaúnde's election in 1963 changed everything. For many villagers it had the effect of dramatically restructuring the energy formula to correspond very closely to that of hypothesis 12:7, which suggests that a successful elaboration of energy facilitators, such as group resources and linkages, heightens the probability of intense protest when the proper preconditions are set. Although solidarity-producing structural and psychological binds resulting from rising capacity and a rising but then falling opportunity had existed for some time (primarily because of the coercive control of the military), with the election of Belaúnde the coercion was temporarily called off. And although opportunities for massive emigration seemed still to be out of the question, with Belaúnde as president the need probably seemed less acute. Belaúnde had promised reform at home—hence, also the promises of peasant opportunities without having to migrate. Moreover, organizational and leadership resources, as exemplified by the activities of Tácunan, had been in the making among the peasantry all along; for, indeed, Tácunan was not the only one of his kind, just one of the more spectacular. Thus into a juncture of "contained social energy" stepped an important energy-facilitating factor, a "group linkage"—Belaúnde himself.

Belaúnde provided convincing logic that the country now was his, and he already had told the peasants of the reforms that he would make if and when that ever occurred. No doubt the peasants considered that he would continue to protect them from the coercive excesses of the police, the land barons, and the army. Belaúnde was an energy-facilitating linkage, his election a catalyst. Although the army continued to be not only highly visible but extremely powerful (and the peasants knew it), the villagers nevertheless saw their special linkage with Belaúnde as effectively neutralizing its coercive power. The land invasions began nearly immediately. The effect of Belaúnde, therefore, was to undermine the stability of the very government he had come to head. One probably will never know how really scared he was running in those first few weeks.

The next critical moment in this first phase of peasant activism is best analyzed with the societal-response variables. Would Belaúnde deceive the peasants and rather than maintain his liberalizing linkage simply pull out and allow the army to go to work? Or, on the other hand, would he maintain that linkage while also attempting to raise peasant opportunities, thereby lowering the intensity of protest energy potential? Within the limitations imposed by his opposition, Belaúnde chose the absorption course and carried out on-the-spot land reforms. As these particular reforms were selective, however, it meant that while one village received land and would therefore find, at least, temporary relief from its frustration-producing binds, another village not so fortunate would not. It would have Belaúnde's promises but nothing to show for them. Opportunity per capita was massively increased for some peasant groups but continued totally unchanged for others. It was this unhappy set of events that actually began to produce the accelerator conditions outlined in hypothesis 12:8 (Unkept promises radicalize protestors). While Belaúnde frantically moved from hot spot to hot spot carrying out reforms, the result was to enhance the probability of intense collective action in villages not covered by them.

The president quickly realized the effect that his actions were having. It was then that he made his decision to journey to Junín, make his plea with Tácunan and others, lay the cards on the table, and tell them what he was up against. He could not stay the coercive hands of the opposition much longer unless the peasants cooperated and gave him time to carry out a *general* reform in the central sierra. His argument seemed convincing. The peasants became aware not only of their president's dilemma but also of the precarious nature of their own position. They gave him the time. He then set to work concentrating in the central sierra all the development programs at his disposal. Although the land reform question remained up in the air, the president did manage, in a general way and for a short run, to substantially improve peasant opportunities.

As a result of the peasants' decision and the president's actions, the peasants' world was restructured in such a way as to begin to reduce some of the binds (increasing absorption while maintaining low coercion). As time wore on many villagers seemed to find themselves settling into the conditions established by hypothesis 3a (moderate solidarity movements produced by rising capacity and static opportunity but with high expectations of future opportunities because of absorptive response by the larger society). Thus the peasants in the central sierra began to be less concerned with invading lands and more pre-occupied about building up their villages, constructing schools, equipping medical posts, founding cooperatives, and digging irrigation networks. In due time opportunity per capita was effectively raised.

A subsequent side effect of the activities necessary to produce the opportunities, however, was a further increase in capacity. Increased education, new experiences, new challenges, and new exposures seemed to do this. It was only a matter of time, therefore, until Belaúnde would have to face the land-reform question in all seriousness or see the accelerator conditions of hypothesis 12:8 rise once again and a new round of intense collective action get underway. We know he tried. How he tried. But the system beat him. By the time he was forced into exile there was, indeed, some indication that the second round of intensive protest in the central sierra was beginning.

Satipo

The shift of the Satipo movement into intense energy forms is explained by the existence of conditions approximating those set by hypotheses 12:4a, 12:6, and 12:7. In the initial stages the peasants were disappointed and, no doubt, further frustrated by their failure to really find in Satipo the opportunities that they had come to expect. Under these conditions, as hypothesis 12:4a suggests, the motivation to collectively protest, at least in the short run, would be enhanced because further opportunities through emigration were perceived not to exist. This aggravated "gap" situation was intensified by the increasingly intemperate coercion and intimidation that the local aristocracy found convenient to apply from time to time on those protestors who did emerge. The model predicts that this combination of conditions would probably lead to an intensification of the collective energy. And so it was. The rhetoric became more agitated, the meetings more frequent, and the protesting group larger. There were other complicating factors: Belaúnde's promises for reform were not only never realized but also his "protective linkage" with Satipo never materialized. This further radicalized the peasantry. It also permitted the local establishment to increase its level of coercion without fear of state reprisal.

Thus, in response to the increasing level of protest among the Satipo peasants, the local authorities once again increased their level of coercion. The PIP and other state agencies concerned with subversion and public order seemed, by their own activities in the area, to give the go ahead. This, in turn, pushed increasing numbers of peasants over the brink into revolutionary preparations. Finally, however, the authorities in Satipo supplied sufficient coercion to shut the protest movement down, jailing many of the leaders and cowing the participants. One sees the local society responding with coercion over absorption, completing the cycle established by hypothesis 12:7.

Although actual protest diminished because of the high degree of coercion, the potential for more protest nevertheless was always there. The "gaps" remained, and even under such heavy restraints the frustration was still given momentary aggressive expression from time to time. But it could be done only after the fashion of sudden spurts of a pressurized garden hose periodically kinked and unkinked.

A more sustained and radical expression of "protest solidarity" could occur only if some factors or series of events were either to reduce or to neutralize the coercive power of the local Satipo authorities. If Belaúnde had stepped in as he did in the sierra, events in Satipo might have transpired along less disruptive lines—aggression with a "wait-and-see" attitude afterward. But the only neutralizing hope for Satipo seemed to lie in the professional revolutionaries; and because of the aggravations that existed they found a ready-made climate for their ambitions.

As a result of the pressures of peasant activism in the sierra, Belaúnde never did extend his aid programs to Satipo. By default, therefore, the linkages that he had established in the sierra, and that there worked for moderation, were picked up in Satipo by revolutionaries who had other ideas in mind. Moreover, their appearance functioned as a kind of catalyst. Thus the greater intensity of the Satipo movement.

If the state had not sent in Elite Ranger reinforcements to handle the "revolution," the Satipo establishment would have indeed collapsed, victim of the forces that it had helped to create. The urban revolutionaries came with resources, a revolutionary ideology, and fighting materiel. These constituted the "energy facilitators" noted in hypothesis 12:7.

SUMMARY AND CONCLUSIONS

An important key to the understanding of protest movements lies in identifying the underlying conditions that make them possible. These conditions are frequently produced by certain "gaps" or discrepancy factors. Many students of revolution and protest have singled out the importance of these factors: Ted Gurr's discrepancy between value expectations and value capabilities,[2] the Feierabends discrepancy between social expectations and social achievements,[3] Chalmers Johnson's discrepancy between values and the division of labor,[4] Frank Young's structural binds, occasioned by gaps between differentiation and relative centrality,[5] Samuel Huntington's gaps between social mobilization and political development,[6] and our own capacity and opportunity variables are six contemporary examples. The discrepancies, gaps, or binds about which they all speak are necessary not only for peasant revolutions but for collective protest action of the much more moderate varieties. The advantage that the capacity and opportunity variables hold over the others, at least, where micro studies of peasants are concerned, lies in their relative ease of empirical measurement in the field.

The existence of the gap, discrepancy, or bind does not insure, however, that the stage for collective action is well set. Under certain conditions the binds may foster the appearance of migration or even resignation. The differentiating key seems to lie in a mediating psychological variable—perceived future opportunities—and the actual availability of migration opportunities. If the proper critical "mix" is set, however, the result is group solidarity. This is the final necessary precondition for a peasant movement, moderate or intense.

Once the preconditions are set, then other variables intervene to help explain why a peasant movement actually occurs and, when it does, why it occasionally appears in moderate and at other times in intense forms. The mediating variables that explain a large degree of the variance are: (1) accelerators, (2) the societal response set encompassing *absorption* and *coercion,* (3) the energy facilitation set embodying *linkages* and *resources,* and (4) catalysts. In general, the hypotheses using these variables and advanced in the study have worked very well in helping us to understand the appearance and intensity of the Peruvian movements. The hypotheses are sufficiently validated, therefore, to merit additional use and testing, and refinement and reelaboration. Methodologically, it is useful to move to quantitative indicators whenever possible.

With these possibilities, and within these limitations, several additional important generalizations are supported by this study.

1. Peasant movements, whether moderate or intense, have a common origin in response to structural discrepancies in the social system.

2. Peasant movements are incipiently moderate. This derives from the fact that structural discrepancies ordinarily occur only slowly. The movements remain moderate as long as increasing information-processing capacity is reflected in increasing opportunities to exercise that capacity.

3. Government action programs among peasants will tend to increase their potential for corporate activism if the impact affects capacity, or opportunity expectations, more so than actual opportunity.

4. Under conditions of increasing structural binds, state coercion as a main stabilizing policy tends to be counter productive in the long run unless the larger society is willing to engage in a campaign of virtual extermination.

5. Peasants in a state of solidarity tend to prefer their own leadership over outside (revolutionary) leadership unless the nation's response to their activities is one of massive deterrence rather than constructive absorption.

6. In situations where a nation wishes to isolate professional revolutionaries and prevent them from "winning the hearts and minds" of peasants who have acquired a state of solidarity, the government would be advised to respond to their activities with a policy of absorption over coercion and effectively to open the doors to opportunity (or, at least, remove the coercive blocks and stand aside). The consequences will tend to be a considerable amount of peasant loyalty and obedience to law and order *after* opportunity has been effectively raised.

Summary and Conclusions

Is modernization, with its associated psychological and structural changes, really worth it? The response is as divided and disjointed as the process itself. Desires notwithstanding, most individuals caught up in the tides of change find the experience to be a disquieting one. The whole process tends to "mobilize" people; and although they develop new abilities and skills, they also acquire new wants and generate new expectations. Reaching out to fulfill these wants and expectations, much of what they touch—their personal harvest or the lack of it—depends on the vested interests that they feel committed to protect, the new ones that they might wish to champion, the extent and rapidity of the modernizing changes that they seek, the development potential of the country in which they live, and the kind of political system that governs them.

Mobilized individuals sometimes engage in collective action. Such action frequently signals the birth of a new social force. If a modernizing country happens to enjoy relatively absorptive, politically developed institutions, it may be possible for the new social forces that modernization spawns to achieve some of their modernizing goals. Fine, therefore, if one is a member of a favored new social force and fortunate enough to live in a politically modernizing country with good development potential. But institutions emphasizing absorption may, and frequently do, sacrifice on the altar of progress older established groups who would like to see less change and more stability. As such groups often have values "incompatible" with modernity, the individuals who compose them are judged to be expendable. Under these conditions, no doubt, they would greatly appreciate less absorption, more rigidity, more "law and order" and, therefore, a preservation of traditional institutional patterns.

The problem is that neither newly mobilized groups nor old elite ones are likely to get exactly what they want out of modernization. Rapid change frustrates both. It engenders clashes, contributes to instability, and may even set the stage for a civil war.

For those whose vision is directed toward the future rather than toward the past, tensions are assuaged considerably if they have moderate—perhaps, we might say realistic—expectations of what lies beyond the horizon. It is unlikely that any nation can meet the extravagant hopes and unrealistic demands of those who expect the visions of tomorrow to have been realized yesterday, or of charismatic leaders who promise rights of passage forthwith. Similarly, those whose sight is directed toward the glories of the past will have a more palatable ordeal of change if their own future expectations, albeit grudgingly, allow for some compromise and accommodation.

296

Regardless of preferences, from all appearances modernization is definitely with us. Barring some cataclysmic event, it will not be turned back, at least, within the foreseeable future. Therefore, in today's "new" countries the social forces that modernization creates will in all likelihood march relentlessly onward.

As the modernization process unfolds, it appears that the long-range tides of its mobilizing impact will continue to caress the lower half of the social pyramid—the new middle class, workers, students, peasants—and the political rhetors of their respective causes. The rigid past—the old lords and their friends—may not exactly become the first casualties of the new world, but they are highly compromised by it. "With the new military junta," explained a Peruvian aristocrat, "I lose half my fortune. With a more radical revolution I might lose my entire fortune and my neck as well." Hence, after years of resistance he finally acquiesced to the lesser of evils, a "preventive" revolution. The oligarchs in Libya, however, were less judicious. They lost it all.

Thus, in general, two of modernization's salient features, the rise of new social forces and their relation to political institutions, have been under special examination in this book. We have investigated why people become socially mobilized, under what conditions they merge into new social forces of varying degrees of strength and intensity, and what the impact on them of certain kinds of political institutions is as well as some of the political and social consequences of their collective actions. Throughout we have kept in mind the political tensions deriving from these rapid changes.

So much for a general summary of content. Now let us list some of the more important generalizations we have advanced.

1. Modernization is accompanied as much by changes in people's attitudes and values as it is in alterations to their environment.

In all the case studies, we found evidence of these changes. Not only did the environment change and become more complex (urbanization, literacy, economic development, differentiation), but many people, particularly the upwardy mobile, adopted new values of empathy, rationality, material acquisitiveness, and aspiration for political efficacy. Numerous other transformations were observed as well. Many of these value and attitudinal changes arose as a product of experience in and exposure to formal education, new ideologies, new forms of communication and work experiences, and macro-economic changes affecting the whole society (the world depression and consequent "forced" industrialization in Brazil and the discovery of oil in Libya are spectacular examples). In Brazil, both Vargas and Goulart attempted to capture the new mood with *trabalhismo*. In Peru, Belaúnde moved to do the same with *acción popular*, and in Libya al-Qaddafi combined the Koran with oil and largely redid Libyan society, economy, and national expectations along lines of "Arab socialism."

2. The appearance of new attitudes and values is accompanied by changes

in wants, aspirations, and desires. To a greater or lesser degree, depending on the developmental possibilities of the nation and the rigidity or openness of its political system, those wants, aspirations, and desires generally tend to outstrip the possibility of their being satisfied. The resulting "gaps"—structural and pychological binds—occasion frustration and sometimes despair. Yet it is the existence of these gaps or binds among recently "mobilized" individuals that also sets the stage for the birth of new social forces. Accordingly, rapid environmental and value change, such as is commonly associated with "modernization," is generally accompanied by the appearance of new groups and classes that demand economic, political, and social rights and opportunities.

Characteristically, the collective mobilization begins first among those most in a position to be affected by, or to affect, their environment. Workers and peasants are, therefore, among the last to become significantly involved. Accordingly, they are also among the last to constitute a social force of significant proportions.

In Peru, it was not until after the heyday of the Apra movement and the organization of workers into labor unions that any large-scale protest arose in the countryside among the peasants. The same was true in Brazil, where *trabalhismo* and the PTB labor movement did not arise until after Getúlio Vargas had done some experimenting with his Estado Nôvo, based mostly on an uptight economic middle class. In Libya, on the other hand, what we have seen is a disaffected "middle class" and junior officer corps rally against and eventually overthrow a monarchy. Libya, therefore, exemplifies a less well-developed stage of social mobilization. Thus now al-Qaddafi and his friends will still have to decide what to do when the Bedouins and villagers, as surely they eventually will, start making their political, social, and economic demands.

Three levels of mobilization and social organization are therefore described in our case studies. First is Brazil, where social mobilization by the early 1950's had dipped down even to the peasantry. Second is Peru, where the peasantry began generating energy in the early 1960's. And third is Libya where, essentially, the "young middle class" is the group constituting the most recently mobilized sector of the society while the Bedouins and villagers are, for the most part, still politically unimportant.

3. Changes in attitudes and values, and alterations in the environment, are generally not accompanied by a compensating development in authoritative and integrating political institutions. The most singular political effect of the early stages of rapid modernization, therefore, is not political development but political decay, a condition accompanied by instability, disorder, corruption, and chaos.

One of the best visible signs that the political system is relatively weak, either because old traditional patterns of governance and control are decaying or because modern ones are simply not up to par, or because—and most probably this is the case—there is both decay and lack of political development at the same time, is the susceptibility of the regime to raids by organized groups within the society. In extreme instances, revolutions have resulted, but in most practical ones it is the military that deals the hand. Interestingly, it is now the military that controls civilian life in all of the case-study countries. In Brazil, the officers have ruled since the ouster of Goulart in 1964. In Peru, they have held sway since 1968 when they forced Belaúnde to flee. In Libya it was in 1969 that the young officers left their desert garrisons to depose King Idris while he sat in a Turkish bath.

And yet, while the failure, or inability, of traditional political institutions to respond favorably to new demands occasions a decline in the legitimacy of the old order, no automatic assurance exists that a more capable, effective, or legitimate "rational-legal" or developed set of institutions will eventually emerge. Thus charismatic leaders *and* military officers frequently sound the attack, sometimes supporting one another, but often being at odds with each other.

4. Charismatic leadership is made possible by a combination of (a) situational factors (characterized by systemwide societal dislocations) affecting large sectors of the population, and (b) personality or personal-quality factors possessed by a potential leader. Situational factors include (i) a decrease in the legitimacy of old traditional patterns of authority, (ii) a relative decline in (but not absence of) the power or willingness of a regime (or international system) in the presence of declining domestic political legitimacy to maintain stability on the basis of coercion, and (iii) the existence of relatively underdeveloped "rational-legal" political institutions capable of absorbing and assimilating new groups and classes. Personality or personal-quality factors of a leader (i) include a capability to, in a sense, exercise economic and social "magic" for the welfare of the governed—or, at least, have them believing that he can, (ii) require an adeptness or flair for "saying it like it really is" (ideology, doctrines, slogans), which reinforce a belief in the previous item, and (iii) generally demand an origin (birth and early rearing, at least) indigenous to the masses.

Situational and some personality factors are clearly evidenced in the life and times of Getúlio Vargas, first as he championed the cause of the economic middle class under the Estado Nôvo, and later when he defected to blue-collar workers with his *trabalhista* encantations. For certain periods Goulart also marginally qualified for both categories, although his constituency seemed to grow increasingly smaller if not more homogeneous and vociferous as a function of time and his inability to perform any magic.

In Peru, there was an appropriate mix of these situational and personality factors during various periods—with Haya de la Torre in the 1930's and 1940's, with Belaúnde in the late 1950's and early 1960's, and at concurrent periods with numerous locals such as Elías Tácunan and other peasant leaders.

In Libya, on the other hand, there have been essentially only two appropriate situational and personality combinations: with Idris, as he helped to wrench Libya away from the Italian occupation, and with al-Qaddafi, as he pulled the same land and its new sons away from the social stagnation, corruption, and elitism that King Idris had permitted to develop.

5. Charismatic leadership is highly unstable. Either by success or failure in achieving his goals, a charismatic leader may lose his charisma. The only way to preserve charisma seems to be in knowing when to make it a legend, by

bowing out of political power (willingly), or by death, or preferably by martyrdom at the hands of enemies, but by doing so only at the apex of success, not at the trough of failure.

6. Charismatic leaders who do not withdraw or who are not removed at a "charisma preserving" time have a tendency not only to delay the emergence of developed rational-legal authority patterns but also to become despots in their own right.

Of all the charismatic leaders in the case studies, only one now survives: al-Qaddafi. Yet he is entering a traumatic period that perhaps augurs for his traveling paths similar to those of other charismatic leaders. Libyan students are upset with his authoritarianism. There is some discontent with his squandering of the nation's treasure on a war of liberation against Israel. As he suffers declining popularity, al-Qaddafi is certainly typical. Of all the great mid-twentieth century nationalist leaders and liberators, for example, only a handful survive (for example, Nyerere in Tanzania and Touré in Guinea, Mao Tse-Tung in China, and Fidel Castro in Cuba)—and this not only because of natural death. Many lost their charisma and succumbed to military coups (for example, Nkhruma of Ghana and Sukarno of Indonesia) such as we have seen in Brazil, Peru, and Libya. One of the main problems with charismatic leaders, we have learned, is that they are much more adept at articulating problems not solved by others (therefore, justifying their own try at attacking the same) than they are in performing the "magic" needed to do so once they take power.

Look at what happened to Goulart. At one time, 500,000 men, women, and students marched in favor of his assuming full presidential powers (thereby eliminating the parliamentary limbo that the Brazilian military had dictated). But it was not long before an equal number marched to rabidly denounce him and show their disaffection for his person. His political impotency (in part due to structural as well as, perhaps, personality factors) was found out. Who would shout "Goulart! Goulart!" today? Not many Brazilians, we suspect. The man has "lost" his charisma.

As these kinds of leaders react to all the discontent about them, frequently they become, if they can, as dictatorial and despotic as the regimes that they replaced. Goulart increasingly moved toward dictatorial tactics in the closing months of his regime. And al-Qaddafi is all the despot that Idris ever was. The difference is, therefore, not so much in degree, if any, as in the kinds of people who are affected.

7. Thus we see that, as with the rise of charismatic leaders, it is the existence of unrequited anxieties, if not outright societal disturbances occasioned by "gap" conditions, that also precede the manifest intervention of the military in politics. Charismatic and military political authority—one with transitory political legitimacy, the other usually struggling to obtain it—rise on essentially the same social conditions. Depending on other factors, the appearance of a charismatic or populist leader may actually be the catalyst that triggers a military coup, especially if the society is at the level of social mobilization and absence of political development that Huntington characterizes as "mass praetorian."

8. The greater the binds that socially mobilized people suffer, and the greater the resistance to change and "bind-relieving" reform that the political and social system under which they live generates, the greater the probability that rapid modernization will be accompanied by severe protests if not attempts for a genuine revolution.

The problem is one of "clearing away the debris and bastions of the past" so that integrating changes can occur. The longer the old order resists, the more the steam builds up among the masses below. In Brazil, resistance in the 1960's was epitomized at one or another time by Carlos Lacerda, the military hardliners, and a frightened middle class. In Peru, resistance came from the land barons, General Odría and his friends, the monied elite and, eventually, even Haya de la Torre, the former champion of change. In Libya the royal house around King Idris, the Sanussi brotherhood, and the powerful Shalhi family (and United States oil men with whom they were in economic alliance) were that country's functional counterparts.

The existence of resistance permitted leaders such as Goulart, Tácunan, and Libya's Bakkush (the reforming prime minister whom Idris fired after a few months of reform) to enlist "true believers" to their cause. The enemy was clearly identifiable. The old order failed to recruit the newly mobilized precisely because it wanted to keep them out. Other leaders with counter points of view were more than willing to take up the slack and therefore found, in many people, a willing audience and a potential source of recruits. The protest mounted. The results were people's rallies, strikes, and marches in Brazil, land invasions in Peru, and riots in Tripoli and Benghazi.

9. The intensity and, perhaps, success of protest, revolution, or general collective action among social forces relate not only to the underlying conditions that produce structural and psychological binds but to the power these forces have vis-à-vis other groups in the society. Mobilized people increase the probability of intensifying any collective action, therefore, to the extent that they are able to: (a) recruit large numbers to their cause; (b) forge protective linkages or alliances with other groups in the society; (c) generate a stimulating and preferably charismatic form of leadership; and (d) amass an ideological, material, and organizational resource base at (e) the same time that the nation's political and social institutions are rigid and resisting reforming change.

Brazil, Libya, and Peru present differential patterns of both intensity and success of protest. For example, Goulart's social forces—mainly the PTB labor movement—obviously failed to create a new Brazil to their own liking. This, in part, was due to the failure of the respective groups to carry off social-protest agitation of sufficient intensity to convince the rest of Brazil to "shape up." Why, therefore, did Goulart and his friends fail to develop enough pressure?

First, although Goulart certainly was capable of recruiting large numbers of people to his cause, and had done so, he also eventually alienated many of his strategically placed left-wing moderate *and* radical supporters because of the way in which he fumbled on the issues of nationalization, basic reforms, and economic development. The resulting declining linkages hurt Goulart's base of power and left him vulnerable to attacks by counter groups when they chose to play their hand. Moreover, Goulart's vitriolic brother-in-law, Brizola, did not help the situation. It was around him that the most radical elements in the labor movement coalesced, thus articulating two groups on the political left, each fragmenting the other. In attempting to sidetrack this pressure from the radical left and preserve the head of steam in his movement, Goulart shifted his position so far that he not only alienated some former colleagues and their respective supporters but he also cast others off with apparent contempt (for example, San Tiago Dantas and Celso Furtado).

Also, Goulart cut himself off from any protective linkages with military soft-liners and moderates (who might have been able to restrain the hand of the hard-liners). Direct raids on military discipline and tradition was a start. For some officers, dining with mutineers, making military cabinet appointments from an "approved list" supplied by the PTB, and rotating commands so as to keep any general from developing a personal following was as incomprehensible as it was intolerable.

If this were not enough, Goulart was consistently unable to "pay off" his blue-collar followers with any of the magic he had so long promised. When the showdown finally came, therefore, Brazil's president was left standing on very loose sand, having reduced his numbers, broken his protective linkages, lost much of his charisma, and failed to develop a tight organizational base as a repository for his ideology, slogans, and rhetoric. In the end he left everyone wondering whether he was a true ideologue with a new plan for Brazil or simply one more in a long line of political opportunists.

With Libya, it seems that the students and other rioters in Tripoli and Benghazi got absolutely nowhere until the repressive solidarity of the military broke down. There was virtually no one elsewhere in Libya with whom to link. The level of social mobilization was yet too low. Thus, while urban Libya remained cowed, or thought that it was, the junior officers, once they had made their decision to pull off the coup, were able to do so without much apparent civilian help, although they did enjoy an enormous amount of middle class civilian sympathy. It therefore might have turned out to be nothing more than a classical "change of the palace Guard." But the young officers, chafing as they were, schooled by radio Cairo and incensed with oligarchical corruption and opportunism, chose to be hand servants to none other than the new Libya that they had come to envision.

In Peru, the peasants had a lot of indigenous leadership going for them as well as the structural and psychological binds needed for social mobilization. The only additional thing that these people apparently required was the neutralizing linkage of Belaúnde (which temporarily removed the military from a role of suppression) to encourage them to spin off into intense forms of collective protest—land invasions and expulsions of landlords. Equally important linkages served to bring benefits in the absence of violence (in the sierra) when Belaúnde adopted a policy of reform as a substitute for revolution. The failure of like linkages in the Satipo area encouraged the "up-tight" generation there to form counter linkages with professional revolutionaries from the MIR, and this enhanced the intensity of protest among immigrant groups in the eastern uplands.

10. Political and social institutions that resist modernizing change radicalize new social forces. Those that promote change radicalize old ones—the traditional elite and many of their middle class friends.

All of the case studies demonstrate the general validity of this observation. Newly mobilized groups want entrance and access to social mobility, political power, and economic benefits. Older established elite groups frequently perceive these wants to be a direct threat to their time-honored privileges and statuses.

In Brazil, workers, students, intellectuals, and peasants protested and sometimes rioted—if they could get away with it—when the political system was hung up and rigid. On the other hand, when Dantas and Furtado were pushing their reforms, Carlos Lacerda and his associates from among those who had "already made it" were bent out of shape. Thus when Goulart brought up the basic reforms issue with determination and tenacity, 500,000 people marched to shout their displeasure. Finally, taking the appropriate cues, the military hard-liners took control of the political system. The upshot, in the Brazilian case, was that a hard-nosed, fairly exclusionary political-military elite ended up at the helm.

With Libya the case is similar except for the outcome. In that Middle Eastern land the champions of new social forces have the upper hand. In the process of their getting it, however, the general patterns of our tenth generalization are evident. As modernization advanced, students rioted and pleaded with King Idris to open up the political system to them and to their like-minded urban compatriots. Under pressure, Idris appointed Bakkush to be a reforming prime minister. But when the new minister actually set his hand to the task of reform, the powerful Shalhi family and others of similar persuasions put sufficient pressure on the king not only to fire the prime minister but also to suppress the energy if not the mood of change that Bakkush had come to articulate. It was left to the junior officers to call the new hand. Since they have done so, it is apparent that many of the old elite have lost nearly everything. Not the least among those involved is King Idris who now has joined the long list of the world's deposed monarchs.

With Peru, the case is also nearly a classical example of these generalizations, even to the point that early champions of change (Apra), when threatened with more of it than they had in mind, became a new force for the resistance. Specifically, however, peasants became radicalized when their energy potential had built up in the absence of any structural changes in the society to relieve it. Yet, as soon as Belaúnde moved to relieve the tension, scores of vested interests, not the least important of which was the old reformer himself, Haya de la Torre, moved to attack him.

11. From these and related observations, therefore, we see that political modernization and political development do not tend automatically to accompany other indices of modernization, such as increased productivity, urbanization, and literacy.

12. The nature of modernization in the twentieth century encourages the surfacing of "socialist" and "developmentalist" ideologies among new social forces. *Trabalhismo, acción popular,* and Arab socialism are examples encountered in the cases of Brazil, Peru, and Libya. Virtually every developing country displays one or another brand with varying degrees of commitment to communalism and public entrepreneurship.

13. In praetorian countries where the only relevant socially mobilized forces consist almost entirely of a traditional oligarchy, the social and political effect of military rule tend to be similar to that of the traditional civilian elite. They may quarrel among themselves but nevertheless generally protect each other's vital interests. Governmental coups are carried out by a succession of officers having less common purpose than personal attachment to one or another camp among the oligarchical class. It is not until the officer corps begins to experience widespread invasions by an upwardly mobile middle class that the effect of military rule shifts from a simple changing of the oligarchical guard to thrusts in social and economic reforms and national development.

The historically low level of modernization and social mobilization in all our countries coincided with a period in each instance that Huntington has referred to as "oligarchical praetorianism." Thus, although both Brazil and Peru suffered frequent military interventions in politics throughout their history, the effect served, until about 1938 in Brazil and about 1965 in Peru, essentially traditional interests. Libya, since its inception as a nation in 1952, had no military coup before 1969, but obviously the military was nevertheless playing a heavily oligarchy-related role in favor of King Idris. This corresponds to the general low level of social mobilization and modernization prior to the respective dates noted above.

14. On the other hand, in praetorian countries in which social mobilization has touched an "economic and professional middle class," the social and political effect of military rule tends to be "left-wing" reformist. Deviations from this generalization may occur if the social origins or reference group of the victorious officers is oligarchical or elitist. In this case, however, "coups-within-coups" can be expected if junior officers are recruited from middle or lower class groups.

Libya is the spectacular example here, although the use of "left wing" may be more unfortunate than accurate. In any event, the young officers under al-Qaddafi certainly are bent on reforming and restructuring the entire social, political, economic, and cultural fabric of their oil-rich nation, but for the benefit of the masses rather than the oligarchy.

Peru, on the other hand, now has a reformist military in power, but social mobilization obviously has dipped down to include more than just an economic middle class. Based on generalization no. 14, we probably would have looked for the appearance of a modernizing military in Peru as early as the late 1930's or early 1940's, since that was the time when an emerging economic middle class was testing its oats. But either traditional recruitment patterns (geared to the elite) helped to maintain military-oligarchy solidarity, or perhaps the phenomenal success of the Apra labor reform movement and its classic confrontation with the military in the 1930's so terrified the oligarchy that it quickly absorbed the economic middle class and made it an ally rather than an enemy, thus altering what might have been a "natural order" of confrontation. In any event, as Peru continues to mobilize, the one certain thing is that the present military is firmly bent on fairly drastic reform measures in favor of itself and the middle and lower classes—at the expense of the traditional elite.

15. A third case of political and social consequences of military rule relates to coups occurring in praetorian countries experiencing rapid mobilization among blue-collar workers and/or peasants. Here the social and political effect of military rule tends to be "right-wing" reformist in social and political areas, but may be expansionary in economic ones. Deviations occur if junior rather than senior officers gain the upper hand in military infighting, particularly if their social origins or ideological reference groups hold the lower classes in some esteem. Brazil fits the general pattern and Peru, partially at least, the "deviation."

16. In praetorian countries with low levels of social mobilization, the military may successfully foster the development of rational-legal political institutions which, after it withdraws from power, might survive it. Libya is the one country for which we could hold out some hope, but time may prove us wrong in that particular case.

17. In praetorian countries with high levels of social mobilization, the military has little capability to establish rational-legal political institutions but may be highly successful in areas measured by aggregate economic indices.

Brazil is the obvious candidate for this general observation, that, in conjunction with the previous discussions, suggests why military leadership, as charismatic leadership, is sometimes volatile and unstable. One military authority may be replaced by another. It may be destroyed by a revolutionary movement. Or it may just keep the country dangling in limbo for an indefinite period—turning politics back to civilians when complexities become overwhelming, only to retrieve them once again when the civilian politicians cannot produce the promised order either.

If either military or charismatic authority is to be replaced by more orderly rational-legal or politically modern forms of government, the first task is to begin to close the gap between social mobilization and political development. As it is unlikely that anyone will be able to stop social mobilization, the key to stability must therefore lie in political development. Yet to accomplish this entails a conscious act as well as an enormous will. Charismatic leaders, just as military officers, frequently have neither.

In Brazil the economy has modernized and the society is struggling to do so; but the political system is hung up and, for some Brazilians, has proven incapable either of governing or of ameliorating the structural and psychological binds which are associated with modernization. It was into this wake, into this dilemma of a decaying political past and a yet undeveloped political present that João Goulart entered and the military ushered him out.

18. We thus see some empirical support for the theoretical assertions that the consequences of military coups (with respect to how officers relate to new

social forces) may be explained by the level of social mobilization existing in a society when a coup occurs, and the reference-group identity of the officers. Increasingly, officers tend to have a "middle class" reference identity. When social mobilization is low, their behavior after a coup tends to be politically radical. They depose old monarchs, traditional oligarchs, and reactionary despots; and then they set up a "socialist" state. When social mobilization has dipped midway down into the social pyramid, officers, when they intervene, tend to constitute a kind of holding action on reform. They may push economic development but still resist participation of peasants and workers in politics. When social mobilization has dipped far enough into the social structure to make even the peasants revolutionary, then the officers take on a decidedly conservative stance. In Brazil we found the officers to be essentially conservative in all matters but economics. In Peru they have been moderately radical reformers. In Libya, on the other hand, the military government is very radical. This corresponds to an apparent differential ranking of the countries with respect to social mobilization, with Brazil highest, followed closely by Peru and then Libya.

19. Political parties, per se, neither enhance nor undermine political development. It is not the existence of parties, therefore, but their nature and function that is crucial for political development. Those parties which do enhance political development are more broad in their constituency than a single social force. They have an institutionalized pattern of leadership succession and change. They are decidedly "absorptive" in their political participation functions. And they are not totally dependent on official government sanction for their existence. As new social forces rise, they attempt to incorporate them under their wing and relieve the binds which so frustrate them. The most successful arrangements in this regard in the developing countries seem to be the "dominant party systems," Mexico being one of the best examples. Unfortunately, none of our case countries has such a system. Brazil has two parties sanctioned by the military—the party of "yes" (MDB "opposition") and the party of "yes sir" (ARENA). Peru has gone esssentially "a-political" as far as parties are concerned, and Libya sports only an officially sponsored semblance of one.

20. As long as rapid modernizing change impinges upon people, as long as traditional political institutions continue to decay and the development of modern ones remains attenuated and skeletal, and as long as new social forces continue to experience serious structural and psychological binds, instability rather than the art of peaceful association will be the most salient political news stories of the contemporary Third World.

Political instability is not inevitable, but as long as conditions exist which foster its occurrence, we must in any case consider the probability of its continuation very great. What observations, therefore, can we make about some of these conditions? For one thing, social mobilization will in all likelihood not reduce its tempo, at least for the next two or three decades. Moreover, people's wants and expectations, and their capacity, will no doubt continue to outstrip any possibility of their being generally satisfied. Compounding this dilemma is the general lag in the development of political institutions and procedures, either because of elite restraint on their absorptive capability or internal weaknesses which have produced the same result. Up to now they have not been able to respond adequately either to demands or pressures. We are led to conclude that their performance in the immediate future will not appreciably improve, although some notable exceptions may occur. The outlook, it would seem, is that if "political stability" is to be achieved, it will be done so either on the basis of a substantial amount of domestic coercion and police power (which may be supported by one or another superpower whose domestic meddling significantly alters the odds in favor of a clientele group selected for support), or by transitory national distractions which reduce people's felt problems in favor of attention toward resisting, or destroying, a perceived threat to national sovereignty and well being (e.g., Egypt and Libya vs. Israel).

Accordingly, if political stability with democracy is one's overriding goal in the Third World, he probably ought not to be overly optimistic about the possibilities of a general realization soon. Yet, it is precisely the instability of the moment, with all its personal tragedies, that may prepare the eventual way for peoples, as much as nations, to develop "an art of peaceful association." Given the conditions of the times, societal restructuring as well as personal retooling seem to be required. Instability and pressure, under some conditions, may enhance both.

If the hearts and minds of people are to be welded to their homeland and to the legitimacy of their political institutions, those institutions will have to serve the interests of more than one class of people, or one set of international alliances. There is more than a little truth to the statement that "there needs to be at least something in it for all." Modernization makes the vision brighter, but the tasks harder. If old formulas no longer work, it is because the conditions on which they rested are no longer with us.

NOTES

NOTES TO THE INTRODUCTION

[1] Samuel P. Huntington, *Political Order in Changing Societies* (New Haven: Yale University Press, 1968), 135.

[2] One of the early modernization volumes looks into the social, cultural, and political implications of being an "old society" while a "new state." See Clifford Geertz, ed., *Old Societies and New States: The Quest for Modernity in Asia and Africa* (New York: The Free Press, 1963).

[3] The "fragment society" concept has been explored from time to time, but its most systematic theoretical and empirical presentation is to be found in Hartz' edited volume, *The Founding of New Societies: Studies in the History of the United States, Latin America, South Africa, Canada, and Australia* (New York: Harcourt, Brace, and World, 1964).

NOTES TO CHAPTER 1

[1] Disclosures on the front foundations came in February and early March of 1967, originating mostly in *The New York Times*. The foreign press picked them up with banner headlines. Much soul searching ensued among social scientists. As an example, see "Report of the Executive Committee," *American Political Science Review, 61* (June 1967), 565–568.

[2] Roberto de Oliveira Campos, *Reflections on Latin American Development* (Austin, Tex.: University of Texas Press, 1967), 67.

[3] A lot of paper has been consumed, especially by anthropologists, on the subjects of "social, cultural, and psychological barriers to change." These do indeed exist, and many of them have been picturesquely portrayed by George M. Foster in *Traditional Cultures: and the Impact of Technological Change* (New York: Harper and Row, 1962). In the present day, however, such an orientation can be overworked. Raymond Firth, for example, has convincingly shown that in the "micro-economic" sphere peasants are well aware of the possibilities of rational economic action and make strong endeavors to better their economic position whenever this is possible. In their own traditional economy they watch alternatives and productivity margins most carefully and switch their productive efforts accordingly. "In the macro-economic field, however, they have not shown the same perspective, primarily because of a lack of understanding of how large-scale commodity markets work and the existence of external competitors with differential advantages." See Raymond Firth, "Social Structure and Peasant Economy: The Influence of Social Structure Upon Peasant Economics," in Clifton R. Wharton, Jr., ed., *Subsistence Agri-*

culture and Economic Development (Chicago: Aldine Publishing Co., 1969), 23–37.

[4] Kling's statement, along with other interesting points on methodology, may be found in "The State of Research on Latin America: Political Science," in Charles Wagley, ed., *Social Science Research on Latin America* (New York: Columbia University Press, 1964). The quotation is from page 197.

NOTES TO CHAPTER 2

[1] David E. Apter, *Some Conceptual Approaches to the Study of Modernization* (Englewood Cliffs, N.J.: Prentice-Hall, 1968), 195–197, 335–337.

Several scholars, such as Apter, have emphasized that modernization and industrialization are not the same thing. For politicians to confuse the two only adds hardship on people who are trained for roles and occupations which their country has neither the resources nor the competitive potential to provide. Modernization, according to Apter, should therefore not be viewed in the tight technological sense that Marion J. Levy, Jr., (*Modernization and the Structure of Societies*) and Walt Rostow, (*The Stages of Economic Growth*) do. Rather, modernization is a more general phenomenon, and one way to get there, but not the only way, is through industrialization. Other means, in which new role structures, patterns of thinking, and integrating institutions which bind them all together, might also work. One practical problem here, of course, is that "alternative" routes to modernization other than industrialization are not at all in vogue today. Moreover, if a country finds it impossible to modernize through industrialization, it is not certain that any alternative schemes will work any better for it.

[2] Walt W. Rostow, *The Stages of Economic Growth* (Cambridge, England: Cambridge University Press, 1964), 73–92.

[3] Wilbert E. Moore, *The Impact of Industry* (Englewood Cliffs, N.J.: Prentice-Hall, 1965), 3.

[4] Apter, *Some Conceptual Approaches*, 3.

[4a] Edward Shils, "Tradition," *Comparative Studies in Society and History*, *13*, No. 2 (April 1971), 122–159.

[5] Everett M. Rogers, *Modernization Among Peasants: The Impact of Communication* (New York: Holt, Rinehart and Winston, 1969), 24–38.

[6] Daniel Lerner, *The Passing of Traditional Society: Modernizing the Middle East* (New York: The Free Press, 1958), 3.

[7] Alex Inkeles, "Making Men Modern: On the Causes and Consequences of Individual Change in Six Developing Countries," *The American Journal of Sociology*, *75*, No. 2 (September 1969), 210.

[8] Neil J. Smelser, "Toward a Theory of Modernization," in Amitai Etzioni and Eva Etzioni, eds., *Social Change* (New York: Basic Books, 1964), 258–274. Refer also to Smelser's "The Modernization of Social Relations," in Myron Weiner, ed., *Modernization: The Dynamics of Growth* (Basic Books, 1966), 110–112.

[9] Albert O. Hirschman, "Obstacles to Development: A Classification and a

Quasi-Vanishing Act," *Economic Development and Cultural Change*, 13, No. 4 (July 1966); reprinted in Harvey Kebschull, ed., *Politics in Transitional Societies* (New York: Appleton-Century-Crofts, 1968), 375.

[10] Lerner, *The Passing of Traditional Society*, 60.

[11] David C. McClelland, *The Achieving Society* (Princeton, N.J.: Van Nostrand, 1961). See also McClelland's "The Impulse to Modernization," in Weiner, ed., *Modernization*.

[12] Weiner, *Modernization*, 5.

[13] G. Lenski, *Power and Privilege, A Theory of Social Stratification* (New York: McGraw-Hill, 1966), 209–210. See also Alex Inkeles, *What is Sociology: An Introduction to the Discipline and Profession* (Englewood Cliffs, N.J.: Prentice-Hall, 1964), 39.

[14] The variables are reviewed on page 44.

[15] George M. Foster, *Traditional Cultures: And the Impact of Technological Change* (New York: Harper and Row, 1962), 120–143.

[16] As a representative sample, see Oscar Lewis, *The Children of Sánchez: Autobiography of a Mexican Family* (New York: Vintage Books, 1961).

NOTES TO CHAPTER 3

[1] Karl Deutsch, "Social Mobilization and Political Development," *American Political Science Review*, 55 (September 1961), 494.

[2] For the origins of this terminology see Edward C. Banfield, *The Moral Basis of a Backward Society* (New York: The Free Press, 1958); and Huntington, *Political Order in Changing Societies*, 24. The practical consequences of the syndrome are outlined by John H. Kautsky, *The Political Consequences of Modernization* (New York: Wiley, 1972), 139–169.

[3] Huntington, *Political Order in Changing Societies*, 4.

[4] Both S. N. Eisenstadt and Samuel P. Huntington have persuasively argued that the major problem confronting today's modernizing societies is the need to create patterns of political organization and procedure, along with other institutions, capable of continuously absorbing the various new social forces which arise as modernization proceeds. Samuel P. Huntington's major ideas may be found in *Political Order in Changing Societies*. Eisenstadt has summarized his thinking in *Modernization, Protest and Change*.

[5] Fred W. Riggs, "The Theory of Political Development," in James C. Charlesworth, ed., *Contemporary Political Analysis* (New York: The Free Press, 1967), 318. Refer also to Riggs' "The Dialectics of Developmental Conflict," *Comparative Political Studies*, 1, No. 2 (July 1968), 197–226.

[6] In "Political Development and Political Decay."

[7] Refer to pages 34–35 of *Political Order in Changing Societies*.

[8] Refer to "The Theory of Political Development," and to "The Dialectics of Developmental Conflict."

[9] The Committee on Comparative Politics of the Social Science Research Council has maintained that political modernization and development can be usefully reduced to the three key concepts of equality, capacity, and *differen-*

tiation. These and related points are expounded in their seventh volume on the subject, *Crises and Sequences in Political Development* (Princeton: Princeton University Press, 1971), by Lucian Pye and his colleagues .

[9a] Robert B. Stauffer, "Great-power Constraints on Political Development," *Studies in Comparative International Development*, 6, No. 11 (1970–1971), 231–251.

[9b] Samuel P. Huntington, "No More Vietnams," *The Atlantic Monthly* (December 1968).

[10] Huntington, *Political Order in Changing Societies*, 264.

[11] Sigmund Neumann, "The International Civil War," *World Politics*, 1, No. 3 (April 1949), 333–334.

[12] Ivo K. Feierabend, Rosalind L. Feierabend, and Betty A. Nesvold, "Social Change and Political Violence: Cross-National Patterns," *The History of Violence in America: A Report to the National Commission on the Causes and Prevention of Violence*, edited by Hugh Davis Graham and Ted Robert Gurr (New York: Bantam Books, 1969), 632–687.

[13] Until recently many social scientists considered "deprivation" alone to be the main motivation for aggression and goal-seeking protest activity. New theorizing gives considerable weight (in addition to *relative* deprivation) to such factors as perceived threat, anticipation of goal achievement, expectations of future opportunities, and present expectations of future frustrations. For an expanded discussion which summarizes some of the literature see Leonard Berkowitz, "The Concept of Aggressive Drive," in L. Berkowitz, ed., *Advances in Experimental Social Psychology*, Vol. II (New York: Academic Press, 1965), and also Berkowitz' more recent article, "The Study of Urban Violence: Some Implications of Laboratory Studies of Frustration and Aggression," *Riots and Rebellion: Civil Violence in the Urban Community* (1968), 39–49, edited by Louis H. Masotti and Don R. Bowen, and reprinted in James C. Davies, ed., *When Men Revolt and Why* (New York: The Free Press, 1971), 182–187.

[14] This is a "bridging problem" of theory with the real world which derives from the fact that a deductive theory cannot be tested directly without the aid of an auxiliary set of assumptions linking its theoretical variables to the required operational indicators. See Hubert M. Blalock, Jr., *Theory Construction: From Verbal to Mathematical Formulations* (Englewood Cliffs, N.J.: Prentice-Hall, 1969), 151–154.

[15] For example, see Bryant Wedge, "The Case Study of Student Political Violence: Brazil, 1964, and Dominican Republic, 1965," *World Politics*, 21, No. 2 (January 1969), 183–206.

[16] Ted Robert Gurr, *Why Men Rebel* (Princeton University Press, 1970). A further consideration of the "frustration-aggression" notion may be found in Leonard Berkowitz, ed., *Roots of Aggression: A Re-examination of the Frustration-Aggression Hypothesis* (New York: Atherton Press, 1968).

[17] Frank W. Young, "A Proposal for Cooperative Cross-Cultural Research on Intervillage Systems," *Human Organization*, 25, No. 1 (Spring 1966), 46–50. See also F. LaMond Tullis, *Lord and Peasant in Peru*, Part I.

[18] See Johan Galtung, "A Structural Theory of Aggression," *Journal of Peace*

Research, No. 2 (1964), 95–119; and Andrzej Malewski, "The Degree of Status Incongruence and its Effects," *Class, Status, and Power,* 2nd ed., Reinhard Bendix and Seymour Martin Lipset, eds. (New York: The Free Press, 1966), 303–308.

[19] Chalmers Johnson, *Revolutionary Change* (Boston: Little, Brown, 1966).

[20] Ibid.

[21] Samuel P. Huntington, *Political Order in Changing Societies* (New Haven, Conn.: Yale University Press, 1968).

[22] Frank W. Young, "A Proposal for Cooperative Cross-Cultural Research on Intervillage Systems."

[23] F. LaMond Tullis, *Lord and Peasant in Peru: A Paradigm of Political and Social Change* (Cambridge, Mass.: Harvard University Press, 1970).

[24] This is the so-called *J*-curve hypothesis articulated by James C. Davies, "The *J*-Curve of Rising and Declining Satisfactions as a Cause of Some Great Revolutions and a Contained Rebellion," in *The History of Violence in America,* ed., Hugh David Graham and Ted Robert Gurr, 690–730. See also Davies' "Toward a Theory of Revolution," *American Sociological Review,* 27 (February 1962).

[25] See Gino Germani, "Stages of Modernization in Latin America," *Studies in Comparative International Development,* 5, No. 8 (1969–1970), 155–173, and Albert O. Hirschman, *Exit, Voice, and Loyalty: Responses to Decline in Firms, Organizations, and States* (Cambridge, Mass.: Harvard University Press, 1970).

[26] Ivo K. Feierabend and Betty Nesvold with Rosalind L. Feierabend, "Political Coerciveness and Turmoil: A Cross-National Inquiry," *Law and Society Review* (August 1970), 93–117. See also analogous observations on "value" and "coercion" theories of integration in Chalmers Johnson, *Revolutionary Change,* Chapter 2.

[27] The point at issue is treated by Chalmers Johnson, *Revolutionary Change,* 99–100, 103–105, and 153–154.

[28] Analogous observations are made by Ted Gurr, "Psychological Factors in Civil Violence," *World Politics,* 20, No. 2 (January 1968), 245–278, and Bryant Wedge, "The Case Study of Student Political Violence: Brazil, 1964, and Dominican Republic, 1965." See also Chalmers Johnson, *Revolutionary Change,* Chapter 5.

[29] Chalmers Johnson, *Revolutionary Change,* 99.

NOTES TO CHAPTER 4

[1] Robert L. Heilbroner, *The Great Ascent: The Struggle for Economic Development in Our Time* (New York: Harper Torchbooks, 1963), 137.

[2] Ibid., 139.

[3] Ndabaningi Sithole, *African Nationalism,* 2nd ed. (London: Oxford University Press, 1968).

[4] Charles W. Anderson, Fred R. von der Mehden, and Crawford Young,

Issues of Political Development (Englewood Cliffs, N.J.: Prentice-Hall, 1967), 179–183. The quotation is found on page 183.

⁵ Claude Ake, *A Theory of Political Integration* (Homewood, Ill.: The Dorsey Press, 1967), 26, has made some instructive remarks on this point.

⁶ Chalmers Johnson, *Revolutionary Change* (Boston: Little, Brown, 1966); Chapter 2 reviews some of the "value" and "coercion" literature on political integration.

⁷ As cited in Dankwart Rustow, *A World of Nations: Problems of Political Modernization* (Washington, D.C.: The Brookings Institution, 1967), 149–150.

⁸ See the observations raised by Seymour Martin Lipset in *The First New Nation: The United States in Historical and Comparative Perspective* (New York: Basic Books, 1963), 170.

⁹ Ann Ruth Willner and Dorothy Willner, "The Rise and Role of Charismatic Leaders," in Harvey G. Kebschull, ed., *Politics in Transitional Societies: The Challenge of Change in Asia, Africa and Latin America* (New York: Appleton-Century-Crofts, 1968), 170.

¹⁰ Argentina, Brazil, Bolivia, Burma, Congo (Leopoldville), Congo (Brazzaville), Dahomey, Dominican Republic, Ecuador, Egypt, El Salvador, Gabon, Ghana, Greece, Guatemala, Honduras, Indonesia, Iraq, Korea, Libya, Mali, Nigeria, Panama, Pakistan, Paraguay, Peru, Sudan, Syria, Thailand, Togo, Turkey, Vietnam.

¹¹ Huntington, *Political Order in Changing Societies,* 194.

¹² The citation comes from Martin Needler, "Political Development and Military Intervention in Latin America," *American Political Science Review, 60,* No. 3 (September 1966), 618. This view is supported by Edwin Lieuwen in a special report to a U.S. Senate Committee, *Survey of the Alliance for Progress: The Latin American Military,* a study prepared at the request of the Subcommittee on American Republics Affairs of the Committee on Foreign Relations, United States Senate. U.S. Government Printing Office, Washington, D.C., 1967.

¹³ Samuel P. Huntington, *Political Order in Changing Societies* (New Haven, Conn.: Yale University Press, 1968), 192–263.

¹⁴ Eric A. Nordlinger, "Soldiers in Mufti: The Impact of Military Rule Upon Economic and Social Change in the Non-western States," *American Political Science Review, 64,* No. 4 (December 1970), 1131–1148; and José Nun, "A Latin American Phenomenon: The Middle Class Military Coup," *Trends in Social Science Research in Latin American Studies* (Berkeley, Cal.: University of California, Institute of International Studies, 1965), 55–99.

¹⁵ Robert M. Price, "A Theoretical Approach to Military Rule in New States: Reference-Group Theory and the Ghanaian Case," *World Politics, 23,* No. 3 (April 1971), 399–430.

¹⁶ It would seem fairly obvious that no single variable, taken alone, would be worth much as a predictor. In addition to the concept of social mobilization vis-à-vis praetorianism, and the qualifying variables of "social origins" or "professional identifications," Alfred Stepan has explored the nature of the

military's institutional organization and recruitment patterns, the size of the military, and the effect upon the military of highly institutionalized military academies which have taken on something of an ideological life of their own (e.g., those in Brazil and Peru). See Stepan's *The Military in Politics: Changing Patterns in Brazil* (Princeton, N.J.: Princeton University Press, 1971), 7–56.

[17] Huntington, *Political Order in Changing Societies*, 228. This view is also held by Martin Needler, "Political Development and Military Intervention in Latin America," and Lieuwen, *Survey of the Alliance for Progress.*

[18] Martin C. Needler, *Political Development in Latin America: Instability, Violence, and Revolutionary Change* (New York: Random House, 1968), 69.

[19] Samuel P. Huntington, *Political Order in Changing Societies*, 151.

[20] Gabriel A. Almond, and G. Bingham Powell, Jr., *Comparative Politics: A Developmental Approach* (Boston: Little, Brown, 1966), 98–127.

[21] Huntington, *Political Order in Changing Societies*, 397–461.

[22] Rustow, *A World of Nations*, 105–132.

[23] Myron Weiner and Joseph LaPalombara, *Political Parties and Political Development* (Princeton, N.J.: Princeton University Press, 1966), 403.

NOTES TO THE INTRODUCTION TO PART III AND TO CHAPTER 5

[1] Victor Alba, *Alliance Without Allies* (New York: Praeger, 1965), cited by George C. Lodge, *Engines of Change: United States Interests and Revolution in Latin America* (New York: Knopf, 1970), 56.

[2] I have written portions of the Brazilian case with the very able research and editorial assistance of Richard Kennedy, my research assistant. His own resources, in addition to the standard library materials, included a personal residence in Brazil from 1964–1966 during which time he collected information from Brazilian publications and personalities.

[3] Many students of Latin American politics have noted the great similarity between Brazil's *Coronelismo* and the nineteenth century machine politics of New York and Chicago. An engaging perspective on Tammany Hall, one of America's most famous political machines, may be found in William L. Riordon, *Plunkitt of Tammany Hall: A Series of Very Plain Talks on Very Practical Politics* (New York: E. P. Dutton, 1963).

[4] Thomas E. Skidmore, *Politics in Brazil, 1930–1964: An Experiment in Democracy* (New York: Oxford University Press, 1967), 33.

[5] Ibid., 73.

[6] Samuel E. Finer characterizes career-enlisted men and officers as being systematically nomadized, "moving from one garrison town to another" (*The Man on Horseback*, p. 9). Alfred Stepan notes that such a characterization does not fit Brazil, however, because transfers out of the state are the exception. Thus strong regional ties are maintained, and frequently a soldier's attachment to the state governor, or at least to the public opinion of his state, is much stronger than anything which the national executive or the congress in Rio (and

now Brasília) could or can elicit (Alfred Stepan, *The Military in Politics: Changing Patterns in Brazil* [Princeton University Press, 1971], 14).

[7] Skidmore, *Politics in Brazil, 1930–1964*, 218.

[8] Ibid., 249.

[9] I have profited by instruction from Brazil's Helio Jaguaribe on several of the points raised in Goulart's shift to the left. See also the notes by Ronald M. Schneider, *The Political System of Brazil: Emergence of a "Modernizing" Authoritarian Regime, 1964–1970* (New York: Columbia University Press, 1971), 73–107.

[10] Roberto Muggiati and Jario Regis, "Quem Derrubou Jango," *Manchete* (Brazil), March 25, 1967, p. 11 (translated by Richard Kennedy).

[11] Ibid., 11.

[12] Ibid.

[13] Ibid. See also Skidmore, *Politics in Brazil*, 264, 285, and 299. Schneider, *The Political System of Brazil*, 91–107 provides extensive notes on civilian as well as military conspiracies.

[14] Muggiati and Regis, "Quem Derrubou Jango," 10; and Skidmore, *Politics in Brazil*, 284–302. A discussion of the March 13 rally may also be found in Stepan, *The Military in Politics*, 195–204.

[15] Skidmore, *Politics in Brazil*, 295, treats some of the points.

[16] Ibid., 297.

[17] Muggiati, "Quem Derrubou Jango," 12.

[18] Ibid., 12.

[19] Ibid. A discussion of the Naval Mutiny, with background notes, may be found in Stepan, *The Military in Politics*, 204–209.

NOTES TO CHAPTER 6

[1] My research assistant, Richard Kennedy, reported that while he resided in Brazil (1964–1966) it was popularly estimated that the soft-liners and moderates together made up over 80 percent of the officer corps. The remaining 20 percent was evenly divided between the "reactionary" and "young Turk" hard-liners. Thus the hard-liners themselves were divided between those who wanted to retain jurisdiction over the political system in order to return Brazil to the *status quo ante*, and those who wanted to retain the political system in order to carry out rapid economic development and institute social reforms. In any event, all hard-liners in a monolithic "conservative camp" does not fit either popular notions or the empirical evidence.

[2] Skidmore, *Politics in Brazil*, 308, and Schneider, *The Political System of Brazil*, 127.

[3] Huntington, *Political Order in Changing Societies*, 233–237.

[4] Skidmore, *Politics in Brazil*, 309.

[5] Roberto de Oliveira Campos, in his *Reflections on Latin American Development* (Austin, Tex.: University of Texas Press, 1967), has relayed some introspective thinking. One item is of particular interest: "I am more and more

convinced that the foundation of the theory of growth has much more to do with psychology, social institutions, and ethical values than with the laws of rational economic behavior" (p. 68). Jaguaribe nevertheless considered that, those insights notwithstanding, the practical effect of Campos' policies was diametrically opposite to those of Celso Furtado, arguing that Campos had proposed a program of social stabilization "with an intrinsic propensity for becoming a colonial fascist regime." See Helio Jaguaribe, *Economic and Political Development: A Theoretical Approach and a Brazilian Case Study* (Cambridge, Mass.: Harvard University Press, 1968), 188. See also the discussion by Schneider, *The Political System of Brazil*, 149–153.

[6] Schneider, *The Political System of Brazil*, 165–173, documents the particulars.

[7] James Nelson Goodsell, "Brazil: The Uncertain Giant," *The Christian Science Monitor*, January 7, 1966, p. 9.

[8] A report tracing the beginning of the problems with students can be found in *O Cruzeiro*, July 15, 1967, pp. 38–45.

[9] *The New York Times*, August 19, 1966.

[10] Schneider, *The Political System of Brazil*, 227.

[11] *Jornal do Brasil*, December 17, 1967, as cited by Schneider, *The Political System of Brazil*, 226.

[12] *The New York Times*, March 3, 1968.

[13] Frances M. Foland, "Whither Brazil," *Inter-American Economic Affairs*, 24, No. 3 (Winter 1970), 60.

[14] *The New York Times*, April 4, 1968.

[15] *The New York Times*, April 8, 1968.

[16] Reported in *Time*, July 5, 1968, p. 34. A backdrop to the growing student-church discontent is catalogued by Schneider, *The Political System of Brazil*, 229–240.

[17] Leslie Warren, "Opposition Gets Bolder in Brazil," *The Christian Science Monitor*, July 15, 1968, p. 10.

[18] Murilo Melo Filho and Roberto Stuckert, *"Brasília/O Campus da Batalha,"* *Manchete* (Rio de Janeiro), September 14, 1968, pp. 12–15.

[19] The riots during these months were not only between students and police. Sometimes bands of students fought each other. *Manchete* (October 19, 1968, pp. 26–31) reports a riot between student conservatives of the CCC ("Committee for Hunting Communists") and liberals from the School of Philosophy of the University of São Paulo.

[20] All major international dailies had extensive commentaries on Brazil for this period. This quotation comes from an editorial in *The Christian Science Monitor*, November 5, 1968.

[21] The reports of police torture have been not only habitual but so persistent that few now believe they have no validity. The only *official* acknowledgement so far has come from a former anti-Goulart military conspirator, Education Minister (1970) Jarbas Passarinho, who stated that to deny that torture had been used in Brazilian jails would be untrue. He added, however, that it was not true to say that there was a systematic policy of torture (*New York Times,*

December 4, 1970). An academic report touching on this and related issues comes from Philippe C. Schmitter, "The Persecution of Political and Social Scientists in Brazil," *PS* (published quarterly by the American Political Science Association), 3, No. 2 (Spring 1970), 123–128. Additional notes may be found in James Nelson Goodsell's "Brazil Brutality? Evidence Builds Up of Political Torture," *Christian Science Monitor*, May 1970. José Yglesias has some corroborating evidence in his "Report from Brazil: What the Left is Saying," *The New York Times Magazine*, December 7, 1969. *Newsweek*, December 8, 1969, p. 68, noted that even the clergy was not immune to the torture chambers. Related references corresponding to subsequent time periods follow in the notes below.

[22] See Schneider, *The Political System of Brazil*, 271–274.

[23] See the reports in *The New York Times*, December 15, 1968, p. 3, and February 27, 1968, p. 5. Also, interpretive coverage is given by James Nelson Goodsell, "Brazil Military Cracks Down," *The Christian Science Monitor*, December 18, 1968.

[24] The dialogue is reported by James Nelson Goodsell, "Militarists Muffle Political Dissent in Brazil," *The Christian Science Monitor*, February 11, 1969, p. 1.

[25] Ibid.

[26] In 1968 the gross national product exceeded $21 billion (an increase of six percent against a population growth of approximately three percent) and industrial production expanded by more than 12 percent. In addition, nearly one million kilowatts were added to the nation's electrical generating capacity.

[27] Azikiwe is quoted in Huntington, *Political Order in Changing Societies*, 48–49.

[28] *The Christian Science Monitor*, March 11, 1969, p. 6.

[29] Ibid.

[30] Ibid.

[31] Ibid.

[32] Some of the names appear in Schneider, *The Political System of Brazil*, 285–286.

[33] *The Christian Science Monitor*, May 10, 1969.

[34] Philippe C. Schmitter ("The Persecution of Political and Social Scientists in Brazil") has made an instructive survey on this particular, and continuing, problem in Brazil.

[35] The three Brazilian Presidents since 1964 provide an interesting example of how the revolution has gone. Castello Branco was a known and respected man even before 1964 and, because of his strategic position in the pre-coup plots, was the natural "swing man" of the revolution. Costa e Silva became president not only because of his revolutionary activities but because he also had the backing of Castello Branco. Médici, on the other hand, became president more for what he *did not* do than for anything he ever did. A compromise candidate, he was selected because he did not have exclusive ties with any of the more powerful officer groups.

[36] *The New York Times*, October 8, 1969, p. 16.

[37] *The New York Times,* December 3, 1969, p. 9.

[38] *The New York Times,* March 11, 1970, p. 2.

[39] Numerous journalistic reports appeared during the period. See *Newsweek* August 17, 1970, p. 94, and *Times of the Americas,* October 7, 1970. A spate of academic publications on the new social-change doctrines of the "radical" church, especially since Vatican II, have also surfaced recently. Among the best are: Ivan Vallier, "Religious Elites: Differentiations and Developments in Roman Catholicism," *Elites in Latin America,* Seymour Martin Lipset and Aldo Solari, eds. (New York: Oxford University Press, 1967), 190–232; Ivan Vallier, *Catholicism, Social Control, and Modernization in Latin America* (Englewood Cliffs, N.J.: Prentice-Hall, 1970); and Henry Landsberger, ed. *The Church and Social Change in Latin America* (Notre Dame, Indiana: University of Notre Dame Press, 1970).

[40] See the report by James Nelson Goodsell, "Tension Rises in Brazil," *The Christian Science Monitor,* December 10, 1971, p. 12.

[41] Figures were reported in *Brazilian Bulletin, 26,* No. 529 (June 1971), 3.

NOTES TO CHAPTER 7

[1] Arthur S. Banks, *Cross-Polity Time-Series Data* (Cambridge, Mass.: The MIT Press, 1971), 8.

[2] Ibid., 59–60.

[3] Ibid., 210–211.

[4] The Northeast is an atypical area in many ways. Whereas the rest of Brazil apparently has abundant natural resources and usually a plentiful supply of water, the Northeast (in 1964) was an area with *no* important resources. Moreover, it was beset by drought and pressed with an exploding population. See Albert O. Hirschman, *Journeys Toward Progress: Studies of Economic Policy-Making in Latin America* (New York: Anchor Books, 1965), 31–129.

[5] For an impressive discussion on the Escola Superior de Guerra along these lines see Stepan, *The Military in Politics,* 172–187.

[6] Inter-American Development Bank, *Socio-Economic Progress in Latin America: Social Progress Trust Fund,* Ninth Annual Report, 1969, p. 241.

[7] For a discussion of this change, see "A Nova Face da Moeda," *Fatos e Fotos* (February 25, 1967), 16–19.

[8] To understand how this frequently works let's use a hypothetical example: Country A and Country B both produce the same product and sell it on the world market for $100A and $100B respectively. Since $1 US=$1 A and $1 US=$1 B, both countries are selling the product on the world market for $100 US. Now, let us assume that Country A devalues its money by 50 percent while Country B keeps its money steady. The change now makes $1 US equal to $2 A. There has been no change in the currency ratio of Country B, of course, which remains equal to $1 US, that is, $1 US=$1 B. What this now means for Country A, however, is that anyone with a given amount of US dollars can buy twice as much of the same product from it as he can from

Country B (each US dollar equals one B dollar but *two* A dollars). Thus the demand for Country A's exports will tend to increase.

On the other hand, the same currency adjustments can also produce a temporary "tariff effect" for domestic industry in Country A. As its citizens must now pay twice as much of their own currency for items which they import from other countries (now that it takes $2A to make $1 US), they are discouraged from importing and therefore turn their purchases toward domestically produced products which, because of the currency adjustment, are more competitive. Demand for import-substitution manufacturing therefore tends to increase. One should note, however, that these benefits only work if Country A's trading partners do not "retaliate" with their own currency adjustments.

[9] *Brazilian Bulletin*, 25, No. 521 (November 1970), 3 (published by the Brazilian Government Trade Bureau).

[10] The Inter-American Development Bank (*Ninth Annual Report*, p. 240) places the deficit in 1966 at 11 percent.

[11] *Brazilian Bulletin*, 25, No. 521 (November 1970), 3.

[12] "Brasil '66" in *Manchete*, March 26, 1966, p. 53.

[13] *Manchete*, March 26, 1966, p. 56.

[14] "Considerable headway has been made in meeting the demand for power. One of the most expressive indices is the rise in per capita consumption of electrical energy from 262 kilowatt-hours in 1961 to 326 kilowatt-hours in 1967." (IDB *Ninth Annual Report*, p. 237). As the other projects mentioned are completed, one can expect further increases.

[15] For selected articles on industrial development in the Northeast, see "*Uma Industria de Base*," *Manchete*, October 12, 1968, pp. 128–131; and "*Os Caminhos do Desenvolvimento*," *Manchete*, August 3, 1968, pp. 142–144.

[16] The growth rate of Gross Domestic Product in 1963 was 1.5 percent; in 1964–1967 it was 3.9 percent; in 1968–1969, an estimated 7 percent (IDB Ninth Annual Report, p. 234).

[17] IDB *Ninth Annual Report*, p. 236.

[18] In 1969, under one such program, 600 families were settled on 18,000 hectares (IDB *Ninth Annual Report*, p. 248).

[19] "The most recent statistics of the IBRA (Brazilian Institute of Agrarian Reform) indicate that, from the beginning of the agrarian reform program to March 1969, 45,226 families have benefited from awards of property deeds or guarantees of land holdings over an area of 921,606 hectares. During this period, 1191 families also benefited from the distribution of privately owned land purchased by the state from individuals or distributed by their owners under official sponsorship. A total of 35,500 hectares was transferred in this way." (IDB *Ninth Annual Report*, pp. 247–248)

On page 249 of the same Report, details are given regarding the 14th Institutional Act (that is, amendment to the Federal Constitution and more recent legislation having to do with agricultural reform).

[20] "Right Wing Prosperity," *Time*, 99, No. 8 (February 21, 1972), 70.

[21] "*Poder Militar Versus Poder Civil*," *O Cruzeiro*, July 15, 1967, pp. 116–117.

[22] *Time,* July 27, 1970, p. 27.

[23] See *"Estes Padres São Subversivos,"* (*Manchete,* July 13, 1968, pp. 40–42) for an article on the leaders of the liberalizing movement among Brazil's Catholic priests.

[24] *The New York Times,* April 29, 1970, p. 40.

[25] Samuel P. Huntington, *Political Order in Changing Societies,* 177–191.

NOTES TO CHAPTER 8

[1] As cited by John Wright, *Libya* (New York: Praeger, 1969), 225.

[2] Ibid., 241.

[3] Ibid., 244.

[4] As cited by James D. Farrell, "Libya Strikes it Rich," *Africa Report, 12,* No. 4 (April 1967), 15.

[5] Wright, *Libya,* 259.

[6] Eric Rouleau, "Oil and Monarchies Don't Mix," *Africa Report, 14* (November 1969), 25.

[7] *Newsweek,* October 20, 1969, p. 56.

[8] Ibid.

[9] Henry Serrano Villard, *Libya: The New Arab Kingdom of North Africa* (Ithaca, New York: Cornell University Press, 1956).

NOTES TO CHAPTER 9

[1] Reported in *Newsweek,* August 30, 1971, p. 38.

[2] *New York Times,* December 21, 1970, p. 2.

[3] A synopsis of the background may be found in Daniel Lerner, *The Passing of Traditional Society* (New York: The Free Press of Glencoe, 1958), 353–397. Confirmation of the CIA involvement comes from Allen W. Dulles, past head of that agency, in *The Craft of Intelligence;* 1st ed. (New York: Harper and Row, 1963), 224.

[4] Interview of Prime Minister al-Maghreby with the *Tripoli Mirror,* September 30, 1969, as reported in "The Libyan Revolution in the Words of its Leaders," *Middle East Journal, 24* (Spring 1970), 211.

[5] As reported in "The Libyan Revolution in the Words of its Leaders," *Middle East Journal, 24* (Spring 1970), 207.

[6] Declaration by an unnamed member of the Revolutionary Command Council, September 10, 1969, and relayed in "The Libyan Revolution in the Words of its Leaders," *Middle East Journal, 24* (Spring 1970), 203.

[7] Reported in *Time,* August 2, 1971, p. 22.

[8] Some of the acrimony appears in Francis Hope, "The Tripoli Hillbillies," *New Statesman, 79* (May 22, 1970), 278.

[9] Comments of an unnamed member of the Revolutionary Command Council in an interview with *Deutsche Welle,* reprinted in "The Libyan Revolution in the Words of its Leaders," *Middle East Journal, 24* (Spring 1970), 218.

[10] Reported in *The Christian Science Monitor,* August 6, 1970.

NOTES TO CHAPTER 10

[1] A discussion of the wide variety of socialist ideas emerging in Libya at this time may be found in Majid Khadduri, *Modern Libya: A Study in Political Development* (Baltimore: Johns-Hopkins Press, 1963), 330–334.

[2] The observations on the Movement of Free Officers were reported by George W. Herald, "The Libyan Oil Revolt," *The New Leader,* September 29, 1969.

[3] Interview of al-Qaddafi with *Le Figaro* and reprinted in *al-Yawim,* October 1, 1969. Reported in "The Libyan Revolution in the Words of its Leaders," *Middle East Journal, 24* (Spring 1970), 204.

NOTES TO CHAPTER 11

[1] I have devoted several pages to these particular peasants in *Lord and Peasant in Peru: A Paradigm of Political and Social Change* (Cambridge, Mass.: Harvard University Press, 1970), 61–69. To my knowledge there is no other published information.

[2] Anthropologists rightfully inform us that the term "peasant" does not precisely describe much, owing to the great diversity in culture, social status, and economic well-being among those so tagged. The people under the glass here are called *campesinos* (peasants) because they derive most of their livelihood from the soil. But a *campesino,* in a social sense, may be either an "indio" or a "cholo," depending on the degree to which he has adopted Western custom. Because the peasants about which the case studies deal are in the process of becoming "Europeanized," they fall in the social class termed *cholo.* The discussion following will help to clarify.

Social stratification is based to some degree on racial variation, but the nature of one's cultural habits is a greater criterion. For example, *mestizo,* a social and cultural status term, literally means "half breed" (Indian-European). But in the areas under study it does not carry pejorative connotations. Thus it is highly possible and quite probable that an obviously "Indian-looking" person will not be considered Indian at all by the people who know him if he participates predominately in the "European" culture of the nation (often called national culture) rather than the folk culture of the countryside. Social stratification in the areas under study could, therefore, be arranged from bottom to top in this way: *indios* (Indians), *cholos* (more folk than national), *mestizos* (more national than folk), and finally, *rubios* or *blancos* (all national). From this it is obvious that race enters the picture but not in a totally rigid way. Racial considerations, however, do heavily impinge on the *zambo* (mixed Indian-Negro and, incidentally, somewhat rare in the sierra). The cholos and indios in the central sierra region often consider the *zambo* inferior no matter what his economic and cultural status may be.

The peasant movements of today are largely among *cholo* peasants (with a few important exceptions in the eastern jungle regions). A *cholo* peasant is one who, while still earning his livelihood from the soil and participating in the folk life of the village, has nevertheless discarded native dress and speaks Spanish as a second language. By way of comparison, the *mestizo* frequently speaks a native language but primarily participates in the European culture of the nation. He is a city or large-town dweller, has a white-collar (or armed forces) job, and generally returns "home" to the peasant village to visit his relatives only on holidays.

While fifteen years ago virtually all peasants in the central sierra were *indios,* today nearly all are *cholos.* Nearly 100 percent of the men are bilingual (Spanish-Quechua), as are a majority of the women. Nearly all the village schools are taught in Spanish, and there is some evidence that the village children now prefer to "forget" their parents' native tongue. According to their fathers they understand but are reluctant to speak it because of the inferior status it connotes. On the other hand, at peasant league conventions politicians and students still attempt to gain rapport with the peasants by "showing off" their ability in one or another native dialect (all ultimately derived from Quechua).

³ An excellent treatise of structural relations on this point is by Julio Cotler, "The Mechanics of Internal Domination and Social Change in Peru," *Studies in Comparative International Development,* 3, No. 12 (1966–67), 229–246.

⁴ Author's translation.

⁵ The most notable successful shut down within this time reference relates to the dramatic peasant movement in the valleys of La Convención and de Lares east of Cuzco. The final acts of retribution were completed just before Belaúnde assumed power in 1963. The movement itself had been building up for at least a decade. The irony of it all, however, was that when the suppression had been completed both the military and Belaúnde's government responded with an impressive revolutionary land reform program which settled virtually all of the peasants' immediate major complaints. Essentially the peasants got what they asked for. But it required the ordeal of a major revolt. They received some satisfaction, however, in knowing that the military was prosecuting several army men who had been especially abusive and whose activities allegedly had provoked the first violent attack on the civil guard and large landowners. Important information, along with a chronology and analysis of the events, may be found in Wesley W. Craig, Jr., "Peru: The Peasant Movement in La Convención," in *Latin American Peasant Movements,* Henry Landsberger, ed. (Ithaca, New York: Cornell University Press, 1969), 274–296. Refer also to Eric Hobsbawm, "A Case of Neo-Feudalism: La Convención, Peru," *Journal of Latin American Studies,* 1, No. 1 (May 1969) 31–50.

⁶ The Apra has been one of the most important political parties in Latin America. Founded by the indomitable Víctor Raúl Haya de la Torre while he was a student exile in Mexico during the 1920's, the party's early Peruvian members prided themselves in having theoretically elaborated all the answers to their country's "undevelopedness" and the "Indian problem." Stripped of its philosophical trappings, the thrust was simple: "While millions of Indians continue to live on a subsistence level, not incorporated into the life of the country, Peru will stagnate."

A sympathetic exposition on Haya de la Torre and his Apra party is found in Harry Kantor, *The Ideology and Program of the Peruvian Aprista Movement* (Washington, D.C.: Savile Books, 1966). Kantor is probably too sympathetic at times and has really failed to note sufficiently the degeneration of Apra in recent years to yet another participant in the rather singular Peruvian political game of "amoral groupism." Apra has grown old and fat and lost much of its reforming zeal. The vacuum was filled by Belaúnde.

[7] As the palace guard wilted with little resistance in the face of army assault troops who surrounded the national palace in the early morning hours, Belaúnde was easily taken. He emerged shouting to the troops: "Traitors to your country!" After a short stay in Argentina, where he had been flown under guard, he took up residence in Massachusetts and began teaching regional planning at Harvard University. In 1971 he was at The American University in Washington, D.C., teaching a course on socio-economic cooperation in Latin America.

[8] The most widely noted expropriation is that of the huge Gildemeister ranch (2,427,600 acres) located near Trujillo. The plantation was turned into one giant cooperative on June 24, 1969, and overnight over 30,000 ranch workers and their families became "cooperativists" rather than ranch hands.

[9] Official translation of the Peruvian government, cited in the *New York Times,* January 26, 1970, p. 73.

[10] Anibal Quijano O., *"El Movimiento Campesino del Perú y sus Líderes,"* *América Latina*, October–December 1965, p. 45.

[11] See Note 6 preceding.

[12] In Anibal Quijano's otherwise excellent study (*"El Movimiento Campesino del Perú y sus Líderes"*), he intimates that most peasant activity in the sierra was organized "top downward" by the National Federation of Peasants of Peru (Fencap), or by the Confederation of Peasants of Peru (CCDP). This latter organization had at its helm numerous militant urban types, some of whom were reported to be communists. The Communal Movement of the Center was beholden to neither of the above organizations and opposed to both. Most Fencap and CCDP activity was concentrated on the coast among the large plantations. It was only after about 1961 that these groups gained an interest in penetrating the backward areas of the sierra. Thus Tácunan's movement and others similar to it elsewhere in the highlands arose on the back of leadership directly related to the peasantry. Frequently peasant sons who had left to work in the mining centers and gained an education outside the village later returned home to lead their people. Accordingly, the Communal Movement of the Center and others like it elsewhere were much more grass roots oriented and less dependent upon urban types for their survival than many peasant groups on the coast. They did not discourage urban linkages when it served their purposes, however. As the decade of the 1960's came to a close, literally scores of small grass roots organizations were being formed, consisting anywhere from 25 to 30 villages each. Sometimes they were affiliated with a large federation; sometimes not. Fencap and the CCDP began making strident efforts after 1961 to bring these peasant organizations under their wing. Sometimes they were successful, other times not.

[13] Literacy tests were rigorously applied, invalidating the vote for most peasants in the sierra although permitting some voting among plantation workers on the coast.

[14] The departmental capital of Huancayo was only approximately 50 miles away, but the ride in bus or truck over the primitive road took from five to seven hours. Of course, one had to walk two to seven hours, depending on his village of origin, just to get to Chongos Alto in order to begin the motorized journey. Yet in 1958 many villagers were taking the ride.

[15] All quotations derive from my conversations with the participants.

[16] Previously, and there were frequent instances when it occurred, whenever a peasant had wanted his son to receive a formal education he had always found it necessary to send him out to a main district capital. These sons usually did not return to their villages of origin to reside. They continued their migration and ended up in the sierra mining complexes or coastal cities. Some even went to the eastern lowlands.

[16a] Illustrative of those dealing with the Mantaro Valley are Harry Tschopik, Jr., *Highland Communities of Central Peru* (Institute of Social Anthropology, Publication No. 5), Washington, D.C.: Smithsonian Institution, 1947, pp. 17–18; and Richard N. Adams, *A Community in the Andes: Problems and Progress in Muquiyauyo* (Seattle: American Ethnological Society, 1959), chapter 6.

[16b] The social consequences of this particular kind of exogenous change factor (commercialization of agriculture) is treated as a key explanatory variable in the peasant movements of Venezuela, by John D. Powell, *Political Mobilization of the Venezuelan Peasant* (Cambridge, Mass.: Harvard University Press, 1971).

[17] *Colonos* are "homesteaders" who settled in Peru's eastern regions.

[18] A discussion of the 1962 and 1963 elections, along with an evaluation of Peru's two most important parties at the time, may be found in Richard W. Patch, "Fernando Belaúnde Terry and Peruvian Politics," in *Latin American Politics*, Robert D. Tomasek, ed. (New York: Anchor Books, 1966), 498–513.

[19] The agrarian reform law approved by the Senate and passed by the Chamber in May 1964 was scarcely what Belaúnde had hoped for when he made his promises to the peasants in the central sierra. Both his own Popular Action party and that of the Christian Democrats, with whom he was allied at the time, were unhappy with the law as it stood because it lacked the kind of details that would favor the peasant farmer. Moreover, it had nothing to say about the villages recuperating their ancestral lands. Once promulgated, both the Popular Action and Christian Democratic parties believed that the law would only radicalize the peasants further. After May 24, the government would find out; on that date the legislation took effect. Even in its weakness Belaúnde designated the departments of Junín and Pasco as the first zones for its application.

[20] These included the Rural Education and "Nuclear School" Program, the Public Health and Sanitation Program, the Joint-Action Project for Indian Integration, the Popular Cooperation Program, the Community Research and Handicraft Development Program, the Community Organization and Property Enrollment Program, the Agrarian Reform and Credit Program, the Agricultural

Extension Program, and the Program for the Development of Cooperatives. Only the Housing and Urbanization Program, directed by the National Housing Council, was solely urban focused. See *Economic Bulletin for Latin America, 13*, No. 2 (1968).

[21] There was considerable confusion in the organization following Tácunan's death. After some infighting among the first lieutenants (compounded with an attempt by Peru's Christian Democrat party to raid the organization for its own political purposes), approximately 80 percent of the delegates and leaders finally reorganized around a new peasant leader, Manuel Canchucaja from the village of Sicaya in the Mantaro valley. It was under Canchucaja's auspices that the May national convention was carried out with some degree of success. Apra politicians declared that the convention had been taken over by the communists. President Belaúnde looked upon the Canchucaja organization very favorably as likewise he had when it was under the command of Tácunan.

[22] Ciro Alegría, *Broad and Alien is the World*, translated by Harriet de Onís (New York: Farrar and Rinehart, 1941).

[23] A short treatise on the origins of the MIR (rebels originally expelled from the Apra party), the wave of guerrilla warfare it launched in the Southeast under Luís de la Puente, and the Centereast under Guillermo Lobatón, may be found in James Petras, "Revolution and Guerrilla Movements in Latin America: Venezuela, Colombia, Guatemala, and Peru," in *Latin America: Reform or Revolution*, James Petras and Maurice Zeitlin, eds. (New York: Fawcett World Library, 1968), 343–350.

NOTES TO CHAPTER 12

[1] Oran R. Young, "Professor Russett: Industrious Tailor to a Naked Emperor," *World Politics, 21*, No. 3 (April 1969), 489–490.

[2] Albert O. Hirschman, "The Search for Paradigms as a Hindrance to Understanding," *World Politics, 22*, No. 3 (April 1970), 329.

[3] In particular I refer to *The Strategy of Economic Development* (New Haven: Yale University Press, 1958) and *Journeys Toward Progress: Studies of Economic Policy-making in Latin America* (New York: Twentieth Century Fund, 1963), Part II.

[4] Hubert M. Blalock, Jr., *Theory Construction: From Verbal to Mathematical Formulations* (Englewood Cliffs, N.J.: Prentice-Hall, 1969), 1.

[5] See Blalock, *Theory Construction*, 151–154.

[6] Ibid., 151.

[7] Frank W. Young, "A Proposal for Cooperative Cross-Cultural Research on Inter-village Systems," *Human Organization, 25* (Spring 1966), 46–50. I have profited from Young's course at Cornell University on "Comparative Peasant Societies" in which he further explored the usage of these three variables.

[8] In addition to the notes in Chapter 2, it may be worthwhile to note that Harold Lasswell's perception of the logical thrust of modernization is the elimination in large part of localized symbolic nuances and their replacement by broad-spectrum, near-universal symbolic structures. See his "The Emerging

Internation Culture," in U.S. International Development Agency, *International Cooperation and Problems of Transfer Adaptation*, Vol. X (Washington, D.C.: U.S. Government Printing Office, 1962).

[9] The norms and values associated with the information symbols, no matter how diverse or complex the symbols are, may be shared broadly and similarly. In such cases the group is said to have a high sense of unity. Or, the symbols may carry quite differing and perhaps mutually contradictory meanings for the members. In this case the group does not have a sense of unity. This particular aspect of the theory is taken up in greater detail under the solidarity variable which follows.

[10] Thus, as David McClelland argues, exposure to symbols of modernity increases the need for achievement only when the exposure is accompanied by a kind of "ideological conversion" of the total group—a condition I will term *solidarity*. See McClelland's *The Achieving Society* (Princeton, N.J.: Van Nostrand, 1961), 411–417.

[11] Blalock, *Theory Construction*, 72.

[12] As an early example, and still one of the best, see Daniel Lerner, *The Passing of Traditional Society* (New York: The Free Press, 1958). In addition, one ought to look at the excellent study by Everett M. Rogers, *Modernization Among Peasants: The Impact of Communication* (New York: Holt, Rinehart and Winston, 1969).

[13] Richard H. Holton, "Changing Demand and Consumption," in Wilbert E. Moore and Arnold S. Feldman, eds., *Labor Commitment and Social Change in Developing Areas* (New York: Social Science Research Council, 1950), 210–216, as cited by Gurr, *Why Men Rebel* (Princeton: Princeton University Press, 1970), 94.

The "demonstration effect" as a cause of discontentment or frustration has been widely discussed in the literature. There is contradictory evidence to suggest both that it does and does not have that effect. After examining an impressive amount of evidence Gurr concludes that "none of the findings indicates that the demonstration effects of other people's material and political culture does not operate. The implication is rather that it raises expectations only in certain circumstances, and that when it does it does not necessarily lead to increased discontent and political violence" (p. 100). Gurr then proceeds to argue that the susceptibility of a group to rising value expectations deriving from exposure to new modes of life varies strongly with the intensity and scope of already existing levels of discontentment or frustration. Thus, while there is a controversy as to whether the exposure provokes discontentment or frustration, there is agreement on the basic premise that under certain conditions exposure is likely to lead to what I call higher levels of information-processing capacity. The tendency would appear to be strongest when a discrepancy already exists between capacity and opportunity.

[14] See, in particular, the moving treatise by Ndabaningi Sithole, *African Nationalism*; 2nd ed. (London: Oxford University Press, 1968); and, also A. H. Cole, "The Relation of Missionary Activity to Economic Development," *Economic Development and Cultural Change*, 9 (January 1961), 120–127.

¹⁵ Frank W. and Ruth C. Young, "Individual Commitment to Industrialization in Rural Mexico," *American Journal of Sociology, 71* (January 1966), 373–383; and Tullis, *Lord and Peasant in Peru*, 84–144.

¹⁶ See Sithole, *African Nationalism*, 1–29; J. Goody and I. Watt, "The Consequences of Literacy," *Comparative Studies in Society and History, 5* (April 1963), 304–345; Lloyd Fallers, "Equality, Modernity, and Democracy in the New States," in *Old Societies and New States: The Quest for Modernity in Asia and Africa*, Clifford Geertz, ed. (New York: The Free Press, 1963), 158–219; and Tullis, *Lord and Peasant in Peru*, 84–114.

¹⁷ The most widely publicized school in Latin America is "Radio Sutatenza" in Colombia. The Maryknoll Fathers have an impressive radiophonic school in operation in Puno (southern Peru) as well. See Everett M. Rogers, *Modernization Among Peasants: The Impact of Communication* (New York: Holt, Rinehart and Winston, 1969), 136–144.

¹⁸ Unidimensional scalograms have been prepared for several score villages. Refer to Tullis, *Lord and Peasant in Peru*, 194; and Frank W. Young, Berkley A. Spencer, and Jan L. Flora, "Differentiation and Solidarity in Agricultural Communities," *Human Organization, 27*, No. 4 (Winter 1968), 344–351.

¹⁹ Young, "A Proposal." See Note number 7.

²⁰ Indicators that have served to operationalize this abstract variable may be found in Young, and others, "Differentiation and Solidarity"; Tullis, *Lord and Peasant in Peru*, Chapter 9; and Wesley W. Craig, Jr., *From Hacienda to Community: An Analysis of Solidarity and Social Change in Peru*, Latin American Program Dissertation Series of Cornell University, No. 6 (Ithaca, New York: By the Program, 1967).

²¹ John T. Dorsey, Jr., "The Bureaucracy and Political Development in Viet Nam," in *Bureaucracy and Political Development*, Joseph LaPalombara, ed. (Princeton, Princeton University Press, 1963), 318–325.

²² Solidarity occurs prior to collective forms of peasant behavior that seek "high-horizon" goals requiring concessions from superior-status groups. The collective behavior may be "moderate" or "intense," conforming to definitions in the text. Some forms of intense behavior are synonymous with revolution.

In seeking a general explanation of what I call "intense collective action," other scholars also have looked for the preconditioning "discrepancy factors." Chalmers Johnson (*Revolutionary Change*) sees them arising from a "disequilibrated social system" in which the division of labor and people's values have fallen out of harmony. Ted Gurr's preconditions (*Why Men Rebel*) are designated "relative deprivation," a psychological state arising out of a discrepancy between the values people expect to attain in life and their capacity to achieve them; and Ivo K. Feierabend, Rosalind L. Feierabend, and Betty A. Nesvold rest their case on "systemic frustration," a condition arising out of a discrepancy between social expectations and social achievement. Refer to their excellent study, "Social Change and Political Violence: Cross-National Patterns," in *The History of Violence in America*, Hugh Davis Graham and Ted Robert Gurr, eds. (New York: Bantam Books, 1969), 632–681.

²³ Albert O. Hirschman, in a provocative little book (*Exit, Voice, and Loyalty*:

Harvard, 1970) has raised similar issues. He has shown that members of organizations (and we might construe this to mean peasants caught in a regional or village system of political, economic, and social organization) have essentially two options (not necessarily mutually exclusive) open to them when they become dissatisfied with the state of existing affairs. These options he calls "voice" and "exit." With the exit option, dissatisfied members simply leave the the organization, migrate, or take their business elsewhere, looking for the satisfactions they could not obtain where they were. With the voice option, however, they chose not to withdraw but rather to remain and work for improvements. Hirschman shows that when the state of existing affairs is considered bad at home but exit is possible, people will leave or withdraw (exit or migrate). On the other hand, "the role of voice would increase as the opportunities for exit decline, up to the point where, with exit wholly unavailable, voice must carry the entire burden of alerting management to its failings" (p. 34).

[24] Ibid., 76.

[25] A collection of essays dealing with some of the technologically related forms of alienation and anomie is by Simon Marcson, ed., *Automation, Alienation, and Anomie* (New York: Harper and Row, 1970).

[26] Edward C. Banfield, *The Moral Basis of a Backward Society* (New York: The Free Press, 1958).

[27] Gurr, *Why Men Rebel*, 83.

[28] Several combinations which produce structural binds are: (1) capacity rises but opportunity remains low and unchanged; (2) opportunity rises, and capacity does also but at a faster rate; (3) capacity rises while opportunity falls; (4) capacity is high while opportunity falls.

[29] Bryant Wedge found in his comparative study of student violence that the "threat-aggression" sequence was a more powerful explanation in intense manifestations than the "frustration-aggression" formula frequently used. See Wedge's "The Case Study of Student Political Violence: Brazil, 1964, and the Dominican Republic, 1965," *World Politics, 21*, No. 2 (January 1969), 183–206. Refer also to Ted Gurr, "Psychological Factors in Civil Violence," *World Politics, 20*, No. 2 (January 1968), 248 note 7.

[30] James C. Davies, "Toward a Theory of Revolution," *American Sociological Review, 27* (February 1962), 6. See also Davies' "The J-Curve of Rising and Declining Satisfactions as a Cause of Some Great Revolutions and a Contained Rebellion," in *The History of Violence in America,* Hugh David Graham and Ted Robert Gurr, eds., 690–730. Gurr also concurs in the "J-Curve" and its effect on political violence with his "progressive deprivation" hypotheses. See *Why Men Rebel*, 52–56.

[31] The "rate of change" on the two variables producing the structural bind is of some importance, because the likelihood is that the more rapid the rate of change the more pronounced will be the level of solidarity at any given level of structural bind. For an engaging discussion on rates, see Richard W. Chadwick and Karl W. Deutsch, "Doubling Time and Half Life: Two Suggested

Conventions for Describing Rates of Change in Social Science Data," *Comparative Political Studies, 1*, No. 1 (April 1968), 139–48.

[32] William Mangin has edited a most fascinating volume on this subject: *Peasants in Cities: Readings in the Anthropology of Urbanization* (Boston: Houghton Mifflin Company, 1970).

[33] Gino Germani has made some important observations on this and related aspects of migration. "A second important illustration of stabilizing mechanisms is provided by mass internal migration. Here again we find a process which is not peculiar to Latin America. It is well known how mass overseas emigration operated as a safety valve in Europe during the nineteenth century. This latent function of emigration as a substitute for revolution, was not so latent, since European political rulers did not fail to make a deliberate use of it as a means to decrease lower-class pressures . . . emigration from the more backward regions is likely to operate in selective terms, giving an outlet precisely to the most active and potentially more 'dangerous' (from a conservative perspective) individuals among the rural population." See Germani's "Stages of Modernization in Latin America," *Studies in Comparative International Development, 5*, No. 8 (1969–70), 171–172. See also Samuel P. Huntington, *Political Order in Changing Societies* (New Haven: Yale University Press, 1968), 281–283, and Hirschman, *Exit, Voice, and Loyalty*, 43, 76, 106, and 111.

[34] Ted Gurr, *Why Men Rebel*, 210.

[35] One of the most dramatic of these episodes deals with "Anthony the Counsellor" and his movement in Brazil's drought-stricken northeast. Euclydes da Cunha's recording of the events has become classic reading in several languages. See his *Rebellion in the Backlands*; translated by Samuel Putnam (Chicago: University of Chicago Press, 1944).

[36] Henry Landsberger has made some instructive observations on this point. Refer to his "The Role of Peasant Movements and Revolts in Development," in *Latin American Peasant Movements*, Henry Landsberger, ed. (Ithaca, N.Y.: Cornell University Press, 1969), 1–61. Refer also to Chapter 3.

[37] Huntington, *Political Order in Changing Societies*, 1–92.

[38] Ted Gurr, "A Causal Model of Civil Strife: A Comparative Analysis Using New Indices," *American Political Science Review, 82*, No. 4 (December 1968), 1105.

[39] A heavy application of coercion under conditions suggested by Figure 8 (rising capacity—static opportunity) may simply produce resignation if the major rhetorical participants are eliminated.

[40] Coercion is a relative term, of course, and is best understood in relation to the strength of peasant organization and the linkages and resources it can draw upon. One formulation has it that the coercive capabilities of a regime are related inversely to the magnitude of violence. There is considerable evidence to support such a contention, of course, and it does have a common-sensical ring of authenticity. After summarizing the literature and reflecting on the equally impressive but contradictory evidence however, Ted Gurr came to the conclusion that a more accurate proposition recognizes that the effectiveness

of a regime's coercive forces and resources is directly related to their size relative to those of the opponents. Thus under some circumstances, application of coercion may produce a curvilinear effect. See Gurr, *Why Men Rebel,* 243–46.

[41] Gurr, "A Causal Model of Civil Strife," 1105.

[42] Gurr, *Why Men Rebel,* 274.

[43] The point at issue is treated by Chalmers Johnson, *Revolutionary Change,* 99–100, 103–105, and 153–154.

[44] Huntington, *Political Order in Changing Societies,* 12–24.

[45] Gurr, *Why Men Rebel,* 298.

[46] Ibid., 293.

[47] From David Apter's "Ideology and Discontent," in *Ideology and Discontent,* David Apter, ed. (New York: The Free Press, 1964).

[48] The function of ideology in conditions similar to those specified in this model is also treated by Johnson, *Revolutionary Change,* 80–87, and Gurr, *Why Men Rebel,* 194–197.

[49] Johnson, *Revolutionary Change,* 99.

[50] Working from his frustration-aggression model, Ted Gurr argues that catalysts "may be categorized according to their inferred psychological effects, for example, according to whether they facilitate interaction among the discontented, or provide the discontented with a sense that violent responses to deprivation are justified, or give them the means to make such responses with maximum effect, or shelter them from retribution." From "A Causal Model of Civil Strife," 1106.

NOTES TO CHAPTER 13

[1] An adequate statistical "test" would require numerous cases, of course, and so the theory cannot be either validated or rejected by the data presented in this book alone. Evidence from 45 villages may be found in Tullis, *Lord and Peasant in Peru.* In that study I also found that villages not involved in movements were also those tending not to have major discrepancy problems.

[2] Gurr, *Why Men Rebel,* 22–58, also reviewed in Chapter 3 under "Modernization and Revolution."

[3] Ivo K. Feierabend et al., "Social Change and Political Violence," 632–681.

[4] Johnson, *Revolutionary Change,* 59–87.

[5] Young, "A Proposal."

[6] Huntington, *Political Order in Changing Societies.*

Bibliography

ADAMS, RICHARD N. *A Community in the Andes: Problems and Progress in Muquiyauyo.* Seattle: University of Washington Press, 1959.

AKE, CLAUDE. *A Theory of Political Integration.* Homewood, Illinois: The Dorsey Press, 1967.

ALBA, VICTOR. *Alliance Without Allies.* New York: Praeger, 1965. Cited by George C. Lodge. *Engines of Change: United States Interests and Revolution in Latin America.* New York: Knopf, 1970.

ALEGRÍA, CIRO. *Broad and Alien is the World.* Translated by Harriet de Onis. New York: Farrar and Rinehart, 1941.

ALMOND, GABRIEL A. "Political Development: Analytical and Normative Perspectives." *Comparative Political Studies, 1,* No. 4 (January 1969), 447–470.

ALMOND, GABRIEL A., and JAMES S. COLEMAN, eds. *The Politics of the Developing Areas.* Princeton, N.J.: Princeton University Press, 1960.

ALMOND, GABRIEL A., and G. BINGHAM POWELL, JR. *Comparative Politics: A Developmental Approach.* Boston: Little, Brown, 1966.

ALMOND, GABRIEL A., and SIDNEY VERBA. *The Civic Culture: Political Attitudes and Democracy in Five Nations.* Boston: Little, Brown, 1965.

ANDERSON, CHARLES W., FRED R. VON DER MEHDEN, and CRAWFORD YOUNG. *Issues of Political Development.* Englewood Cliffs, N.J.: Prentice-Hall, 1967.

ANDREWS, WILLIAM G., and URI RA'ANAN. *The Politics of the coup d'etat: Five Case Studies.* New York: Van Nostrand, Reinhold, 1969.

ANGELL, ALAN. "Chile: The Difficulties of Democratic Reform." *International Journal, 24,* No. 3 (Summer 1969), 515–528.

APTER, DAVID E. *Ghana in Transition,* revised edition. New York: Atheneum, 1963.

————. "Ideology and Discontent." *Ideology and Discontent.* Edited by David E. Apter. New York: The Free Press, 1964.

————. *The Politics of Modernization.* Chicago: The University of Chicago Press, 1965.

————. "The Role of Traditionalism in the Political Modernization of Ghana and Uganda." *World Politics, 13,* No. 1 (October 1960), 45–68.

————. *Some Conceptual Approaches to the Study of Modernization.* Englewood Cliffs, N.J.: Prentice-Hall, 1968.

BAKLANOFF, ERIC N., ed. *New Perspectives of Brazil.* Nashville, Tenn.: Vanderbilt University Press, 1966.

_____.*The Shaping of Modern Brazil*. Baton Rouge, La.: Louisiana State University Press, 1969.

BANFIELD, EDWARD C. *The Moral Basis of a Backward Society*. New York: The Free Press, 1958.

BANKS, ARTHUR S. *Cross-Polity Time-Series Data*. Cambridge, Mass.: The MIT Press, 1971.

BENGUR, ALI R. "Financial Aspects of Libya's Oil Economy," *Finance and Development* (Quarterly publication of the International Monetary Fund and the International Bank for Reconstruction and Development), March 1967.

BENDIX, REINHARD. "Tradition and Modernity Reconsidered." *Comparative Studies in Society and History*, 9, No. 3 (April 1967), 292–346.

BENDIX, REINHARD, and SEYMOUR MARTIN LIPSET, eds. "Karl Marx's Theory of Social Classes." *Class, Status, and Power: Social Stratification in Comparative Perspective*, second edition. Edited by Reinhard Bendix and Seymour Martin Lipset. New York: The Free Press, 1966, 6–11.

BERKOWITZ, LEONARD. "The Concept of Aggressive Drive." *Advances in Experimental Social Psychology*. Edited by Leonard Berkowitz. Vol. 2. New York: Academic Press, 1965.

_____, ed. *Roots of Aggression: A Re-examination of the Frustration-Aggression Hypothesis*. New York: Atherton Press, 1968.

_____. "The Study of Urban Violence: Some Implications of Laboratory Studies of Frustration and Aggression." *Riots and Rebellion: Civil Violence in the Urban Community* (1968). Edited by Louis H. Masotti and Don R. Bowen, and reprinted in James C. Davies, ed. *When Men Revolt and Why*. New York: The Free Press, 1971.

BILL, JAMES. "The Military and Modernization in the Middle East." *Comparative Politics*, 2, No. 1 (October 1969), 41–62.

BINDER, LEONARD, JAMES S. COLEMAN, JOSEPH LaPALOMBARA, LUCIAN W. PYE, SIDNEY VERBA, and MYRON WEINER. *Crises and Sequences in Political Development*, Princeton, N.J.: Princeton University Press, 1971.

BLACK, C. E. *The Dynamics of Modernization: A Study in Comparative History*. New York: Harper and Row, 1966.

BLALOCK, HUBERT M., JR. *Theory Construction: From Verbal to Mathematical Formulations*. Englewood Cliffs, N.J.: Prentice-Hall, 1969.

BONILLA, FRANK. "A National Ideology for Development: Brazil." *Expectant Peoples: Nationalism and Development*. Edited by K. H. Silvert. New York: Random House, 1963, 232–264.

BOURRICAUD, FRANÇOIS. *Power and Society in Contemporary Peru*. Translated by Paul Stevenson. New York: Praeger, 1970.

"Brazil: Government by Torture." *Look* (July 14, 1970), 70–71.

Brazilian Bulletin (published by the Brazilian Government Trade Bureau). various monthly issues.

BREESE, GERALD. *Urbanization in Newly Developing Countries.* Englewood Cliffs, N.J.: Prentice-Hall, 1966.

————, ed. *The City in Newly Developing Countries: Readings on Urbanism and Urbanization.* Englewood Cliffs, N.J.: Prentice-Hall, 1969.

BREHM, JACK W., and ARTHUR R. COHEN. *Explorations in Cognitive Dissonance.* New York: Wiley, 1962.

BRODE, JOHN. *The Process of Modernization: An Annotated Bibliography on the Sociocultural Aspects of Development.* Cambridge, Mass.: Harvard University Press, 1969.

BROWN, CHARLES E. "The Libyan Revolution Sorts Itself Out," *Africa Report,* December 1969, pp. 12–15.

BROWN, ROBERT. *Explanation in Social Science.* Chicago: Aldine Publishing Company, 1963.

BROWN, ROBERT WYLIE, "Libya's Rural Sector," *African Report,* April 1967, pp. 16–18.

BUCKLEY, WALTER, ed. *Modern Systems Research for the Behavioral Scientist.* Chicago: Aldine Publishing Company, 1968.

BURNS, E. BRADFORD. *Nationalism in Brazil: A Historical Survey.* New York: Praeger, 1968.

CAMPOS, ROBERTO DE OLIVEIRA. *Reflections on Latin American Development.* Austin, Texas: University of Texas Press, 1967.

CECIL, CHARLES O. "The Determinants of Libyan Foreign Policy," *Middle East Journal, 19* (Winter 1965), 20–34.

CHADWICK, RICHARD W., and KARL W. DEUTSCH. "Doubling Time and Half Life: Two Suggested Conventions for Describing Rates of Change in Social Science Data." *Comparative Political Studies, 1,* No. 1 (April 1968), 139–145.

CHAPANIS, N. P., and A. CHAPANIS. "Cognitive Dissonance: Five Years Later." *Psychological Bulletin, 61,* No. 1 (January 1964), 1–22.

CHAPLIN, DAVID. "Peru's Postponed Revolution." *World Politics, 20,* No. 3 (April 1968), 393–420.

CHARLESWORTH, JAMES C., ed. *Contemporary Political Analysis.* New York: The Free Press, 1967.

CLINTON, RICHARD LEE. "The Modernizing Military: The Case of Peru." *Inter-American Economic Affairs, 24,* No. 4 (Spring 1971), 43–66.

COLE, A. H. "The Relations of Missionary Activity to Economic Development." *Economic Development and Cultural Change, 9,* No. 2 (January 1961), 120–127.

COLEMAN, JAMES S., ed. *Education and Political Development.* Princeton, N.J.: Princeton University Press, 1965.

COLEMAN, JAMES S., and CARL G. ROSBERG, JR., eds. *Political Parties and National Integration in Tropical Africa.* Berkeley: University of California Press, 1964.

COOLEY, JOHN K. "Libya Rocks Mideast." *The Christian Science Monitor,* September 3, 1969, p. 1.

_____. "Libyan Coup Well Prepared?" *The Christian Science Monitor,* September 3, 1969, p. 1.

_____. "Nasser Hails Libya Coup Leaders." *The Christian Science Monitor,* September 9, 1969.

_____. " 'Made in Libya' Power Seizure Surprises Arab Observers." *The Christian Science Monitor,* October 24, 1969, p. 5.

_____. "Libyan Rulers Take Time." *The Christian Science Monitor,* October 28, 1969, p. 2.

_____. "U.S. Continues to Train Libyan Pilots Despite Closedown Order." *The Christian Science Monitor,* November 1, 1969, p. 4.

_____. "Army Rulers' Reforms Win Public Acceptance in Libya." *The Christian Science Monitor,* November 3, 1969, p. 6.

_____. "U.S., Britain Face Libya Conflicts." *The Christian Science Monitor,* December 13, 1969, p. 4.

_____. "Few Arab Chiefs Rise to Call for 'Summit.' " *The Christian Science Monitor,* July 31, 1971.

COSTA, FLAVIO (Interviewing Luis Viana Filho). "A Revolucao Precisa de Autocritica." *Manchete,* September 28, 1968, pp. 184–185.

COTLER, JULIO. "The Mechanics of Internal Domination and Social Change in Peru." *Studies in Comparative International Development,* 3, No. 12 (1967–1968), 229–246.

COTLER, JULIO, and FELIPE PORTOCARRERO. "Peru: Peasant Organizations." *Latin American Peasant Movements.* Edited by Henry A. Landsberger. Ithaca, New York: Cornell University Press, 1969, 297–322.

COUTINHO, BENEDITO. "Poder Militar Versus Poder Civil." *O Cruzeiro,* July 15, 1967, pp. 116–117.

CRAIG, WESLEY W., JR. *From Hacienda to Community: An Analysis of Solidarity and Social Change in Peru.* Latin American Program Dissertation Series of Cornell University, No. 6. Ithaca, New York: By the Program, 1967.

_____. "Peru: The Peasant Movement of La Convencion." *Latin American Peasant Movements.* Edited by Henry Landsberger. Ithaca, N.Y.: Cornell University Press, 1969, 274–296.

DAHRENDORF, RALF. *Class and Class Conflict in Industrial Society.* Stanford, California: Stanford University Press, 1959.

DALAND, ROBERT T. *Brazilian Planning: Development, Politics, and Administration.* Chapel Hill, North Carolina: University of North Carolina Press, 1967.

DAVIES, JAMES C. "The J-Curve of Rising and Declining Satisfactions as a Cause of Some Great Revolutions and a Contained Rebellion." *The History of Violence in America: A Report to the National Commission on the Causes and Prevention of Violence.* Edited by Hugh Davis Graham and Ted Robert Gurr. New York: Bantam Books, 1969, 690–730.

──────. "Toward a Theory of Revolution." *American Sociological Review,* 27, No. 1 (February 1962), 5–19.

──────. *When Men Revolt and Why.* New York: The Free Press, 1969.

DELGADO, CARLOS. "An Analysis of 'Arribismo' in Peru." *Human Organization,* 28, No. 2 (Summer 1969), 133–139.

DEUTSCH, KARL W. *The Nerves of Government: Models of Political Communication and Control.* New York: The Free Press, 1963.

──────. "Social Mobilization and Political Development." *American Political Science Review,* 55, No. 3 (September 1961), 493–514.

DEUTSCH, KARL W., and RICHARD L. MERRIT. *Nationalism and National Development: An Interdisciplinary Bibliography.* Cambridge, Mass.: M.I.T. Press, 1970.

DIAMANT, ALFRED. Political Development: Approaches to Theory and Strategy." *Approaches to Development: Politics, Administration and Change.* Edited by John D. Montgomery and William J. Siffin. New York: McGraw-Hill, 1966.

DOBYNS, HENRY F. *The Social Matrix of Peruvian Indigenous Communities.* Cornell-Peru Project Monograph. Ithaca, N.Y.: Department of Anthropology, Cornell University, 1964.

DORSEY, JOHN T., JR. "The Bureaucracy and Political Development in Viet Nam." *Bureaucracy and Political Development.* Edited by Joseph LaPalombara. Princeton, N.J.: Princeton University Press, 1963, 318–359.

DUBNIC, VLADIMIR REISKY DE. *Political Trends in Brazil.* Washington, D.C.: Public Affairs Press, 1968.

──────. "Trends in Brazil's Foreign Policy." *New Perspectives of Brazil.* Edited by Eric N. Baklanoff. Nashville: Vanderbilt University Press, 1966.

DULLES, ALLEN W. *The Craft of Intelligence,* first edition. New York: Harper and Row, 1963.

DULLES, JOHN W. F. "Post-Dictatorship Brazil: 1930–1964." *New Perspectives of Brazil.* Edited by Eric N. Baklanoff. Nashville: Vanderbilt University Press, 1966.

DURKHEIM, EMILE. *The Division of Labor in Society.* Glencoe, Illinois: The Free Press, 1949.

EDWARDS, DAVID V. *International Political Analysis.* New York: Holt, Rinehart and Winston, 1969.

EICHER, CARL K., and LAWRENCE W. WITT, eds. *Agriculture in Economic Development.* New York: McGraw-Hill, 1964.

EISENSTADT, S. N. *Modernization: Protest and Change.* Englewood Cliffs, N.J.: Prentice-Hall, 1966.

ESMAN, MILTON J. "The Politics of Development Administration." *Approaches to Development: Politics, Administration and Change.* Edited by John D. Montgomery and William J. Siffin. New York: McGraw-Hill, 1966, 59–112.

"*Estes Padres São Subversivos.*" *Manchete,* July 13, 1968, pp. 40–42.

ETZIONI, AMITAI, and EVA ETZIONI, eds. *Social Change*. New York: Basic Books, 1964.

EVANS-PRITCHARD, E. E. *The Sanusi of Cyrenaica*. Oxford: Oxford University Press, 1949.

EVANS, ROBERT D. "The Brazilian Revolution of 1964: Political Surgery Without Anaesthetics." *International Affairs, 44*, No. 2 (April 1968), 267–281.

EVANS, TREFOR. "The New Libya: Coming to Terms with Revolution in the Arab World," *The Round Table, 70*, No. 239 (1970), 265–273.

FALLERS, LLOYD. "Equality, Modernity, and Democracy in the New States." *Old Societies and New States: The Quest for Modernity in Asia and Africa*. Edited by Clifford Geertz. New York: The Free Press of Glencoe, 1963, 158–219.

FARRELL, JAMES D. "Libya Strikes it Rich," *Africa Report, 12*, No. 4 (April 1967), 8–15.

FEIERABEND, IVO K., BETTY NESVOLD, and ROSALIND L. FEIERA-BEND. "Political Coerciveness and Turmoil: A Cross-National Inquiry." *Law and Society Review*, August 1970, pp. 93–117.

_____. "Social Change and Political Violence: Cross-National Patterns." *The History of Violence in America: A Report to the National Commission on the Causes and Prevention of Violence*. Edited by Hugh Davis Graham and Ted Robert Gurr. New York: Bantam Books, 1969, 632–687.

FEIT, EDWARD. "Military Coups and Political Development: Some Lessons from Ghana and Nigeria." *World Politics, 20*, No. 2 (January 1968), 179–193.

FESTINGER, LEON. *A Theory of Cognitive Dissonance*. Evanston, Illinois: Row, Peterson, 1957.

FINER, SAMUEL E. *The Man on Horseback: The Role of the Military in Politics*. New York: Praeger, 1962.

FINKLE, JASON L., and RICHARD W. GABLE, eds. *Political Development and Social Change*. New York: Wiley, 1966.

FIRTH, RAYMOND. "Social Structure and Peasant Economy: The Influence of Social Structure Upon Peasant Economies." *Subsistence Agriculture and Economic Development*. Edited by Clifton R. Wharton, Jr. Chicago: Aldine Publishing Company, 1969, 23–37.

FOLAND, FRANCES M. "Whither Brazil?" *Inter-American Economic Affairs, 24*, No. 3 (Winter 1970), 43–68.

FOSSUM, EGIL. "Political Development and Strategies for Change." *Journal of Peace Research, 1* (1970), 17–31.

FOSTER, GEORGE M. "Peasant Society and the Image of Limited Good." *American Anthropologist, 67*, No. 2 (April 1965), 293–315.

_____. *Traditional Cultures: The Impact of Technological Change*. New York: Harper and Row, 1962.

FREY, FREDERICK W. *The Turkish Political Elite*. Cambridge, Mass.: M.I.T. Press, 1965.

FRIEDRICH, CARL J. "Political Leadership and the Problem of the Charismatic Power." *Journal of Politics*, 23, No. 1 (February 1961), 3–24.

"From the Parrot's Perch." *Time*, July 27, 1970, p. 27.

FURTADO, CELSO. *The Economic Growth of Brazil: A Survey From Colonial to Modern Times*, translated by Richard W. de Aquiar and Eric Charles Drysdale. Berkeley: University of California Press, 1965.

GALTUNG, JOHAN. "A Structural Theory of Aggression." *Journal of Peace Research*, No. 2 (1964), 95–119.

GEERTZ, CLIFFORD, ed. *Old Societies and New States: The Quest for Modernity in Asia and Africa*. New York: The Free Press, 1963.

GERMANI, GINO. "Stages of Modernization in Latin America." *Studies in Comparative International Development*, 5, No. 8 (1969–1970), 155–173.

GERSCHENKRON, ALEXANDER. "Economic Backwardness in Historical Perspective." *The Progress of Underdeveloped Areas*. Edited by B. F. Hoselitz. Chicago: The University of Chicago Press, 1952, 3–29.

GIBBS, JACK P., and WALTER T. MARTIN. "Urbanization, Technology and the Division of Labor: International Patterns." *American Sociological Review*, 27, No. 5 (October 1962), 667–677.

GODSELL, GEOFFREY. "Libya's Big Splash' for Arab Power Role." *The Christian Science Monitor*, September 3, 1971.

_____. "Libyans 'Forced out of Cocoon.' " *The Christian Science Monitor*, September 4, 1971.

"Going for a Ride with Brazil's Guerrilleros." *Atlas*, August 1970, pp. 49–51.

GOLINO, FRANK RALPH. "Patterns of Libyan National Identity." *Middle East Journal*, 24 (Summer 1970), 338–352.

GOODSELL, JAMES NELSON. "Brazil Brutality? Evidence Builds Up of Political Torture." *The Christian Science Monitor*, May 1970.

_____. "Brazil Military Cracks Down." *The Christian Science Monitor*, December 18, 1968.

_____. "Brazil: The Uncertain Giant." *The Christian Science Monitor*, January 7, 1966, p. 9.

_____. "Militarists Muffle Political Dissent in Brazil." *The Christian Science Monitor*, February 11, 1969, p. 1.

_____. "Tension Rises in Brazil." *The Christian Science Monitor*, December 10, 1971.

GOODY, J., and I. WATT. "The Consequences of Literacy." *Comparative Studies in Society and History*, 5 (1962-1963), 304–345.

GROSS, LLEWELLYN, ed. *Sociological Theory: Inquiries and Paradigms*. New York: Harper and Row, 1967.

GUDIN, EUGENIO. *Analise de Problemas Brasileiros*. Rio de Janeiro: Agir, 1965.

GUSFIELD, JOSEPH. "Tradition and Modernity: Misplaced Polarities in the Study of Social Change." *American Journal of Sociology*, 72, No. 4 (January 1967), 351–362.

GURR, TED ROBERT. "A Causal Model of Civil Strife: A Comparative Analysis Using New Indices." *American Political Science Review*, 62, No. 4 (December 1968), 1104–1124.

————. "Psychological Factors in Civil Violence." *World Politics*, 20, No. 2 (January 1968), 245–278.

————. *Why Men Rebel*. Princeton, N.J.: Princeton University Press, 1970.

HAGEN, EVERETT E. *On the Theory of Social Change: How Economic Growth Begins*. Homewood, Illinois: Dorsey Press, 1962.

HAH, CHONG-DO, and JEANNE SCHNEIDER. "A Critique of Current Studies on Political Development and Modernization." *Social Research*, 35, No. 1 (Spring 1968), 130–158.

HALLER, ARCHIBALD O. "Urban Economic Growth and Changes in Rural Stratification: Rio de Janeiro 1953–1962." *América Latina*, 10, No. 4 (October–December 1967), 48–67.

HALPERN, JOEL M., and JOHN BRODE. "Peasant Society: Economic Changes and Revolutionary Transformation." *Biennial Review of Anthropology*, 1967. Edited by Bernard J. Siegel and Alan R. Beals. Stanford: Stanford University Press, 1967.

HALPERN, MANFRED. *The Politics of Social Change in the Middle East and North Africa*. Princeton, N.J.: Princeton University Press, 1963.

HARBISON, FREDERICK, and CHARLES A. MYERS. *Education, Manpower and Economic Growth: Strategies of Human Resource Development*. New York: McGraw-Hill, 1964.

HARING, C. H. *Empire in Brazil: A New World Experiment With Monarchy*. Cambridge, Mass.: Harvard University Press, 1958.

HARTZ, LOUIS. *The Founding of New Societies: Studies in the History of the United States, Latin America, South Africa, Canada, and Australia*. New York: Harcourt, Brace, and World, 1964.

HEILBRONER, ROBERT. *The Great Ascent: The Struggle for Economic Development in Our Time*. New York: Harper and Row, 1963.

HEMPEL, CARL G. *Aspects of Scientific Explanation and Other Essays in the Philosophy of Science*. New York: The Free Press, 1965.

HERALD, GEORGE W. "The Libyan Oil Revolt." *The New Leader*, September 29, 1969.

HILL, R. W. *A Bibliography of Libya*. Department of Geography Research Papers, No. 1 (Newcastle-upon-Tyne, England: University of Durham, 1959).

HIRSCHMAN, ALBERT O. *Exit, Voice, and Loyalty: Responses to Decline in Firms, Organizations, and States*. Cambridge, Mass.: Harvard, 1970.

————. *Journeys Toward Progress: Studies of Economic Policy-Making in Latin America*. New York: The Twentieth Century Fund, 1963.

————, ed. *Latin American Issues: Essays and Comments*. New York: The Twentieth Century Fund, 1961.

_____. "Obstacles to Development: A Classification and a Quasi-vanishing Act." *Economic Development and Cultural Change, 13*, No. 4, Part 1 (July 1965), 385–393.

_____. "The Search for Paradigms as a Hindrance to Understanding." *World Politics, 22*, No. 3 (April 1970), 329–343.

_____. *The Strategy of Economic Development.* New Haven, Conn.: Yale University Press, 1958.

HOBSBAWM, ERIC J. "A Case of Neo-Feudalism: La Convención, Peru." *Journal of Latin American Studies, 1*, No. 1 (May 1969), 31–50.

HOFFER, ERIC. *The True Believer: Thoughts on the Nature of Mass Movements.* New York: Harper and Row, 1951.

HOLTON, RICHARD H. "Changing Demand and Consumption." *Labor, Commitment, and Social Change in Developing Areas.* Edited by Wilbert E. Moore and Arnold S. Feldman. New York: Social Science Research Council, 1960, 201–216.

HOPE, FRANCIS. "The Tripoli Hillbillies: Are Libya's Young Rulers Working in a Void?" *New Statesman*, May 22, 1970, pp. 727–729.

HOPKINS, JACK W. *The Cooperacion Popular Movement in Peru.* Atlanta, Georgia: Emory University, Department of Political Science, 1967.

HOROWITZ, IRVING LOUIS. *Revolution in Brazil: Politics and Society in a Developing Nation.* New York: E. P. Dutton, 1964.

HOROWITZ, IRVING LOUIS, JOSUÉ DE CASTRO, and JOHN GERASSI, eds. *Latin American Radicalism: A Documentary Report on Left and Nationalist Movements.* New York: Random House, 1969.

HOWE, MARVINE. "Libyan Leader Shows Some Reserve Toward Arab Federation." *New York Times*, December 21, 1970.

HUNTER, GUY. *Modernizing Peasant Societies: A Comparative Study in Asia and Africa.* New York: Oxford University Press, 1969.

HUNTINGTON, SAMUEL P., ed. *Changing Patterns of Military Politics.* New York: The Free Press, 1962.

_____. "No More Vietnams." *The Atlantic Monthly*, December 1968.

_____. "Political Development and Political Decay." *World Politics, 17*, No. 3 (April 1965), 386–430.

_____. "The Political Modernization of Traditional Monarchies." *Daedalus, 95*, No. 3 (Summer 1966), 763–788.

_____. *Political Order in Changing Societies.* New Haven, Conn.: Yale University Press, 1968.

_____. "Social and Institutional Dynamics of One-Party Systems." *Authoritarian Politics in Modern Society: The Dynamics of Established One-Party Systems.* Edited by Samuel P. Huntington and Clement H. Moore. New York: Basic Books, 1970, 3–47.

_____. *The Soldier and the State: The Theory and Politics of Civil-Military Relations.* Cambridge, Mass.: Harvard University Press, 1957.

HUNTINGTON, SAMUEL P., and CLEMENT H. MOORE, eds. *Authoritarian Politics in Modern Society: The Dynamics of Established One-Party Systems*. New York: Basic Books, 1970.

HUREWITZ, J. C. *Middle East Politics: The Military Dimension*. New York: Praeger, 1969.

HYMAN, HERBERT H. "The Value Systems of Different Classes: The Social-Psychological Contribution to the Analysis of Stratification." *Class, Status and Power: Social Stratification in Comparative Perspective*, second edition. Edited by Reinhard Bendix and Seymour Martin Lipset. New York: The Free Press, 1966, 488–499.

IANNI, OCTAVIO. *Crisis in Brazil*. Translated by Phyllis B. Eveleth. New York: Columbia University Press, 1970.

INKELES, ALEX. "Making Men Modern: On the Causes and Consequences of Individual Change in Six Developing Countries." *The American Journal of Sociology*, 75, No. 2 (September 1969), 208–225.

Inter-American Development Bank. *Socio-Economic Progress in Latin America*. Social Progress Trust Fund, Ninth Annual Report, 1969.

International Bank for Reconstruction and Development. *The Economic Development of Libya*. Baltimore: The Johns Hopkins Press, 1960.

JACOBS, DAN N., ed. *The New Communisms*. New York: Harper and Row, 1969.

JAGUARIBE, HÉLIO. *Economic and Political Development: A Theoretical Approach and a Brazilian Case Study*. Cambridge, Mass.: Harvard University Press, 1968.

_____. "Political Strategies of National Development in Brazil." *Studies in Comparative International Development*, Vol. 3, Annual Register (1967–1968).

JANOWITZ, MORRIS. *The Military in the Political Development of New Nations*. Chicago: University of Chicago Press, 1964.

JOHANSSON, BERTRAM B. "Libyans Gain Arab Standing." *The Christian Science Monitor*, May 20, 1971.

_____. "Corruption Loses Hold in Libya." *The Christian Science Monitor*, June 25, 1971.

JOHNSON, CHALMERS. *Revolutionary Change*. Boston: Little, Brown, 1966.

JOHNSON, HARRY M. "Ideology and the Social System." *International Encyclopedia of the Social Sciences*, Vol. 7. New York: The Macmillan Company and the Free Press, 1968, 76–85.

JOHNSON, JOHN J., ed. "The Military." *Continuity and Change in Latin America*. Stanford: Stanford University Press, 1964, 136–160.

_____. *The Military and Society in Latin America*. Stanford: Stanford University Press, 1964.

_____, ed. *The Role of the Military in Underdeveloped Countries*. Princeton: Princeton University Press, 1962.

KAHL, J. A. *The Measurement of Modernism: A Study of Values in Brazil and Mexico*. Published for the Institute of Latin American Studies. Austin, Tex. and London: University of Texas Press, 1968.

KANTOR, HARRY. *The Ideology and Program of the Peruvian Aprista Movement*. Washington, D.C.: Savile Books, 1966.

KAUTSKY, JOHN H. *Communism and the Politics of Development: Persistent Myths and Changing Behavior*. New York: Wiley, 1968.

_____. *The Political Consequences of Modernization*. New York: Wiley, 1972.

KEBSCHULL, HARVEY, ed. *Politics in Transitional Societies: The Challenge of Change in Asia, Africa and Latin America*. New York: Appleton-Century-Crofts, 1968.

KEITH, AGNES NEWTON. *Children of Allah*. Atlantic-Little, Brown, 1966.

KHADDURI, MAJID. *Modern Libya: A Study in Political Development*. Baltimore: Johns Hopkins Press, 1963.

KLING, MERLE. "The State of Research on Latin America: Political Science." *Social Science Research on Latin America*. Report and Papers of a Seminar on Latin American Studies in the United States held at Stanford, California, July 8–August 23, 1963. Edited by Charles Wagley. New York: Columbia University Press, 1964.

KUHN, THOMAS L. *The Structure of Scientific Revolutions*, second edition, enlarged. Chicago: The University of Chicago Press, 1970.

KUNKEL, JOHN H. *Society and Economic Growth: A Behavioral Perspective of Social Change*. New York: Oxford University Press, 1970.

LAMBERT, WILLIAM W., and WALLACE E. LAMBERT. *Social Psychology*. Englewood Cliffs, N.J.: Prentice-Hall, 1964.

LANDSBERGER, HENRY A., ed. *The Church and Social Change in Latin America*. Notre Dame, Ind.: University of Notre Dame Press, 1970.

_____. "The Role of Peasant Movements and Revolts in Development." *Latin American Peasant Movements*. Edited by Henry A. Landsberger. Ithaca, N.Y.: Cornell University Press, 1969, 1–61.

LaPALOMBARA, JOSEPH, ed. *Bureaucracy and Political Development*. Princeton, N.J.: Princeton University Press, 1963.

LaPALOMBARA, JOSEPH, and MYRON WEINER, eds. *Political Parties and Political Development*. Princeton, N.J.: Princeton University Press, 1966.

LASSWELL, HAROLD. "The Emerging Internation Culture." In U.S. International Development Agency, *International Cooperation and Problems of Transfer Adaptation*. Science, Technology and Development: United States Papers Prepared for the United Nations Conference on the Application of Science and Technology for the Benefit of the Less Developed Areas, Vol. 10. Washington, D.C.: U.S. Government Printing Office, 1962.

LEE, JOHN M. "Strict Government in Libya Making Life Uneasy for 4,700 Americans." *New York Times*, November 10, 1970.

LEFF, NATHANIEL H. *Economic Policy-Making and Development in Brazil, 1947–1964.* New York: Wiley, 1968.

LEITES, NATHAN, and CHARLES WOLF, JR. *Rebellion and Authority: An Analytic Essay on Insurgent Conflicts.* Chicago: Markham Publishing Company, 1970.

LENSKI, G. *Power and Privilege, A Theory of Social Stratification.* New York: McGraw-Hill, 1966.

LERNER, DANIEL. *The Passing of Traditional Society: Modernizing the Middle East.* New York: The Free Press of Glencoe, 1958.

LEVY, MARION J., JR. *Modernization and the Structure of Societies: A Setting for International Affairs.* Princeton, N.J.: Princeton University Press, 1966. Two Volumes.

LEWIS, OSCAR. *The Children of Sanchez: Autobiography of a Mexican Family.* New York: Vintage Books, 1961.

"Libyan Revolution in the Words of Its Leaders." *Middle East Journal, 24* (Spring 1970), 203–219.

LIEUWEN, EDWIN. "Survey of the Alliance for Progress: The Latin American Military." A study prepared at the request of the Subcommittee on American Republics Affairs of the Committee on Foreign Relations, United States Senate. Washington, D.C.: U.S. Government Printing Office, 1967.

LIPSET, SEYMOUR MARTIN. *The First New Nation: The United States in Historical and Comparative Perspective.* New York: Basic Books, 1963.

————. *Political Man: The Social Bases of Politics.* New York: Doubleday, 1960.

————. *Revolution and Counter Revolution: Change and Persistence in Social Structures.* New York: Basic Books, 1968.

LIPSET, SEYMOUR MARTIN, and STEIN ROKKAN, eds., *Party Systems and Voter Alignments: Cross-National Perspectives.* New York: The Free Press, 1967.

LODGE, GEORGE C. *Engines of Change: United States Interests and Revolution in Latin America.* New York: Knopf, 1970.

LORETO, SILVIO. *"Reforma Agraria no Brasil—Implicações Sociológicas." Revista Brasileira de Estudos Políticos,* No. 27 (July 1969).

LUPSHA, PETER. "Explanation of Political Violence: Some Psychological Theories vs. Indignation." *Politics and Society, 2,* No. 1 (Fall 1971), 89–104.

MALEWSKI, ANDRZEJ. "The Degree of Status Incongruence and its Effects." *Class, Status, and Power,* second edition. Edited by Reinhard Bendix and Seymour Martin Lipset. New York: The Free Press, 1966, 303–308.

MALLAKH, RAGAEI EL. "The Economics of Rapid Growth: Libya." *Middle East Journal, 23* (Summer 1969), 308–320.

MANGIN, WILLIAM, ed. *Peasants in Cities: Readings in the Anthropology of Urbanization.* Boston: Houghton Mifflin, 1970.

MARCSON, SIMON, ed. *Automation, Alienation, and Anomie.* New York: Harper and Row, 1970.

MARCUS, J. T. "Transcendence and Charisma." *Western Political Quarterly,* *14,* No. 1, Part 1 (March 1961), 236–241.

MARKOVITZ, IRVING LEONARD, ed. *African Politics and Society: Basic Issues and Problems of Government and Development.* New York: The Free Press, 1970.

MARTZ, JOHN D. "Doctrine and Dilemmas of the Latin American 'New Left'." *World Politics, 22,* No. 2 (January 1970), 171–196.

MAY, JOHN ALLAN. "Occidental Wins Libyan Oil Pact." *The Christian Science Monitor,* October 13, 1970.

MAYNARD, EILEEN A. *Patterns of Community Service Development in Selected Communities of the Mantaro Valley, Peru.* Socio-Economic Development of Andean Communities, Report No. 3, Cornell-Peru Project. Ithaca, New York: Department of Anthropology, Cornell University, 1964.

MATOS MAR, JOSÉ. *El Valle de Yanamarca.* Departamento de Antropología Publicación No. 18, Universidad Nacional Mayor de San Marcos, Facultad de Letras. Lima, Peru: By the Department, 1964.

McALISTER, LYLE N. "Changing Concepts of the Role of the Military in Latin America." *Annals of the American Academy of Political and Social Science, 360* (July 1965).

————. "Recent Research and Writings on the Role of the Military in Latin America." *Latin American Research Review, 11* (Fall 1966), 5–36.

McCLELLAND, DAVID C. "The Impulse to Modernization." *Modernization: The Dynamics of Growth.* Edited by Myron Weiner. New York: Basic Books, 1966.

————. *The Achieving Society.* Princeton: Van Nostrand, 1961.

McKINNEY, JOHN C. *Constructive Typology and Social Theory.* New York: Appleton-Century-Crofts, 1966.

MEHDEN FRED R. VON DER. *Politics of the Developing Nations.* Englewood Cliffs, N.J.: Prentice-Hall, 1964.

MELO FILHO, MURILO. "Brasil '66." *Manchete,* March 26, 1966, p. 53.

MELO FILHO, MURILO, and ROBERTO STUCKERT. "Brasília/O Campus da Batalha." *Manchete,* September 14, 1968, pp. 12–15.

MERKL, PETER H. "Political Cleavages and Party Systems." *World Politics, 21,* No. 3 (April 1969), 469–485.

MILLIKAN, MAX F., and DAVID HAPGOOD. *No Easy Harvest: The Dilemma of Agriculture in Underdeveloped Countries.* Boston: Little, Brown, 1967.

MILNE, R. S. "Elections in Developing Countries." *Parliamentary Affairs, 18,* No. 1 (Winter 1964–1965), 53–60.

MOORE, WILBERT E. *The Impact of Industry.* Englewood Cliffs, N.J.: Prentice-Hall, 1965.

MOORE, WILBERT E. and ARNOLD S. FELDMAN, eds. *Labor Commitment and Social Change in Developing Areas.* New York: Social Science Research Council, 1960.

MUGGIATI, ROBERTO, and JARIO REGIS. "Quem Derrubou Jango." *Manchete*, March 25, 1968.

MYRDAL, GUNNAR. *Asian Drama*. New York: Twentieth Century Fund, 1968.

_____. *The Challenge of World Poverty: A World Anti-Poverty Program in Outline*. New York: Pantheon Books, 1970.

NASSER, DAVID. "O Dia em que Jango Caiu." *Manchete*, October 28, 1967.

NEEDLER, MARTIN C. "Political Development and Military Intervention in Latin America." *American Political Science Review, 60*, No. 3 (September 1966), 616–626.

_____. *Political Development in Latin America: Instability, Violence and Revolutionary Change*. New York: Random House, 1968.

NESS, GAYL D. *The Sociology of Economic Development: A Reader*. New York: Harper and Row, 1970.

NETTL, J. P. *Political Mobilization: A Sociological Analysis of Methods and Concepts*. New York: Basic Books, 1967.

NEUMANN, SIGMUND. "The International Civil War." *World Politics, 1*, No. 3 (April 1949).

NIEDERGANG, MARCEL. "Revolutionary Nationalism in Peru." *Foreign Affairs, 49*, No. 3 (April 1971), 454–463.

NORDLINGER, ERIC A. "Soldiers in Mufti: The Impact of Military Rule Upon Economic and Social Change in the Non-Western States." *American Political Science Review, 61*, No. 2 (June 1967), 417–427.

NUN, JOSÉ. "A Latin American Phenomenon: The Middle Class Military Coup." *Trends in Social Science Research in Latin American Studies*. Berkeley, Cal.: University of California, Institute of International Studies, 1965, 55–99.

NYE, J. S. "Corruption and Political Development: A Cost-Benefit Analysis." *American Political Science Review, 61*, No. 2 (June 1967), 417–427.

PACKENHAM, ROBERT A. "Approaches to the Study of Political Development." *World Politics, 17*, No. 1 (October 1964), 108–120.

PARSONS, TALCOTT. *The Social System*. Glencoe, Ill.: The Free Press, 1951.

"Part of What Was Wrong." *Time*, July 3, 1964, pp. 22–23.

PATCH, RICHARD W. "Fernando Belaúnde Terry and Peruvian Politics." *Latin American Politics*. Edited by Robert D. Tomasek. New York: Anchor Books, 1966, 498–513.

PAYNE, ARNOLD. "Peru: Latin America's Silent Revolution." *Inter-American Economic Affairs, 20*, No. 3 (Winter 1966), 69–78.

PAYNE, JAMES L. *Labor and Politics in Peru: The System of Political Bargaining*. New Haven, Conn.: Yale University Press, 1965.

PELT, ADRIAN. *Libyan Independence and the United Nations: A Case of Planned Decolonization*. New Haven, Conn.: Yale University Press, 1970.

PERALVA, OSWALDO. "Quem Ameaca o Brasil: Esquerda ou Direita?" *Realidade*, February, 1968.

PERINBANAYAGAM, R. S. "The Dialectics of Charisma." *The Sociological Quarterly* (Summer 1971), 387–402.

PERLMUTTER, AMOS. "The Praetorian State and the Praetorian Army: Toward a Taxonomy of Civil-Military Relations in Developing Polities." *Comparative Politics, 1*, No. 3 (April 1969), 382–404.

PETRAS, JAMES. "Revolution and Guerrilla Movements in Latin America: Venezuela, Guatemala, Colombia, and Peru." *Latin America: Reform or Revolution*. Edited by James Petras and Maurice Zeitlin. Greenwich, Conn.: Fawcett Premier, 1968, 329–369.

PINHEIRO, LAERTE (Interviewing Albuquerque de Lima). "Os Caminhos do Desenvolvimento." *Manchete*, August 3, 1968, pp. 142–144.

POPPINO, ROLLIE E. *Brazil: The Land and the People*. New York: Oxford University Press, 1968.

————. "Imbalance in Brazil." *Current History*, February 1963. Philadelphia: Current History, Inc.

POTTER, JACK M., MAY N. DIAZ, and GEORGE M. FOSTER, eds. *Peasant Society: A Reader*. Boston: Little, Brown, 1967.

POWELL, JOHN D. *Political Mobilization of the Venezuelan Peasant*. Cambridge, Mass.: Harvard University Press, 1971.

PRICE, ROBERT M. "A Theoretical Approach to Military Rule in New States: Reference-Group Theory and the Ghanaian Case." *World Politics, 23*, No. 3 (April 1971), 399–430.

PUTNAM, ROBERT D. "Toward Explaining Military Intervention in Latin American Politics." *World Politics, 20*, No. 1 (October 1967), 83–110.

PYE, LUCIAN W. *Aspects of Political Development*. Boston: Little, Brown, 1966.

————, ed. *Communications and Political Development*. Princeton, N.J.: Princeton University Press, 1963.

————, ed. *Crises and Sequences in Political Development*. Princeton, N.J.: Princeton University Press, 1971.

————. "The International Gap." *Modernization*. Edited by Myron Weiner. New York and London: Basic Books, 1966, 337–347.

————. "Party Systems and National Development in Asia." *Political Parties and Political Development*. Edited by Joseph LaPalombara and Myron Weiner. Princeton, N.J.: Princeton University Press, 1966, 369–398.

————. *Politics, Personality and Nation Building: Burma's Search for Identity*. New Haven, Conn.: Yale University Press, 1962.

PYE, LUCIAN W., and SIDNEY VERBA, eds. *Political Culture and Political Development*. Princeton, N.J.: Princeton University Press, 1965.

QUIJANO OBREGÓN, ANIBAL. "*El Movimiento Campesino del Perú y sus Líderes*." *América Latina, Año* VIII, No. 4 (1965), 43–65.

_____. "Tendencies in Peruvian Development and Class Structure." *Latin America: Reform or Revolution.* Edited by James Petras and Maurice Zeitlin. Greenwich, Conn.: Fawcett Premier, 1968, 289–328.

RATNAM, K. J. "Charisma and Political Leadership." *Political Studies, 12* (October 1964).

REDFIELD, ROBERT. *The Folk Culture of Yucatan.* Chicago: University of Chicago Press, 1941.

RIGGS, FRED. "Agraria and Industria—Toward a Typology of Comparative Administration." *Toward a Comparative Study of Public Administration.* Edited by W. J. Siffin. Bloomington, Ind.: Indiana University Press, 1957.

_____. *Administration in Developing Countries: The Theory of Prismatic Society.* Boston: Houghton Mifflin, 1964.

_____. "The Theory of Political Development." *Contemporary Political Analysis.* Edited by James C. Charlesworth. New York: The Free Press, 1967, 317–349.

_____. "The Dialectics of Developmental Conflict." *Comparative Political Studies, 1,* No. 2 (July 1968), 197–226.

ROCKEFELLER, NELSON. *The Rockefeller Report on the Americas: The New York Times Edition.* Chicago: Quadrangle Books, 1969.

ROGERS, EVERETT M., in association with Lynne Svenning. *Modernization Among Peasants: The Impact of Communication.* New York: Holt, Rinehart and Winston, 1969.

ROSTOW, WALT W. *The Stages of Economic Growth: A Non-Communist Manifesto.* Cambridge, England: Cambridge University Press, 1964.

ROTH, GUENTHER. "Personal Rulership, Patrimonialism, and Empire-building in the New States." *World Politics, 20,* No. 2 (January 1968), 194–206.

ROULEAU, ERIC. "Oil and Monarchies Don't Mix." *Africa Report, 14* (November 1969), 24–27.

RUDNER, RICHARD S. *Philosophy of Social Science.* Englewood Cliffs, N.J.: Prentice-Hall, 1966.

RUDOLPH, LLOYD I., and SUSANNE HOEBER RUDOLPH. "The Political Role of India's Caste Associations." *Pacific Affairs, 33,* No. 1 (March 1960), 5–22.

RUNCIMAN, W. G. *Social Science and Political Theory.* Cambridge, England: Cambridge University Press, 1963.

RUSTOW, DANKWART A. "Modernization and Comparative Politics: Prospects in Research and Theory." *Comparative Politics, 1,* No. 1 (October 1968), 37–51.

_____. *A World of Nations: Problems of Political Modernization.* Washington, D.C.: The Brookings Institution, 1967.

SANDERS, THOMAS G. "The Church in Latin America." *Foreign Affairs, 48,* No. 2 (January 1970), 285–299.

SARDA, ROSINHA. "Afinal, O Que Há Com Os Estudantes?" *O Cruzeiro,* July 15, 1967.

SCARROW, HOWARD A. *Comparative Political Analysis: An Introduction.* New York: Harper and Row, 1969.

SCHMITTER, PHILIPPE C. "The Persecution of Political and Social Scientists in Brazil." *PS* (Published quarterly by the American Political Science Association), 3, No. 2 (Spring 1970), 123–128.

SCHNAIBERG, ALLAN. "Measuring Modernism: Theoretical and Empirical Explorations." *American Journal of Sociology, 76,* No. 3 (November 1970), 399–425.

SCHNEIDER, RONALD M. *The Political System of Brazil: Emergence of a "Modernizing" Authoritarian Regime, 1964–1970.* New York: Columbia University Press, 1971.

SCHULTZ, THEODORE W. *Transforming Traditional Agriculture.* New Haven, Conn.: Yale University Press, 1964.

SCHWEINITZ, KARL D., JR. "Growth, Development, and Political Modernization." *World Politics, 22,* No. 4 (July 1970), 518–540.

SCOTT, JAMES C. "The Analysis of Corruption in Developing Nations." *Comparative Studies in Society and History, 11,* No. 3 (June 1969), 315-341.

_____. "Corruption, Machine Politics, and Political Change." *American Political Science Review, 63,* No. 4 (December 1969), 1142–1158.

SCOTT, ROBERT E. "Political Parties and Policy-Making in Latin America." *Political Parties and Political Development.* Edited by Joseph LaPalombara and Myron Weiner. Princeton, N.J.: Princeton University Press, 1966, 331–368.

SELLTIZ, CLAIRE, and others. *Research Methods in Social Relations,* revised edition. New York: Holt, Rinehart and Winston, 1962.

SHARABI, HISHAM. "Libya's Pattern of Growth." *Current History,* January 1963.

SHERRILL, KENNETH S. "The Attitudes of Modernity." *Comparative Politics, 1,* No. 2 (January 1969), 184–210.

SHILS, EDWARD. "The Concentration and Dispersion of Charisma: Their Bearing on Economic Policy in Underdeveloped Countries." *World Politics, 11,* No. 1 (October 1958), 1–19.

_____. "The Concept and Function of Ideology." *International Encyclopedia of the Social Sciences,* Vol. 7. New York: The Macmillan Company and The Free Press, 1968, 66–75.

_____. "Tradition." *Comparative Studies in Society and History, 13,* No. 2 (April 1971), 122–159.

SIEKMAN, PHILIP. "When Executives Turned Revolutionaries." *Fortune.* September 1964.

SIGMUND, PAUL E., ed. *The Ideologies of the Developing Nations,* revised edition. New York: Praeger, 1967.

SILVERT, KALMAN H., ed. *Expectant Peoples: Nationalism and Development.* New York: Random House, 1963.

SITHOLE, NDABANINGI. *African Nationalism,* second edition. London: Oxford University Press, 1968.

SKIDMORE, THOMAS E. *Politics in Brazil: 1930–1964. An Experiment In Democracy.* New York: Oxford University Press, 1967.

SMELSER, NEIL J. "The Modernization of Social Relations." *Modernization.* Edited by Myron Weiner. New York and London: Basic Books, 1966, 110–121.

_____. *Theory of Collective Behavior.* New York: Free Press of Glencoe, 1963.

_____. *Social Change in the Industrial Revolution: An Application of Theory to the British Cotton Industry.* Chicago: University of Chicago Press, 1959.

_____. "Toward a Theory of Modernization." *Social Change: Sources, Patterns and Consequences.* Edited by Amitai Etzioni and Eva Etzioni. New York: Basic Books, 1964, 258–274.

SOARES, GLAUCIO ARY DILLON. "Economic Development and Class Structure." *Class, Status, and Power: Social Stratification in Comparative Perspective,* second edition. Edited by Reinhard Bendix and Seymour Martin Lipset. New York: The Free Press, 1966, 190–199.

_____. "The Political Sociology of Uneven Development in Brazil." *Revolution in Brazil: Politics and Society in a Developing Nation.* Edited by Irving Louis Horowitz. New York: Dutton, 1964, 164–195.

STAUFFER, ROBERT B. "Great-Power Constraints on Political Development." *Studies in Comparative International Development,* 6, No. 11 (1970–71), 231–251.

STAVENHAGEN, RODOLFO, ed. *Agrarian Problems and Peasant Movements in Latin America.* New York: Anchor Books, 1970.

STEIN, STANLEY J. *Vassouras: A Brazilian Coffee County, 1850–1900.* Cambridge, Mass.: Harvard University Press, 1957.

STEPAN, ALFRED. *The Military in Politics: Changing Patterns in Brazil.* Princeton, N.J.: Princeton University Press, 1971.

_____. "The Military's Role in Latin American Political Systems." A review of the works of John J. Johnson, Edwin Lieuwen, and Robert Gilmore. *Review of Politics,* 28 (October 1965), 564–568.

"*O Terror Mata em São Paulo.*" *Manchete,* October 19, 1968, pp. 26–31.

THOMAS, FREDERICK C., JR. "The Libyan Oil Worker." *Middle East Journal,* 15 (Summer 1961).

TOENNIES, FERDINAND. *Community and Society—Gemeinschaft and Gesellschaft.* Translated and edited by Charles P. Loomis. East Lansing, Mich.: The Michigan State University Press, 1957.

TSCHOPIK, HARRY, JR. *Highland Communities of Central Peru.* Institute of Social Anthropology, Publication No. 5. Washington, D.C.: Smithsonian Institution, 1947.

TORREY, GORDON H., and JOHN F. DEVLIN. "Arab Socialism." *Journal of International Affairs,* 19, No. 1 (1965), 47–62.

TRISKA, JAN F. "The Socialist World System in Search of a Theory." *The New Communisms.* Edited by Dan N. Jacobs. New York: Harper and Row, 1969, 18–46.

TSANTIS, ANDREAS C. "Political Factors in Economic Development." *Comparative Politics,* 2, No. 1 (October 1969), 63–78.

TUCKER, ROBERT C. "The Theory of Charismatic Leadership." *Daedalus,* 97, No. 3 (Summer 1968), 731–756.

TURNER, RALPH E. "The Industrial City: Center of Cultural Change." *Cities and Society,* second edition. Edited by Paul K. Hatt and Albert J. Reiss, Jr. Glencoe, Ill.: The Free Press, 1951, 189–200.

TULLIS, F. LAMOND. *Lord and Peasant in Peru: A Paradigm of Political and Social Change.* Cambridge, Mass.: Harvard University Press, 1970.

United Nations Economic Commission for Latin America. *Economic Survey of Latin America,* issues from 1963–1970. New York: United Nations.

VALLIER, IVAN. *Catholicism, Social Control, and Modernization in Latin America.* Englewood Cliffs, N.J.: Prentice-Hall, 1970.

_____. "Religious Elites: Differentiations and Developments in Roman Catholicism." *Elites in Latin America.* Edited by Seymour Martin Lipset and Aldo Solari. New York: Oxford University Press, 1967, 190–232.

VERNON, RAYMOND. *The Dilemma of Mexico's Development: The Roles of the Private and Public Sectors.* Cambridge, Mass.: Harvard University Press, 1963.

VILLARD, HENRY SERRANO. *Libya: The New Arab Kingdom of North Africa.* Ithaca, New York: Cornell University Press, 1956.

WAGLEY, CHARLES, ed. *Social Science Research on Latin America.* New York: Columbia University Press, 1964.

WARD, ROBERT E., and DANKWART A. RUSTOW. *Political Modernization in Japan and Turkey.* Princeton, N.J.: Princeton University Press, 1964.

WARREN, LESLIE. "Opposition Gets Bolder in Brazil." *The Christian Science Monitor,* July 15, 1968, p. 10.

WEBER, MAX. *Charisma and Institution Building.* Edited with an introduction by S. N. Eisenstadt. Chicago: University of Chicago Press, 1968.

_____. *From Max Weber: Essays in Sociology.* Translated by H. H. Gerth and C. Wright Mills. New York: Oxford University Press, 1946.

_____. *The Protestant Ethic and the Spirit of Capitalism.* Translated by Talcott Parsons. New York: Scribner, 1958.

WEDGE, BRYANT. "The Case Study of Student Political Violence: Brazil, 1964, and Dominican Republic, 1965." *World Politics,* 21, No. 2 (January 1969), 183–206.

WEINER, MYRON, ed. *Modernization.* New York and London: Basic Books, 1966.

_____. "Political Integration and Political Development." *New Nations: The Problem of Political Development, The Annals,* 358 (March 1964), 53–62.

_____. *The Politics of Scarcity: Public Pressure and Political Response in India.* Chicago: University of Chicago Press, 1962.

WELCH, CLAUDE, E., JR., ed. *Political Modernization: A Reader in Comparative Political Change.* Belmont, California: Wadsworth, 1967.

_____. *Soldier and State in Africa: A Comparative Analysis of Military Intervention and Political Change.* Evanston, Ill.: Northwestern University Press, 1970.

WHARTON, CLIFTON R., JR., ed. *Subsistence Agriculture and Economic Development.* Chicago: Aldine Publishing Co., 1969.

WHYTE, WILLIAM FOOTE. "Rural Peru: Peasants as Activists." *Trans-Action,* 7, No. 1, Whole No. 51 (November 1969), 37–47.

WHYTE, WILLIAM FOOTE, and LAWRENCE K. WILLIAMS. *Toward an Integrated Theory of Development: Economic and Noneconomic Variables in Rural Development.* New York State School of Industrial and Labor Relations Paperback No. 5. Ithaca, N.Y.: Cornell University, February 1968.

WILLIAMS, EDWARD J. "Latin American Catholicism and Political Integration." *Comparative Political Studies,* 2, No. 3 (October 1969), 327–348.

WILLNER, RUTH N., and DOROTHY WILLNER. "The Rise and Role of Charismatic Leaders." *New Nations: The Problem of Political Development, The Annals,* 358 (March 1965), 68–88.

WRAITH, RONALD, and EDGAR SIMPKINS. *Corruption in Developing Countries.* London: George Allen and Unwin, Ltd., 1963.

WOLF, ERIC R. *Peasants.* Englewood Cliffs, N.J.: Prentice-Hall, 1966.

WRIGHT, JOHN. *Libya.* New York: Praeger, 1969.

YGLESIAS, JOSÉ. "Report from Brazil: What the Left is Saying." *The New York Times Magazine,* December 7, 1969.

YOUNG, FRANK W. "A Proposal for Cooperative Cross-Cultural Research on Intervillage Systems." *Human Organization,* 25, No. 1 (Spring 1966), 46–50.

YOUNG, FRANK W., and RUTH C. YOUNG. "Individual Commitment to Industrialization in Rural Mexico." *American Journal of Sociology,* 71, No. 4 (January 1966), 373–383.

YOUNG, FRANK W., BERKLEY A. SPENCER, and JAN L. FLORA. "Differentiation and Solidarity in Agricultural Communities." *Human Organization,* 27, No. 4 (Winter 1968), 344–351.

YOUNG, JORDAN M. "Brazil." *Political Forces in Latin America: Dimensions of the Quest for Stability,* second edition. Edited by Ben G. Burnett and Kenneth F. Hohnson. Belmont, California: Wadsworth Publishing Company, Inc., 1970, 557–595.

YOUNG, ORAN R. "Professor Russett: Industrious Tailor to a Naked Emperor." *World Politics,* 21, No. 3 (April 1969), 486–511.

AUTHOR INDEX

SUBJECT INDEX

Absorption, social and political, 40, 67-68, 95. *See also* Variables, societal responses

Accelerators, 280; relationship of, to protest and revolution, 68. *See also* Variables, accelerators

Acción Popular (Peru), *see* Parties, political, *Acción Popular*

Achievement motivation, relationship of, to modernity, 29. *See also* "Need achievement" virus

African socialism, *see* Socialism, African

Agency for International Development, 72

Aggression, related to frustration, 61-65; related to threats, 64. *See also* Frustration-aggression

Agitation peasant, in Peru, 244ff

Agrarian Reform, *see* Reform, agrarian

Agriculture, related to processes of structural change, 31; to socialist ideologies, 77; decline of, in Brazil during Kubitschek era, 177. *See also* Development, agricultural

Ainus, Hairy, 34

Aleixo, Pedro, 130

Algeria, 196

Allende, Salvador, 60

Alliance for Progress, 242

Alves, Marcio Moreira, 146

America, history of unappropriate for Third World countries, 4. *See also* United States

American and Foreign Power Company, 124, 128

American Council of Learned Societies, 252

American Telephone and Telegraph Company, 122, 128

Amoral familism, 266

Amoral groupism, 50, 96

Analysis, longitudinal versus cross-sectional, 18-19; relationship of, to variables and theory, 7-21. *See also* Variables

Anderson, Jack, 60

Anselmo, José, 130, 167

Anthropologists, social, 40

APRA (*Aprista* party in Peru), *see* Parties, political, APRA

Arab socialist union, 223

Arabs, *see* Libya

ARENA (Aliança Renovadora Nacional-Brazil), *see* Parties, political, ARENA

Argentina, 40, 88

Ascription, relationship of, to modernity, 29

Attitudes and values, relationship of, to modernization, 24-29, 33, 37

Authority, charismatic, 79, 80, 95; emergence of, 80-84; political consequences of, 80-84;

Christian Democracy, 78; in
Peru, 250
Cities: relationship of, to modernization, 36
Civil Service, in Libya, 195
Class conflict: relationship of,
to revolution, 64
Clergy, protests loss of civil liberties in Brazil, 141; objections
of, to military rule in Brazil,
178. *See also* Câmara, Dom
Helder; Catholic Church
Coercion, 67-68, 278, 285,
329n40; relationship of, to
revolution, 62-63, to stability,
72, 95; in Brazil, 176-178; impact of, on intensity of collective action, 278; impact of,
upon organizational efforts,
282; hypotheses related to,
285; effect of, upon peasant
movements, 289-294
Coffee, growers of, in Brazil,
111; exports of, in Brazil, 118
Cold War, 7
Colonialism, 2, 39; relationship
of, to modernization, 3, 33;
in Libya, 218. *See also* Imperialism
Colonization, in Brazil, 174;
programs related to, 247
Colonos, in Peru, 247-248
Communal Movement of the
Center (Peru), 291-293,
323n12. *See also* Peru, peasant
movements in
Communism, relationship of,
to ideology, 76; appeal of, to
some elite modernizers, 77;
negative aspects of, in relationship to nationalism, 78, 101;

in Brazil, 112, 114, 115, 118,
126, 127, 128, 142, 165, 179;
in the Sudan, 209; in Peru,
243
Community development, in
Peru, 233, 246
Conspiracies, military, relationship of, to revolution, 64;
among political machines in
Brazil, 111-112; against Goulart,
126-129
"Conspiracy" theory of revolution, 62
Convención Valley, 242, 322n5
Coronelismo, 108, 110
Corruption, 88, 118, 122, 199;
relationship of, to modernization, 99, 100
Costa e Silva, Artur, 127, 317n35;
presidential regime of, 141-151
Coups, military, 86-87, 103; relationship of, to political development, 87; relationship of,
to political parties, 95-96; in
Brazil, 112, 113; probability
of success of, 166; in Libya,
222-225, 302; in Peru, 242-
243, 247
Cuba, 59, 60, 87, 118, 120
Culture of poverty, 40. *See also*
Peasants
Cyrenaica (Libya), 185, 187,
188, 190ff *passim;* regional defense force in, 200, 202, 205,
210, 220
Czar, of Russia, 93

Dantas, San Tiago, 122, 123,
161, 168, 302, 303; economic
stabilization program of, 123ff
Debts, foreign, 118

Decay, political, in Brazil, 113, 115; in Libya, 210-211, 219-230

Democracy, 99; difficulty of achieving, 52; relationship of, to economic development, 107; relationship of, to political stability, 307

Depression, world-wide economic, 111

Deprivation, relative, 64, 74, 107, 311n13. *See also* Frustration-aggression

Desio, Professor Ardito, 196

Demonstration effects, 326n13

Development, agricultural, 7, 9-14. *See also* Agriculture

Development, economic, 52; relationship of, to modernization and industrialization, 25, to psychological changes, 37, to foreign aid, 61, to military regimes, 103, and to democracy, 107; in Brazil, 172-173; in Libya, 197-199

Development, political, 65, 96, 298; difficulty of achieving, 51-52; superpower constraints on, 58-61; models of, 59; relationship of, to foreign aid, 61, to military coups, 86-88, and to political parties, 96-98; requirements of, 155; in Brazil, 176-178, 181; in Libya, 219-225

Differentiation, 38, 65; relationship of, to political modernization, 31, 33, 53-54, to psychological changes, 37, and to political development, 56-61

"Diffusionism," 32-36, 258;

relationship of, to modernization, 43-44

Dissonance, cognitive, 34-36, 44

Disturbances, social, arising from modernization, 38. *See also* Violence; Revolution; Authority, military; and Authority, charismatic

Dominican Republic, 61

Dutra, Eurico, president of Brazil, 129

Dutra, Tarsol, education minister in Brazil, 144

Economic development, relationship of, to democracy, 107; in Brazil, 152-153. *See also* Development, economic

Economic Middle Class (Brazil), increases in expectations of, 158; opportunities of, 159

Economists, 8, 40

Education, compulsory, 35; Brazilian cuts in budget for, 144; in Libya, 195; in Peru, 238; radio schools fostering, 258. *See also* Schools

Egypt, 59, 88, 93

Einstein, Albert, 20, 22

Eisenhower, Dwight D., 205

Elections, 111; in Brazil, 110, 114, 117, 140, 179; in Libya, 191; in Peru, 242, 243, 291

Elite Rangers, Peruvian, 294

Elites, modernizing, 101; traditional, 101; modernizing, in Peru, 232

Emigration, in Peru, 240-241, 248; explanation of, 267

Empathy, 28, 36

Energy facilitators, relationship

299-300; failure of traditional, during rapid modernization, 168. *See also* Authority, charismatic; Authority, traditional; Leadership, charismatic; and Military

Leadership, charismatic, 69, 85, 95, 96, 100-102, 108, 299-300; definitions of, 79-80; relationship of, to processes of environmental change, 81-82, to military coups, 89, to military authority, 93, to political parties, 97, and to Goulart, 126; political and social consequences of, 83-84; assets and liabilities of, 169; in Libya, 220-222. *See also* Leadership

Legitimacy, political, difficulty of traditional authority to maintain, 52. *See also* Authority, traditional

Liberal Alliance (Brazil), 111

Liberation Front (Political Party, Peru), 242

Libya, 59, 87, 88, 105, 185-225, 297-307 *passim;* early occupiers of, 187-188; Italian colonists in, 188, 189; sense of pre-independence nationhood in, 188-189; post independence elections in, 191; post-independence conflicts in, 192; princes of, challenge the throne, 193; discovery of oil in, 195-198; educational improvements in, 197; corruption in, 199; effect of Arab-Israeli war on, 201-202; political modernization in, 201-202; disaffection of

military in, 202-203; military rule in, 204-225; confiscation by, of property of Italians, 206; socialism in, 206; political modernization in, 207-210; political thinking of the military in, 207-210; economic decay in, 210-211; National purification of, 210-212; revenues from oil exports in, 211; conflict of, with Israel, 212; union with Egypt and Syria, 213; underground water in, 214; political effects of economic development in, 219-225; charismatic leadership in, 220-222

Linkages, 69, 282-285; of military officers with civilians in Brazil, 166. *See also* Variables, energy facilitators

Links, motivational, between environmental or psychological factors and revolution, 64

Literacy, 33, 35, 36, 107; in Libya, 191, 195, 197; tests of, for voting rights (Peru), 324n13. *See also* Education

Lobatón, Guillermo, 250

Louis Philippe, King, 93

Luis, Washington, 111, 112, 113

Al-Maghreby, Prime Minister, of Libya, 209

Maghrib, modernization in the, 217-225

Mantaro Valley, 324n16a

Mao Tse-tung, 80, 300

Markets, 13, 15, 17, 101-102, 260

Marx, Karl, 100